SUPPLEMENT III, Part 2
Philip Roth to Louis Zukofsky
and
Cumulative Index

AMERICAN WRITERS
A Collection of Literary Biographies

LEA BAECHLER

A. WALTON LITZ

General Editors

SUPPLEMENT III, Part 2
Philip Roth to Louis Zukofsky
and
Cumulative Index
to Volumes 1–4 and
Supplements I, II, and III

Charles Scribner's Sons / New York

Maxwell Macmillan Canada / Toronto
Maxwell Macmillan International / New York   Oxford   Singapore   Sydney

Copyright © 1991 by Charles Scribner's Sons

Library of Congress Cataloging-in-Publication Data

American writers: a collection of literary biographies.

   Suppl. 3 edited by Lea Baechler and A. Walton Litz.
   The 4-vol. main set consists of 97 of the pamphlets
originally published as the University of Minnesota
pamphlets on American writers; some have been rev. and
updated. The supplements cover writers not included in
the original series.
   Includes bibliographies.
   Contents: v. 1. Henry Adams to T.S. Eliot — v. 2.
Ralph Waldo Emerson to Carson McCullers — [etc.] —
Supplement[s] — [etc.] — 3, pt. 1. John Ashbery to
Walker Percy. 3, pt. 2. Philip Roth to Louis Zukofsky.
   1. American Literature — History and criticism.
2. American literature — Bio-bibliography. 3. Authors,
American — Biography. I. Unger, Leonard, ed.
II. Baechler, Lea. III. Litz, A. Walton. IV. University
of Minnesota. Pamphlets on American writers.
PS129.A55   810'.9   73-1759
ISBN 0-684-19196-2 (Set)
ISBN 0-684-19356-6 (Part 1)
ISBN 0-684-19357-4 (Part 2)

Charles Scribner's Sons   Maxwell Macmillan Canada, Inc.
Macmillan Publishing Company   1200 Eglinton Avenue East
866 Third Avenue   Suite 200
New York, New York 10022   Don Mills, Ontario M3C 3N1

Macmillan Publishing Company is part of the Maxwell Communication Group of Companies.

Impression

1   2   3   4   5   6   7   8   9   10

PRINTED IN THE UNITED STATES OF AMERICA

Philip Roth

1933–

THE EPIGRAPH TO Philip Roth's *The Facts: A Novelist's Autobiography* (1988) is courtesy of Nathan Zuckerman, the narrative persona of much of Roth's later fiction: "And as he spoke I was thinking, *the kind of stories that people turn life into, the kinds of lives that people turn stories into.*" The epigraph, Roth's decision to use a fictional character who is himself a fiction writer to introduce his autobiography, and the whole body of Roth's work testify to the dynamic interrelationship, sometimes symbiotic and sometimes problematic, between the author's life and his art. Roth has identified this cross-fertilization as his chief artistic concern, what he calls "the relationship between the written and the unwritten world." Particularly in his fiction from the mid 1970's on, starting with *My Life as a Man* (1974), he examines how the "unwritten world" of life experiences becomes transformed in literature and how the "written world" of literature can affect courses of action taken in life.

Given this preoccupation, it is not surprising that Roth's stories often treat writers whose stories—both their personal histories and the fictions created from them—resemble his own in many ways. It is tempting, but dangerous, to read his work as thinly veiled autobiography. True, Roth has assiduously mined his life and background for ore-bearing material, but, he admits, he has "looked only for what could be

transformed" by "turning the flame up under my life and smelting stories out of all I've known." Rather than autobiographical confession, the works should be seen as what Tony Tanner, borrowing a phrase from William Carlos Williams, terms "fictionalized recall."

The events thus recalled typically document the struggle of the self to realize autonomy in some restrictive environment, often by trying to frame an account of its own history and development. In the novella "Goodbye, Columbus," this account takes the form of Neil Klugman's post mortem examination of his first serious love affair; in *Portnoy's Complaint*, it takes the form of a logorrheic outburst to a psychoanalyst; in *My Life as a Man* and the Zuckerman novels, it takes the form of a writer's attempt to compose himself through the act of writing—to exorcise demons from his life, or to impart some sense to it, by putting it into literary form. In these works especially, strategies for narrative expression become strategies for self-discovery and self-definition. Since the characters' strivings parallel the author's, Roth produces a literature that is both psychologically and aesthetically self-conscious. Roth and his protagonists, most of all his writer–characters, face the dilemma of choosing between two antithetical styles of personality and narrative expression: that of the polished, high-minded, restrained, and responsible intellectual, whom he calls "the nice Jewish boy," and that of the brash, crude, and rebellious iconoclast, whom he dubs "the Jewboy."

As the terms suggest, the conflicting impulses behind the personal and artistic choices derive from Roth's history as a Jew growing up in mid-twentieth-century America. Philip Milton Roth was born on March 19, 1933, to Herman and Bess Finkel Roth in Newark, New Jersey. His mother came from a native Jewish-American family; his father, whose parents had emigrated from Austria-Hungary, was an insurance salesman for Metropolitan Life whose career prospects, Roth feels, were limited because he was Jewish. The Roths lived in the Weequahic section of Newark, then an almost entirely Jewish neighborhood. Roth has remarked that this milieu accounts not only for the material but also for the manner and even the motive in much of his writing. Of his long, uncensored interchanges with boyhood friends he says, "I associate that amalgam of mimicry, reporting, kibbitzing, disputation, satire, and legendizing from which we drew so much sustenance with the work I now do. . . . Also, those millions of words were the means by which we either took vengeance on or tried to hold at bay the cultural forces that were shaping us." Thus, early on, there emerges a dominant theme in Roth's life and writings: a need for personal freedom and autonomy as well as a wariness of, at times a hostility toward, conditioning forces. And, significantly, young Roth sees linguistic self-expression as the means of asserting his independence against those forces.

 To complicate matters, these forces were often loving ones toward which he felt the deepest of loyalties: a cohesive community and a nurturing family. Roth recalls, "In our lore, the Jewish family was an inviolate haven against every form of menace, from personal isolation to gentile hostility. . . . *Hear, O Israel, the family is God, the family is One.* Family indivisibility, the first commandment." Any act of self-assertion that threatened the family's solidarity or harmony— indeed, any act of exploration that ventured beyond the bounds of family values—could arouse a deep sense of guilt. If anything about his father weighed on him, Roth explains, it was "his limitless pride in me. When I tried not to disappoint him, or my mother, it was never out of fear of the mailed fist or the punitive decree, but of the broken heart."

Roth would later represent the conflict he felt between filial loyalty and personal or artistic self-realization in the portraits of Gabe Wallach, Alexander Portnoy, David Kepesh, Peter Tarnopol, Nathan Zuckerman, and the child narrator of "Looking at Kafka," who wonders, "Can it possibly be true (and can I possibly admit) that I am coming to hate [my father] for loving me so?" As a boy, though, Roth generally vented his rebellious impulses in conversation with his friends; everywhere else he was, as he describes it, "a good, responsible, well-behaved boy, controlled (rather willingly) by the social regulations of the self-conscious and orderly lower-middle-class neighborhood where I had been raised, and mildly constrained still by the taboos that had filtered down to me, in attenuated form, from the religious orthodoxy of my immigrant grandparents." But although he says he submitted to these controls "rather willingly," Roth also speaks of his high-school years as time served in a "minimum-security institution."

After graduating from Weequahic High School in January 1950, Roth worked as a stock clerk in a Newark department store until he enrolled that September as a prelaw student at Newark Colleges of Rutgers, the "unprestigious little downtown branch of the state university" that Neil Klugman attended. Despite the appeal of the urban heterogeneity of the student body to his "liberal democratic spirit," Roth was chafing under the yoke of parental supervision and aching to get away from home, determined not "to become encased in somebody else's idea of what I should be.'' He transferred to Bucknell University as a sophomore in September 1951. Although he had the chance to pledge the predominantly gentile Theta Chi fraternity, he joined Sigma Alpha Mu, a Jewish fraternity, because he felt less constrained among students whose ''style was familiar.'' For him and the other ''Sammies,'' assimilation was not an issue, nor was the observance of Jewish holidays and dietary laws. ''The Jews were together,'' Roth says, ''because they were profoundly different but otherwise like everyone else.''

During this time, Roth was becoming seriously interested in literature. His first published story, ''Philosophy, Or Something Like That,'' appeared in 1952 in *Et Cetera,* the college literary magazine he helped to found. In the winter of 1952 he resigned from Sigma Alpha Mu to devote his extracurricular energies to editing and writing fiction for it. Despite entertaining friends with mimicry and anecdotes of characters from his boyhood, Roth at this early stage never thought of turning the familiar material into literature: ''How could Art be rooted in a parochial Jewish Newark neighborhood having nothing to do with the enigma of time and space or good and evil or appearance and reality?'' His writing was doggedly ''sensitive'' and ''serious,'' intended to demonstrate his compassionate understanding that life was a sad and serious business. There were no Jews, and there was no comedy: ''the last thing I wanted to do was to hand anybody a laugh in literature.'' But, as in his boyhood, Roth had to give expression to the other side of his nature: soon the reviews and editorial columns of *Et Cetera* revealed his penchant for satire and what he calls ''a flash of talent for comic destruction.'' In his last two years at Bucknell, he wrote nearly as much satire as fiction.

Roth was gaining sexual as well as literary experience that he would draw upon for characters and situations in his novels. His attempt to carry on an affair without the knowledge of a moralistic landlady gives rise to a central episode in *When She Was Good.* Also, for about six weeks in the spring of 1954, Roth and his girlfriend believed that she was pregnant. He was resigned to marrying her, giving up his dreams of graduate school as a Fulbright or Marshall scholar, and staying on at Bucknell as a salaried teaching assistant. In the great relief of learning that there was no pregnancy, Roth forswore the ''encumbering responsibilities'' of monogamy in favor of the freedom to pursue adventures, erotic and otherwise. But the episode stayed with him: the voluntary, self-sacrificing bondage he envisioned for himself and his sense of the disappointment it would have brought is rendered in the Herz marriage in *Letting Go*; his passion for personal freedom and his conscious decision to renounce obligations in favor of exploits prefigure numerous protagonists, especially the young David Kepesh in *The Professor of Desire.*

Roth graduated magna cum laude from Bucknell in 1954 with a B.A. in English and was elected to Phi Beta Kappa. He then entered the graduate program at the University of Chicago, where he received an M.A. in 1955 and formed a neophyte's devotion to Henry James, Gustave Flaubert, and the masters of psychological realism. While there, he published ''The Contest for Aaron Gold'' in *Epoch;* the story was later selected for inclusion in *The Best American Short Stories of 1956.* Roth next enlisted in the army and worked for the public information officer of Walter Reed Army Hospital in Washington, D.C. Within a year he was discharged because of a back injury suffered during basic training, an episode that served as a source for ''Novotny's Pain.'' In 1956 he returned to the University of Chicago as a Ph.D. candidate and instructor of English. During the next three years, he published reviews, satire, and fiction, including the stories collected in *Goodbye, Columbus.*

An event occurred in the fall of 1956 that had

greater impact on Roth's life, and literature: he met Margaret Martinson Williams, a divorced ex-waitress four years his senior whose two children lived with their father in Arizona. Her difficult life, hard-bitten self-reliance, and troubled family history would furnish Roth with raw materials for the characters Martha Reganhart, Lucy Nelson, Maureen Johnson Tarnopol, and others. The woman also fascinated the sheltered and impressionable young man because she was so different from all he had known. At the time he was attached to someone very like Brenda Patimkin in "Goodbye, Columbus." But just as Nathan Zuckerman in Peter Tarnopol's "useful fiction" chooses Lydia Ketterer over Sharon Shatzky, and his author Tarnopol forsakes Dina Dornbusch for "his angry nemesis" Maureen, so Roth rejected the Jewish girl from suburban north Jersey for Margaret. And just as the characters spurn the girl who represents a life too easy and undemanding, a selling short of one's destiny, so Roth severed the connection that "had inevitably to resolve into a marriage linking me with the safe enclosure of Jewish New Jersey. I wanted a harder test, to work at life under more difficult conditions." Like Zuckerman and Tarnopol, he got the chance.

After Margaret had an abortion in early 1957, the relationship deteriorated into acrimonious feuding. Roth spent the summer of 1958 traveling alone in Europe. Rather than return to Chicago and finish his degree, he moved to New York City and lived off the first payment of the fellowship Houghton Mifflin had awarded him for the manuscript of *Goodbye, Columbus*. He took up again with Margaret, who had moved to Manhattan and begun working at *Esquire*. Soon afterward, she told Roth that she was pregnant. He disbelieved her, but she presented what appeared to be medical proof. According to Roth, the way Maureen in *My Life as a Man* tricks Peter into believing that she is pregnant almost exactly parallels the deception Margaret prac-

ticed on him in February of 1959: "Those scenes represent one of the few occasions when I haven't spontaneously set out to improve on actuality." Maureen bought a urine specimen from a pregnant woman and submitted it for a pregnancy test. Philip Roth and Margaret Williams were married on February 22, 1959.

While his personal life was foundering, Roth's literary career was being launched in spectacular fashion in 1959. A Guggenheim Fellowship and a National Institute of Arts and Letters grant followed the fellowship from Houghton Mifflin. Roth won the *Paris Review*'s Aga Khan Award for "Epstein," and "The Conversion of the Jews" was chosen for *The Best Short Stories of 1959. Goodbye, Columbus*, Roth's first collection of short stories, was published in May 1959 and won the Jewish Book Council of America's Daroff Award; in 1960 it received the National Book Award. Also in 1960, "Defender of the Faith" appeared in *The Best Short Stories of 1960* and *The O. Henry Memorial Award Prize Stories of 1960*. That year Roth joined the faculty of the Writers' Workshop at the University of Iowa. In 1962 *Letting Go* was published, with the dedication "For Maggie," and Roth received a Ford Foundation grant to write plays. He and Margaret moved back to New Jersey, where Roth was writer-in-residence at Princeton from 1962 to 1964.

By the end of 1962, Roth was legally separated from his wife and had moved from Princeton to New York City. Margaret refused to grant him a divorce and continued to live in Princeton, receiving about half of his income in alimony. Roth entered a period of "intense psychoanalysis" that provided "a model for reckless narrative disclosure of a kind I hadn't learned from Henry James," one he would later draw on for *Portnoy's Complaint*. He also began a romantic relationship of "mutual convalescence" with a tender, quieter, more gentile gentile whose character can be seen in the later novels. The year

1967 saw the publication of *When She Was Good,* which Roth based on Margaret's account of her upbringing. The book, he says, became a means "to look backward and discover the origins of that deranged hypermorality" by which he felt Margaret had ensnared and exploited him. The fictional catastrophe was to seem eerily fatidic: Margaret was killed on May 19, 1968, in a car accident in Central Park. Roth said that, on hearing the news, he was "transfixed at first by the uncanny overlapping of the book's ending with the actual event." As Tarnopol does later, he felt disbelief, even suspicion that it was a trick by his wife, and then an "immeasurable relief." The morning after the funeral, Roth chillingly recounts in his autobiography:

I walked over to Central Park and tried to find the spot where the car was said to have crashed and killed her. It was a splendid spring morning and I sat on the grass nearby for about an hour, my head raised to take the sun full in my face. Like it or not, that's what I did: gloried in the sunshine on my living flesh. "She died and you didn't," and that to me summed it up. I'd always understood that one of us would have to die for the damn thing ever to be over.

But for Roth it was not over so easily. After Margaret, the idea of being married, or of being bound to anyone, became intolerable. In his work it took him years of "hapless experimentation" to purge himself of his rage. *My Life as a Man* (1974) was largely an attempt to purge his feelings by converting them into literature. The numerous false starts and reworkings, Roth has admitted, almost broke his will: "The only experience worse than writing it . . . would have been for me to have endured that marriage without afterward having been able to find ways of reimagining it into a fiction with a persuasive existence independent of myself."

The years since Margaret's death, however, have been relatively peaceful ones. Roth and the British actress Claire Bloom have lived together since 1975 and share a rather quiet private life in a 200-year-old Connecticut farmhouse. The period since the mid 1970's has been one of great productivity—stories, novels, novellas, a book of essays and interviews, general editorship of Penguin Books' "Writers from the Other Europe" series, and an autobiography. His life, however, has not been without trial. In the summer of 1989 Roth underwent quintuple-bypass heart surgery. Worse, in the spring of 1987, at the height of his creative powers, he had suffered what he still terms "a breakdown." Painful complications from knee surgery led to despondency and insomnia. He began taking Halcion, a sleeping pill, and Xanax, a tranquilizer, but his mental state rapidly worsened. Unknown to him and his doctors, the drugs were interacting to produce hallucinations, panic, and even thoughts of suicide. Roth believed that he was going mad, and even after the cause of his distress was discovered, he continued for months to feel a "helpless confusion" about the course and meaning of his life. In order to recover the clarity, energy, and direction he had lost, he began retracing his steps, reviewing his personal history in *The Facts.*

Significantly, *The Facts* ends with Roth at thirty-five, just released from the psychic and financial burdens of a catastrophic marriage, sensing the end of his thralldom to his literary masters and the achievement of his own narrative voice in *Portnoy's Complaint,* restlessly anticipating the future, and yet looking twelve years into the past: back to the time when he felt the "exhilarating, adventurous sense of personal freedom" and artistic awakening—back to the time when he was about to meet Margaret and was beginning to write the stories of *Goodbye, Columbus.*

For those early stories, Roth drew largely on the memories, experiences, characters, and neighborhood folklore of his Newark boyhood. He also shows the devotion of a young writer to literary heroes. Believing "fiction writing to be something like a religious calling, and literature a kind of sacrament," he follows the high priests of realism, the great exemplars of morally serious fiction—Henry James, Gustave Flaubert, Leo Tolstoy, and T. S. Eliot. Among more recent Americans, F. Scott Fitzgerald, Saul Bellow, Isaac Bashevis Singer, and Bernard Malamud are apparent as models. The need for personal freedom and the suspicion of normative controls that Roth felt as a youth inform the five short stories in *Goodbye, Columbus*. Each is built around a morally significant action that a character decides to undertake in the face of social or institutional opposition. As in James, the characters define themselves by their brave decisions and their willingness to live with the consequences. As Roth explains it, each of the central figures "is seen making a conscious, deliberate, even willful choice *beyond* the boundary lines of his life, and just so as to give expression to what in his spirit will not be grimly determined, by others, or even by what he had himself taken to be his own nature."

The collection is rather uneven; the budding author was criticized by Alfred Kazin, Leslie Fiedler, Irving Howe, and others for hammering home his moral points too urgently and emphatically. Still, the chronological order of the stories' first publication dates suggests Roth's rapid development as a writer, for it is also the order of the pieces from least to most accomplished. The earliest and weakest of the stories is "You Can't Tell a Man by the Song He Sings." The impress of J. D. Salinger is obvious in this brief tale of a sensitive adolescent's discovery of hypocrisy in the adult world. The good and dutiful boy who submits to authority is punished for a fight; his reform-school acquaintances flee the scene. Further, he learns that the episode will become a permanent part of his record. Concluding that the school is less interested in doing justice than in maintaining appearances and finding scapegoats,

he recognizes the disparity between espoused ideals and actual practice.

"The Conversion of the Jews" also takes up the theme of freedom versus conformity, especially unthinking acquiescence to authority. The opponents are schematically drawn, and named, in the inquisitive young Ozzie Freedman and the dogmatic yeshiva teacher Rabbi Binder. Ozzie's curiosity leads him to question the religious orthodoxy, complacency, and xenophobia of his family and community. In particular, he is unconvinced by the rabbi's claim that the Virgin Birth was biologically impossible: If God could make the world in six days, Ozzie argues, He could make a woman have a baby without intercourse. Ozzie's reward for freethinking is a slap in the face from his mother at home and one from the rabbi at the yeshiva. Angry and humiliated, Ozzie goes to the roof of the building. When he realizes the power he has over the terrified adults below, he forces them all to kneel and proclaim their belief in Jesus. After rebuking his mother and the rabbi, "You should never hit anybody about God," he makes an exultant leap into the firemen's net. Although marred by a simplistic treatment of good and bad, a strained resolution, and a heavy-handed underscoring of "message," the story presents issues that pervade the later work.

The lone individual is again pitted against the community's morality, if not theology, in "Epstein." Here the rebellious maverick is not a yeshiva boy but a despondent man of fifty-nine who, after a lifetime of hard work and dutiful service to his family, finds his life empty. Making what Roth calls "a final struggle" against "exhaustion, decay, and disappointment," Epstein begins an adulterous affair with a widow across the street. Unfortunately, their attachment comes to light, as does a rash around Epstein's genitals. After being comically and humiliatingly exposed before his family, Epstein seeks solace at the widow's. There he suffers a heart attack in the midst of her ministrations. The story ends as Epstein is taken off in an ambulance with his wife, who feels vindicated by this judgment upon him, and a doctor, who assures her that he can treat the rash "so it'll never come back." By implication, neither will Epstein's chance for vital existence.

Roth based the work on a tale of neighborhood adultery that his father recounted one evening when Roth was about fourteen. What aroused his sympathy was the plight of an individual in conflict not just with his family and community, but also with himself. Epstein's adultery, Roth has said, does not "square with the man's own conception of himself." Having offended against his own self-image as well as against community standards, the hero complains, "I don't even feel any more like Lou Epstein." Roth's use of sex as the means of rebellion and the grounds for comedy looks forward to *Portnoy*, where once again the attempt at rebellion only intensifies the sense of guilty entrapment.

In "Defender of the Faith," conflict with an antagonist catalyzes the central character's conflict with himself. The story is set on a stateside army base in 1945, when the horrors of the Holocaust were just becoming known and the appeals for Jewish solidarity were all but irresistible. Battleworn Sergeant Nathan Marx, trying to recover his emotional equilibrium after two years of fighting in Europe, must decide how to deal with Private Sheldon Grossbart, a fellow Jew for whom he feels a personal aversion. Grossbart, by appealing to their common Jewish identity, constantly pressures Marx to give him and two other Jewish privates special favors. Marx makes a few exceptions that seem harmless. Discovering that Marx is vulnerable, Grossbart pushes for more and more special treatment, which Marx finds hard to deny. But when Grossbart uses information he received from Marx to change his orders from an assignment in the Pacific theater to one at Fort Monmouth, New Jersey, Marx employs a deception of his own to ensure that the original assignment stands. To Marx, Grossbart's exploitation of his Jewishness is dangerous as well as contemptible because it feeds anti-Semitic stereotypes. Ironically, he defends the faith by denying appeals to Jewish bonds he had been conditioned to honor.

Ironically, too, Roth's story prompted the same outraged accusations of betrayal from the Jewish community that Marx's action drew from Grossbart. Throughout his career, Roth has been attacked for self-hatred, anti-Semitism, or, at the very least, breaking ranks. He has portrayed Jewish characters who are greedy, lustful, manipulative, self-serving, and neurotic—not because they are Jews but because they are human. He also has drawn Jewish characters who are conscientious, intelligent, sensitive, and caring—not because they are Jews but because they are human. His most successfully realized characters are all these at once, and wrestle with themselves to achieve some delicate balance.

The conflict between secular assimilationism and devout orthodoxy is central to "Eli, the Fanatic." In fact, the conflict becomes centered *in* Eli Peck. When a yeshiva of displaced German Jews moves into Woodenton, an affluent suburb in mid-century America, the acculturated Jews there are embarrassed by the black garb of the "fanatics" and also fearful of the gentile community's reaction. The Americanized Jews deputize Eli, a successful attorney, to make the orthodox Jews conform to the ways of Woodenton or leave. Eli is at first willing to serve as their ambassador, but contact with the yeshiva precipitates a crisis of identity that leads twice to "what his neighbors forgivingly referred to as 'a nervous breakdown.' " In his negotiations with Leo Tzuref ("trouble" in Yiddish), Eli begins to sense a previously unrealized need for something beyond the spiritual emptiness and cultural rootlessness of his community. He tries to hold out against these feelings and finally prevails upon one of the "greenhorns" to give up his religious garb for Eli's new suit. Later, Eli finds the man's black clothes on his doorstep. On the day his son is born, he dons the black garb of his forefathers and walks through the town to the hospital. Eli's adoption of the black clothing does not signal a religious conversion so much as an acceptance of the suffering and separateness, the persecutions borne for the sake of an identity, that are part of his heritage. At the hospital it is assumed that Eli has had another breakdown. He is seized at the nursery window and given a sedative shot. The story ends: "The drug calmed his soul, but did not touch it down where the blackness had reached."

The novella "Goodbye, Columbus" also treats the lure of affluent assimilation and the strains caused by class differences among Jews. Although Brenda was a girl when the Patimkins moved from Newark to Short Hills, the chasm between her background and Neil Klugman's looms large, "as though the hundred and eighty feet that the suburbs rose in altitude above Newark brought one closer to heaven." Even the mundane expressions of value are telling. His Aunt Gladys, with whom Neil lives, pushes canned fruit so that it won't go to waste. Mr. Patimkin consumes fresh fruit ravenously and always has a conspicuous abundance on hand. When Brenda's little sister, Julie finds Neil helping himself to fruit, she accuses him of stealing, as if he has been caught trespassing in a world where he does not belong.

Neil, like Fitzgerald's Gatsby before him, sees the woman as embodying life's richest possibilities, the American dream of wealth and status. But, unlike Gatsby, he recognizes her deficiencies and understands that her allure depends in part on what she symbolizes to him. He feels deep ambivalence about Brenda and the world she represents. Undeniably drawn to it, cowed by it, he also resents it—and her. He resents her offhand, disparaging remarks about Newark. He resents her nose job. He resents the fact that she

asks him nothing about himself until her mother wants information. Most of all, he resents the way that she and her family unthinkingly treat him as they do their maid. Part of Neil's desire to possess Brenda is the desire to settle a score. He beds her for the first time on the night that he is left baby-sitting Julie. "How can I describe loving Brenda? It was so sweet, as though I'd finally scored that twenty-first point." Brenda, for her part, uses sex with Neil as a form of rebellion against her mother.

From their first meeting at poolside, when Brenda has Neil hold her glasses so she can dive, he associates her with water and tropical settings. She is "a sailor's dream of a Polynesian maiden," and Short Hills at dusk is "rose-colored, like a Gauguin stream." His susceptibility to such images and his sense that they represent a world closed to him cause him to feel an affinity with the little black boy who comes from the ghetto to the Newark Public Library where Neil works to stare at Gauguin prints in art books. In a prophetic dream, he and the boy are the only crew members on a ship anchored off a tropical island. Suddenly the ship begins to drift out to sea, and as they try futilely to stop it, the native women on shore keep calling out "Goodbye, Columbus . . ." Neil had heard the phrase on Ron Patimkin's record bidding farewell to Ohio State. In his dream it portends his loss of Brenda and of the American dream he pursued in her. Whenever he senses Brenda slipping away, Neil tries to bind her to him. Afraid of losing her when she returns to Radcliffe and afraid of proposing marriage, Neil pressures her into getting a diaphragm as a token of commitment to him. Brenda, fearful of the implication, balks at first but then assents. When she leaves it at home, her mother finds it. Her parents' disapproval makes Brenda feel that she must break off with Neil. Faced with the choice between his world and theirs, she predictably chooses theirs.

After a final confrontation in Boston, Neil

stands before Lamont Library at Harvard, wishing he could see inside his reflection in a window and know what it was "that had turned pursuit and clutching into love, and then turned it inside out again." Neil has, in a sense, been left outside looking in, but he is trying to look into himself as well. He is both James Gatz of *The Great Gatsby*, drawn to the "service of a vast, vulgar, and meretricious beauty," and Nick Carraway, who tells the story, reflecting on its meaning and looking for direction. And like Nick, Neil ends up between two worlds, a part of neither.

Letting Go (1962), Roth's first novel, treats the lives of four unmoored characters who drift together, apart, together, and apart again as the tide of circumstance carries them. Roth has said that for them "it isn't a matter of sinking or swimming—they have, as it were, to invent the crawl." Gabe Wallach, Paul and Libby Herz, and Martha Reganhart are struggling desperately not to sink, but they are not sure how best to stay afloat: by holding on to someone who may pull them under, or by letting go. Weighty epigraphs from Thomas Mann, Simone Weil, and Wallace Stevens clarify the problem at issue: that we expect more of people then they will be able to give us, while each of us, acting from "the unalterable necessity / Of being the unalterable animal," frustrates the needs and expectations of others.

Gabe and Paul represent two main types of response. The novel opens with a letter that Gabe's mother had written to him on her deathbed. In it, she confesses to using the guise of beneficence to control and manipulate people, especially Gabe's father: "I was always doing things for another's good. The rest of my life I could push and pull at people with a clear conscience." After reading the letter, Gabe vows not to interfere in others' lives, or let them interfere in his. His distrust of involvement causes him to drift into other people's lives until they begin to need him; then he tries to withdraw.

In this way, Gabe becomes involved in the marital problems of Paul and Libby Herz. Libby is the embodiment of "agonized yearning" for a happiness that she does not know how to find. Paul justifiably feels both oppressed by and responsible for Libby's unmet needs. They come to see Gabe as an "agent of deliverance" who will take Libby away and make her happy. Gabe has encouraged such fantasies by revealing his attraction to Libby and at one point kissing her; but when deeper commitment looms, he retreats. He then gravitates into a relationship with Martha, a divorced waitress and mother of two. She is for him "the escape hatch" through which he flees from his emotionally dependent father and Libby; at the same time, she uses him to avoid Sid Jaffee, a persistent suitor whose demands for a permanent tie frighten her. At first, at least sexually, Gabe and Martha seem well suited. But when the difference in their backgrounds begins to show and Martha starts having expectations of Gabe, he starts looking to Sid the way Paul had looked to him.

Despite bouts of escapism, Paul, like Gabe, embraces obligation and responsibility, somewhat as a martyr embraces the rack. He marries Libby in part because he can thus "make himself a better man." His joyless commitment is a source of pain for Libby, who was hoping for love and happiness. Paul tells her, "If I can't feel what I have to, I *do* what I have to." When she asks him how he can, he replies, "I force myself." He begins to crack under the weight of his and Libby's unfulfillable expectations. On the pretext of seeing his dying father, who had cut him off when he married a gentile, Paul goes to New York. There, swayed by his Uncle Asher, who presents the extreme case for letting go— "Nobody owes nobody nothing"—he decides to leave Libby.

At his father's burial Paul has an epiphanic vision of life as sacrifice, beyond human understanding of order and justice. He returns to

Libby, and they resolve to adopt a baby. At this point, most of the principals have had enough of drifting and resolve at least to be resolved. Paul wants to love Libby. Martha wants to make a conventional home for her children, and she tells Gabe that she will marry Sid. And Gabe, with the former threats to his independence looking for sustenance elsewhere, wants "something to hang on—to hang on *to*." Fired by a wish to be of service, he becomes involved in the Herzes' attempt to buy a baby from an ignorant and impoverished couple. He has the ulterior motive of proving his worth and good intentions: "he did not want it said by others—or by himself *to* himself—that he had gone less than all the way once again." But when the success of his enterprise is threatened, Gabe rashly takes the baby and forces a confrontation with the parents. The result is that the Herzes almost lose the child and Gabe suffers a breakdown. The novel closes with another letter of farewell and confession, this time one in which Gabe admits to Libby that he has used people for his own ends while ostensibly acting on their behalf. "I can't bring myself yet to ask forgiveness," he tells her. "If you've lived for a long while as an indecisive man, you can't simply forget, obliterate, bury, your one decisive moment. . . . You see, I thought at the time that I was sacrificing myself."

The Jamesian overtones here are unmistakable, but not unexpected, for as graduate students both Gabe and Roth cherished the James who was a "lover and interpreter of the fine amenities of brave decisions." Roth has remarked that the serious, ruminative tone and balanced sentences are "the language of a preoccupation with conscience, responsibility, and rectitude rather grindingly at the center of *Letting Go.*" Characters often apprehend one another through some nuance of manners, a revealing action, or a telling detail. Jamesian structural and narrative devices are evident in ficelles such

as the Horvitzes and in the shifting, imperfect centers of consciousness.

In *Letting Go,* Roth makes particular use of *The Portrait of a Lady.* Gabe and Libby discuss their situation indirectly by commenting on the novel. Clearly, its main story is relevant: Isabel Archer's quest for freedom leads to its restriction and the mature recognition that one must live with the binding consequences of uninformed decisions. Libby is critical at first of Isabel's desire "to alter what can't be altered" and to push and pull people "with an absolutely clear conscience." Hearing this phrase, Gabe realizes that Libby has read his mother's letter, which he had left in the book, and he uses the example of Isabel to chide her about Paul: "She shows herself to have a lot of guts in the end. It's one thing marrying the wrong person for the wrong reasons; it's another sticking it out with them." Ironically, the courage to make a commitment and keep it is precisely what Gabe lacks and Libby works toward.

Letting Go displays a greater sense of moral ambiguity and mixed natures than do Roth's previous works, a less rigorous division into sheep and goats, in part because the people it presents are deeply ambivalent about the claims of conscience and interpersonal responsibility. But for Lucy Nelson of *When She Was Good* (1967), nothing is morally ambiguous, no natures are mixed, and no claim admits of ambivalence. The book takes its title from "The Little Girl with a Curl": "When she was good she was very, very good / And when she was bad she was horrid." In Lucy's eyes, as in the example of the little girl in the nursery rhyme, there is no middle ground: people are either very, very good or horrid— *period.* The ironic twist is that Lucy herself becomes horrid, as well as pitiable, in her grim determination to be very, very good, and to make everyone around her cleave to the same standard.

The novel, set in Protestant, Midwestern, small-town America and taking a lower-middle-class girl as its center of interest, seems anomalous; Roth, in fact, once described it as his "book with no Jews." But the preoccupation with what is good and who sets the standards links it closely with his other fiction: "the question of who or what shall have influence and jurisdiction over one's life has been a concern in much of my work. From whom shall one receive the Commandments? The Patimkins? Lucy Nelson?" Presuming their own goodness or rightness, the characters attempt to remake others in their own image, as, in their various ways, Brenda does with Neil, Gabe's mother does with his father, Lucy does with Roy Bassart, and Sophie Portnoy does with little Alex.

Roth portrays Lucy as a victimizer but also as a victim of the incongruities between her family environment and the values of the larger society. In particular, he examines the destructive effects of traditional sex roles, with man as the authoritative protector and woman as the submissive helpmate. Sadly for Lucy, she accepts the model unconditionally and is driven to self-righteous desperation, violent anger, and finally death by her frustration at living among people who refuse to play their assigned parts.

Faced with a weak, self-effacing grandfather and a reckless, self-pitying father, Lucy learns from an early age to do everything for herself. Seeking a protective and prescriptive moral order, she becomes involved with Roman Catholicism as an adolescent and dedicates herself to St. Teresa of Lisieux's example of "submission, humility, silence and suffering." But one night when Lucy is fifteen, her father comes home drunk and creates a scene. She calls upon St. Teresa and Jesus for help in making him stop. When she gets no reply, she calls the police, who arrest her father. She is not visibly moved by the episode, prompting him to call her "Stone! Pure stone!"—but she is deeply scarred and humiliated. She decides then that she "hates suffering as much as she hated those who made her suffer."

Lucy becomes obsessed with moral rectitude and loses the capacity for sympathy; in fact, she sees mercy as reprehensible, a failure to combat evil. At this point, she begins to show signs of real psychological disturbance. She sees slights, threats, or injustices to herself everywhere. She becomes involved with the dreamy and unmotivated Roy Bassart because he is the first boy who has taken a real interest in her, because as an ex-soldier he seems mature, and because his more affluent, conventional family represents the kind of life she has missed. Soon, though, she begins to despise him as a younger version of her father. Just as she is about to escape her family and begin an independent life at a nearby college, she learns that she is "in trouble." Rather than undergo the abortion that she wants, she forces Roy to "do his duty" and marry her.

The marriage goes from terrible to worse. Lucy sees herself as the only force for decency in a depraved world of "fiends and monsters" conspiring against her. News that her father has been jailed for theft sends her into a rage in which she confuses Roy and her father, or at least unleashes her fury at her father against Roy. Terrified at her insane outburst, Roy flees with their son to his Uncle Julian's. Lucy follows, and in a vicious confrontation that accelerates from verbal to physical violence, she collapses. She escapes from her grandfather's house, where she is recovering, and wanders delirious in the snow, hallucinating scenes from her earlier life and plotting to steal her son back. She is found frozen to death by the spot where Roy had first seduced her, clutching to her cheek a letter that her father had written to her mother, begging forgiveness.

If "Goodbye, Columbus" recalls Fitzgerald and *Letting Go* invokes James, *When She Was Good* echoes *Madame Bovary,* Flaubert's tale of a provincial woman chafing under a drab life, surrounded by weak men, caught and destroyed by her own illusions as much as by circumstances. It also resembles the naturalistic fiction of Theodore Dreiser, Frank Norris, and Stephen Crane. In seeking to rise above the "coarse and banal" life around her, Lucy is doomed to failure by hereditary and environmental factors; these initiate a downward spiral that, once set in motion, feeds on itself and accelerates. Every attempt to escape her fate only hastens it. Lucy vows while giving birth that "her child would never know what life was like in a fatherless house," but her fanatical devotion to making Roy the man her father wasn't emasculates him and precipitates the catastrophe that will cause the child to grow up in a motherless house. Roth even conveys the mood of entrapment by using unrelievedly conventional, hackneyed, cliché-ridden prose to present the characters' thought and actions, thus suggesting the stunted possibilities and spent alternatives of the world Lucy struggles to transcend. Ironically, the town where she lives and dies is Liberty Center.

When She Was Good marks the end of the first phase of Roth's literary career, one in which he rather self-consciously wrote "complicated fictions of moral anguish" of the sort that also appealed to the young Peter Tarnopol. But the weightiness and oppressive atmosphere of his first two novels began to weigh on Roth—the fun was missing from his fiction, and from the act of writing. The five years between *Letting Go* and *When She Was Good* is the longest hiatus of his career; the latter novel required eight drafts and thousands of pages of revisions, a task so draining that Roth even talked of giving up writing. Moreover, the reviews of the final product were disappointing and often misdirected. Many declared the book "irrelevant" to the social upheavals of the late 1960's, whereas Roth felt that an examination of the destructive power of self-righteous conviction was quite pertinent to Vietnam-era America. Many saw the change of venue as an ill-advised attempt by Roth to abandon what he did best in order to demonstrate his versatility, whereas Roth was trying to extend his examination of guilt and goodness, freedom and duty.

After the arduous years spent on his "gloomy" first two novels, Roth was "aching to write something freewheeling and funny," to "get in touch with another side of [his] talent." That side—anarchic, irreverent, satiric—was allowed to play now and then in "Epstein," the depiction of Leo Patimkin, and the scenes with Asher Herz, but was largely suppressed in favor of the high seriousness of James and Flaubert. Yet while he was laboring over the tortured tale of Lucy Nelson, Roth was also, as a sort of antidote, making "abortive forays" into what emerged later as *Portnoy's Complaint* (1969). These included an untitled scatological slide show (begun in 1966); "The Jewboy" (begun in 1962), a bit of folkloric fantasy; *The Nice Jewish Boy* (begun in 1964), a realistic play; and an autobiographical "Portrait of an Artist" (begun in 1966). The general subject, Roth explains, was "the argument between the Abel and Cain of my own respectable middle-class background." But *Portnoy* is "a novel in the guise of a confession," not "a confession in the guise of a novel." Roth depicts not himself but a character torn between two powerful impulses contained within "the range of Jewish possibilities." The book has "less to do with 'freeing' me from my Jewishness or my family," he says, "than with liberating me from an apprentice's literary models."

Actually, Roth discovered a voice more distinctively his own by broadening his range of models to include complementary types, the raucous and unrestrained as well as the high-minded and morally serious. Drawing on Philip Rahv's terms, Roth identifies the first type as "redskins" and the second as "palefaces." He neatly characterizes himself as a "redface": "*fundamentally ill at ease in, and at odds with, both worlds*"—a sort of literary analogue to Neil

Klugman. But Roth experiences the tension as artistically invigorating. Now he can draw on Henny Youngman as well as Henry James, on Arnold G. and Jake the Snake of his Newark boyhood as well as Flaubert, on native American humorists as well as Tolstoy and Conrad: "being a redface accounts as much as anything for the self-conscious and deliberate zigzag that my own career has taken, each book veering sharply away from the one before."

Portnoy's Complaint seems to mark an exceedingly sharp zig after the zag of *When She Was Good*. But, as Roth points out, both dramatize "the problematic nature of moral authority," especially as incarnated in a dominating female. Both show a passion for freedom from the past leading the protagonist into "a bondage more gruesome and ultimately insupportable." Both show emotionally troubled adult children who are oppressed less by their parents than by their rage against them. The difference, of course, is that Roth radically alters the setting, voice, tone, and treatment of his theme: "not until I had got hold of guilt . . . as a comic idea, did I begin to feel myself lifting free and clear of my last book." Despite surface similarities to the nightclub routines of Mort Sahl or Lenny Bruce, Roth's dark comedy was influenced not so much by stand-up comics as by "a sit-down comic named Franz Kafka and a very funny bit he does called 'The Metamorphosis.' " Roth also draws on Kafka's "Letter to His Father," which he asked his students at Penn to use as a model for an imaginary letter to their parents; "I took the assignment on myself," he recalls, "and wrote a novel."

Kafka's is a comedy of guilt, proscription, blockage, and entrapment—of absurd worlds where authority is unreasoning and strategies for contending with it are self-defeating. Similarly, Portnoy tightens the cords that bind him by flailing about trying to get loose. As Roth explains it, "Portnoy's pains arise out of his refusal to be bound any longer by taboos which, rightly or wrongly, *he* experiences as diminishing and unmanning. The joke on Portnoy is that for him breaking the taboo turns out to be as unmanning in the end as honoring it. Some joke."

At first the taboos were unclear. As a little boy, Alex inhabited a Kafkaesque world of punishment without crime, guilt without apparent offense. He recalls his mother locking him out of the apartment for being bad; as he hammered on the door, begging to be let back in and promising to reform, he wondered, "But what is it I have done?" He only knew that pleasurable things were proscribed for unfathomable reasons. After watching a snowstorm he turned from the window and asked hopefully, "Momma, do we believe in winter?" As Alex gets older, he discovers that the taboos pertain mostly to food and sex, which become linked in his mind as means of rebellion. After his mother browbeats him into promising never again to eat hamburgers and french fries, he races to the bathroom in a fit of defiant fury to "grab that battered battering ram to freedom"; on another occasion he masturbates with a piece of liver that becomes the family dinner.

As an adult, Portnoy substitutes *shickses* for nonkosher foods and masturbation as the tools of revolt; they represent the polar opposite of the ingrained Jewish standards of restraint and renunciation. This campaign for liberation proves just as self-thwarting as the earlier ones. The more inhibited Portnoy feels by the guilt his parents have instilled in him, the more he strikes back through obscenity and sexual profligacy; doing so only makes him feel more guilty, which makes him strike back more. And so the cycle intensifies until it culminates in the wordless "pure howl" that ends his diatribe to his analyst, Dr. Spielvogel. Spielvogel's "punchline" reply—"Now vee may perhaps to begin Yes?"—indicates the viciously circular nature of Portnoy's complaint. The patient laments being "torn by desires that are repugnant to my conscience, and a conscience repugnant to my desires."

Portnoy's erotic life receives a triple-whammy in Israel. There the tormented soul finds taboos aplenty; a dearth of *shickses,* against whom he uses sex as a way of "settling [ethnic] scores"; and a strapping young woman named Naomi who closely resembles his mother at that age. He tries to force himself on her, but he proves impotent and she overpowers him. Humiliated, Portnoy submits to a tongue-lashing for being a perverse "self-hating Jew" who hides behind satiric humor. Here Roth is having some fun with his critics; he had faced these charges himself, and would again for *Portnoy.*

In "On the Air" (1970) talent scout Milton Lippman says that a talent scout must be attuned to "the strange"—"he doesn't make things happen, *he only points them out!*" In the essay "Writing American Fiction" (1960) Roth claims a similar role for the contemporary fictionist, who "has his hands full in trying to understand, describe, and then make *credible* much of American reality." When he tries in *Our Gang* (1971) not simply to understand and describe Richard Nixon, but to *satirize* him, he really has to exert himself. In conversations with Random House executives, he began answering charges of distortion and bad taste even before the book was published. There is, as he noted, a long tradition of American political satire that relies on shocking, tasteless distortion, the "dye dropped onto the specimen to make vivid traits and qualities otherwise only faintly visible to the naked eye." To criticism that the satire might prove ineffectual, Roth argued that writing satire is "a literary, not a political act." It is "moral rage transformed into comic art" and should be judged as such, not according to its power to bring about change.

But, judged as art, the satire is decidedly uneven. Roth does display a wonderful gift of mimicry, capturing Nixon's speech patterns, intonations, obsequious modesty, and self-serving casuistry; he also expands the target to include the mind set of "Tricky Dixon's" gang as well as the gullibility and self-importance of the news media. Sensing political opportunity in the abortion issue, Tricky professes his belief in "the sanctity of human life" and "the rights of the unborn." When Lt. William Calley is convicted in the slaughter of unarmed Vietnamese villagers, Tricky finds the soldier's actions consistent with a belief in the sanctity of human life: none of the women was known to be pregnant at the time of her death.

Another crisis erupts when the Boy Scouts protest that if Tricky supports the rights of the unborn, he must be in favor of sex. Tricky and his gang devise a plan to massacre the demonstrating scouts and blame the entire episode on Curt Flood, a black baseball player who threatened the American way of life by being the first to sue for free agency. Before his schemes, which include the invasion of Denmark, can come to fruition, Tricky is assassinated by being stuffed fetuslike into a large, fluid-filled plastic bag. Nearly everyone confesses to the crime. When last seen, Tricky is "on the comeback trail" in hell, running a smear campaign against Satan for the office of Devil. But despite some undeniably funny moments and direct hits, *Our Gang* often suffers from being strained, unmeasured, and heavy-handed—from Roth's not knowing what to cut and when to leave off.

Baseball becomes the main vehicle in *The Great American Novel* (1973) for comic attacks on institutionalized greed, bureaucratic ineptitude, xenophobia, racism, promotional schemes, anti-Communist paranoia, and just about any feature of the mid-century American landscape that illustrates the disparity between espoused ideals and actual practice. The progression from *Portnoy's Complaint* to *Our Gang* to *The Great American Novel* marks what Roth described as "my increased responsiveness to, and respect for, what is unsocialized in me." As the focus broadens from personal to impersonal, from the neurotic individual to the particular administration to the nation's "mythic sense of itself," the humor becomes less satiric and, says Roth, more "satyric": "The comedy in *The Great American Novel* exists for the sake of no higher value than comedy itself; the redeeming value is not social or cultural reform, or moral instruction, but *comic inventiveness*. Destructive, or lawless, playfulness—and for the fun of it."

The book demonstrates Roth's tremendous range and willingness to take risks. The votary of Flaubert and James here abandons the vows of the paleface priesthood for the barbaric—even obscene—yawp of the redskins. The raucous and ribald laughter, as Bernard Rodgers observes, has its roots in the oral storytelling traditions of the old Southwest that Roth studied at Chicago with Napier Wilt and Walter Blair, pioneer scholars in native American humor. Apparent in Roth's novel are the use of crude vernacular; the emphasis on masculine pastimes; the comic exploitation of physical discomfort and scatology; the hyperbole and mythologizing, especially about feats of physical prowess; the anecdotal style and episodic structure; the lack of psychological depth in character development; and the use of the frame-tale setting.

That setting is the most interesting part of the book. "Call me Smitty," the Prologue begins. Smitty is Word Smith, a foul-mouthed, funny, possibly paranoid and senile eighty-seven-year-old sportswriter with a love of verbal gymnastics that matches his love of baseball. Like a latter-day Ishmael, he has survived to tell the tale of the defunct Patriot League, supposedly an equal partner with the National and American Leagues until the end of World War II. The historical existence of the league is being covered up through a sort of universal—or national—tacit agreement, because to chronicle its destruction

would be to expose the forces of corruption, cynicism, and expediency that belie the national myth. The story of the extinction of the Patriot League, then, is the story of a dying America. The Prologue, in which Smitty tries to justify his undertaking, is enlivened by his earthy, exuberant play with language and his engaging parodies of Hawthorne, Melville, Twain, Hemingway, and others who might be considered contenders for the title "Great American Novelist."

Smitty goes on to recount the trials of the Ruppert Mundys, a team owned in its glory days by Glorious Mundy. After his death, the war-profiteering new owners lease the home stadium to the government and force the Mundys to leave Port Ruppert (named for the park in Newark where Philip and his dad watched baseball) and wander like the ancient Israelites in the wilderness of foreign fields. Soon Glorious's Mundys are sick of transit and give over to assorted dissipations. Despite the biblical parallels and mythic overtones lent by such players' names as Red Kronos, Gil Gamesh, and Deacon Demeter, the third-person narrative loses much of the stylistic verve and energy of the first-person prologue. Roth, or Smitty, tries to compensate with a frantic heightening of the action, relating events so farfetched that the reader can no longer credit them. Moreover, it is not clear how the extreme implausibilities—on the field or off—are to be taken, for Roth fails to establish whether Smitty is intentionally writing a fiction or distractedly spinning out a paranoid fantasy that he takes for history.

Like Melville and Hawthorne, whom he calls "my precursors, my kinsmen," Smitty attempts, in Roth's words, "to imagine a myth of an ailing America"; Roth says that his own attempt has been "to imagine a book about imagining that American myth." In grounding Smitty's fabrications in historical events, by mixing actual players and commissioners with invented ones, he tries to establish "a continuum between the credible incredible and the incredible credible.'' In *The Breast* (1972), Roth posits an incredible event that the reader and the protagonist must accept as reality. Professor David Kepesh has, unaccountably, been transformed into a disembodied 155-pound female breast. Although published before *The Great American Novel, The Breast* was written after it. The focus shifts back from public to private life. Roth also returns to his most characteristic narrative strategy, one that he dropped with mixed results in the previous two works: encouraging the reader to identify with a central character by showing the world as it looks and feels to that person.

Kepesh is another of those characters ''whose moorings have been cut, and who are swept away from their native shores and out to sea.'' His predicament, Roth notes, is similar to that of earlier characters, but ''with a difference: his unmooring can't be traced (much to his dismay, too) to psychological, social, or historical causes.'' Not that Kepesh doesn't try. A rational humanist, he even feels an ''intellectual responsibility'' to uncover the cause and meaning of his metamorphosis; thus he considers and rejects a number of explanations for his predicament. He even entertains the notion that fiction is to blame, that his condition is really a hallucination inspired by his teaching of Gogol's ''The Nose'' and Kafka's ''The Metamorphosis.'' Ironically, he appreciates the absurd and inexplicable in literature but cannot abide it in life: insisting on a plausible answer, he convinces himself very rationally that he is insane. Ultimately, Kepesh discounts this hypothesis as well. He reasons too coherently to be crazy.

In searching his character for clues to his fate, Kepesh recognizes what Roth has described as ''the struggle to accommodate warring (or, at least, contending) impulses and desires, to negotiate some kind of inner peace or balance of power . . . between the ethical and social yearnings and the implacable, singular lusts for the flesh and its pleasures.'' In this way he recalls Lou Epstein and Alexander Portnoy while anticipating Peter Tarnopol and Nathan Zuckerman. On the one hand, he realizes that ''the social constraint practiced by and large by the educated classes provided me with genuine aesthetic and ethical satisfactions.'' On the other hand, he acknowledges his need to indulge the lustful Dionysian side of his nature. In fact, in the months preceding his metamorphosis, he was troubled by the waning of his desire for Claire, a lovely and tender young woman who had made his life ''orderly and stable'' for the first time since his disastrous marriage. He hits upon the notion that his transformation results from the ''trauma'' of undeserved happiness—''my guilt!''

Roth is parodying the all-purpose diagnosis of Portnoy's complaint. It does not finally strike Kepesh as very persuasive, either. He comes to accept the reality of his condition, which includes his inability to understand it. As Roth says, ''To try to unravel the mystery of 'meaning' here is really to participate to some degree in Kepesh's struggle—and to be defeated, as he is.'' And yet in defeat Kepesh is what the author calls his ''first heroic character.'' Kepesh's victory, or consolation prize, is learning to take responsibility for the management of his inner self, regardless of outer circumstances. He closes his account with a line from Rainer Maria Rilke: ''. . . You must change your life.''

Roth has said that he envisions Wallach, Portnoy, and Kepesh

as three stages of a single explosive projectile that is fired into the barrier that forms the boundary of the individual's identity and experience: that barrier of personal inhibition, ethical conviction and plain, old monumental fear beyond which lies the moral and psychological unknown. Gabe Wallach crashes up against the wall and collapses; Portnoy proceeds on through the fractured mortar, only to become lodged there, half in, half out. It remains for Kepesh to pass right on through the bloodied hole, and out the other end, into no-man's-land.

With Peter Tarnopol of *My Life as a Man* (1974), Roth first presents a character who tries to orient himself in no-man's-land—to understand and shape the chaos of his life—through the act of writing about it.

Tarnopol has a compulsion to tell and retell the story of how he squandered his manhood and youthful promise by marrying Maureen Johnson, a disturbed and destructive woman about five years his senior. He first offers two "Useful Fictions" as attempts to objectify his experience and then the autobiographical "My True Story." For the fictions he created an alter ego named Nathan Zuckerman, himself an author whose life in many particulars resembles Tarnopol's—and Roth's. In "Salad Days," the first "Useful Fiction," a third-person narrator relates from an "amused, Olympian point of view" the early personal history of Zuckerman: his protected Jewish childhood; his precocity in school; his inflated sense of himself in college, where he attains moral seriousness and literary ambitions; his erotic adventures with Sharon Shatzky, a cruder and more carnal Brenda Patimkin; and his brief stint in the peacetime army. But near the end of this tale of youthful self-absorption he writes, "He would begin to pay . . . for the contradictions: the stinging tongue and the tender hide, the spiritual aspirations and the lewd desires, the soft boyish needs and the manly, the *magisterial* ambitions."

Zuckerman suffers from the same duality as many of Roth's characters, including Tarnopol, who is, after all, writing autobiographical fiction. Sensing the inadequacy of the voice in "Salad Days" to recount the horrors to come, Tarnopol switches to a "grave and pensive" first-person account in "Courting Disaster," the second "Useful Fiction." There Zuckerman tells of his tortured relationship with Lydia Ketterer,

which parallels Tarnopol's with Maureen and Roth's with Margaret. Zuckerman chooses Lydia over Sharon because she appeals to his literary sensibilities; having survived a sordid upbringing invests her with enormous moral "glamor." Also, somewhat like Paul Herz, he invests *himself* with moral glamor by dutifully assuming responsibility for her. As if to prove himself to himself, he embraces a woman who has become repugnant to him. The marriage ends in Lydia's suicide and Zuckerman's flight to Italy with her semiliterate daughter, now his mistress.

Tarnopol indicates through Zuckerman's disappointment with the narrative that his fiction, too, has failed to purge, placate, or even illuminate his demons. In a statement that remarkably anticipates Roth's rationale for *The Facts*, Tarnopol determines "to forsake the art of fiction for a while and embark upon an autobiographical narrative." Roth employs various stratagems to make Peter seem real. As Zuckerman's creator and the author of the two fictions, he, like his history, appears genuine by comparison. His embarrassed confession that he married Maureen because he was influenced by great literature seems to be the "real-world" antecedent for Zuckerman's comparable blunder; it also seems to distinguish Tarnopol's life from literary invention. As an added structural twist, Roth has Tarnopol have Zuckerman make *himself* seem real by complaining that his life would be more richly patterned and clearly meaningful if it were fiction.

Although biographical parallels and structural ploys encourage one to regard Tarnopol's "True Story" as true, it is another of Roth's useful fictions—an attempt to master personal experience by ruminating on it and reshaping it as art. Roth reveals Tarnopol's fictionality by making him a patient of Dr. Spielvogel, Portnoy's analyst—a neat little bit of intertextuality that subverts some of the trompe l'oeil. A more telling distinction is that Tarnopol's experiences render him impotent for years as both a writer and a man, whereas Roth continues to publish prolifically. The crucial similarity between Roth and Tarnopol is not in the overlapping details of their marriages but in their need to reexamine, redirect, or even regain themselves through writing about the trauma.

Roth's description of Tarnopol's endeavor reveals the key link between them:

the presentation or description of himself is what is most problematical—and what remains unsolved . . . Tarnopol's attempt to realize himself with the right words . . . is what's at the heart of the book, and accounts for my joining his fictions about his life with his autobiography. When the novel is considered in its entirety, I hope it will be understood as Tarnopol's struggle to achieve a description.

Of course, it is also Roth's, as well as a chance to stand at one remove, exploring the relationship between life and artistic representation.

At the end of *My Life as a Man*, Tarnopol sees himself as fated to repeat old patterns: although released from Maureen by a car accident, he is still trapped in himself: "This me who is me being me and none other!" That sense of what Roth calls "characterological enslavement" pervades *The Professor of Desire* (1977), the story of David Kepesh before his metamorphosis. His inability to alter his character or his fate is underscored by our knowledge of what happens to him, but, as Roth says, the book does not "bear a necessary relationship to *The Breast*." Rather, he imagines "the details that had formed the realistic underpinnings of a very surreal story." Until the conclusion, there is little foreshadowing of Kepesh's transformation.

Kepesh's complaint is a familiar one: an internecine warfare between "the measured self" and "the insatiable self." The failure to achieve an inner peace, though, is rendered more poignantly here than in any of Roth's previous work.

Kepesh is acutely sensitive to the pain and disorientation caused by his dual nature. His account begins, "Temptation comes to me first in the conspicuous personage of Herbie Bratasky," a coarse, outrageous young comic and master of ceremonies at his parents' Catskills resort hotel whom David idolizes as a boy. Yet while he acknowledges the call of the wild, he tries to resist it, here through the formality of his language. His bouts of frantic self-indulgence typically elicit self-recrimination, expiatory gestures, and pledges to make amends. At college, literature gives him the means to rationalize, if not to reconcile, his opposing natures: he takes Macaulay's description of Steele—"A rake among scholars, a scholar among rakes"—along with selected bits of Byron's poetry and Kierkegaard's *Either/Or* as guides for action.

Kepesh often sees the alternatives represented in pairs of people. When he is a boy, there is his dutiful and responsible father to match Herbie. When he is in London on a fellowship, there are the voracious, hedonistic Birgitta and the tender, sensitive, conscience-stricken Elisabeth. In his professional life, there are the raunchy, uninhibited poet Ralph Baumgarten and the fastidious, elegantly restrained Arthur Schonbrunn. Most important, there are the lustful, shallow, adventurous Helen, whom he marries and divorces, and the calm, orderly, tender Claire, with whom he tries to rebuild his life after bouts with Helen have left him an impotent analysand of Dr. Frederick Klinger. Birgitta and Helen stimulated and shared his impetuous craving for ever more of the exciting, the unknown, the forbidden; Claire offers him hope of peace from the consuming appetites he fears as "inimical to [his] overall interests"—"No more *more*."

Kepesh also sees the scholar as protection against the rake. Afraid of losing himself in a life of excess with Birgitta, he retreats into the academic rigors of graduate school. Later he uses scholarly pursuits to buffer himself against Helen, although he realizes that these may in part be "evasions" and laments, "Oh, why must it be Helen and Birgitta at one extreme or life with a lemon at the other?" He alludes here to Kafka, one of his literary heroes, who epitomized self-denial in claiming that "the only fit food for a man is half a lemon." Kepesh addresses the same issues in his literary criticism that obsess him in his life—Kafka's "preoccupation with spiritual starvation," for example. In the "sexual despair" induced by his dichotomous nature, he sees an analogue to Kafka's blocked, thwarted K's "banging their heads against invisible walls." A literary Portnoy whose conscience and desires are mutually repugnant, Kepesh understands that the walls are internal. Even in his aesthetic tastes, he is drawn to different poles: not only Kafka's surrealistic fables of obstruction, guilt, and punishment but also Chekhov's muted, realistic stories of romantic disillusionment. He also focuses on what confounds him in life; he is writing "an essay on license and restraint in Chekhov's world," with particular attention to Chekhov's "perverse pessimism" about the chances for achieving "personal freedom."

For a time it seems as if Kepesh finds in literature and in Claire the means to integrate his contending selves. When they travel to Europe together, he works on lectures that show how his emotional life and his readings have informed each other; he becomes a "professor of desire." But in Venice he decides to conceal from Claire his adventures there with Birgitta some ten years earlier, whereupon Birgitta becomes all he can think of. The two visit Kafka's grave, in Prague, as Roth did in 1972. In this new setting, just when he thinks he has quelled his old demons, Kepesh dreams that he is led by Herbie Bratasky to visit Kafka's aged whore. She asks him through Herbie whether he "would like to inspect her pussy . . . She submits that it might hold some literary interest for you." The grotesque incongruity here reveals that in Kepesh's

psyche, the scholar and the rake remain unreconciled. And the dream association of Kafka's grave with Kafka's whore indicates that Kepesh still links sexuality with the death of his better self.

David and Claire return to an idyllic farmhouse in the Catskills where, for a time, he enjoys the balm of her placid tenderness. His father and a friend, a survivor of the death camps, come for a visit, and Claire is wonderfully sensitive to their emotional needs. A surprise visit from Helen, unhappy in her outwardly perfect new marriage and still craving *more*, triggers the same response in him: he feels "the lovely blandness of a life with Claire" begin "to cloy, to pall," and he knows that soon the complacent scholar "will give way to Herbie's pupil, Birgitta's accomplice, Helen's suitor, yes, to Baumgarten's sidekick . . . to the would-be wayward son and all he hungers for."

The novel ends in the early morning with David, after a night of bad dreams, reaching out for Claire and pressing his lips "in a desperate frenzy" to her breast, knowing that his humanity and wholeness depend on fixing his desire in *her*, and yet sensing it slip away into "fear of transformations yet to come." Despite the adumbration of Kepesh's metamorphosis and echoes of Kafka's story, the tone and treatment in the last section of the book are Chekhovian. Roth infuses the late-summer retreat with the pathos of the dying season, and of dying love. More than anywhere before, he shows a compassionate understanding of the poignancy of longing and loss; a sense of the passing of all things before they are realized; "a feel," as Kepesh says of Chekhov, "for the disillusioning moment and for the processes wherein actuality pounces upon even our most harmless illusions, not to mention the grand dreams of fulfillment and adventure."

David Kepesh is finally unable to integrate the polar extremes of his nature. Similarly, Roth says of himself, "one of my continuing problems as a writer has been to find the means to be true to these seemingly inimical realms of experience that I am strongly attached to by temperament and training.'' Previously, he had tended to objectify this artistic problem as a personal dilemma for his characters. With *The Ghost Writer* (1979), he treats the artistic problem directly. Nathan Zuckerman, sans Tarnopol, looks back more than twenty years to the time when he, like Roth, was twenty-three and writing the stories that would be collected in his first book. Nathan has had a falling out with his father, a Newark chiropodist whose loving pride and high expectations have become a burden. In Victor Zuckerman's opinion, ''Higher Education,'' Nathan's most ambitious story, presents a disparaging picture of Jews. The father enlists the prestigious Judge Leopold Wapter to influence the son to suppress his story and redirect his imagination. Nathan hears the same criticisms that Roth did after publishing ''Defender of the Faith''; and among the questions Judge Wapter poses is essentially the same one that Roth had to field at Yeshiva University in 1962: ''If you had been living in Nazi Germany in the thirties, would you have written such a story?'' A self-styled ''Nathan Dedalus,'' Zuckerman vows to fly past the nets of family, church, and state on wings of his own making.

Somewhat ironically, his flight takes him ''off and away seeking patriarchal validation elsewhere.'' As in *The Professor of Desire,* the alternatives are embodied in a pair of contrasting characters: Felix Abravanel, a larger-than-life, self-publicizing, self-indulgent Maileresque author aloft ''in the egosphere''; and E. I. Lonoff, a composite figure with elements of Bernard Malamud, Isaac Bashevis Singer, and Isaac Babel, whose characters are ''masters of renunciation'' and whose fictions are dour ''visions of terminal restraint.'' Nathan had met Abravanel three years earlier, but feeling certain that the literary lion was ''not in the market for a twenty-three-year-old son,'' he mailed his four published stories to

Lonoff and received an invitation to visit ''the most famous literary ascetic in America'' at home in the Berkshires. As the novel opens, young Nathan, ''already contemplating [his] own massive *Bildungsroman*,'' arrives to submit himself ''for candidacy as nothing less than E. I. Lonoff's spiritual son.'' He looks around at the austerity and seclusion, everything reserved for the ''transcendent calling,'' and thinks, ''This is how I will live.''

What Roth identifies as a central question in his works, ''who or what shall have influence and jurisdiction over one's life,'' here becomes primarily an aesthetic issue. The impressionable Nathan is ready to embrace Lonoff uncritically as his mentor, but Lonoff realizes that his way of resigned disillusionment, patience, and self-denial may not be Nathan's way: ''an unruly personal life will probably better serve a writer like Nathan. . . . His work has turbulence—that should be nourished.'' Lonoff has read Nathan well.

Nathan is also drawn to Amy Bellette, a beautiful and mysterious young woman he meets at Lonoff's. Is she a student, another disciple, a mistress—or all three? At night he fantasizes about her and masturbates on the daybed in Lonoff's study. To expiate his sin, he reads ''The Middle Years,'' a story by Henry James about a dying novelist who narrowly missed greatness. The man's deathbed utterance he recognizes as the quotation pinned above Lonoff's desk: ''Our doubt is our passion and our passion is our task. The rest is the madness of art.'' Hearing Lonoff's and Amy's voices in the room above, Zuckerman stands on the thick volume of James to facilitate eavesdropping. Amy is tempting Lonoff, but Lonoff, himself a master of renunciation, returns to his wife's room. Zuckerman is astonished, and like young Roth in ''Writing American Fiction,'' chagrined at the thinness of his own imagination: ''If only I could invent as presumptuously as real life! . . . But,'' he wonders, "if I ever did, what then would they think of me, my father and his judge? How would my elders hold up against that? And if they couldn't . . . just how well would I hold up against being hated and reviled and disowned?"

To answer the challenge to his imagination posed by "real life," and to answer his elders, Nathan invents another fantasy about Amy: she is Anne Frank alive. This useful fiction provides him with a morally unassailable precedent for placing his art ahead of his family and vindicates him before the court of Wapter, who had advised him to raise his Jewish consciousness by seeing the Broadway production of *The Diary of Anne Frank* and to present Jews favorably in his fiction. In Nathan's reverie, Amy–Anne writes, as he does, not to present a representative sampling of Jews or to improve their public image but to "educate herself." Like Nathan Dedalus, she declares to the family and the world at large, *"I don't feel in the least bit responsible for any of you."* After escaping death and immigrating to America, she learns that her father has survived to publish her work. Realizing that it will have far greater impact if she is believed dead, she decides not to be reunited "with the loving father who must be relinquished for the sake of his child's art."

The next morning, Nathan is "continually drawn back into the fiction" he has spun about Amy. He even imagines marrying her and thus being exonerated before his elders, for who would accuse the husband of Anne Frank of anti-Semitism? Nathan's musings are disrupted by Hope Lonoff's sudden outburst. Amy's presence, and thirty-five years of sacrificing herself to the closed, brooding Lonoff's needs, finally prove too much. To Amy as she leaves, Hope says: "There is his religion of art, my young successor: rejecting life! *Not* living is what he makes his beautiful fiction *out* of! And you will now be the person he is not living with!" As Lonoff calmly prepares to go out and retrieve Hope, he directs Nathan to paper for making notes on what he has witnessed. "It could be an interesting story. You're not so nice and polite in your fiction. . . . You're a different person." "Am I?" Nathan asks. Lonoff, as though administering confirmatory rites, gravely shakes the young writer's hand and says, "I should hope so."

Over the morning mail from assorted self-seekers and cranks, Lonoff had said to Hope, "Let Nathan see what it is to be lifted from obscurity. Let him not come hammering at our door to tell us that he wasn't warned." His remark becomes the epigraph for *Zuckerman Unbound* (1981). It and his comment on Nathan's niceness prove prophetic. Thirteen years have passed, and Nathan has achieved notoriety along with his first commercial success, *Carnovsky,* his *Portnoy's Complaint.* He has taken a page, as it were, from Abravanel as well as from Lonoff. As Zuckerman has zigzagged, so has Roth: the shift from the modulated, reflective tone of *The Ghost Writer* to the manic edginess of this book befits the sudden disruptions in the life of the new literary celebrity. Gossip columnists invent affairs for him, television personalities make jokes about him, marginal types and perverts insult and proposition him through his answering service, and someone threatens to kidnap his mother. He is followed by one Alvin Pepler, an embittered former quiz-show contestant who believes he was the victim of an anti-Semitic conspiracy to install a WASP as champion. Like Smitty, Pepler wants to write a book that shows "in detail, step by step, the decline of every decent American thing into liars and lies." Of course, he could use Zuckerman's help.

Moreover, Zuckerman has lost his "levelheaded Laura," another of Roth's orderly, practical, generous women with whom life begins to get dull. She tells him, "having written a book like that, you had to go. That's what writing it was all about." What was a personal dilemma for David Kepesh becomes a personal and artistic dilemma for Nathan Zuckerman, because the question of what kind of books he will write is bound up with the question of what kind of husband or son he will be.

Aside from outraging the Jewish community, *Carnovsky* deeply wounds Zuckerman's mother, whom even old friends take for Mrs. Carnovsky, and it effectively destroys his relationship with his brother and father. Dr. Zuckerman's dying word to Nathan is—"Bastard." When Nathan later tries to comfort and advise his miserable brother, who is sinking under the burden of an unhappy marriage and the legacy of paternal expectations, Henry curses him for sacrificing their parents to write a "liberating" book. Nathan admits inwardly that "he'd known it all along. . . . But he'd written it anyway." The novel ends with Nathan being driven by an armed chauffeur through the wreckage of what was once his family's Newark neighborhood. In fighting to free himself from the constraints of his past, he has succeeded all too well: there seems nothing left of it for him to hold on to. Zuckerman unbound is also Zuckerman unmoored.

The author of *Carnovsky* is shown in the process of learning lessons that the author of *Zuckerman Unbound* has absorbed. One is self-doubt. The mock heroic title implicitly satirizes authorial self-importance. Zuckerman is no Prometheus, willingly bearing the god's wrath for giving fire, civilization, and the arts to man. He must question whether his gifts, the stories, are worth the pain he suffers, and causes. Another is self-discipline, for the written world imposes a set of constraints as restrictive as the unwritten world's: "It may look to outsiders like a life of freedom. . . . But once one's writing it's *all* limits," says Zuckerman bound. "Bound to a subject. Bound to make sense of it. Bound to make a book of it." And bound to be misread, the harshest lesson. Zuckerman is dismayed that a great portion of the reading public "cannot distinguish between the illusion and the illusionist." Roth experienced the same vexation when Portnoy's complaint was taken for his, but he can now be playful: in making the point through Zuckerman he simultaneously unmakes it by encouraging readers to identify his situation with the character's.

In defending "Epstein," Roth explained that he was "interested in how—and why and when—a man acts counter to what he considers to be his 'best self,' or what others assume it to be, or would like it to be." This collision between the individual and a set of unmanageable expectations is the central conflict in Roth, one that often triggers a crisis of identity in which the main character must reexamine his or her own motives, methods, and values in redefining the self. *The Anatomy Lesson* (1983) finds Zuckerman four years older and in the throes of just such a crisis. He has not been able to complete "a page worth keeping" since his father's deathbed rebuke. "What he'd made his fiction from was gone. . . . Without a father and a mother and a homeland, he was no longer a novelist. No longer a son, no longer a writer."

According to critic Milton Appel, he never was much of one. Appel's hatchet job on Zuckerman in *Inquiry* is, for all practical purposes, Irving Howe's "Philip Roth Reconsidered" in the December 1972 *Commentary,* an indictment of the author on charges of vulgarity, mediocrity, shallowness, and cultural treason. Appel vents, in the voice of the Jewish intellectual community, the anger and disappointment of Nathan's father. Just as Howe asked, "but who can doubt that Portnoy's cry . . . speaks in some sense for Roth?" so Appel contends that the difference between characters and their authors is not what "grown-ups" pretend to their students. Although Zuckerman fights back, Appel's attack hurts all the more deeply because it echoes his own doubts: "But suppose he's right. . . . What if twenty years of writing has just been so much helplessness before a . . . lowly, inconsequential compulsion that I've dignified with all my principles.'' Worse, one for which he loses a brother and a father, and hurts his mother deeply. He knows that she died not blaming him, but not understanding.

Zuckerman's complaint involves physical as well as psychological distress: for a year and a half he has suffered from debilitating neck and shoulder pain, undiagnosable like Novotny's. And, like Portnoy "locked up in self," he becomes "ensnared by the selfness" of his agony. Also feeling Kepesh's need to account for his affliction, he considers and rejects undischarged filial anger or guilt over *Carnovsky* as an explanation. Perhaps, he thinks, the pain is a message from his buried self to "escape the clutches of self-justification . . . learn to lead a wholly indefensible, unjustifiable life—and learn to like it." To Zuckerman, this translates into giving up writing, which the bodily pain, the father's curse, and the lack of subject make impossible anyway.

Zuckerman comes to believe that, aside from damaging and exploiting other people's lives, his writing has prevented him from living his own. He attempts to pursue the unjustifiable life and escape his pain through drugs, sex, and alcohol, but to no avail. In his "search for the release from self," he hits upon the idea of becoming a doctor: "So busy diagnosing everybody else there's no time to overdiagnose yourself." As if to undo a spell, he travels back to Chicago, the site of his graduate-school initiation into the coven of writers, and tries to enlist the help of an old roommate, now a physician, in getting into medical school. On a visit to a Jewish cemetery with the friend's father, a drunken and deranged Nathan tries to assault the old man, whom he sees as "the last of the fathers demanding to be pleased." He falls on a gravestone, severely injures his mouth, and winds up in the hospital. There he likes to accompany the interns on their rounds and contemplate sharing in their "indispensable work . . . . as though he still believed that he could unchain himself from a future as a

man apart and escape the corpus that was his.'' So the novel ends, with another image of "characterological enslavement": Zuckerman bound to his corpus—both his body and his writings— and thus to their identity: author.

Zuckerman Bound (1985) becomes the title for the Zuckerman trilogy and "Epilogue: The Prague Orgy," a paranoid vision of the spiritual depravity that results from the suppression of freedoms. The story, in the form of entries from Zuckerman's notebooks, is a variation of James's "The Aspern Papers" by way of Kafka. At the request of Zdenek Sisovsky, a Czech writer he meets in New York, Zuckerman travels to Prague to recover the unpublished Yiddish stories of Sisovsky *père*. "This," the son assures him, "is not the Yiddish of Sholem Aleichem. This is the Yiddish of Flaubert." Unfortunately, the son's wife, Olga, has the stories and, out of hatred for the man who abandoned her, intends to keep them. The only way to get them, Sisovsky believes, is for Zuckerman to seduce her. In Prague, Zuckerman finds himself in a grotesque "comedy of manners" that the artists and intellectuals have fashioned out of their oppression. He is the Jamesian character, "only ears—and plans, an American gentleman abroad, with the bracing if old fashioned illusion that he is playing a worthwhile, dignified, and honorable role."

Zuckerman comes to question his own motives in the affair. Is he trying to prove his literary idealism, show solidarity with European Jewry, play the good son by proxy and expiate sins against the father? Perhaps he, like Olga, is motivated only by *touha*, a longing for "the absent thing." And what if the stories aren't any good? Olga, too embittered and apathetic to require payment or seduction, gives them to Zuckerman. They are confiscated by the authorities before he can get them out of the country. With the degeneration of his mission into "a personal fiasco," Zuckerman concludes: "No, one's story isn't a skin to be shed—it's inescapable. . . . the ever-recurring story that's at once your invention and the invention of you.''

The possibility of reinventing your story and yourself, and the *touha* for a new mode of life, are at the heart of *The Counterlife* (1986), a sort of Menippean satire in which Roth, and Zuckerman, create characters who express a range of viewpoints in a running debate on the writer's enterprise. Every perspective is opposed, or at least qualified, by others, and none is finally proved authoritative, for the different stories that make up the book expose one another as fictions and challenge one another's validity as representations of reality. Roth masterfully combines traditional psychological realism and a poststructuralist fascination with interlocking, self-subverting structures. As a result the authenticity of each compellingly presented account is undercut until the reader, like the main characters, is certain of little aside from the transforming power of fiction.

Point of view shifts from story to story, and sometimes within a story. ''Basel'' is a third-person narrative in which Henry has fallen in love with a Swiss woman, Maria. He has inherited from his father not only heart disease but a sense of duty that requires him to reject her for his unloved wife and their children. The dual legacy proves fatal. Henry's heart condition worsens from the emotional strain of his decision, and the drugs he takes for it make him impotent. For the sake of a compensatory affair, he risks dangerous surgery that would get him off the drugs, and dies. Nathan, guilty over not having tried to stop his brother, takes notes he made from Henry's outpourings to him and begins to transform them into ''a puzzle for his imagination to solve''—a story.

In the first-person ''Judea,'' Henry is physically recovered and ethnically reborn. On vacation in the Holy Land, he experiences a sudden, overpowering conversion to Judaism, as a heritage more than as a religion. He leaves his family and takes up life in the mountains with a band of militant Zionists. Nathan, married to an Englishwoman named Maria who is expecting their first child, visits Henry as the ambassador from home and is generally derided as the epitome of all that is wrong with the diaspora Jew. In particular, Henry disdain's Nathan's self-absorbed, self-deprecating fictions about oppression by Momma and Poppa, whereas Nathan sees Henry's action as a belated rebellion against their father—one that ironically subjugates him to a patriarchal code even more rigid. Henry stands for the patriot's ''certainty'' that he learned in the hills, Nathan for the artist's ''doubt'' that he learned in Lonoff's study. Nathan realizes that his motives for the visit are not pure: The writer in him wants to exploit what is ''far and away Henry's most provocative incarnation.''

''Aloft'' finds Nathan flying back to Maria and writing Henry a long letter in which he opines that for European Jews, Zionism is ''the construction of a counterlife that is one's own antimyth,'' a reflection of ''the will to remake reality'' and the ''urge to self-renovation.'' He also writes to an Israeli friend who had urged him in the name of Jewish interests not to use his Middle East adventures as the basis for satire; Nathan replies that social concerns do not warrant curbing free artistic expression. At this point, he is accosted by a character from ''Judea'' who pursues self-liberation by enacting the wildest, most anarchic impulses in *Carnovsky*. Claiming Nathan as a father figure, ''Jimmy'' Lustig attempts to hijack the plane as part of a manic jest and is brutally overpowered, possibly killed, by Israeli security, who seize Nathan as an accomplice. He concedes to himself that sometimes social welfare does justify even violent censorship of the unchecked imagination.

''Gloucestershire'' opens in the first person with Nathan facing Henry's dilemma in ''Basel.'' Nathan, however, contemplates the potency-restoring heart surgery as a way *into* marriage and fatherhood. Maria tries to talk him out of it, because she is suspicious—that he is confusing love with longing for the absent thing, that he will put her in a book (as someone obviously does), that he is already fictionalizing her in the "unwritten world" (which "Gloucestershire" of course is not) by making her into something she isn't. But he, like the Zionists, has envisioned a counterlife and will not be denied. The narrative switches to the third person with Henry as the center of consciousness. Nathan has died without their having made up after their father's death. In Nathan's apartment, he finds Draft #2 of an untitled book with an untitled chapter corresponding to "Aloft" and other chapters called "Basel," "Judea," and "Christendom"; this last appears to be Nathan's "dream of escape" into a new life. Henry is enraged to see his marital woes recounted, and appalled to see that Nathan's pregnant wife is given the name of *his* Maria. He leaves "Christendom" but discards most of the rest in a trash can off the New Jersey Turnpike. Next Nathan's Maria is heard answering questions posed by an unidentified voice. She has read "Christendom"; like Henry she sees the longing for a new life, and like Henry she resents the way Nathan distorted her and her family to work through his obsessions. Her resentment, though, is softened by love and insight. She identifies the voice as Nathan's ghost's and speaks movingly of the vacancy he has left in her life. She will keep him a presence by talking with him, as they used to when he was impotent and conversation was their only form of eros. She tells him, "It's my turn now to invent you."

"Christendom," told in the first person, has Nathan returning to Maria after leaving Henry in Judea and making notes on the encounter during a quiet flight home; in other words, "Judea," discarded in "Gloucestershire," is now presented as the unwritten world's raw material for Nathan's "narrative factory, where there is no clear demarcation dividing actual happenings eventually consigned to the imagination from imaginings that are treated as having actually occurred." But Nathan is as sick of reprocessing the same old personal history as he was in *The Anatomy Lesson;* he has conceived a counterlife with Maria and their child. Unfortunately, anti-Semitism in the family—subtle in her mother, blatant in her sister—and a display of British bigotry in a restaurant ignite an argument between Nathan and Maria that uncovers all the tensions stemming from their different ages, temperaments, and backgrounds—"the unevadable past." Nathan fears that she will leave him "completely otherless and reabsorbed within," alone with no voices but his own "ventriloquizing."

Reflexively, his imagination takes over and composes her farewell letter. There she cleverly presents herself not as the woman who is leaving his life but as the character who is leaving his fiction. She critiques him as an author and a man for the way he has used others and supports her point by citing an appropriate page reference from "Judea," the story supposedly on the same plane of reality as "Christendom." She says that she had expected more from his counterlife—not that he would "reenact the dead past"; but that he would rebel against *his* author and remake his life. Nathan's letter of reply presents a new twist on "characterological enslavement": one cannot escape being a character, but can exert some shaping influence. Because "one invents one's meanings, along with impersonating one's selves," he tells her, they two can be authors who help to write their own story; the story admits of variation, but from their fate—to be part of a fiction—there is no escaping. And so, Roth tells us, it is in the unwritten world: we are characters in a story shaped by our families, our experiences, our society, history—and by our own attempts to impersonate viable selves. We cannot withdraw from the condition of being inscribed. We should not withdraw from the struggle to help write the inscription.

The Facts (1988) begins with a letter to Zuckerman in which Roth explains his reasons for writing an autobiography. He needs to rediscover himself by taking a new approach. "Until now," he writes, "I have always used the past as the basis for transformation . . . a kind of intricate explanation to myself of my world." That attempt at explanation is his fiction. But just as Nathan becomes sick of "cultivating hypothetical Zuckerman's . . . to decipher his existence," so Roth in 1987 became "sick of fictionalizing myself further" and undertook *The Facts* as *his* "counterlife." He closes the letter by asking Zuckerman whether he should publish it.

Roth, of course, recognizes that he can never present "the facts" unshaped by his imagination and unreliable memory, free from subjective bias in the selection and treatment of materials. To call his autobiography *The Facts* is begging the question, and he admits that he could have been "both less ironic and more ironic by calling it *Begging the Question*." One also suspects that *The Facts* does not present the plain, unvarnished truth because it is so highly varnished. The prose, with its studiously precise and even recondite diction, rather stuffy tone, and carefully balanced hypotactic constructions, suggests that Roth is often as interested in building elaborate verbal structures, or in achieving calculated effects, as in recapturing how something happened and felt.

The Facts closes with Zuckerman's reply to Roth. His advice: "Don't publish—you are far better off writing about me than 'accurately' reporting your life." He points out that Roth can be both more interesting and more truthful in fiction, where he is less constrained by filial respect and the unwritten world's code of decency, discretion, and decorum. In particular, he distrusts the treatment of Roth's family life: where is the conflict that explains the development of an artist where a dentist or a lawyer should have

been? What spurred Portnoy's complaint, or Zuckerman's counterlife? Roth has left out the facts that account for the fiction. As a novelist himself, Zuckerman declares: "you, Roth, are the least completely rendered of all your protagonists." Roth reached a similar conclusion when trying to write *Portnoy:* "the more I stuck to the actual and the strictly autobiographical, the less resonant and revealing the narrative became."

Zuckerman ends by admitting that he and Maria are very worried about what is coming next. He is aware of his absurd position: on the one hand, arguing that Roth should use him as the best means of "self-confrontation" is self-interested pleading for his own existence; on the other hand, that existence would be an ordeal fraught with heightened, fantastical versions of Roth's unresolved traumas, complexes, and conflicts. Nathan had told Maria at the end of *The Counterlife* that the pastoral was not his genre, and he knows better than anyone that it is not Roth's either. Without the conflict—the struggle to discover and define oneself in the face of redoubtable opposition—there can be no Zuckerman the author/character, for there can be no Roth the character/author.

With the exchange of letters, the real subject of *The Facts* becomes, as in most of the fiction, not Roth's life so much as the interrelationship between life and literature. The movement back and forth between Roth and Zuckerman, facts and imaginative reconstruction, replicates the movement that produced the stories, the novels, the essays, and the autobiography—a movement between "the written and the unwritten world" that promises more of fictional distillations and factual models from Philip Roth.

Deception (1990) purposely confounds the models and distillations. The title refers not only to the deception inherent in any illicit love affair, and in any work of fiction, but also to the elaborate hide-and-seek game that Roth plays with his readers. He presents a series of contrapuntal dialogues between unidentified voices, chiefly those of an American novelist named Philip—who has created characters named "Portnoy," "Lucy Nelson," "Maureen Tarnopol," "E. I. Lonoff," and "Nathan Zuckerman"—and an English woman with whom he is having an adulterous affair. Roth says he wanted to capture the "peculiar intimacy which is unlike any other, having to do with hiding," and to present talking and listening as the essence of that intimacy. Philip says of himself, "I listen. I'm an ecouteur—an audiophiliac. I'm a talk fetishist." His lover replies, "Ummm. It *is* erotic, you just sitting there listening." Their affair draws energy from verbal as well as sexual play: the lovers play "reality shift" by changing positions, as when the woman pretends to be biographer interviewing a friend (played by Philip) of the late Nathan Zuckerman. Roth has said he plays such games with Claire Bloom to get ideas for how to handle scenes or bits of dialogue.

The question of what is real and what is fiction gets a new twist when Philip's wife finds a notebook with the dialogues as entries. She contends that Philip is having an affair with the woman who served as the model for Maria; Philip maintains that the woman exists only as a character in his imagination. His wife asks if he would then save her from embarrassment by changing the name "Philip" to "Nathan" for publication. He replies, "Would I? No. It's not Nathan Zuckerman. . . . The *novel* is Zuckerman. The notebook is me." "You just told me it's not you," she counters. He responds, "No, I told you it is me, imagining." After he storms out, defending himself on the grounds of artistic rather than sexual freedom, he has another conversation with the woman—their first in over two years; his novel has been published, and they discuss the relation between their real and fictionalized affairs. Philip playfully warns her that their conversation could become part of his next novel, as it apparently does. All this

suggests that the woman is real—at least in Philip's life—but to an imagination as playful as his, or Roth's, the final conversation could be just a final deception.

Philip's wife is understandably frustrated by his insistent confounding of fact and fiction, and some of Roth's critics are similarly vexed. *The New York Times* reviewer (March 11, 1990) commented that Roth's audience "must surely be growing impatient for the author to stop analyzing his imagination and start exercising it, if he hasn't dissected it beyond repair by now." But this kind of analysis and dissection is Philip Roth's preferred form of imaginative exercise. Having published *Patrimony*, a book of nonfiction about his father, in 1991, he plans a novel on a subject yet to be specified, in which, no doubt, he will continue to explore the boundary between the written and the unwritten world.

Selected Bibliography

WORKS OF PHILIP ROTH

BOOKS

Goodbye, Columbus. Boston: Houghton Mifflin, 1959.

Letting Go. New York: Random House, 1962.

When She Was Good. New York: Random House, 1967.

Portnoy's Complaint. New York: Random House, 1969.

Our Gang. New York: Random House, 1971.

The Breast. New York: Holt, Rinehart and Winston, 1972.

The Great American Novel. New York, Holt, Rinehart and Winston, 1973.

My Life as a Man. New York: Holt, Rinehart and Winston, 1974.

Reading Myself and Others. New York: Farrar, Straus and Giroux, 1975.

The Professor of Desire. New York: Farrar, Straus and Giroux, 1977.

The Ghost Writer. New York: Farrar, Straus and Giroux, 1979.

A Philip Roth Reader. New York: Farrar, Straus and Giroux, 1980.

Zuckerman Unbound. New York: Farrar, Straus and Giroux, 1981.

The Anatomy Lesson. New York: Farrar, Straus and Giroux, 1983.

Zuckerman Bound: A Trilogy and Epilogue. New York: Farrar, Straus and Giroux, 1985.

The Counterlife. New York: Farrar, Straus and Giroux, 1986.

The Facts: A Novelist's Autobiography. New York: Farrar, Straus and Giroux, 1988.

Deception. New York: Simon and Schuster, 1990.

Patrimony: A True Story. Simon and Schuster, 1991.

UNCOLLECTED STORIES

"Philosophy, Or Something Like That." *Et Cetera,* May 1952, pp. 5, 16.

"The Box of Truths." *Et Cetera,* October 1952, pp. 10–12.

"The Fence." *Et Cetera,* May 1953, pp. 18–23.

"Armando and the Fraud." *Et Cetera,* October 1953, pp. 21–32.

"The Final Delivery of Mr. Thorn." *Et Cetera,* May 1954, pp. 20–28.

"The Day It Snowed." *Chicago Review* 8:34–45.

"The Contest for Aaron Gold." *Epoch* 5-6:37–51 (Fall 1955).

"Heard Melodies Are Sweeter." *Esquire,* August 1958, p. 58.

"Expect the Vandals." *Esquire,* December 1958, pp. 208–228.

"The Love Vessel." *Dial I* 1:41–68 (Fall 1959).

"Good Girl." *Cosmopolitan,* May 1960, pp. 98–103.

"The Mistaken." *American Judaism* 10:10 (Fall 1960).

"Novotny's Pain." *New Yorker,* October 27, 1962, pp. 45–56. Revised and reprinted in *The Philip Roth Reader.*

"Philip Roth Papers." *Quarterly Journal of the Library of Congress* 27:343–344 (1970).

"Psychoanalytic Special." *Esquire,* November 1963, p. 106.

"On the Air." *New American Review* 10:7–49 (August 1970).

MANUSCRIPT PAPERS

The major collection of Roth's manuscripts and correspondence is at the Library of Congress.

BIBLIOGRAPHY

Rodgers, Bernard F. *Philip Roth: A Bibliography.* 2nd ed. Metuchen, N.J.: Scarecrow Press, 1984.

BIOGRAPHICAL AND CRITICAL STUDIES

BOOKS

Baumgarten, Murray, and Barbara Gottfried. *Understanding Philip Roth.* Columbia: University of South Carolina Press, 1990.

Bloom, Harold, ed. *Philip Roth: Modern Critical Views.* New York: Chelsea House, 1986.

Jones, Judith P., and Guinevera A. Nance. *Philip Roth.* New York: Ungar, 1981.

Lee, Hermione. *Philip Roth.* London and New York: Methuen, 1982.

McDaniel, John N. *The Fiction of Philip Roth.* Haddonfield, N.J.: Haddonfield House, 1974.

Meeter, Glenn. *Philip Roth and Bernard Malamud: A Critical Essay.* Grand Rapids, Mich.: William B. Eerdmans, 1968.

Milbauer, Asher Z., and Donald G. Watson, eds. *Reading Philip Roth.* Houndmills, Basingstoke, Hampshire: Macmillan, 1988.

Pinsker, Sanford. *The Comedy That "Hoits": An Essay on the Fiction of Philip Roth.* Columbia: University of Missouri Press, 1975.

———, ed. *Critical Essays on Philip Roth.* Boston: G. K. Hall, 1982.

Rodgers, Bernard F., Jr., *Philip Roth.* Boston: Twayne, 1978.

Searles, George J. *The Fiction of Philip Roth and John Updike.* Carbondale: Southern Illinois University Press, 1985.

ARTICLES OR BOOK SECTIONS

Allen, Mary. "Philip Roth: When She Was Good She Was Horrid." In her *The Necessary Blankness: Women in Major American Fiction of the Sixties.* Urbana: University of Illinois Press, 1976. Pp. 70–96. (Reprinted in Bloom.)

Bettelheim, Bruno. "Portnoy Psychoanalyzed." *Midstream* 15:3–10 (June–July 1969). Reprinted in Bloom.

Detweiler, Robert. "Philip Roth and the Test of the Dialogic Life." In *Four Spiritual Crises in Mid-Century American Fiction*. University of Florida Monographs no. 14. Gainesville: University of Florida, 1963. Pp. 25–35.

Donaldson, Scott. "Philip Roth: The Meanings of *Letting Go*." *Wisconsin Studies in Contemporary Literature* 11:21–35 (Winter 1970).

Fiedler, Leslie A. "Jewish-Americans Go Home." In his *Waiting for the End*. New York: Stein and Day, 1964. Pp. 89–103.

Guttman, Allen. "Philip Roth and the Rabbis." In his *The Jewish Writer in America: Assimilation and the Crisis of Identity*. New York: Oxford University Press, 1971. Pp. 64–76. Reprinted in Bloom.

Howe, Irving. "Philip Roth Reconsidered." *Commentary*, December 1972, pp. 69–77. Reprinted in Bloom.

Isaac, Dan. "In Defense of Philip Roth." *Chicago Review* 17, no. 2–3:84–96 (1964).

Kazin, Alfred. "The Earthly City of the Jews." In his *Bright Book of Life: American Novelists and Storytellers from Hemingway to Mailer*. Boston: Little, Brown, 1973. Pp. 144–149.

Olderman, Raymond M. *Beyond the Waste Land: The American Novel in the Nineteen-Sixties*. New Haven: Yale University Press, 1972. Pp. 2–3.

Podhoretz, Norman. "Laureate of the New Class." *Commentary* 54:4,7 (December 1972).

Raban, Jonathan. "The New Philip Roth." *Novel* 2:153–163 (Winter 1969).

Shechner, Mark. "Philip Roth." *Partisan Review*, 41, no. 3:410–427 (1974).

Siegel, Ben. "The Myths of Summer: Philip Roth's *The Great American Novel*." *Contemporary Literature* 17:171–190 (Spring 1976).

Solotaroff, Theodore. "Philip Roth and the Jewish Moralists." *Chicago Review* 13:87–99. (Winter 1959).

Tanner, Tony. "Fictionalized Recall—or 'The Settling of Scores! The Pursuit of Dreams!' " In his *City of Words: American Fiction 1950–1970*. New York: Harper & Row, 1971. Pp. 295–321. Reprinted in Bloom.

Trachtenberg, Stanley. "The Hero in Stasis." *Critique* 7:5–17. (Winter 1964/1965). Reprinted in Bloom.

Wisse, Ruth. "Requiem in Several Voices." In her *The Schlemiel as Modern Hero*. Chicago: University of Chicago Press, 1971. Pp. 108–124; see 118–121.

Wolff, Geoffrey. "Beyond Portnoy." *Newsweek*, August 3, 1970, p. 66.

—*PETER L. COOPER*

Sam Shepard

1943–

SAM SHEPARD WRITES plays about power—about individuals' attempts to gain or exert power over one another physically, emotionally, spiritually, psychologically. He seems to have embraced the age-old precept that all drama arises from conflict and has made it the central device in his dramaturgy. Yet Shepard also intuits the centrality of power as an informing principle of American culture, and thus integrates this essential struggle for dominance with cultural icons of power: mythic figures, material objects, historical characters, and social and cultural institutions. Using the stage and, later, film, as his media, he has gravitated to the genres that, in turn, have the greatest power for an audience—the immediate, proximal force of theatrical performance and the larger-than-life potency of the screen.

Samuel ("Steve") Shepard Rogers III was born on November 5, 1943, in Fort Sheridan, Illinois—an army base where his mother, Jane Elaine Schook Rogers, was living while his father, an army pilot, was serving in Italy. The eldest of three children, Steve moved with his family often, residing in South Dakota, Utah, Florida, and Guam before his father left the army, and the family finally settled in southern California. After spending some time in South Pasadena, a suburb of Los Angeles, they moved to an avocado ranch in Duarte, where Shepard spent his teenage years. This dual of exposure—to the culture of urban California and to western agricultural life—would have a lasting influence on the dramatist, whose fascination with popular images of the West as well as those of the southern California life-style animates many of his works.

After graduating from high school, Shepard spent three semesters at Mount San Antonio Junior College in Walnut, California, with the notion of becoming a veterinarian. While studying education and agricultural science, he drifted into theater, acting in campus productions of Mary Chase's *Harvey* and Thornton Wilder's *The Skin of Our Teeth.* He was introduced to Samuel Beckett's *Waiting for Godot,* and was struck by its freedom from conventional theatrical form and language, although he maintains he did not understand the play. When a touring group, the Bishop's Company Repertory Players, advertised local auditions, Shepard took advantage of the opportunity to explore theater as an alternative to the stable yet stultifying small-town life he knew. While traveling throughout New England with the Players, he changed his name from Steve Rogers to Sam Shepard, thereby crystallizing the new identity he was creating apart from his family traditions. The process of self-discovery and self-fashioning later became a central motif in his work, one often connected with an artist figure trying to find an identity within society.

Shepard left the Players to go to New York City, where he became involved with the downtown art scene, especially music. Through an old friend from California, Charles Mingus, Jr. (son of the jazz musician), he found a job at the Village Gate, a jazz club in Greenwich Village. There Shepard met Ralph Cook, the founder of Theater Genesis, who produced his first two plays, *Cowboys* and *The Rock Garden,* in 1964. Although they were roundly panned by the uptown critics, Shepard's plays were championed by *Village Voice* critic Michael Smith, who established Shepard as a new, exciting talent. Buoyed by Smith's support, Shepard began churning out plays for the growing number of off-off-Broadway theaters emerging at the time, garnering three Obies (annual awards for excellence in off-off- and off-Broadway theater) by 1966. Between 1964 and 1971, nearly twenty Shepard dramas opened in New York, and small theaters around the country began to produce his plays as well. He also attracted the attention of filmmakers, including Michelangelo Antonioni, who commissioned Shepard to work on the screenplay for *Zabriskie Point* (1970), based on Antonioni's original story outline.

In 1969, Shepard married actress O-Lan Johnson, with whom he had a son, Jesse Mojo, in 1970. In the words of Shepard's biographer Don Shewey, "By May 1971 Sam Shepard had been in New York slightly less than eight years. He'd gotten about as much out of it as a twenty-seven-year-old playwriting college dropout from small-town California could ever have dreamed." But New York had also taken its toll on the playwright, who had become heavily involved in drugs, had had an affair with the rock musician Patti Smith, and had begun to succumb to the impersonality and materialism of the city. Shepard decided to leave New York, and took his wife and son to England, where they lived for four years.

While living abroad, Shepard began to think carefully about his work and his life as an artist, exploring particularly closely his attitudes toward America and American culture. In an important interview conducted in England in 1974 with director Kenneth Chubb and the editors of *Theatre Quarterly,* which is reprinted in *American Dreams: The Imagination of Sam Shepard,* edited by Bonnie Marranca, he explained, "It wasn't until I came to England that I found out what it means to be an American. Nothing really makes sense when you're there, but the more distant you are from it, the more the implications of what you grew up with start to emerge." Living outside of London, Shepard wrote *The Tooth of Crime* (1972; dates are of first production), a play that brings together his view of growing up in America and his grasp of American violence and competitiveness, all filtered through the dominant cultural force of rock music. Shepard later claimed that one of his motives for going to England was to fulfill a lifelong ambition of becoming a rock and roll star, but this dream did not materialize. Instead, Shepard broadened his theatrical capabilities, writing and directing his play *Geography of a Horse Dreamer* (1974); this experience helped him to understand the nuances of working with actors and adjusting scripts for them.

In the *Theatre Quarterly* interview, Shepard expressed the desire "to try a whole different way of writing now, which is very stark and not so flashy and not full of a lot of mythic figures and everything, and try to scrape it down to the bone as much as possible." This new form—which he admitted "could be called realism, but not the kind of realism where husbands and wives squabble and that kind of stuff"—subsequently dominated his work for both stage and screen.

Shepard and his family returned from England in 1974 and settled in California, where he formed an association with the Magic Theater in San Francisco—a group that would premiere many of his works, including *Angel City* (1976),

Buried Child (1978), and *True West* (1980). Shortly after his return, he received a telephone call from the musician Bob Dylan, who wanted Shepard to write the screenplay for the film of his upcoming Rolling Thunder tour. Shepard agreed, but his involvement with the tour proved to be a lesson in the idiosyncrasies of fickle star personalities. Shepard kept a journal of the tour, which he later published as the *Rolling Thunder Logbook* (1977). The film, *Renaldo and Clara,* was eventually released in 1978, with Shepard appearing intermittently. Although the experience probably turned Shepard away from his rock-star fantasies forever, it ironically led to his movie career; the director Terrence Malick learned of his work on the Dylan film, and after meeting him decided to cast him in one of three starring roles in the film *Days of Heaven* (1978).

As Ross Wetzsteon points out in his introduction to Shepard's collection *Fool for Love and Other Plays* (1984), ''It's a peculiarly American irony that this playwright who has so frequently dealt with the captivity of the artist by commerce, who has so often shown how our myths have been corrupted by our media, should at last come to widespread public attention as a movie star.'' Shepard has appeared in a number of successful Hollywood movies, including *Resurrection* (1980), *Raggedy Man* (1981), *Frances* (1982), *Country* (1984), and the screen version of his play *Fool for Love* (1985), among others, and received an Academy Award nomination for his portrayal of Chuck Yeager in *The Right Stuff* (1983). *Frances* and *Country* starred Jessica Lange, for whom Shepard left and later divorced his wife O-Lan.

After returning from England, Shepard turned his creative energies toward the family. He wrote a series of obliquely autobiographical dramas about American families, starting with *Curse of the Starving Class* (1977) and culminating in the last drama he wrote on this theme, *A Lie of the Mind* (1985). In 1979, Shepard received the Pu-

litzer Prize for his play *Buried Child.* Family themes are further explored in *Far North* (1989), the first film Shepard both wrote and directed. Since 1978, he also collaborated with the actor and director Joseph Chaikin on a series of performance pieces on themes of love and hate, life and death, including *Tongues* (1978), *Savage/Love* (1979) and *The War in Heaven* (1985).

Following the production of *A Lie of the Mind,* Shepard's attention was directed predominantly toward film. Having grown up strongly influenced by film, Shepard in his stage work always reflected a cinematic sensibility, particularly in terms of his scenic structure and his use of striking visual images. The transition to film, through the roles of screenwriter, actor, and then director, was thus a natural development for him. *Far North* displays remarkable continuity with his later plays, and indicates his potential to affect this medium in the years to come, as he has influenced American theater over the past quarter century.

After Michael Smith's groundbreaking review of Shepard appeared in *The Village Voice* in 1964, theater critics began to pay increasing attention to the prolific young dramatist. By the late 1960's theater periodicals such as *Yale/Theatre* were featuring the first analytical views of his work, and by the late 1970's academic journals such as *Modern Drama* were including pieces on the plays. In 1981 the first book devoted to the study of Shepard was published: *American Dreams: The Imagination of Sam Shepard,* a collection of critical essays and personal commentary. This work, and the various longer studies and individual scholarly essays that began to appear subsequently, helped to establish a positive critical reputation for the author as well as to introduce a wider readership to his plays, most of which have been published.

Common to many of these pieces, however, is an admission of bafflement on the part of critics. Ross Wetzsteon, for example, recalls in the in-

troduction to *Fool for Love and Other Plays,*
"The first moment I was stunned by Shepard's
stagecraft—the final image of *La Turista,* the
American Place Theater, 1967. . . . in the theater we instinctively ask 'what is the playwright
trying to *say?*' and, in spite of my increasing
enchantment, I didn't have the vaguest idea what
it was.'' Scholars have long grappled with Shepard's dramaturgy, trying to explain it, to account
for it in a logical, coherent, and orderly way. As
Richard Gilman notes in his introduction to the
Shepard collection *Seven Plays* (1981), "most
critics find it hard clearly to extract . . . ideas
from Shepard's plays, many of which are . . .
extraordinarily resistant to thematic exegesis."
The work continually eludes them, perhaps for
the simple reason that Shepard's plays intentionally eschew logic, cohesion, and order. Unlike
the work of other writers, Shepard's dramas cannot be neatly categorized by genre, style, or authorial technique. In fact, critics even directly
contradict each other in their efforts to explain
the trajectory of his career. Gilman writes,
"More than that of any important playwright I
know, Shepard's work resists division into periods, stages of growth or development''; by contrast, Wetzsteon assures us that "Shepard's work
can be roughly divided into three periods."

Wetzsteon's sense of three periods, or genres,
of plays (roughly corresponding to the years
1964 to the late 1960's; the early 1970's to 1976;
and 1977 to the mid 1980's) offers a starting
point for analysis, however. He identifies these
divisions as the early one-acts (the "abstract collages''), the plays concerned with artist figures,
and the family plays. Lynda Hart's acute observation in *Sam Shepard's Metaphorical Stages*
that Shepard's dramaturgy inverts the historical
development of modern drama, by moving from
postmodernism and absurdism through expres-
sionism to modified realism, also provides a generic framework to help contextualize the
dramas.

Scholars and critics alike have noted the recurring motifs, character types, and action sequences that thread through Shepard's plays. In
response to a question posed by Kenneth Chubb
in the 1974 *Theatre Quarterly* interview, Shepard remarked, "You accumulate the experience
of having written all those other plays, so they're
all in you somewhere. But sometimes it gets in
the way—you sit down and you find yourself
writing the same play, which is a drag. Terrible
feeling when you suddenly find yourself doing
the same thing over and over again." Yet these
repetitions can disclose what is compelling for an
author—what he has not fully exorcized or expressed and so must confront in new or slightly
different ways.

Having produced over forty plays in the United
States and abroad, and having received numerous prestigious awards for his writing, Shepard
holds a very prominent position among American playwrights. Yet his plays remain extremely
controversial, not only for their style, which originally departed radically from the tradition of
American realism, but for several key areas of
their content. Shepard has always focused on the
"Anglo male American," and audiences and
critics have had difficulty with the brutality of the
American men he portrays, as well as with his
depiction of minorities and women.

In his interview with Chubb, Shepard comments on one of his earliest produced, but unpublished plays: "*Dog* [1965] was about a black
guy—which later I found out it was uncool for a
white to write about in America. It was about a
black guy on a park bench, a sort of *Zoo Story*
[Edward Albee]–type play." Shepard also ran
into difficulties with the initial production of *Operation Sidewinder,* which had been optioned by
the Yale Repertory Theatre for its 1968–1969
season. According to Don Shewey, the play

kicked off a full-blown campus crisis when a
committee of the six black students at the Yale

Drama School demanded it be canceled because ''the play is full of stereotypes about black men.'' (The original version of the play, published in *Esquire* in May 1969, had the black revolutionaries sitting in an orange Cadillac watching a black-power speech by Stokely Carmichael on TV.)

Shewey reports that Shepard withdrew the play ''not because he agreed with their assessment but because he declined to have his play become the scapegoat for grievances between the black students and the university faculty.''

A number of Shepard's critics have also observed the limited, stereotyped portrayal of women in his plays. Doris Auerbach in *Sam Shepard, Arthur Kopit, and the Off Broadway Theater* asserts that ''the female characters . . . are mere macho fantasies of familiar female stereotypes, castrating mothers and devouring sex goddesses.'' Bonnie Marranca, in a section of her introduction to *American Dreams* subtitled ''The Zero Gravity of Women,'' states:

One of the most problematic aspects of the plays is Shepard's consistent refusal or inability, whichever ever the case may be, to create female characters whose imaginative range matches that of the males. Women are the background of the plays: they hang out and make themselves useful for chores while the men make the decisions, take risks, face challenges, experience existential crises. Women are frequently abused, and always treated as subservient to men, their potential for growth and change restricted. For a young man Shepard's portrayal of women is as outdated as the frontier ethic he celebrates.

These problems of race and gender persist in Shepard's later work. His family plays dramatize only the lives of white rural Americans, and although the 1985 play *A Lie of the Mind* and the 1988 screenplay *Far North* attempt to depict women with greater breadth and complexity,

they still appear tied to men and centered on their domestic lives.

When Shepard started writing plays in the early 1960's, he had had little formal theatrical experience and minimal contact with dramatic literature. In the 1974 *Theatre Quarterly* interview he explains:

I didn't really have any references for the theatre, except for the few plays that I'd acted in. But in a way I think that was better for me, because I didn't have any idea about how to shape an action into what is seen—so the so-called originality of the early work just comes from ignorance. I just didn't know.

However, Shepard acknowledges here as elsewhere a number of authors whose work he admires, or whose style he has imitated in some way. In addition to recounting the story of reading Beckett's *Waiting for Godot*, he confesses to having written a bad Tennessee Williams imitation while in college, and claims Bertolt Brecht as his favorite playwright. Richard Gilman in his introduction to *Seven Plays* ''sometimes suspects Shepard of wanting to be thought *sui generis*, a self-creation,'' but believes he ''must . . . have been influenced by Jack Gelber's 1959 play *The Connection*, . . . by [Harold] Pinter and, more recently, by Edward Bond,'' although ''he has never mentioned'' these individuals. With the appearance of additional interviews and the recent publication of Shepard's correspondence with Joseph Chaikin, the eclectic breadth of his reading and artistic exploration begins to emerge, revealing a surprising array of influential figures, including Jack Kerouac, Lawrence Ferlinghetti, Edward Albee, the beat poets, the French symbolist poets, Carlos Castaneda, Werner Herzog, and Fyodor Dostoyevski.

Shepard is unique among major dramatists for his accession to prominence with a series of one-act plays—a form he continued to use regularly until he began to write his family plays, all of which have two or more acts. In a short essay, "Time" (1975), reprinted in *American Dreams,* he comments bitterly on the professional conflicts that that intuitive choice of form presents:

In the realm of experimental writing for the theatre, a young writer is gradually persuaded that the "one act" form is a stepping stone toward the creation of "full-length" plays . . . [that] alone can serve as proof of his literary value to the public. . . . The cultural machine that encourages young writers to experiment, in the same breath encourages them to quickly grow out of it and start producing "major works." . . . Another part of this syndrome is the difficulty a playwright has in returning to attempts at shorter works after having "accomplished" one or two longer plays. . . . Rarely is it seen for what it is—a part of the gradually unfolding process of a playwright's total work.

When considering Shepard's plays, then, we must adjust our preconceived notions of "important" drama and examine the total impact of each piece in the theater, not using a predetermined guide for measuring greatness by length or scope.

Shepard's observations about the way he writes plays appear closely related to the form and content of the plays themselves. In the *Theatre Quarterly* interview with Chubb, Shepard remarked that in his early plays, he "wasn't really trying to shape it [the "stuff," or content] or make it into any big thing." He explained: "I would have like a picture, and just start from there. A picture of a guy in a bathtub [*Chicago*], or of two guys on stage with a sign blinking [*Cowboys #2*]." In an essay entitled "Language, Visualization and the Inner Library" (1977), reprinted in *American Dreams,* Shepard recalls, "I can't even count how many times I've heard the line, 'Where did the idea for this play come from?' I never can answer it because it seems totally back-assward. Ideas emerge from plays—not the other way around." He goes on to describe the process of writing as being something like watching a movie:

The picture is moving in the mind and being allowed to move more and more freely as you follow it. . . . I'm taking notes in as much detail as possible on an event that's happening somewhere inside me. The extent to which I can actually follow the picture and not intervene with my own two-cents worth is where inspiration and craftsmanship hold their real meaning. If I find myself pushing the character in a certain direction, it's almost always a sure sign that I've fallen back on technique and lost the real thread of the thing.

Shepard creates his characters by a similar process of observation: "In my experience the character is visualized, he appears out of nowhere in three dimensions and speaks. He doesn't speak to me because I'm not in the play. I'm watching it. He speaks to something or someone else, or even to himself, or even to no one." Yet, somewhat contradictorily, he also believes in the close connection between his playwriting and acting: "The similarity between the actor's art and the playwright's is a lot closer than most people suspect. In fact the playwright is the only actor who gets to play all the parts."

Shepard's views of acting were undoubtedly shaped in part through his association beginning in the mid 1960's with the Open Theater director and writer Joseph Chaikin. Don Shewey notes that

Chaikin's influence, direct or indirect, on off-off-Broadway playwrights—what they wrote and how it was performed—in the early sixties equaled the effect that Lee Strasberg's gospel of Method acting had a decade before on Broadway drama, to which the Open Theater was in part an innovative response.

Chaikin trained actors in workshops devoted to what Shewey calls "sound-and-movement improvisations.'' These exercises, known as ''transformations,'' were designed to help the actor express ''the emotional undercurrents that accompany everyday behavior.'' According to Richard Gilman, ''a transformation exercise was an improvised scene—a birthday party, survivors in a lifeboat, etc.—in which after a while, and suddenly, the actors were asked to switch immediately to a new scene and therefore to wholly new characters.'' The call for these abrupt transitions could come from an external source (the teacher/director), or an internal source (an actor already within the scene or just entering the scene).

Shepard incorporated the concept of transformation scenes directly into such plays as *Cowboys #2* (1967), *The Holy Ghostly* (1969), *Mad Dog Blues* (1971), and *Back Bog Beast Bait* (1971). In *Cowboys #2*, two young men dressed all in black, Chet and Stu, transform themselves into two old men, Clem and Mel. The action begins with an offstage voice (external source):

MAN NUMBER ONE: [*Off left*] It's going to rain.
STU: Do you think so?
CHET: What?
STU: Uh, rain?
CHET: Oh . . . sure. Maybe.

. . . .

STU: . . . Why don't you go over there and see if you can see any cloud formations? (internal source)
[*He points downstage. Chet gets up and crosses downstage like an old man. He stands center and looks up at the sky, then speaks like an old man.*]
CHET: Well, well, well, well. I tell ya, boy. I tell ya. Them's some dark ones, Mel. Them's really some dark ones.
STU: [*Talking like an old man*] Dark, eh? How long's it been since ya seen 'em dark as that?

After playing old men for a while, the characters change back again, this time resorting to a Beckettian sequence to pass the time:

[*Chet sits abruptly. There is a pause, then Stu starts doing jumping calisthenics, clapping his hands over his head. He faces Chet as he does this.*]
STU: Clap, clap, clap. Clapping, clapping. Clap.
CHET: What are you doing?
STU: This?
CHET: That.
STU: Oh. Well, you remember yesterday?
CHET: Yesterday what?
STU: Remember yesterday when I was sitting and my feet fell asleep?
CHET: Yeah.
STU: Well, this is for that.

As the young men alternate roles, they not only transform but playact within the roles, imagining a cowboys-and-Indians battle of the sort little boys create or that crops up in B-grade westerns:

[*They make gun noises and fire at imaginary Indians.*]
STU: Fire!
CHET: Fire!
STU: Damn! Look like Apaches!
CHET: Some of 'em's Comanches, Clem!

. . . .

STU: Fire!
CHET: Atta baby!
[*Stu grabs his shoulder, screams and falls back. Chet stands and yells out at the audience, firing his rifle.*]
You lousy redskinned punks! Think you can injure my buddy? Lousy red assholes! Come back and fight!

In the intensity of this imaginary scene, Chet loses his old-man's voice, calling our attention to the fluidity of these roles and their ephemerality: the actors pass easily from one to the next and add them on or discard them at will.

In *The Holy Ghostly*, father and son characters named Pop and Ice are enmeshed in a quintessential generational conflict that gets acted out with similar role-playing: Pop takes on the voice of an old rancher, Ice that of a tough young cowboy. *Mad Dog Blues* features two friends, Kosmo and Yahoodi, who move around "an open, bare stage," yet pretend, in a series of "visions," that they are in San Francisco, in the jungle, on a pirate ship on the ocean, and on an island with buried treasure. They play with such mythic and cultural figures as Marlene Dietrich, Mae West, Paul Bunyan, Jesse James, and Captain Kidd, while simultaneously struggling with their own love/hate relationship—a problem they share with many other Shepard personae:

KOSMO: Get away from me! Get out of here! Go on! Take your trip! Go as far away as you can! Get out of my sight!
[*Yahoodi takes off . . .*]
No! Yahoodi! I'm sorry! Come back! I need you! We're brothers! Yahoodi! I love you.

Back Bog Beast Bait also incorporates one of the central improvisatory sequences in transformation exercises: the transition from human character to animal character. Two hired guns, Slim and Shadow, have been retained to kill a mysterious and elusive monster that has been terrorizing the bayou swamp country. The power struggle that ensues involves the transformative force of the monster, who seems to be able to drive the human characters mad; they turn into various animals—a coyote, a bull, a wildcat, an owl, and an alligator—all perhaps latent elements of their human identities, elements that are metaphorically indicative of their fundamental natures.

In his 1977 essay "Language, Visualization and the Inner Library" (collected in *American Dreams*), Shepard explains, "The reason I began writing plays was the hope of extending the sensation of *play* (as in 'kid') on into adult life. If 'play' becomes 'labor,' why play?" The one-act collages *Cowboys #2* and *Mad Dog Blues*

perfectly exemplify this quality of play, as the characters romp around the stage in different roles, pretending to be in faraway places. Shepard claims these early dramas evolved from his own play with his friend Charles Mingus, Jr., in their assumed roles of urban cowboys in New York. Yet this extension of life into work does not fully explain the form of expression Shepard selected. In the 1974 *Theatre Quarterly* interview Shepard clarifies this point: "I always like the idea that plays happened in three dimensions, that here was something that came to life in space rather than in a book."

What is crucial here, of course, is Shepard's selection of the dramatic form not only for its playfulness and multivocal potential, but also because of its realization on stage, with all the techniques and potential for audience impact that the theater holds. Shepard talks frequently about other art forms, especially music and the visual arts, and he has incorporated these into his work in numerous ways—creating characters based on rock stars, integrating music into the plays, writing a drama (unpublished and unproduced) about the painter Jackson Pollock. The stage seems the natural home for Shepard's work, as it is the best medium by which he can employ many art forms simultaneously, to their full effect. In a brief note on "American Experimental Theatre" written for *Performing Arts Journal* in 1977 (collected in *American Dreams*), Shepard remarks that

the only thing which still remains and still persists as the single most important idea [after the turbulent 1960's] is the idea of consciousness. How does this idea become applicable to the theatre? For some time now it's become generally accepted that the other art forms are dealing with this idea to one degree or another. That the subject of painting is seeing. That the subject of music is hearing. That the subject of sculpture is space. But what is the subject of theater which includes all of these and more? It may be that the territory available to a theatrical event is so vast that it has to be narrowed down to ingredients like plot, character, set, costume, lights, etc., in order to fit it into our idea of what we know. Consequently, anything outside these domains is called "experimental."

Shepard's inventive use of the stage, which called on these various art forms as well as on more conventional theatrical devices, catapulted him to prominence among avant-garde playwrights of the late 1960's. In *Fourteen Hundred Thousand* (1966), a couple, Tom and Donna, are building a bookcase to hold her extensive collection (the number in the title) of books, with the intermittent help of their friend Ed. With tools, lumber, and sawdust scattered about the stage, Tom perches on a stool putting shelves in place. At first a seemingly naturalistic environment, the stage suddenly becomes a surreal space as the lights change quickly from blue to white and the shelves mysteriously fall. To the accompaniment of the repeated slamming of the one door in the back wall, the lights change, two other characters (Mom and Pop) arrive with armfuls of books that they place in piles around the stage and then sit on, and the three other characters attempt to carry on a "normal" conversation about what Ed's cabin in the woods is like, how Donna got the books, and how the construction is progressing. Finishing the bookcase becomes an obsession for Tom, as the shelves keep falling and Ed waffles on his offer to help complete it. Donna and Tom subsequently lose their tempers and start dueling with each other, using large paintbrushes to splatter each other with white paint. The stark stage environment, the striking use of lighting and special effects, and the visceral action of the paint fight combine to make *Fourteen Hundred Thousand* an intriguing yet estranging play—one to which the audience responds primarily on a sensory level.

Exploiting ideas developed by the "found art"

movement, Shepard also invokes the notion of "stage pictures" to create striking visual tableaux with his scenic descriptions. *The Unseen Hand* (1969) features "an old '51 Chevrolet convertible, badly bashed and dented, no tires and the top torn to shreds" center stage, while *4-H Club* (1965) plays in a kitchen set "littered with paper, cans and various trash." And, as noted earlier, Shepard's mental image of "a guy in a bathtub" led to the creation of *Chicago* (1965), a play which takes place around Stu in his bathtub, as his girlfriend Joy and their friends come and go and finally arrive with fishing gear that they dangle off the edge of the stage.

Shepard seemed to revel in the pure theatricality the stage allows, especially during the 1970's, before his transition to the family plays. *Operation Sidewinder,* a show so large in scope that it could not be produced by off-Broadway theaters, opened at Lincoln Center in 1970 to mixed reviews, but audiences marveled at the six-foot-long mechanical sidewinder snake constructed for the production, with its blinking eyes, undulating body, and mean rattle. In *Forensic and the Navigators* (1967), two exterminators arrive "dressed like California Highway Patrolmen, with gold helmets, gas masks, khaki pants and shirts, badges, boots, gloves, and pistols. They carry large tanks on their backs with hose and nozzle attachments." At the end of the play, in the course of which the exterminators attempt to foil an anarchist plot, the stage directions indicate that

blue smoke starts drifting onto the stage. It keeps up until the stage is completely covered and all you can hear are the voices of the actors. It gradually pours over into the audience and fills up the entire theater. . . . It could change colors in the course of filling the place up, from blue to pink to yellow to green.

Some critics, like Ellen Oumano (*Sam Shepard: The Life and Work of an American*

Dreamer), feel that such endings fail to resolve the action, but this complaint may well spring from a traditional desire for narrative closure. Since Shepard rejected narrative in his early work, instead approaching the stage on a more visceral, sensory level, the final images he envisioned have the potential for even greater impact than that effected by a satisfactorily neat plot resolution. In "Visual Histrionics: Shepard's Theatre of the First Wall," Toby Silverman Zinman analyzes the endings of Shepard's plays by comparing them to the concept of the "silhouette" described by Peter Brook at the end of his influential theoretical book, *The Empty Space* (1968):

I know of one acid test in the theatre. . . . When a performance is over, what remains? Fun can be forgotten, but powerful emotion also disappears and good arguments lose their thread. When emotion and argument are harnessed to a wish from the audience to see more clearly into itself—then something in the mind burns. The event scorches on to the memory an outline, a taste, a trace, a smell—a picture. It is the play's central image that remains, its silhouette, and if the elements are rightly blended this silhouette will be its meaning, this shape will be the essence of what it has to say.

Shepard seems intuitively to have grasped the power of the silhouette and to have employed it, usually at the end of his plays, to make a lasting impression on his audience. *Red Cross* (1966) takes place in a totally white environment, a motel cabin with two twin beds with white linens. Carol and Jim recount, in monologues (already a central element of Shepard's dramaturgy), events in their lives. Early in the play, Carol tells about a skiing accident she once had and her memory of one spot of blood in the snow. After she leaves to get groceries, Jim discovers he is infested with crab lice and worries about Carol's reaction. At the end of the play Carol returns, having realized she has crabs and thinking she caught them in the motel. As she expresses her extreme distress Jim turns to face her, and we see "a stream of blood running down his forehead." This striking final visual image, linked to Carol's verbal narrative of the accident, creates a kind of unity for the play and becomes the silhouette that makes this piece memorable.

Zinman discusses the silhouette in *La Turista*, the same final picture that convinced Ross Wetzsteon of Shepard's dramatic power. In this, his first two-act play, Shepard uses a setting similar to that of *Red Cross:* two twin beds in a motel room, this time in Mexico. In act 1, Salem and Kent (note the cultural resonance of their "brand" names), two American tourists, are suffering from dysentery, also known as "la turista." A Mexican boy brings help in the person of the local doctor and his son, who perform bizarre witch-doctor and voodoo routines to cure their patients. Act 2, which chronologically precedes act 1, finds Salem and Kent in an American hotel room, preparing for their trip to Mexico. Kent is suffering from a psychological disorder this time, and the doctor arrives dressed in a Civil War uniform. The temporal disjunction leads to an elemental conflict between doctor and patient, as Kent tries desperately to escape the physician's medical machinations. He grabs hold of a rope and swings across the stage over the doctor's head. "He lands on the ramp behind DOC and runs straight toward the upstage wall of the set and leaps right through it, leaving a cut-out silhouette of his body in the wall. The lights dim out as the other three stare at the wall." This remarkable ending left the audience awed; they did not understand it, but the impact of the final image was undeniably powerful.

Shepard's striking use of visual images may well be matched by his incorporation of arresting musical sequences. Many of Shepard's plays feature music, often performed live, as in *Melodrama Play* (1967), for which he envisioned the band "suspended from the ceiling in a cage over the audience's head," and in *A Lie of the Mind*, in which the contributions of the bluegrass group the Red Clay Ramblers, "structuring bridges between scenes, underscoring certain monologues, and developing musical 'themes' to open and close the acts" convinced Shepard "that this play needs music. Live music. Music with an American backbone" (*A Lie of the Mind*). In 1977 Shepard told Kenneth Chubb that "music's really important, especially in plays and theatre—it adds a whole different kind of perspective, it immediately brings the audience to terms with an emotional reality. Because nothing communicates emotions better than music, not even the greatest play in the world."

Shepard's interest in music dates back to his childhood, when his father used to listen to Dixieland jazz and play in an amateur band. Shepard soon surpassed his father's skill as a drummer, and for several years he performed in New York with the Holy Modal Rounders, a folk-rock group. His intensive exposure to jazz through his work at the Village Gate and his cognizance of the centrality of rock music to American youth culture in the 1960's may account for his incorporation of music as a theme, a structuring device, and as a live (or recorded) presence in his plays. *Mad Dog Blues, Melodrama Play,* and *Cowboy Mouth* (1971) all feature rock musicians as central characters and explore the pressures and conflicts in the life of a rock star. Shepard describes Kosmo in *Mad Dog Blues* as a "rock-and-roll star. Dressed in a green velvet satin cape with tight blue velvet pants, teased hair and no shirt. He carries a conga drum." Kosmo explains his first "vision" to his friend Yahoodi: "It came to me in music. It was like ole rhythm-and-blues and gospel, a cappella, sort of like The Persuasions but with this bitchin' lead line. Like a Hendrix lead line. Like a living Hendrix lead line right through the middle of it."

Shepard's set description for *Melodrama Play*

calls for two large posters upstage, one of Robert Goulet, the other of Bob Dylan, both with no eyes. Duke Durgens has had an overnight success with his song "Prisoners, Get Up out of Your Homemade Beds." But Duke's manager is pressuring him for a follow-up hit and has locked him in a room to force him to compose. Duke's brother Drake, and his companion Cisco, hired by the manager, show up to help Duke. It turns out that, unknown to anyone, Duke had stolen the hit tune from his brother Drake, passing it off as his own. Shepard adds a menacing bodyguard, fraternal conflict, and rock interludes as Brechtian disruptions to the action, creating a piece whose thematic and characterological resonances recur in many later plays, including *The Tooth of Crime* (1972) and *True West* (1980).

Cowboy Mouth, possibly the best known of Shepard's early plays, is notorious not so much for its content per se as for the story of its composition and production. In 1970 Shepard had met the poet/musician Patti Smith through his work with the Holy Modal Rounders and they embarked on a highly publicized affair. Don Shewey maintains that "allowing for some poetic exaggeration, the play provides a documentary account of their life together." Shewey quotes Shepard as explaining, "I'd never written a play with somebody before, and we literally shoved the typewriter back and forth across the table," each writing his or her own dialogue. The American Place Theatre's production of the work was short-lived, however, for Shepard "realized [he] didn't want to exhibit [himself] like that, playing [his] life onstage."

In the play, Slim (Shepard) has been kidnapped by Cavale (Smith) who sees in him the potential to be "a rock-and-roll Jesus with a cowboy mouth." The two play out a love/hate struggle, Cavale holding Slim captive in her chaotic apartment while he cries, "You've stolen me away from my baby's cradle! . . . I have a wife and a life of my own! Why don't you let me go!

I ain't no rock-and-roll star. That's your fantasy.'' Cavale, whose idols are the French symbolist poets Gérard de Nerval and François Villon, tries to explain her vision of a savior for their generation:

People want a street angel. . . . Somebody to get off on when they can't get off on themselves. I think that's what Mick Jagger is trying to do . . . what Bob Dylan seemed to be for a while. . . . It's like . . . well, in the old days people had Jesus and those guys to embrace. . . . But it's too hard now . . . and the old God is just too far away. He don't represent our pain no more. His words don't shake through us no more. Any great motherfucker rock-n'-roll song can raise me higher than all of Revelations. We created rock-n'-roll from our own image. . . . It's like . . . the rock-n'-roll star in his highest state of grace will be the new savior . . . rocking to Bethlehem to be born. [Note the somewhat confused and perhaps ironic final allusion to William Butler Yeats's poem ''The Second Coming''].

Despite Shepard/Slim's protestations that he is not the ''rock-and-roll Jesus with the cowboy mouth,'' the notion of becoming a rock star still intrigued Shepard, and, as mentioned earlier, this fascination is part of what motivated him to go to England, where he wrote what some critics believe is his strongest creative effort, *The Tooth of Crime.* In many ways *The Tooth of Crime* is an outgrowth of *Cowboy Mouth,* particularly in the characterization of the rock star Hoss, a fading rock-and-roll Jesus, and the allusion to symbolist poetry in the titular reference to the poem ''Anguish'' (1887) by Stéphane Mallarmé (in *Poems* [1951], translated by Roger Fry):

For Vice, having gnawed by nobleness inborn,
Has marked me like you with its sterility,
But whilst in your breast of stone there is
      dwelling
A heart that the tooth of no crime can wound,

I fly, pale, undone, and by my shroud haunted,
And fearing to die if I but sleep alone.

The Tooth of Crime brings together two rock-star characters, Hoss and Crow, in an elemental struggle for dominance that also invokes transitions in American youth culture between the early 1960's and the mid 1970's, the isolation of the artist, and the inherent violence in our society. Doris Auerbach in *Sam Shepard, Arthur Kopit, and the Off Broadway Theater* reads this play as Shepard's most Brechtian work, not only for its quintessential use of song to comment on the action, but also for its clear link to Brecht's early drama *In The Jungle of Cities* (1922), a play subtitled ''The Fight Between Two Men in the Gigantic City of Chicago.'' Attracted to Brecht's sense of American capitalism as combative, Shepard transforms the conflict between Brecht's central characters Garga and Shlink into the struggle for power between Hoss and Crow.

Hoss, ''in black rocker gear with silver studs and black kid gloves,'' enters a stage empty except for ''an evil-looking black chair with silver studs and a very high back,'' the ''throne,'' a metonymic signifier for the power struggle at the heart of the play. He performs a song which is to sound ''like 'Heroin' by the Velvet Underground.'' Throughout act 1, Hoss, isolated with his entourage to determine when the time is right for his next hit (a word which takes on double meaning as both a musical success and a violent attack), nervously evaluates his current status. He consults his astrologer, Star-Man, a science fiction–like character who ''shouldn't look like *Star Trek,* more contemporary silver.'' Star-Man advises against a move, because of the precarious astral balance. Angered, Hoss demands information about his competition.

STAR-MAN: . . . Mojo Rootforce is the only one close enough to even worry about.
HOSS: Mojo? That fruit? What'd he knock over?

STAR-MAN: Vegas, Hoss. He rolled the big one.
HOSS: Vegas! He can't take Vegas, that's my
    mark! That's against the code!

Just a few minutes into the play, the audience
realizes the diction of these characters is distinctive; they speak a slang dialect all their own, and
the audience is forced to understand by context
what this language means.

Hoss next calls on the disc jockey Galactic
Jack, whose *Billboard*–type charts can pinpoint
Hoss's position. By describing him as "dressed
like a 42nd Street pimp," Shepard evokes a
strong association between financial exploitation
and the music industry, expanding on his rudi-
mentary development of the same theme in
Melodrama Play. Hoss at one point announces,
"They're all countin' on me. The bookies, the
agents, the Keepers. I'm a fucking industry. I
even affect the stocks and bonds."

Reveling in his belief in his own omniscience,
Galactic Jack presents himself as "heavy duty
and on the whim. Back flappin', side trackin',
finger poppin', reelin' rockin' with the tips on
the picks in the great killer race," and pre-
dicts, "A shootin' star, baby. High flyin' and no
jivin'. You is off to number nine." But Hoss's
sidekick and gun moll Becky arrives and changes
the situation as she announces, "Eyes sussed
somebody's marked you. . . . One a' the Gyp-
sies"—a reference to those who operate as
renegades outside "the code," the rules which
control the game that Hoss is playing for dear
life.

Hoss spends the rest of act 1 preparing for the
arrival of this "Gypsy marker"—this outside
threat—by practicing knife-fight maneuvers with
a dummy that bleeds at each hit. He calls on Doc
to administer a drug dose, and sardonically remarks to Doc and Becky,

Look at me now. Impotent. Can't strike a kill
unless the charts are right. Stuck in my image. . . . Waiting for a kid who's probably just

like me. Just like I was then. . . . And I gotta off
him. . . . We're fightin's ourselves. . . . Suicide, man. . . . Blow your fuckin' brains
out. . . . Stick a gun in your fuckin' mouth and
pull the trigger. . . . Jimmy Dean was right.
Drive the fuckin' Spider till it stings ya' to death.
Crack up your soul! Jackson Pollock! Duane All-
man! Break it open! Pull the trigger!

One of Shepard's central themes in this play,
integral to his exploration of the artist figure (as
well as later in his analysis of the individual in
the family), is the artificiality and ephemerality
of the self—of one's individual identity. Shepard
posits the self here as a superficial construct, like
the onion that Ibsen's titular character Peer Gynt
peels away layer by layer to reveal an empty
core. Hoss remarks to Becky, "Ya' know, you'd
be O.K., Becky, if you had a self. So would I.
Something to fall back on in a moment of doubt
or terror or even surprise."

At the opening of act 2, Crow enters, picking
up on this theme in his first song: "But I believe
in my mask—The man I made up is me / And I
believe in my dance—And my destiny." Crow
"looks just like Keith Richard. He wears high-
heeled green rock and roll boots, tight greasy
blue jeans, a tight yellow t-shirt, a green velvet
coat, a shark tooth earring, a silver swastika
hanging from his neck and a black eye-patch
covering the left eye." His dialect is even more
imagistic: "Got the molar chomps. Eyes
stitched. You can vision what's sittin'. Very ra-
zor to cop z's sussin' me to be on the far end of
the spectrum."

Again nodding to Brecht and his passion for
the elemental theatricality of the boxing ring,
Shepard stages the battle between Hoss and Crow
as a boxing match in three rounds, complete with
bells and a referee. Shepard wrote some of his
greatest poetic dialogue for this scene, matching
diction and rhythm perfectly with the characters
and their strengths. In round 1, Crow succeeds in

painting a fallacious picture of Hoss as a weak, maladjusted youth:

Pants down. The moon show. Ass out the window. Belt lash. Whip lash. Side slash to the kid with a lisp. The dumb kid. The loser. The runt. The mutt. The shame kid. Kid on his belly. Belly to the blacktop. Slide on the rooftop. Slide through the parkin' lot. Slide kid. Shame kid. Slide. Slide.

In round 2, Hoss tries to make a comeback, slipping into a black/country voice (continuing Shepard's technique of role play and transformation), exposing the weakness in Crow's musical style:

You could use a little cow flop on yer shoes, boy. Yo' music's in yo' head. You a blind minstrel with a phoney shuffle. You got a wound gapin' 'tween the chords and the pickin'. Chuck Berry can't even mend you up. You doin' a pantomime in the eye of a hurricane. . . . You lost the barrelhouse, you lost the honkey-tonk. You lost your feelings in a suburban country club the first time they ask you to play "Risin' River Blues" for the debutante ball. You ripped your own self off and now all you got is yo' poison to call yo' gift. You a punk chump with a sequin nose and you'll need more'n a Les Paul Gibson to bring you home.

But the referee calls the round a draw, and they move on to round 3. Here, Crow goes for the kill, exposing Hoss's inability to find a style, a musical persona of his own:

Can't get it sideways walkin' the dog. Tries trainin' his voice to sound like a grog. Sound like a Dylan, sound like a Jagger, sound like an earthquake all over the Fender. Wearin' a shag now, looks like a fag now. Can't get it together with chicks in the mag. Can't get it together for all of his tryin'. Can't get it together for fear that he's dyin'. Fear that he's crackin' busted in two.

Busted in three parts. Busted in four. Busted and dyin' and cryin' for more. Busted and bleedin' all over the floor. All bleedin' and wasted and tryin' to score.

After the Ref calls it "a T.K.O.," Hoss tries to salvage his career, asking Crow to help him become a Gypsy: "Just help me into the style. I'll develop my own image. I'm an original man. . . . I just need some help." But Hoss cannot take on a style, cannot change personas like the chameleon Crow, who acknowledges, "The image is my survival kit." With what he believes is the only possible authentic, original gesture, Hoss finally shoots himself, leaving Crow behind to try to sustain his new position of prominence before succumbing to a similar fate: "Now the power shifts and sits till a bigger wind blows."

The Tooth of Crime, in addition to its depiction of the music world as comprised of electric, life-on-the-fast-track action, reveals Shepard's ambivalent nostalgia for the America of his youth—the era of the 1950's and early 1960's, captured more innocently in films like *American Graffiti* (1973). Through the character of Hoss, Shepard recounts a story based on his own experiences as a youth:

We all went out to Bob's Big Boy in Pasadena to cruise the chicks and this time we got spotted by some jocks from our High School. . . . There were eight of 'em, all crew cut and hot for blood. This was the old days ya' know. So they started in on Cruise 'cause he was the skinniest. Smackin' him around and pushin' him into the car. . . . Moose told 'em to ease off but they kept it up. . . . Girls and dates started gathering around until we was right in the center of a huge crowd a' kids. Then I saw it. This was a class war. These were rich white kids from Arcadia who got T-birds and deuce coupes for Xmas from Mommy and Daddy. All them cardigan sweaters and chicks with ponytails and pedal pushers and bubble hairdo's. Soon as I saw that I flipped out. I found my strength. I started kickin' shit, man. . . . Moose and Cruise went right into action. It was like John Wayne, Robert Mitchum and Kirk Douglas all in one movie. . . . We had all eight of 'em bleedin' and cryin' for Ma right there in the parking lot at Bob's Big Boy.

The combination of American dialect and icons with raw violence and energy epitomizes Shepard's sense of his culture. In a 1985 interview conducted by Wetzsteon for *The Village Voice* (reprinted in *File on Shepard*), Shepard explained, "I felt it was important that an American playwright speak with an American tongue, not only in a vernacular sense, but that he should inhabit the stage with American being. The American playwright should snarl and spit, not whimper and whine." The violence that inheres in many of his plays is likewise integral to his concept of America. He said in a *New York Times* interview in 1984 (reprinted in *File on Shepard*):

I think there's something about American violence that to me is very touching. In full force it's very ugly, but there's also something very moving about it, because it has to do with humiliation. There's some hidden, deeply-rooted thing in the Anglo male American that has to do with inferiority, that has to do with not being a man, and always, continually having to act out some idea of manhood that invariably is violent. This sense of failure runs very deep—maybe it has to do with the frontier being systematically taken away, with the guilt of having gotten this country by wiping out a native race of people, with the whole Protestant work ethic. I can't put my finger on it, but it's the source of a lot of intrigue for me.

As several critics have astutely observed, many of Shepard's images (American and other) come straight from film, rather than from original literary or historical sources. Don Shewey

notes that the playwright has "loved the movies" ever since his childhood. However, Shepard's stints as a screenwriter on various projects helped him to realize clearly his distaste for Hollywood and the movie industry and to explode this American icon from the inside out. In *Motel Chronicles* (1982), one of Shepard's two collections of poetry and short prose pieces (the other is *Hawk Moon* [1973]), he includes a poem dated "Hollywood, 1981," which opens with the line, "they ooze and call each other 'darlings.'" In *Angel City* (1976), a play indebted to Eugène Ionesco's *Rhinoceros,* Rabbit Brown, a screenplay "doctor," arrives in Hollywood to consult on a new major disaster movie, but finds himself trapped by the studio executives (much like the musicians in *Melodrama Play*). All the creative staff are working feverishly to come up with a blockbuster before a mysterious disease, threatening the entire city, converts them all to lizards. Shepard's metaphor here, of course, is the corrupting, transformative power of the movie industry. Through the character Miss Scoons, he voices his disquieting realization about the relation of his work to this quintessentially American industry: "The urge to create works of art is essentially one of ambition. The ambition behind the urge to create is no different from any other ambition. To kill. To win. To get on top." A few years later, Shepard made this same kind of ambition part of the central conflict in *True West,* between the brothers Austin and Lee, each of whom is trying to write a Hollywood screenplay.

The movie memories, the car culture, the conflict, and the period images of dress and attitude all coalesce in a picture of a quintessentially Shepardian American environment. He had experimented with this atmosphere earlier in *The Unseen Hand,* set in Azusa ("Everything from 'A' to 'Z' in the USA), California. Blue Morphan, a magically immortal cowboy, draws the connection between the 1950's era and the ethos of the mythic American West: "A car's like a good horse. You take care a' it and it takes care a' you.'' The latter-day cowboys must preserve that former America, as strong men with a mission.

Yet in play after play, that mission runs up against the dark, apocalyptic aura hanging over Shepard's dramaturgy. The trajectory of numerous characters' stories, like Carol's in *Red Cross,* starts on a jubilant note but plummets to a violent, destructive conclusion. This is the overall arc of *Icarus's Mother* (1965), a play that begins bucolically, with four friends relaxing after a Fourth of July picnic, waiting for the evening fireworks. The pastoral American scene is disrupted, however, by the arrival of an airplane flying low overhead, which the characters interpret as the pilot's desire to communicate with them. While Pat and Jill go off for a walk, Howard and Bill try sending smoke signals to the pilot, via the barbecue. The pilot skywrites "$E = MC^2$," but then inexplicably crashes into the water below. In an extended monologue, Frank describes in graphic detail the plane's descent:

Heading straight for the top of the flat blue water. Almost touching in slow motion and blowing itself up six inches above sea level to the dismay of ducks bobbing along. And lighting up the air with a gold tint and a yellow tint and smacking the water so that waves go up to five hundred feet in silver white and blue. Exploding the water for a hundred miles in diameter around itself. Sending a wake to Japan. An eruption of froth and smoke and flame blowing itself up over and over again. . . . The water goes up to fifteen hundred feet and smashes the trees, and the firemen come. The beach sinks below the surface. The seagulls drown in flocks of ten thousand. . . . And the pilot bobbing in the very center of a ring of fire that's closing in. His white helmet bobbing up and bobbing down. His hand reaching for his other hand and the fire moves in and covers him up.

This nuclear vision, clearly linked to the atomic bomb dropped on Hiroshima, proves fascinating entertainment for the holiday spectators.

This same menacing atmosphere hangs over *Action,* staged in a post-apocalyptic setting with characters camping out in a cabin after some form of holocaust. As a small Christmas tree blinks continuously at the rear of an almost bare stage, the characters consume a holiday dinner consisting only of the turkey that they have managed to raise and kill. This juxtaposition of Americana—fireworks, Christmas trees, and holiday turkeys—to a sense of barren foreboding and destruction reveals the complexity of Shepard's feelings about his country.

For all his interest in America, unlike many dramatists of the 1960's, Shepard is rarely discussed as a political playwright. His work is often distinguished from that of his contemporaries at the Living Theatre, which produced *Paradise Now* in 1968, or his colleagues at the Open Theatre, who produced Megan Terry's *Viet Rock* in 1966, both patently political. Yet the mood and tone of plays like *Icarus's Mother* suggest a political consciousness at work that, if not always overtly exercised in Shepard's drama, nevertheless seems integral to his identity as an American author. Shepard's most obviously political speech appears in *Operation Sidewinder,* a play written in 1968 and reflecting the anarchist energy of the time. The Young Man, hired by a group of Black Panther–like characters to capture the sidewinder snake/computer for their revolutionary plot, speaks of his alienation from America's political leaders, their rhetoric, and their actions:

It was like all that oppression from the month before had suddenly cracked open and left me in space. The election oppression: Nixon, Wallace, Humphrey. The headline oppression every morning with one of their names on it. . . . And I was all set to watch "Mission: Impossible" when

Humphrey's flabby face shows up for another hour's alienation session. Oh please say something kind to us, something soft, something human, something different, something real, something—so we can believe again. His squirmy little voice answers me, "You can't always have everything your way." And the oppression of my fellow students becoming depressed . . . "We're not going to win. There's nothing we can do to win." This is how it begins, I see. We become so depressed we don't fight anymore. We're only losing a little, we say. It could be so much worse. The soldiers are dying, the Blacks are dying, the children are dying. . . . Everything must be considered in light of the political situation. No getting around it.

The political content of Shepard's drama has a broader and more pervasive scope than *Operation Sidewinder* demonstrates, however. Recently, in both his stage and film work (especially in *Country*), he has focused on the economic plight of American farmers, whose barren lives in America's heartland reflect their long struggle against poverty. He shares with Brecht a general mistrust of the capitalist system, epitomized by his exposés of the music and film industries.

Curse of the Starving Class, Buried Child, True West, Fool for Love (1983), and *A Lie of the Mind* comprise the one universally recognized unit in Shepard's dramaturgy, the family plays. Family themes, however, run throughout the Shepard canon, from his first produced play, *The Rock Garden* (the final scene from which was included in the long-running Broadway revue *Oh! Calcutta!*), through *The Holy Ghostly, The Tooth of Crime* and the unpublished work *Little Ocean* (1974), which explores pregnancy through the experiences of three women.

Critics had long noted Shepard's avoidance of traditional American realist drama, much of which is family-centered (Eugene O'Neill's

Long Day's Journey into Night and Tennessee Williams's *Cat on a Hot Tin Roof* are just two examples); in a November 1988 interview in *Esquire* he comments on why he came to these plays later in his career: "I always did feel a part of that tradition but *hated* it. I couldn't stand those plays that were all about the 'turmoil' of the family. And then all of a sudden I realized, well that was very much a part of my life, and maybe that has to do with being a playwright, that you're somehow snared beyond yourself." Yet these later plays rarely display the theatrical conventions we associate with "kitchen sink" and "dining room table" dramaturgy. Shepard's families are rural, often agriculturally sustained, but the emphasis in the plays is more on the strange psychology of the family relations, especially those of the father(s) and the children, than on the particular geographical setting or financial wherewithal of the characters. *Curse of the Starving Class, Buried Child, True West,* and *Fool for Love* have been called a "family tetralogy"— works thematically linked by their exploration of various facets of family dynamics. These plays, although complete and often extremely successful works in their own right, also seem to be rehearsals for *A Lie of the Mind*—a drama that initially ran over four hours in performance and seems to try to pull together all the familial images and characters of the other four pieces.

Stanley Kauffmann's review of *Curse of the Starving Class* in *The New Republic* (April 8, 1978, reprinted in *American Dreams*) finds that the play "starts as sweaty, cartoon-character comedy—people living wildly and uncaringly in a poverty they . . . don't take very seriously," but "ends as a paean to agrarian values, to those who love Nature and Space and Simple Things and who are being forced off their land by exploitative commercial combines." He believes that the "ending is simply not in the play's beginning"; but the drama nevertheless merits serious attention, despite the dramaturgic flaws

Kauffmann exposes. In the play, Shepard shows that he can transpose his creative, poetic style to a domestic milieu, weaving motifs of hunger and familial inheritance throughout the action. The parents, Ella and Wesley, each make feeble efforts to sustain their children, Emma and Weston, but finally give up and try to sell the family farm behind each other's backs. Shepard elucidates his sense of family identity here, significantly through the voice of the son, Weston: "It was good to be connected by blood like that. That a family wasn't just a social thing. It was an animal thing. It was a reason of nature that we were all together under the same roof. Not that we had to be but that we were supposed to be."

Buried Child, winner of the 1979 Pulitzer Prize for drama, solidified and refined the style and tone of Shepard's familial environment. The aging alcoholic patriarch, the vague, ineffective mother, and the estranged, psychologically and/or physically wounded children all come together in a sordid world of incest, abuse, and neglect. Shelley, a visitor (and therefore a more "objective" outsider through whose eyes we can understand and evaluate the familial machinations) at the home of her boyfriend Vince, at first believes the house is "like a Norman Rockwell cover or something," but the external facade of idealized American family life soon gives way. The mystery of the titular buried child in the backyard—whose it is, what happened to it, and what it symbolizes for Vince's family, and, by analogy, the American family—is interwoven with Shepard's portrait of home life in the heartland, which inevitably betrays its Rockwellian exterior.

True West, by many accounts Shepard's most commercially popular and accessible play, narrows the focus to examine in depth the fraternal bond. Austin, an Ivy League–educated writer, and Lee, a drifter and petty criminal, confront each other at their childhood home, where Austin is house-sitting while their mother vacations in Alaska (one of the possible "true wests" of the title). *True West* stands out among Shepard plays both for its humor and for its crystallization of the theme of the split self—a motif that pervades Shepard's work. In one of the funniest scenes in contemporary drama, Austin, who wants to change places in life with his brother Lee, has stolen every toaster in the neighborhood—just to prove he can do it—and proceeds to set every one to work, popping bread all over the stage: "There's gonna' be a general lack of toast in the neighborhood this morning. Many, many unhappy, bewildered breakfast faces. I guess it's best not to even think of the victims. Not to even entertain it."

The two brothers, in classic doppelgänger fashion, are two halves of a whole—each the inverse of the other. They battle for supremacy, for the embodiment of a unified identity. This same struggle defines *Fool for Love*, but the equation shifts in the latter play to operate on a sexual scale, as two lovers, May and Eddie, who have discovered they may be half brother and half sister, spar with each other in a "can't-live-with, can't-live-without" relationship. In addition, the four family plays revolve around the father/son dynamic, which is always fraught with conflict, but which also shows the inescapability of familial resemblance.

Fraternal doubling, love/hate relationships, and attempts to come to grips with the father all swirl together in *A Lie of the Mind*. With so many themes to develop, so many character bonds to explore, Shepard for the first time uses two families onstage simultaneously, linked by the marriage of one's daughter, Beth, with the other's son, Jake. Each family occupies a slightly raised platform space, one stage right, one stage left. In between, the "stage is wide open, bare, and left at floor level. The impression should be of infinite space, going off to nowhere." This region comes to represent not only a geographical distance between the families, but the vast gulf between individuals, even those joined as closely as a married couple. As we come to understand each character's misconceptions, preconceived notions, and fantasies—their "lies of the mind"—we also see them trying to grapple with their fundamental identities, defined, to a large extent, by their family roles as wife/mother, husband/father, son/brother, daughter/sister. A basic inability to understand themselves and to communicate with each other dooms these individuals, however, to lives that will always be lies.

The impossibility of family communication finds its most graphic illustration in *A Lie of the Mind* in the character of Beth, who has been severely beaten and left for dead by her husband, Jake. The manifestation of Beth's injury, which resembles aphasia, renders her unable to speak coherently, yet she desperately tries to communicate, using garbled or disjointed phrases, cries, and oblique images. The irony here is that Beth's brain damage renders her better able than the rest of the characters to understand others and express her emotions. She explains to her brother-in-law Frankie, whom she mistakes for her husband:

This—this is my father. He's given up love. Love is dead for him. My mother is dead for him. Things live for him to be killed. Only death counts for him. Nothing else. This—this . . . This is me. This is me now. The way I am. Now. This. All. Different. I—I live inside this. Remember. Remembering. You. You—were one. I know you. I know—love. I know what love is. I can never forget. That. Never.

The power with which Shepard commands language may well be his greatest strength as a dramatist. Each of his characters has a distinctive voice, diction, idiolect. In "Language, Visualization and the Inner Library" (collected in *American Dreams*), Shepard defines words "as tools of imagery in motion." He believes that

the power of words for me isn't so much in the delineation of a character's social circumstances as it is in the capacity to evoke visions in the eye of the audience. . . . Words as living incantations and not as symbols. Taken in this way, the organization of living, breathing words as they hit the air between the actor and the audience actually possesses the power to change our chemistry. . . . I have a feeling that the cultural environment one is raised in predetermines a rhythmical relationship to the use of words. In this sense, I can't be anything other than an American writer.

Selected Bibliography

WORKS OF SAM SHEPARD

PLAY COLLECTIONS
Seven Plays (1981), *Fool For Love and Other Plays* (1984), and *The Unseen Hand and Other Plays* (1986), all in Bantam editions, contain most of Shepard's dramas published to date. The exceptions are *Shaved Splits*, which is included in the 1971 edition of *The Unseen Hand; The Sad Lament of Pecos Bill on the Eve of Killing His Wife*, published along with the 1983 edition of *Fool for Love;* and *A Lie of the Mind* and *The War in Heaven*, which were published together in 1987.

Five Plays. Indianapolis: Bobbs-Merrill, 1967.

The Unseen Hand and Other Plays. Indianapolis: Bobbs-Merrill, 1971.

Mad Dog Blues and Other Plays. With an introduction by Michael McClure. New York: Winter House, 1972.

The Tooth of Crime and Geography of a Horse Dreamer. New York: Grove Press, 1974.

Angel City and Other Plays. With an introduction by Jack Gelber. New York: Urizen Books, 1976.

Buried Child and Seduced and Suicide in B^b. New York: Urizen Books, 1979.

Four Two-Act Plays. New York: Urizen Books, 1980.

Seven Plays. With an introduction by Richard Gilman. New York: Bantam, 1981.

Chicago and Other Plays. New York: Urizen Books, 1981.

Fool For Love and The Sad Lament of Pecos Bill on the Eve of Killing his Wife. San Francisco: City Lights, 1983.

Fool For Love and Other Plays. With an introduction by Ross Wetzsteon. New York: Bantam, 1984.

The Unseen Hand and Other Plays. With an introduction by Shepard. New York: Bantam, 1986.

A Lie of the Mind and The War in Heaven: Angel's Monologue. New York: New American Library, 1987. (*The War in Heaven* written with Joseph Chaikin.)

OTHER WRITINGS

Hawk Moon: A Book of Short Stories, Poems, and Monologues. Los Angeles: Black Sparrow Press, 1973; New York: Performing Arts Journal Publications, 1981.

Rolling Thunder Logbook. New York: Viking, 1977.

Motel Chronicles. San Francisco: City Lights, 1982. Prose and poetry.

Joseph Chaikin and Sam Shepard: Letters and Texts, 1972–1984. Edited by Barry Daniels. New York: New American Library, 1989.

BIOGRAPHICAL AND CRITICAL STUDIES

Auerbach, Doris. *Sam Shepard, Arthur Kopit, and the Off Broadway Theater.* Boston: Twayne, 1982.

Bigsby, C. W. E. *A Critical Introduction to Twentieth-Century American Drama.* Vol. 3. Cambridge: Cambridge University Press, 1985.

Chubb, Kenneth, et al. "Metaphors, Mad Dogs, and Old Time Cowboys." *Theatre Quarterly* 4, no. 15:3–16 (1974).

Dungan, John, ed. *File on Shepard.* Portsmouth, N.H.: HEB, 1989.

Erben, Rudolf. "Women and Other Men in Sam Shepard's Plays." *Studies in American Drama, 1945–Present,* 2:29–41 (1987).

Falk, Florence. "The Role of Performance in Sam Shepard's Plays." *Theatre Journal,* 33:182–198 (May 1981).

Hart, Lynda. *Sam Shepard's Metaphorical Stages.* Westport, Conn.: Greenwood, 1987.

King, Kimball, ed. *Sam Shepard: A Casebook.* New York: Garland, 1988.

Londre, Felicia Hardison. "Sam Shepard Works Out: The Masculinization of America." *Studies in American Drama, 1945–Present,* 2:19–27 (1987).

Marranca, Bonnie, ed. *American Dreams: The Imagination of Sam Shepard.* New York: Performing Arts Journal Publications, 1981.

Mottram, Ron. *Inner Landscapes: The Theater of Sam Shepard.* Columbia: University of Missouri Press, 1984.

Oumano, Ellen. *Sam Shepard: The Life and Work of an American Dreamer.* New York: St. Martin's, 1986.

Parker, Dorothy, ed. *Essays on Modern American Drama: Williams, Miller, Albee, and Shepard.* Toronto: University of Toronto Press, 1987.

Rabillard, Sheila. "Sam Shepard: Theatrical Power and American Dreams." *Modern Drama,* 30:58–71 (March 1987).

Savran, David. "Sam Shepard's Conceptual Prison: *Action* and *The Unseen Hand.*" *Theatre Journal,* 36:57–73 (March 1984).

Shewey, Don. *Sam Shepard.* New York: Dell, 1985.

Whiting, Charles. "Digging Up *Buried Child.*" *Modern Drama,* 31:548–556 (December 1988).

Wilcox, Leonard. "Modernism vs. Postmodernism: Shepard's *The Tooth of Crime* and the Discourses of Popular Culture." *Modern Drama,* 30:560–573 (December 1987).

Zinman, Toby Silverman. "Sam Shepard and Super-Realism." *Modern Drama,* 29:423–430 (September 1986).

———. "Visual Histrionics: Shepard's Theatre of the First Wall." *Theatre Journal,* 40:509–518 (December 1988).

—*J. ELLEN GAINOR*

Susan Sontag

1933–

Writing is a mysterious activity. One has to be, at different stages of conception and execution, in a state of extreme alertness and consciousness and in a state of great naiveté and ignorance.
(Sontag, interview with Geoffrey Movius, 1975)

Writing criticism has proved to be an act of intellectual disburdenment as much as of intellectual self-expression.
(Sontag, *Against Interpretation,* 1966)

More than any other writer today, Susan Sontag has suffered from bad criticism and good publicity.
(William Phillips, *Partisan Review*, 1969)

*E*SSAYIST, CRITIC, reviewer, sometimes educator, editor, novelist, short-story writer, screenwriter, and director of films, Susan Sontag has been called "the Dark Lady of American letters." She has suffered at the hands of critics who are mystified and dismayed by her maverick range of reference, her unruly yet intensely focused attention on so many different topics. Sontag wants to be alert, at any cost, to what is happening around her; her description of what Roland Barthes is up to (from "Remembering Barthes," in *Under the Sign of Saturn*) might describe her own writing enterprise:

It was not a question of knowledge (he couldn't have known much about some of the subjects he wrote about) but of alertness, a fastidious transcription of what *could* be thought about something, once it swam into the stream of attention.

A random sampling of Sontag's subjects over the period since the mid 1960's will begin to convey the voracity of her attention and the intensity with which she casts her eye/I around her surroundings. Often writing on topics jealously guarded or defensively spurned by traditional academics, Sontag has considered Camp, Ingmar Bergman, Walter Benjamin, Antonin Artaud, Roland Barthes, happenings, Nazi propaganda art, Diane Arbus, pornography, Albert Camus, Georg Lukács, Jean-Paul Sartre, Jean Genet, Vietnam, Israel, cancer, and AIDS.

The sheer volume of her collected canon may startle and dismay those who simply cannot believe anyone could write so much so quickly. Since the 1960's Sontag has published four collections of essays—*Against Interpretation* (1966), *Styles of Radical Will* (1969), *On Photography* (1977), and *Under the Sign of Saturn* (1980); two novels—*The Benefactor* (1963) and *Death Kit* (1967); a collection of short stories—

I, etcetera (1978) and two extended essay-meditations on cancer and AIDS—*Illness as Metaphor* (1978) and *AIDS and Its Metaphors* (1989). She also has written and directed four films: *Duet for Cannibals* (1969), *Brother Carl* (1971), *Promised Lands* (1974)—a documentary on the Yom Kippur War of 1973—and *Unguided Tour* (1983).

Embattled and conciliatory, courting "intellectual disburdenment" as well as "intellectual self-expression," Sontag flirts with a position she felt Georg Lukács achieved: "the difficult feat of being both marginal and central in a society which makes the position of the marginal intellectual almost intolerable." Like Claude Lévi-Strauss, the subject of her 1963 essay "The Anthropologist as Hero," Sontag is "in control of, and even consciously exploiting, [her] own intellectual alienation." For her, alienation, detachment, even revulsion can be empowering because these stances create a necessary distance between herself and her subjects; this ambivalence becomes the enabling fiction of her critical enterprise. Positioned on the margin, Sontag earns the right to be "central" and to see her "subjects" with dispassionate clarity and acuity.

This tension is played out in Sontag's canon as she moves from viewing art as autonomous in the 1960's—divorced from the historical forces that produced it—to a belief in the 1970's that art can never be severed from its politics. In her work of the late 1970's, she moves toward a lyrical, elegiac "intellectual self-expression"—one that focuses on the life spent, the life lived. Sontag's journey from the margin to the center enables her to claim the more personal and less guarded voice we begin to hear in *Under the Sign of Saturn*, particularly when she writes about Walter Benjamin, Antonin Artaud, and Roland Barthes.

Like Benjamin, one of her favorite writers, Sontag is herself "under the sign of Saturn"—a phrase she uses to describe Benjamin's temperament in the title essay:

The mark of the Saturnine temperament is the self-conscious and unforgiving relation to the self, which can never be taken for granted. The self is a text—it has to be deciphered. (Hence, this is an apt temperament for intellectuals.) The self is a project, something to be built. (Hence, this is an apt temperament for artists and martyrs, those who court "the purity and beauty of a failure," as Benjamin says of Kafka.) And the process of building a self and its works is always too slow. One is always in arrears to oneself.

A comparatist whose literary performances in her essays link her to Michel de Montaigne, Robert Burton, Ralph Waldo Emerson, and Barthes, Sontag asserted in a 1989 interview with Kenny Fries that *AIDS and Its Metaphors* was "a literary performance," having "more to do with Emerson than Randy Shilts." Though said in a defensive moment, this statement is telling for what it reveals about Sontag's larger project of "building [or inventing] a self" in her essays and in the public arena. In a 1975 interview with Geoffrey Movius, she confided:

My life is my capital, the capital of my imagination. I like to colonize. . . . There is only so much revealing one can do. For every self-revelation, there has to be a self-concealment. A life-long commitment to writing involves a balancing of these incompatible needs.

Like her predecessors, Sontag balances her economy of self-disclosure—her public self-fashioning—with that of keeping her private self inviolate.

Sontag is committed to a "poetics of thinking," a phrase she uses to describe Barthes. We experience a mind in the process of approaching its subject; although she sometimes gives the impression of having had the last word on a given topic, her discourse is, in fact, expansively open-ended. Her syntheses, rather than her extended arguments, convey a quick, omnivorous, and inventive mind—one that resists the safety of closure.

Sontag invites her readers to try to follow the often slippery trajectory toward her subjects—the threads toward and around them. Not particularly interested in sustaining an extended argument, Sontag's exposition seems to stop and start. Many of her essays might be called "Notes Toward an Argument." Extended comparisons and examples bring us close to her subjects and then, sometimes, paradoxically distance us from them. Sontag's comparisons between writers force them into competition with one another or into a new and startling relation. For example, in her essay "The Literary Criticism of Georg Lukács," Sontag compares Lukács and Benjamin only to expose the gap between them:

The notion about allegory in the first essay is based on ideas of the late Walter Benjamin, and the quotations from Benjamin's essay on allegory leap off the page as examples of a type of writing and reasoning much finer than that of Lukács. . . . Benjamin shows us what Lukács as a literary critic might have been.

Sontag also positions her subjects in triangular configurations that allow her to call into question linear presentations of literary or cultural history, the notion that literary "influence" is traceable to a particular historical lineage. Influences and connections are mediated in strange ways—and by unexpected forces. Dispensing with simple "cause and effect" paradigms, Sontag questions how we recognize connections between writers, sensibilities, and centuries. For example, in her introduction to *A Roland Barthes Reader* (1982), Sontag positions Barthes in relation to André Gide and Jean-Paul Sartre—two writers who, at first glance, could not be more opposed:

Gide and Sartre were, of course, the two most influential writer-moralists of this century in France, and the work of these two sons of French Protestant culture suggests quite opposed moral and aesthetic choices. But it is just this kind of polarization that Barthes, another Protestant in revolt against Protestant moralism, seeks to avoid. Supple Gidean that he is, Barthes is eager to acknowledge the model of Sartre as well. While a quarrel with Sartre's view of literature lies at the heart of his first book, *Writing Degree Zero . . .* , an agreement with Sartre's view of the imagination, and its obsessional energies, surfaces in Barthes's last book, *Camera Lucida*.

Valorizing the distance between Gide and Sartre, while showing us that in Barthes this gap becomes fused as he, the "supple Gidean," embraces Sartre, Sontag subverts conventional connections and illustrates how the gaps and dissonances become links. Gide and Sartre thus become two versions of Barthes while remaining in competition with one another. Of course, Sontag's orchestration of this competition, as the composer/conductor, allows her momentarily to upstage both of them. In these moments, Sontag's presence as "critic" competes with her subjects, threatening to eclipse their autonomy.

Sontag makes a similar move in her 1963 essay "Sartre's *Saint Genet*":

Thus the whole discussion of Genet may be read as a dark travesty on Hegel's analysis of the relations between self and other. Sartre speaks of the works of Genet as being, each one of them, small editions of *The Phenomenology of Mind*. Absurd as it sounds, Sartre is correct. But it is also true that all of Sartre's writings as well are versions, editions, commentaries, satires on Hegel's great book. This is the bizarre point of connection between Sartre and Genet; two more different human beings it would be hard to imagine.

Sartre's whole discussion of Genet—the very grounds for his writing about Genet—is thus mediated by G. W. F. Hegel, whose presence in both their canons makes the encounter possible and inevitable.

In Sontag's work we see a mind deftly concentrating on the moment of encounter with the subject at hand, yet firmly rooted in a Western tradition of learning at the end of the twentieth century—"one that presumes an endless discourse anterior to itself," another phrase she uses to describe Barthes. As William Phillips aptly pointed out in a 1969 review of Sontag's work for *Partisan Review:*

All Susan Sontag's writing has these two sides: a skeptical mind steeped in the unsolved problems that make up the history of thought and a strong, almost willed, feeling for change and discovery, and for new ideas that are attractive because they cannot be insured by history.

Born on January 16, 1933, in New York City, the eldest daughter in a family of Polish Jewish heritage, Sontag describes herself in a 1988 profile for *Time* magazine as "a psychologically abandoned child." She and her younger sister were taken care of by aunts while her father, who was a fur trader, and her mother, who was a teacher, traveled in China. Her father died of tuberculosis on one of these trips; in her 1987 autobiographical story "Pilgrimage," which appeared in *The New Yorker,* Sontag recalls that her "hard-to-imagine" father died "exotically elsewhere." She pays homage to this world elsewhere and the father she never knew in her short story "Project for a Trip to China":

After M. returned to the United States from China in early 1939, it took several months for her to tell me my father wasn't coming back. I was nearly through the first grade, where my classmates believed I had been born in China.

When Sontag was six, her mother took the family to Tucson, Arizona, where it was hoped Susan would find some relief from her asthma.

In 1945 her mother remarried; Sontag would later describe her stepfather as "a handsome, bemedalled and beshrapnelled Army Air Forces ace who'd been sent to the healing desert to cap a year-long hospitalization (he'd been shot down five days after D Day)." A year later the family moved to Los Angeles, where Sontag remained until she graduated from high school in 1948, at the age of fifteen.

A reserved, independent, and solitary child, Sontag maintains that she was "a demon reader from earliest childhood." Upon arriving in Los Angeles, she notes in "Pilgrimage," "I tracked down a real bookstore . . . where I went every few days after school to read on my feet through some more of world literature—buying when I could and stealing when I dared." Books clearly provided her an escape from the quotidian; she called them her "household deities," her "spaceships." Her passion for collecting books continues: her personal library is said to contain many thousands of volumes. Sontag also sought out the best journals of the time; at the age of thirteen, she frequented "an international newsstand where militant browsing yielded *Partisan Review, Kenyon Review, Sewanee Review, Politics, Accent, Tiger's Eye,* [and] *Horizon.*" Around this time, she began keeping a journal and even tried her hand at what she later self-consciously called "imitation stories."

Precocious, wildly brilliant, and perhaps deprived of a traditional childhood, Sontag had a passion for foreign movies and concerts. She and her gifted peers, she later claimed, "debated the merits of the Busch and the Budapest Quartets . . . ; discussed whether it would be immoral, given what I'd heard . . . about Gieseking's Nazi past, to buy his Debussy recordings; tried to convince ourselves that we had liked the pieces played on the prepared piano by John Cage . . . ; and talked about how many years to give Stravinsky."

"Pilgrimage" serves to fuse Sontag's early

childhood interests in European literature and contemporary film and music with her adult critical concerns. Much like Henry James's memoir, *A Small Boy and Others* (1913), Sontag's invites us to entertain a connection between her temperament and her critical and artistic sensibilities. The memoir implies that her own writing career was inevitable because of the sort of childhood she had—because she was a "fervid, literature-intoxicated child."

After graduating from high school in 1948, Sontag spent a year at the University of California at Berkeley, then transferred to the University of Chicago, where she received her B.A. in 1951. In 1950 she met Philip Rieff, whom she married after knowing him for ten days. In 1952 their son, David, was born. During the mid 1950's Sontag was at Harvard and Reiff at Brandeis; she completed an M.A. in English in 1954, one in philosophy the following year, and finished her doctoral exams in philosophy (although she never in fact completed her doctorate). During their time in the Boston area, Sontag and Rieff collaborated on *Freud: The Mind of the Moralist;* the book, published in 1959, the year Sontag and Rieff were divorced, has Rieff as the only author. By all accounts this arrangement was by mutual consent.

In 1957 Sontag received a grant from the American Association of University Women that enabled her to spend a year in France, where she studied at the University of Paris. When she returned home, she worked briefly as an editor of *Commentary* in New York (where she has made her permanent home). She also was a lecturer in philosophy at City College and Sarah Lawrence College. Between 1960 and 1964 Sontag was an instructor in the religion department at Columbia University; she also spent the academic year 1964–1965 as writer-in-residence at Rutgers University. This appointment came on the heels of her first novel, *The Benefactor*. When asked in a 1979 interview with Paul Brennan about

"the university life she left behind," Sontag replied: "I got tired of the academic world. I thought I would just repeat myself." Ironically, some of Sontag's critics might feel more comfortable if she did repeat herself occasionally.

Sontag began writing essays, reviews, and fiction at the age of twenty-eight; since the early 1960's her essays and stories, collected and uncollected, have appeared consistently and rapidly in periodicals such as *The New Yorker, Atlantic Monthly, Partisan Review, Harper's, New York Review of Books, Commentary, Nation, American Review, Esquire*, and *Playboy*. Sontag was only thirty-one when "Notes on 'Camp' " appeared in *Partisan Review* in 1964. This essay, along with "Against Interpretation," of the same year, made her something of a celebrity overnight. In 1974, Louis D. Rubin noted that Sontag's "utterances" on "Camp" "were . . . greeted with the kind of adulation previously reserved for such critics and sages as W. H. Auden, Marianne Moore, Simone de Beauvoir, and Norman Mailer."

Two weeks after the essay appeared, an edited version of it was published in *Time* magazine. Although this second publication undoubtedly put Sontag in the limelight, she made clear in her interview with Paul Brennan that she had nothing to do with this reprinting:

I wrote it for a small literary magazine. I was astonished to discover that two weeks later it was an article in *Time* magazine. But I didn't do it. I never co-operated with any of the digests or amplifications. Yet it got reprinted, discussed and digested and misquoted and I was represented as having written a manifesto or even having invented it, which wasn't true at all.

Sontag's anatomy of "Camp" begins in an expository mode, replete with definitions and examples, but soon becomes "the form of jottings, rather than an essay." We are told that "the essence of Camp is its love of the unnatural: of artifice and exaggeration.'' In this canon Sontag includes Tiffany lamps, *Swan Lake,* Bellini's operas, and ''certain turn-of-the-century picture postcards.'' Her concerns in the 1960's with '' 'style' over 'content' '' and '' 'aesthetics' over 'morality' '' emerge as she defends camp's ability to turn ''its back on the good-bad axis of ordinary aesthetic judgment.'' As an aesthetic phenomenon, camp is ''disengaged, depoliticized—or at least apolitical.''

We also see that Sontag needs to set herself up as a privileged, and necessarily disengaged, observer of this sensibility—''one who is strongly drawn to Camp, and almost as strongly offended by it.'' This cultivated ambivalence entitles Sontag to bring this taste to the foreground of American culture:

For no one who wholeheartedly shares in a given sensibility can analyze it; he can only, whatever his intention, exhibit it. To name a sensibility, to draw its contours and to recount its history, requires a deep sympathy modified by revulsion.

Sontag is thus empowered by her marginality and her alienated position. These become the conditions of her willingness to take on subsequent subjects in her essays.

''Notes on 'Camp' '' also appears in Sontag's first collection of essays, *Against Interpretation* (1966), which contains twenty-six essays written between 1961 and 1965. Her subjects serve to predict the concerns of her work over the next twenty-five years. Sontag's interest in European writers and issues emerges in this collection, in which she takes on the work of Simone Weil, Albert Camus, Michel Leiris, Lévi-Strauss, Lukács, Sartre, Genet, and Nathalie Sarraute. Her longtime interest in film also comes to the foreground in her pieces about Robert Bresson, Jean-Luc Godard, Alain Resnais, science fiction film, and Jack Smith's *Flaming Creatures*—a film she places in the tradition of ''the poetic cinema of shock.'' Smith's film, she acknowl-

edges, has been received with ''indifference,'' ''squeamishness,'' and ''downright hostility'' ''by almost everyone in the mature intellectual and artistic community.'' Sontag numbers herself with its supporters: ''a loyal coterie of filmmakers, poets, and young 'Villagers.' ''

By the mid 1960's Sontag's interest in films and filmmaking was well defined. In 1967 she was one of the judges at the Venice Film Festival, and that same year she participated in the selection of films for the New York Film Festival. In 1968 she began working on her first film, *Duet for Cannibals.* Made in Sweden, the film was screened in 1969 at both the Cannes Film Festival and the New York Film Festival.

Against Interpretation also includes essays on theater and performance art; Sontag wrote about Eugene Ionesco, Lionel Abel's *Metatheatre: A New View of Dramatic Form,* Artaud, and ''happenings''—improvised spectacles/performances she called ''a cross between art exhibit and theatrical performance.'' Always alert to the intertexts and links between artistic projects and aesthetics, Sontag links these ''happenings'' to Artaud's ''theatre of cruelty'':

What goes on in the Happenings merely follows Artaud's prescription for a spectacle which will eliminate the stage, that is, the distance between spectators and performers, and ''will physically envelop the spectator.'' In the Happening this scapegoat is the audience.

An essay such as ''Happenings: An Art of Radical Juxtaposition'' reminds us how much Sontag in the early 1960's promoted, defined, and made visible avant-garde art that is now acknowledged by the academy and mainstream culture.

Perhaps the most famous and controversial essays in the collection are ''Against Interpretation'' and ''On Style.'' They are also the most useful for defining Sontag's privileging of aesthetics over morality and for her belief at this time that art could somehow be divorced from its social and historical circumstances of production. Arguing from a defensive, seemingly anti-intellectual, and probably anti-academic position, Sontag becomes an advocate for a shockingly conservative "formalism" that looks at times like an aestheticism akin to the "impressionism" of Oscar Wilde, Algernon Swinburne, or Arthur Symons or the "practical" criticism of T. S. Eliot and his followers. Oddly, in Sontag's scheme these two forms of criticism do not clash.

In "Against Interpretation" Sontag argues that we need to dismantle the well-ingrained split between "form" and "content." At the moment, she maintains, all we focus on is "content"—an impulse that we soon learn makes it impossible for us to see the work at hand. Sontag attributes the all too pervasive dichotomy between "form" and "content" to "the Greek theory of art as mimesis or representation":

It is through this theory that art as such . . . becomes problematic, in need of defense. And it is the defense of art which gives birth to the odd vision by which something we have learned to call "form" is separated off from something we have learned to call "content," and to the well-intentioned move which makes content essential and form accessory.

Interpretation thus becomes a colonizing of the text—an imperialist translation that, in good structuralist terms, robs the "work" of its autonomy: "Plucking a set of elements . . . from the whole work, . . . the interpreter, without actually erasing or rewriting the text, is altering it. But he can't admit to doing this. He claims to be only making it intelligible, by disclosing its true meaning."

Older versions of this impulse are less troubling to Sontag; we discover that her real quarrel is with academics in the 1960's, particularly structuralists in literature departments:

The old style of interpretation was insistent, but respectful; it erected another meaning on top of the literal one. The modern style of interpretation excavates, and as it excavates, destroys; it digs "behind" the text, to find a sub-text which is the true one. The most celebrated and influential modern doctrines, those of Marx and Freud, actually amount to elaborate systems of hermeneutics, aggressive and impious theories of interpretation.

Interpretation thus becomes the philistine's "revenge of the intellect upon art." This revenge, Sontag implies, is motivated by fear of the unknown, the untamable, the unmanageable:

Real art has the capacity to make us nervous. By reducing the work of art to its content and then interpreting that, one tames the work of art. Interpretation makes art manageable, conformable.

Sontag calls instead for a "criticism" that would pay homage to the work itself: "Equally valuable would be acts of criticism which would supply a really accurate, sharp, loving description of the appearance of a work of art." She concludes, "In place of a hermeneutics we need an erotics of art."

While we might understand Sontag's rightful indignation toward academics who seem to have forgotten how to see art, the implications of her own way of seeing need to be taken up. "On Style," published in 1965, continues the debate set up in "Against Interpretation" and serves to highlight some of the ways in which Sontag's position, both as critic and cultural historian, seems slippery and downright dangerous in its avoidance of historical context.

In "On Style" Sontag argues that "art is not only about something; it is something." Calling for the autonomy of the work of art, she asserts: "A work of art is a thing in the world, not just a text or commentary on the world." Although Sontag is advocating that we know art through our experience of it, she comes close to asking us to divorce our experience from the historical moment in which we have our appreciation. She also is willing to ignore the historical nexus of forces surrounding its production. A case in point is her defense of Leni Riefenstahl:

To call Leni Riefenstahl's *The Triumph of The Will* and *The Olympiad* masterpieces is not to gloss over Nazi propaganda with aesthetic lenience. The Nazi propaganda is there. But something else is there, too, which we reject at our loss. Because they project the complex movements of intelligence and grace and sensuousness, these two films of Riefenstahl (unique among works of Nazi artists) transcend the categories of propaganda or even reportage. And we find ourselves—to be sure, rather uncomfortably—seeing "Hitler" and not Hitler, the "1936 Olympics" and not the 1936 Olympics. Through Riefenstahl's genius as a filmmaker, the "content" has—let us even assume, against her intentions—come to play a purely formal role.

Sontag's embrace of Riefenstahl's "style" over her "content" seems irresponsible, amoral, and a way of retreating to "the Ivory Tower" so defended by some of Riefenstahl's contemporaries in the 1930's. It is also a position Sontag would revise in the 1970's when she reconsidered Riefenstahl in "Fascinating Fascism" (1974, in *Under the Sign of Saturn*). Given her subsequent critique of Riefenstahl and her incisive indictment of Diane Arbus in *On Photography,* Sontag's advocacy here seems naive or hollow: "A work of art, so far as it is a work of art, cannot—whatever the artist's personal intentions—advocate anything at all. The greatest artists attain a sublime neutrality." What is most troubling here is the extent to which Sontag wants to have it both ways; after calling for "neutrality" and "the autonomy of art," she concludes that this position "does not preclude but rather invites the examination of works of art as

historically specifiable phenomena." Historicizing, however, occurs through an examination of the relationship between "stylistic decisions" and "historical development." Content is still not factored into her scheme.

Sontag also manages to argue for the primacy of "the autonomy of the aesthetic" and for a division between our moral responses to "something in art" and those we have to "an act in real life." Yet, a few pages later, she maintains that "the qualities which are intrinsic to the aesthetic experience (disinterestedness, contemplativeness, attentiveness, the awakening of the feelings) and to the aesthetic object (grace, intelligence, expressiveness, energy, sensuousness) are also fundamental constituents of a moral response to life." Finally, although Sontag claims, in contrast with José Ortega y Gasset, that we should not isolate "aesthetic from moral response," her own responses to Riefenstahl seem to do just this. Sontag wants the roar of art, and its silence, to come in and out of the Ivory Tower at will:

To become involved with a work of art entails, to be sure, the experience of detaching oneself from the world. But the work of art itself is also a vibrant, magical, and exemplary object which returns us to the world in some way more open and enriched.

"Against Interpretation" and "On Style" lay the groundwork for Sontag's embrace and defense of avant-garde art in the 1960's. Her persona—marginal, detached from the mainstream—allows her to champion works that most people would not acknowledge, let alone study in the academy. Later, she would abandon this need and position, as she confided in the interview with Paul Brennan:

Avant-garde has become institutionalized. It is official high culture. It is supported by museums and foundations. It doesn't need defending the way it did ten or fifteen years ago. It has also exhibited its real limits. Dead ends. Just doing things for the sake of doing them. . . . When I was much younger I thought the word experimental or *avant-garde* or formalist had more meaning than I think now. Now I'm interested in getting away from those labels.

Sontag's second collection of essays, *Styles of Radical Will,* appeared in 1969. Comprising eight essays written between 1966 and 1968, the volume addresses the function of "art" and philosophy as spiritual markers in an age burdened by "an almost insupportable burden of self-consciousness." Sontag also takes on the relationship between film and theater, Ingmar Bergman's *Persona* and Godard, and she offers us an insight into her politics during the late 1960's.

At the end of "On Style," Sontag had addressed "the presence of the inexpressible" in art, concluding that "the most potent elements in a work of art are, often, its silences." These "silences" are taken up again in "The Aesthetics of Silence" (1967), the first essay in *Styles of Radical Will.* Sontag begins the essay with a simple, seemingly axiomatic, declaration: "Every era has to reinvent the project of 'spirituality' for itself." The rest of the essay seeks to map the trajectory of this reinvention and its relationship to the artist's quest for transcendence. "In our time," the artist becomes the mystic who must seek "self-estrangement" or "disburdenment":

As the activity of the mystic must end in a *via negativa,* a theology of God's absence, a craving for the cloud of unknowing beyond knowledge and for the silence beyond speech, so art must tend toward anti-art, the elimination of the "subject" (the "object," "the image"), the substitution of chance for intention, and the pursuit of silence.

Silence, however, is actually a presence: "a full void, an enriching emptiness, a resonating or eloquent silence." The artist's insistence on achieving this "enriching emptiness" becomes a kind of spiritual disburdenment; and only through this process can the artist achieve "transcendence."

Since art replaces the mystery of religion, Sontag believes that the artist's "strategies of impoverishment"—his willed silences—must be seen as "an energetic secular blasphemy: the wish to attain the unfettered, unselective, total consciousness of 'God.' " The artist in Sontag's scheme is in flight from "impure," "contaminated," "exhausted" language—hence the embrace of silence. Language is "fallen," and thus undesirable.

Sontag's artist is also in flight from history:

Behind the appeals for silence lies the wish for a perceptual and cultural clean slate. And, in its most hortatory and ambitious version, the advocacy of silence expresses a mythic project of total liberation. What's envisaged is nothing less than the liberation of the artist from himself, of art from the particular artwork, of art from history, of spirit from matter, of the mind from its perceptual and intellectual limitations.

Here Sontag entertains the possibility of a world in which an artist "compensate[s] for [his] ignominious enslavement to history . . . [by] exalt[ing] himself with the dream of a wholly ahistorical, and therefore unalienated, art." While such a dream might have seemed possible in the 1960's, by the 1990's such a sentiment probably sounds hollow even to Sontag.

Sontag's essay on the Romanian philosopher Emil M. Cioran, " 'Thinking Against Oneself': Reflections on Cioran" (1967), also takes up the "burden of self-consciousness": "Ours is a time in which every intellectual or artistic or moral event is absorbed by a predatory embrace of consciousness: historicizing." The tendency to place every artistic event in a historical/linear continuum, Sontag contends, makes us blind to the intrinsic value of the events themselves:

The human mind possesses now, almost as second nature, a perspective on its own achievements that fatally undermines their value and their claim to truth. For over a century, this historicizing perspective has occupied the very heart of our ability to *understand* anything at all. Perhaps once a marginal tic of consciousness, it's now a gigantic, uncontrollable gesture—the gesture whereby man indefatigably patronizes himself.

Sontag attributes this excessive concern with historicizing to the downfall in the early part of the nineteenth century of the age-old project of philosophical system-building. We are, she maintains, "standing in the ruins of thought and on the verge of the ruins of history and of man himself."

After Hegel, Sontag suggests, we have two responses to our fallen condition. We have "the rise of ideologies—aggressively antiphilosophical systems of thought, taking the form of various 'positive' or descriptive sciences of man." In this camp we find Marx and Freud. In addition, Sontag identifies "a new kind of philosophizing: personal (even autobiographical), aphoristic, lyrical, anti-systematic," typified by Søren Kierkegaard and Ludwig Wittgenstein. Identifying Cioran as a twentieth-century version of Nietzsche, Sontag points out that for him, because we are in a fallen state, "there is no return, no going back to innocence." This leads Cioran in his meditations to pursue "impossible states of being, unthinkable thoughts," to look toward "the end of thought." Cioran, we are told, rages against history, but, like Nietzsche, "doesn't reject historical thinking because it is false. On the contrary, it must be rejected because it is true—a debilitating truth that has to be overthrown to allow a more inclusive orientation for human consciousness."

At the end of the essay Sontag compares Cioran to the avant-garde composer John Cage, who, unlike Cioran, was "able to jettison far more of the inherited anguish and complexity of this civilization." This comparison takes us back to Sontag's endorsement of the aesthetic of silence, as Cage is held up as someone who is able to transcend the agonies of civilization.

Ironically, in the two final essays of the collection, "What's Happening in America" (1966) and "Trip to Hanoi" (1968), Sontag demonstrates her own need to come to terms with "the inherited anguish and complexity of this civilization." The commentary at the beginning of her essay about Cioran aptly describes her own project:

More and more, the shrewdest thinkers and artists are precocious archaeologists of these ruins-in-the-making, indignant or stoical diagnosticians of defeat, enigmatic choreographers of the complex spiritual movements useful for individual survival in an era of permanent apocalypse.

"What's Happening in America" (1966) is Sontag's response to a questionnaire sent to her and others by the editors of *Partisan Review*. Her response is a biting, stinging indictment of American foreign policy, American "power," and American "life." A few quotations will set the tone: "Everything that one feels about this country is, or ought to be, conditioned by the awareness of American *power:* of America as the arch-imperium of the planet, holding man's biological as well as his historical future in its King Kong paws." Or "America was founded on a genocide, on the unquestioned assumption of the right of white Europeans to exterminate a resident, technologically backward, colored population in order to take over the continent." America, in short, is a "violent, ugly, and unhappy country."

Perhaps the most poignant critique of white/

Western imperialism occurs in Sontag's by now well-known statement in ''What's Happening in America'' (1966):

The white race *is* the cancer of human history; it is the white race and it alone—its ideologies and inventions—which eradicates autonomous civilizations wherever it spreads, which has upset the ecological balance of the planet, which now threatens the very existence of life itself.

While we might be tempted to applaud her metaphor—a metaphor she would exhaustively critique in *Illness as Metaphor*—for its illumination of something unspeakable in a code we all understand, it has dangerous implications. As George P. Elliott pointed out in 1978:

There is only one thing to do about a cancer, right? Destroy it. Destroy or be destroyed. That is implicit in the metaphor. If Hitler or Idi Amin had said this, one would know how to take it, but since it was the High Priestess of the New Sensibility, one is supposed to think she did not really mean it at all.

Sontag's politics in the 1960's were colored by this burden of seeing ''the white race'' as ''the cancer of human history.'' Indeed, her trip to Vietnam in 1968 is saturated with the angst of this inheritance. ''Trip to Hanoi'' embodies in its very form—preamble, followed by journal entries, followed by commentary—the tension between Sontag's Eurocentric perspective and her need to see the ''signs'' of Vietnam as ''other'' and inaccessible before imagining their authenticity. Sontag believes that she must disburden herself of her American ''identity'' in order to see her surroundings, yet, as the essay demonstrates, this proves impossible.

The Vietnam that, before my trip to Hanoi, I supposed myself imaginatively connected with, proved when I was there to have lacked reality. During these last years, Vietnam has been sta-

tioned inside my consciousness as a quintessential image of the suffering and heroism of ''the weak.'' But it was really America ''the strong'' that obsessed me—the contours of American power, of American cruelty, of American self-righteousness. In order eventually to encounter what was there in Vietnam, I had to forget about America; even more ambitiously, to push against the boundaries of the overall Western sensibility from which my American one derives. But I always knew I hadn't made more than a brief, amateurish foray into the Vietnamese reality. And anything really serious I'd gotten from my trip would return me to my starting point: the dilemmas of being an American, an unaffiliated radical American, an American writer.

Sontag's description of her initial dislocation, discomfort, and ignorance establish her as someone who fiercely wants to read the Vietnamese; and like a Puritan, who does ''good works'' in the hope of being granted salvation, she will earn the right to have a glimpse of this culture and its gestures. Here we see Sontag exploiting and politicizing her alienation, finding a way in precisely because she has been on the outside.

What Sontag begins to see with great clarity is that the Vietnamese do not suffer from the Western burden of experiencing ''the isolation of a 'private self.' '' They are not prey to ''thinking against [themselves].'' Cary Nelson points out that Sontag needs to be vicariously released from the burden of her own selfhood: ''In the course of the essay's 'interior journey,' Vietnam 'becomes an ideal other' not only because it 'offered the key to a systematic criticism of America' but also because it offered an otherness inimical to the very notion of selfhood.''

By the end of the essay, however, Sontag is recalled to her Western selfhood and its possibilities; she also displays an exuberant optimism: ''An event that makes new feelings conscious is always the most important experience a person can have.'' Sontag writes from the margin to the center, recording with great self-consciousness and confidence her journey toward the belief that ''unfocussed unhappiness in modern Western culture could be the beginning of *real* knowledge—by which I mean the knowing that leads simultaneously to action and to self-transcendence, the knowing that would lead to a new version of human nature in this part of the world.'' Sontag's politics here allow her to embrace a kind of humanism—one that might account for the confusion over her politics in the 1980's. When Sontag denounced communism—particularly the Soviet version—as ''fascism with a human face'' in a 1982 speech in New York, leftists felt betrayed and viewed this position as a repudiation of her sympathies with Cuba and Vietnam in the 1960's. Sontag addressed this public outcry some years later when she was quoted on the subject in a 1989 *New York Times* article by Richard Bernstein:

''I couldn't believe that that was taken as a kind of mea culpa,'' she said of her 1982 speech. Like many others in the mid-1960's, she said, she had hoped that ''some of the small countries, like Cuba and Vietnam, could evolve toward socialism in a non-Stalinist way.''

A careful reading of Sontag's earlier writing might also serve as a good corrective, for Sontag did not wholly embrace the aims and methods of these revolutions. In ''Trip to Hanoi,'' for example, when she thought about the Cuban revolution and her three-month Cuban stay in 1960, she concluded: ''Almost all my comparisons turn out favorable to the Cubans, unfavorable to the Vietnamese—by the standard of what's useful, instructive, imitable, relevant to American radicalism.''

As president of the American Center of PEN, the international writers' organization (1988–1989), Sontag continued to be outspoken against fascist repression of intellectuals and writers.

When Salman Rushdie received a death threat from the Ayatollah Khomeini for publishing his novel *The Satanic Verses,* Sontag testified on March 8, 1989, before a subcommittee of the Senate Foreign Relations Committee. Severely critical of President Bush's lack of formal response to this threat, in a Freedom-to-Write Bulletin (PEN, 1989) Sontag attacked the priorities of U.S. foreign policy and its implications for freedom of expression in America and all over the world:

Some ''chilling effect'' seems inevitable. At least for a while, there is likely to be a great deal of self-censorship—certainly on matters relating to the Islamic religion, and probably on a host of other topics which can provoke strong, and potentially violent, reaction. Most of these decisions—the book not written; the manuscript rejected; the book order not made, by individual or school or library—will be hidden from public view.

Sontag's response to Rushdie is of a piece with her responses in the 1970's to writers, such as the Cuban poet Heberto Padilla, who have been imprisoned or threatened for their activities.

In the 1970's Sontag moved away from the belief that art operates in a realm separate from ethics and moral action. She no longer sees art as autonomous, divorced from a political and social nexus of forces. This concern surfaces in Sontag's collection of essays *On Photography,* which appeared in 1977 and includes seven essays published between 1973 and 1977 in *The New York Review of Books.* A best-seller, *On Photography* won the 1977 National Book Critics Circle Award for criticism.

Sontag sets the tone for her indictment/ examination of photography, the photographer, and those who view the medium in her preface: ''It all started with one essay—about some of the problems, aesthetic and moral, posed by the omnipresence of photographed images.'' In these essays it becomes clear that the slippery separation between the realms of the aesthetic and the moral (real and implied) that Sontag endorsed in *Against Interpretation* and *Styles of Radical Will* is no longer desirable or possible. Calling photography "an ethics of seeing," Sontag asks us to reimagine our relationship—a relationship at once intimate and distant—to the proliferation of "images" around us. Photographs (looking at them and taking them) alter our way of appropriating knowledge about the world: "The most grandiose result of the photographic enterprise is to give us the sense that we can hold the whole world in our heads—as an anthology of images."

Collecting photographs—assembling an archive—becomes a kind of consumerism, in keeping with a phase of late capitalism. "To photograph," Sontag maintains "is to appropriate the thing photographed. It means putting oneself into a certain relation to the world that feels like knowledge—and, therefore, like power." Photographs can also empower their owners, particularly when they function as secondhand agents of surveillance; photography—the possibility of a record of someone's transgression—confers power on institutions, such as prisons, mental institutions, and police forces, that hope to control, curtail, punish, or survey a particular population. "Starting with their use by the Paris police in the murderous roundup of Communards in June 1871," Sontag notes in a moment of analysis reminiscent of Foucault, "photographs become a useful tool of modern states in the surveillance and control of their increasingly mobile populations." Sontag's prescience has been borne out by the function of video cameras and news crews today; the very concept of "undercover activity" has been destroyed by the ubiquitous presence of the anchor person.

For Sontag, photography becomes a kind of colonizing or imperialism in its assumption that everything is worth capturing: "There is an aggression implicit in every use of the camera. . . .

From its start, photography implied the capture of the largest possible number of subjects. Painting never had so imperial a scope." Photography is equally pernicious as a force that democratizes or ignores distinctions between subjects: "Taking photographs has set up a chronic voyeuristic relation to the world which levels the meaning of all events."

Photographs also invite us to entertain the illusion that we can possess the past as well as certain areas of space: "As photographs give people an imaginary possession of a past that is unreal, they also help people to take possession of space in which they are insecure." Photographs allow us to document our journeys and, paradoxically, distance us from them: "A way of certifying experience, taking photographs is also a way of reusing it—by limiting experience to a search for the photogenic, by converting experience into an image, a souvenir."

The desire to document one's life, Sontag suggests, is particularly important for people who have lost a sense of connection to their past:

People robbed of their past seem to make the most fervent picture takers, at home and abroad. Everyone who lives in an industrialized society is obliged gradually to give up the past, but in certain countries, such as the United States and Japan, the break with the past has been particularly traumatic.

While photography seems to promise access to a "whole" and linear view of events, it in fact privileges the fragment and the gap between things and events:

Photography reinforces a nominalist view of social reality as consisting of small units of an apparently infinite number—as the number of photographs that could be taken of anything is unlimited. Through photographs, the world becomes a series of unrelated, freestanding particles; and history, past and present, a set of anecdotes and *faits divers*. The camera makes reality atomic, manageable, and opaque.

Without an accompanying narrative/narrator, however, there can be no real record of the past; photography can only "actively promote nostalgia," for it is "an elegiac art, a twilight art."

Sontag is also interested in the political implications of contemporary photojournalism: "Photographs cannot create a moral position, but they can reinforce one." The "record" of what happens does not implicitly include a "reading" of its significance. In fact, the act of making the record is about nonintervention—about a refusal to make one's allegiance to a particular ideology visible.

Part of the horror of such memorable coups of contemporary photojournalism as the pictures of a Vietnamese bonze reaching for the gasoline can, of a Bengali guerrilla in the act of bayoneting a trussed-up collaborator, comes from the awareness of how plausible it has become, in situations where the photographer has the choice between a photograph and a life, to choose the photograph. The person who intervenes cannot record; the person who is recording cannot intervene.

A political consciousness must name, describe, and interpret an event before "photographic evidence" can serve to enforce or illuminate a moral position:

There can be no evidence, photographic or otherwise, of an event until the event itself has been named and characterized. . . . Without a politics, photographs of the slaughter-bench of history will most likely be experienced as, simply, unreal or as a demoralizing emotional blow.

Repeated exposure to photographs of certain atrocities can in fact make us numb to the moral and political implications of an event we once understood: "The vast photographic catalogue of misery and injustice throughout the world has given everyone a certain familiarity with atrocity, making the horrible seem more ordinary— making it appear familiar, remote. . . , inevitable."

Sontag explores the implications of her contention that "photographic knowledge of the world . . . can, finally, never be ethical or political knowledge" in her extended discussion of the aesthetic and moral problems raised by Diane Arbus' photographs. In "America, Seen Through Photographs, Darkly" Sontag documents how American photographs and photographers, beginning with Alfred Stieglitz and his work, have "moved from affirmation to erosion to, finally, a parody of Whitman's program." Whitman's program called for a democratization of experience and people.

In her discussion of Edward Steichen's 1955 exhibit "Family of Man," and Diane Arbus' 1972 retrospective, Sontag critiques the Whitmanesque implications of their respective desires to level the human condition—to deny historical and social differences in their subjects. Steichen's collection of photographs, she points out, attempts "to prove that humanity is 'one' and that human beings, for all their flaws and villainies, are attractive creatures." Arbus, on the other hand, photographs only "assorted monsters and borderline cases." Her work "does not invite viewers to identify with the pariahs and miserable-looking people she photographed. Humanity is not 'one.' " Sontag concludes that despite their different subjects, both shows "rule out a historical understanding of reality":

. . . "The Family of Man" denies the determining weight of history—of genuine and historically embedded differences, injustices, and conflicts. Arbus's photographs undercut politics just as decisively, by suggesting a world in which everybody is an alien, hopelessly isolated, immobilized in mechanical, crippled identities and relationships. The pious uplift of Steichen's photograph anthology and the cool dejection of the Arbus retrospective both render history and politics irrelevant.

Sontag implicitly calls for a poetics that has a discernible politics. In "On Style" she had argued for the artist's right to achieve "a sublime neutrality"; a decade later, Arbus' desire for neutrality is untenable. Sontag also had maintained that works of art do not advocate a political or moral position. In the 1970's she suggested that artistic projects and productions must be seen in relation to the historical and political circumstances of their production. Sontag's new position may be attributed, or so she argues in "Fascinating Fascism" (1974), to the shift from an elite's reception for these works to a mass culture's:

Art that seemed eminently worth defending ten years ago, as a minority or adversary taste, no longer seems defensible today, because the ethical and cultural issues it raises have become serious, even dangerous, in a way they were not then. The hard truth is that what may be acceptable in elite culture may not be acceptable in mass culture, that tastes which pose only innocuous ethical issues as the property of a minority become corrupting when they become more established. Taste is context, and the context has changed.

In "On Style" Sontag had defended the "style" or "form" of Leni Riefenstahl's films *Triumph of the Will* and *The Olympiad,* arguing that these two films "transcend the categories of propaganda or even reportage." Nearly a decade later, she makes the opposite argument as she examines the "fascist longings in our midst." Sontag can no longer separate the content of these films from their form; she also insists that we recover their historical perspective and the circumstances of their production. Riefenstahl

made four of her six films for the Nazi government; she was a close friend of Hitler and of Goebbels. Her films were financed by the Nazi government. Sontag is clearly concerned with the implications of the "current de-Nazification" of Riefenstahl and the claim that she is an "indomitable priestess of the beautiful." Sontag, who once championed "the complex movements of intelligence and grace and sensuousness" in Riefenstahl's work, in the mid 1970's faults the public for not seeing "the continuity [between Riefenstahl's] political and aesthetic ideas"—a continuity she once saw fit to ignore:

The force of her work being precisely in the continuity of its political and aesthetic ideas, what is interesting is that this was once seen so much more clearly than it seems to be now, when people claim to be drawn to Riefenstahl's images for their beauty of composition. . . . Somewhere, of course, everyone knows that more than beauty is at stake in art like Riefenstahl's.

Sontag concludes her discussion of Riefenstahl by saying she hopes the current attraction to the themes of a fascist aesthetic will pass. Finally, however, she is not sanguine: "Fascism may be merely fashionable, and perhaps fashion with its irrepressible promiscuity of taste will save us. But the judgments of taste themselves seem less innocent."

When questioned about her two assessments of Riefenstahl in a 1975 interview with Robert Boyers and Maxine Bernstein for *Salmagundi,* Sontag argued that her two positions were not incompatible:

My point in 1965 was about the formal implications of content, while the recent essay examines the content implicit in certain ideas of form. . . . The paragraph about Riefenstahl in "On Style" is correct—as far as it goes. It just doesn't go very far. While it is true that her films in some sense "transcend" the propaganda for which they are the vehicle, their specific qualities show how their aestheticizing conception is itself identical with a certain brand of propaganda.

Sontag's maneuvering here is slippery; instead of addressing the implications of her reversal on Nazi propaganda art, she argues (unconvincingly) for a consistency to her thinking on the subject of aesthetics and politics: "I would still argue that a work of art, *qua* work of art, cannot advocate anything. But since no work of art is in fact only a work of art, it's often more complicated than that." Arguing that she never really separated an aesthetic response from a moral one, Sontag begs the issue of the separation by noting: "Though I continue to be as besotted an aesthete and as obsessed a moralist as I ever was, I've come to appreciate the limitations—and the indiscretion—of generalizing either the aesthete's or the moralists's view of the world without a much denser notion of historical context."

In 1977 Sontag was diagnosed with breast cancer. In the wake of a subsequent mastectomy and chemotherapy treatments, she wrote *Illness as Metaphor,* a critique of the metaphors surrounding cancer and other diseases. Not concerned with "what it is really like to emigrate to the kingdom of the ill and live there," Sontag wants, instead, to examine the mythologies surrounding the cancer patient and the disease itself. Comparing cancer to tuberculosis, the Romantic's malady, Sontag notes:

Both the myth about TB and the current myth about cancer propose that one is responsible for one's disease. But the cancer imagery is far more punishing. . . . The view of cancer as a disease of the failure of expressiveness condemns the cancer patient; it expresses pity but also conveys contempt.

In *Illness as Metaphor,* Sontag makes her thesis known immediately; having done this, she displays a Renaissance habit of mind, taking a pronounced pleasure in the play of orchestrating literary allusions to support her extended comparison between the discourse surrounding tuberculosis and that associated with cancer. Her literary map is wide-reaching: Charles Dickens, John Keats, Franz Kafka, Leo Tolstoy, William Blake, Mikhail Lermontov, Thucydides, and W. H. Auden are among those she cites.

In *Illness as Metaphor* Sontag critiques the implications of treating cancer patients as victims. The myths surrounding the disease are well known: patients are responsible for developing cancer; certain character types are predisposed to the illness; and patients are certainly to blame if they do not recover. Cancer metaphors, Sontag contends, contribute to this assignment of blame. The language surrounding cancer, she maintains, is that of military warfare. One's body is under "siege." Cancer cells are "invasive." They "colonize." The body must draw on its "defenses," must "mobilize" against the "enemies."

Having called "the white race . . . the cancer of human history" when raging against American involvement in Vietnam, Sontag is sensitive a decade later to the continual abuse of this metaphor in political discourse. The cancer metaphor, she notes, is "implicitly genocidal." Moreover, it is a metaphor that is necessarily reductive: "Only in the most limited sense is any historical event or problem like an illness. And the cancer metaphor is particularly crass. It is invariably an encouragement to simplify what is complex and an invitation to self-righteousness, if not to fanaticism."

A decade later, Sontag published *AIDS and Its Metaphors,* which was reissued in a single volume with *Illness as Metaphor* in 1990. Sontag believes that AIDS may be seen as a sequel to cancer in the public's imagination: "In recent years some of the onus of cancer has been lifted by the emergence of a disease whose charge of stigmatization, whose capacity to create spoiled identity, is far greater.'' The military metaphors associated with AIDS, Sontag points out, have a different resonance than those used to describe cancer because they address causality: ''In the description of AIDS the enemy is what causes the disease, an infectious agent that comes from the outside.'' Like cancer, AIDS is described as ''an invasion.'' However, ''when the focus is transmission of the disease, an older metaphor, reminiscent of syphilis, is invoked: pollution.'' While cancer is ''a disease of the body's geography,'' AIDS, by definition, ''depends on constructing a temporal sequence of stages.''

Sontag also asserts that while the cancer patient may say ''Why me?'' the person who tests positive for the HIV virus rarely wonders ''Why me?'' Although she wants to make the point that AIDS ''is linked to an imputation of guilt''—and those who have the virus know how they got it—she runs the risk of being greatly insensitive to those who may still wonder why they have been ''condemned'' to an early death. She also assumes that everyone who contracts the virus is ''educated''—that is, knows how it is transmitted. This Eurocentric elitist stance does not take into account large numbers of people here in the United States and in Third World countries who really may not know what ''safe sex'' is or why they should practice it. This same population also may not know that the HIV virus can be spread through intravenous drug use. In short, her stance assumes that the largest population—actual and potential—of people with AIDS in this country and other parts of the world, such as Africa, know the various ways the virus is transmitted. Sontag's local reading, presented under the guise of a global perspective, verges on the offensive.

Sontag does not greatly enhance our knowledge of AIDS as ''a medical condition, whose consequences are a spectrum of illnesses.'' But she does suggest that the discourse surrounding AIDS forces us to revise the myth that we can fashion ourselves in the moment:

The fear of AIDS imposes on an act whose ideal is an experience of pure presentness (and a creation of the future) a relation to the past to be ignored at one's peril. Sex no longer withdraws its partners, if only for a moment, from the social. It cannot be considered just a coupling; it is a chain, a chain of transmission, from the past.

In her 1986 short story ''The Way We Live Now,'' Sontag conveys the image of the chain in her long opening sentence—a sentence, made up of embedded clauses, that brings an ill ''he'' into focus, with an unnamed illness, only to surround him with the speculations of his well and concerned friends in the chain:

At first he was just losing weight, he felt only a little ill, Max said to Ellen, and he didn't call for an appointment with his doctor, according to Greg, because he was managing to keep on working at more or less the same rhythm, but he did stop smoking, Tanya pointed out, which suggests he was frightened, but also that he wanted, even more than he knew, to be healthy, or healthier, or maybe just to gain back a few pounds, said Orson, for he told her, Tanya went on, that he expected to be climbing the walls (isn't that what people say?) and found, to his surprise, that he didn't miss cigarettes at all and revelled in the sensation of his lungs' being ache-free for the first time in years.

''The Way We Live Now'' turns out to be about ''learning how to die'': ''Sexuality is a chain that links each of us to many others, unknown others, and now the great chain of being has become a chain of death as well.'' But Sontag's chain of death is one that suggests connection as well as separation. Her poignant and powerful inscription of loss and stillness in ''The Way We Live Now'' must be seen in the context of her style of telling the story—a style that insists on linking the living and the dead, that slowly circles around the community's reactions to those about to die.

In *AIDS and Its Metaphors,* Sontag implicitly addresses the chain of death when she considers "the amplitude of the fantasies of doom that AIDS has inspired." AIDS, she concludes "may be extending the propensity for becoming inured to vistas of global annihilation which the stocking and brandishing of nuclear arms has already promoted."

Finally, at the end of the book she asks that we abandon the use of military imagery and metaphors to describe AIDS and its consequences: "About the metaphor, the military one, I would say, if I may paraphrase Lucretius: Give it back to the war-makers." D. A. Miller, in a 1989 review essay entitled "Sontag's Urbanity," attacks her for advocating this position:

Unwilling to specify which war metaphors are particularly demoralizing to people with AIDS, Sontag characteristically rejects them all, as all contributing equally powerfully to "the excommunication and stigmatizing of the ill." . . . In doing so, she forgets how well one such military metaphor—the one conveyed in the word "polemic" . . . served her as a cancer patient, beset by debilitating myths of "responsibility" and "predisposition." She also overlooks how vital another such metaphor—the one conveyed in the word . . . militancy . . .—is proving to people with AIDS and to the AIDS activism of which they stand at the center.

To date, Sontag's essays have received more critical acclaim than her fiction. This is not surprising, for while Sontag has written several stunning short stories—"Debriefing" and "The Way We Live Now" come to mind—her novels, *The Benefactor* and *Death Kit,* are less compelling. Her critics have been particularly harsh about her novels. Jay Parini, for example, called *The Benefactor* a "stiff, almost unreadable novel." He was equally critical of Sontag's second attempt to write a novel: "One marvels at Sontag's willingness to type out such a novel." The protagonists in her two novels turn inward in quest of an escape from this world; solipsistically self-absorbed, they relish their nihilism. Her characters may embody, in part, her own need for isolation and alienation, but in her novels, unlike her essays, these postures do not lead to any heightened desire or ability for self-expression.

Hippolyte, the protagonist/narrator of *The Benefactor,* and Diddy, the protagonist of *Death Kit,* are in flight from themselves, from the world around them, and from consciousness itself. Courting Sontag's own flirtation with "disburdenment" and "silence," they both, to quote Sontag on Cioran, engage in "thinking against [themselves]." Hippolyte, in his early sixties, is in an undetermined European city, writing his autobiography. He narrates a series of dreams that become a blueprint of his life as he attempts to act them out. "I am surprised," Hippolyte asserts, "dreams are not outlawed. What a promise the dream is! How delightful! How private! And one needs no partner. . . . Dreams are the onanism of the spirit." As Hippolyte moves between his dreams and their fulfillment in his life, *The Benefactor* chronicles his search for silence, stillness, and disengagement from the life around him. The novel ends with an endorsement of stasis and a view of Hippolyte's paralysis, though in Sontag's vision, there are no regrets:

I shall conclude not by describing an act, nor with one of my favorite ideas, but with a posture. Not with words, but with silence. With a photograph of myself, myself as I sit here after finishing this page. It is winter. You may imagine me in a bare room, my feet near the stove, bundled up in many sweaters, my black hair turned grey, enjoying the waning tribulations of subjectivity and the repose of a privacy that is genuine.

In *Death Kit,* Diddy also is caught between living in his dreams or fantasies and living in this world. The novel involves his frantic need to know if he killed a workman in a train tunnel; Diddy, who is on a train to a conference, imagines that when the train stalls, he has left it and murdered a workman he meets in the tunnel. When he turns to Hester, a blind woman he has met on the train, to ask "Did he?" she assures him he has not left the train compartment. The rest of the novel shows him becoming progressively more locked into himself—unable to separate his actions from his fantasies. Although Sontag claimed in a 1968 interview with James Toback that *Death Kit* "could have been called *Why Are We in Vietnam?* because it gets into the kind of senseless brutality and self-destructiveness that is ruining America," it is hard to imagine Diddy's dilemma as an objective correlative for America's involvement in Vietnam in the 1960's. The novel seems mired in the personal, regressive, solipsistic world of the protagonist.

In 1978, the year *Illness as Metaphor* appeared, Sontag published her first collection of short stories, *I, etcetera*, which contains eight stories written between 1963 and 1977 and published in the pages of *American Review, The Atlantic, Harper's Bazaar, The New Yorker, Partisan Review*, and *Playboy*. Although some of these stories were written at the time she was composing her two novels, they need to be differentiated from *The Benefactor* and *Death Kit*. Unlike the characters in her novels, those in her short stories make efforts to connect with their surroundings. Even when they are most distant from this world, one senses that this estrangement is not desirable or acceptable. The stories in *I, etcetera* may best be described as meditative, parodic, and autobiographical. Some flirt with plots and become parodic, such as "Doctor Jekyll," which Michael Wood maintains is a cousin of Henry James's "The Beast in the Jungle" with its emphasis on "the unlived life." "The Dummy" imitates a science fiction story,

as the narrator makes a dummy/double who will live his life for him. "American Spirits" critiques the Emersonian myth that one can fashion oneself in the moment and the American myth that one can "light out for the territory."

Two of the most powerful stories in the collection—"Project for a Trip to China" and "Debriefing"—seem to address, if obliquely, Sontag's own experiences. In "Project for a Trip to China," Sontag collects notes about her upcoming trip to China—her preparations for the journey take her back in time through family history. Her father had died in China; his invisibility becomes a palpable presence:

My father keeps getting younger. (I don't know where he's buried. M. says she's forgotten.)

An unfinished pain that might, just might, get lost in the endless Chinese smile.

. . . .

He died so far away. By visiting my father's death, I make him heavier. I will bury him myself.

Her own decipherment of the "signs" of China becomes her way to achieve disburdenment: "How impatient I am to leave for China! Yet even before leaving, part of me has already made the long trip that brings me to its border, traveled about the country, and come out again."

In "Debriefing," Sontag also confronts a death, that of a friend who committed suicide by jumping into the Hudson River:

How I groaned under the burden of our friendship. But your death is heavier.

Why you went under while others, equally absent from their lives, survive is a mystery to me.

Sontag cannot answer this mystery; but she does not retreat into silence and stillness, as she would have her protagonists do in her novels.

Two years after *I, etcetera* appeared, Sontag published another collection of essays: *Under the Sign of Saturn*. These seven essays, written between 1972 and 1980, represent a departure from her earlier collections of essays, not so much in subject as in treatment. Although the two best-known essays are those on the German filmmakers Leni Riefenstahl and Hans-Jürgen Syberberg, the other five—literary portraits with a deeply elegiac cast to them—seem curiously personal, unguarded, openly lyrical, less polemical and combative. These essays do not defend; they quietly celebrate. As biography, Sontag's portraits (of Antonin Artaud, Walter Benjamin, and Elias Canetti) and her farewells (to Paul Goodman and Roland Barthes) move delicately between the facts of the life lived and the public offerings of this life. In her obituary of Goodman (1972, in *Under the Sign of Saturn*), for example, Sontag notes:

I admired his courage, which showed itself in so many ways—one of the most admirable being his honesty about his homosexuality in *Five Years,* for which he was much criticized by his straight friends in the New York intellectual world; that was six years ago, before the advent of Gay Liberation made coming out of the closet chic. . . . Like Andrew Breton, to whom he could be compared in many ways, Paul Goodman was a connoisseur of freedom, joy, pleasure. I learned a great deal about those three things from reading him.

In Sontag's portraits, one senses her complicated attachment to these figures. As Elizabeth Hardwick points out in her introduction to *A Susan Sontag Reader:*

The labyrinthine perfectionism, the pathos of a "dissatisfied" spirit like Walter Benjamin came to her, I think, as a model, and certainly as an object of *love,* the word in no way out of bounds. It is love that makes her start her essay on Ben-

jamin by looking at a few scattered photographs. . . . The wish to find Benjamin as a face is touching, subjective, venerating. And this is the mood of much of her recent work, particularly the majestic honoring of Barthes and the homage to Canetti, himself a great and complicated "admirer" of his own chosen instances of genius.

Sontag's tribute to Benjamin, "Under the Sign of Saturn," (1978) is loving and gentle; it is also incisive and astute in its comprehensive analysis of the relationship between his temperament and his work. She gives us a clear sense of how his style illuminates the way his mind works, how he is someone who has lived with his work and habit of mind for a long time:

His sentences do not seem to be generated in the usual way; they do not entail. Each sentence is written as if it were the first, or the last. . . . Mental and historical processes are rendered as conceptual tableaux; ideas are transcribed in extremis and the intellectual perspectives are vertiginous. His style of thinking and writing, incorrectly called aphoristic, might better be called freeze-frame baroque. This style was torture to execute. It was as if each sentence had to say everything, before the inward gaze of total concentration dissolved the subject before his eyes. Benjamin was probably not exaggerating when he told Adorno that each idea in his book on Baudelaire and nineteenth-century Paris "had to be wrested away from a realm in which madness lies."

Sontag's affinity with Benjamin begins to explain why she is also so drawn to Artaud (see "Approaching Artaud," 1973, in *Under the Sign of Saturn*). As she approaches their lives and writings, their projects seem curiously similar:

Some of Artaud's accounts of his Passion of thought are almost too painful to read. He elaborates little on his emotions—panic, confusion, rage, dread. His gift was not for psychological understanding . . . but for a more original mode of description, a kind of physiological phenomenology of his unending desolation. Artaud's claim in *The Nerve Meter* that no one has ever so accurately charted his "intimate" self is not an exaggeration. Nowhere in the entire history of writing in the first person is there as tireless and detailed a record of the microstructure of mental pain.

Sontag's obituary of Barthes also pays homage to his life by charting his various self-transcriptions. Barthes's self-fashioning, like Artaud's, is connected, in part, to the influence that theater exerted on him: "In his youth, he founded a university theater group, reviewed plays. And something of the theater, a profound love of appearances, colors his work when he began to exercise, at full strength, his vocation as a writer." Sontag's own concerns with self-fashioning—with her economy of self-disclosure—implicitly emerge when she describes Barthes's work, in "Remembering Barthes" (1980, in *Under the Sign of Saturn*), as "an immensely complex enterprise of self-description":

His sense of privacy was expressed exhibitionistically. Writing about himself, he often used the third person, as if he treated himself as a fiction. The later work contains much fastidious self-revelation, but always in a speculative form (no anecdote about the self which does not come bearing an idea between its teeth), and dainty meditation on the personal; the last article he published was about keeping a journal.

Sontag, whose next work is a novel and a new collection of short fiction, is also engaged in "fastidious self-revelation." No longer interested in writing essays, she confided to Helen Benedict: "I feel I can make better use of my talents writing in a freer, more emotionally direct way. There must be some puritanism in me that has lashed me to the essay for so long; I find essays extremely difficult to write." Sontag's disclosures in her memoir may be "speculative" like Barthes's self-revelations, or they may be veiled and indirect, like some of Henry James's pronouncements in his memoirs. What is certain is that they will be eagerly greeted by those anxious for the latest instructions from this formidable presence in American letters on how to approach her life and work.

Selected Bibliography

PRIMARY WORKS

FICTION

The Benefactor. New York: Farrar, Straus, Giroux, 1963.

Death Kit. New York: Farrar, Straus, Giroux, 1967.

I, etcetera. New York: Farrar, Straus Giroux, 1978.

"The Way We Live Now," *New Yorker*, November 24, 1986, pp. 42–51.

ESSAYS

Against Interpretation. New York: Farrar, Straus, Giroux, 1966.

Trip to Hanoi. New York: Farrar, Straus, Giroux, 1968.

Styles of Radical Will. New York: Farrar, Straus, Giroux, 1969.

On Photography. New York: Farrar, Straus, Giroux, 1977.

Illness as Metaphor. New York: Farrar, Straus, Giroux, 1978.

Under the Sign of Saturn. New York: Farrar, Straus, Giroux, 1980.

A Susan Sontag Reader, With introduction by Elizabeth Hardwick. New York: Farrar, Straus, Giroux, 1982.

AIDS and Its Metaphors. New York: Farrar, Straus, Giroux, 1989.

MEMOIR

"Pilgrimage." *New Yorker*, December 21, 1987, pp. 38–54.

FILM SCRIPTS

Duet for Cannibals: A Screenplay. New York: Farrar, Straus, Giroux, 1970.

Brother Carl: A Filmscript. New York: Farrar, Straus, Giroux, 1974.

FILMS

Duet for Cannibals. (1969). Written and directed by Sontag. Black and white, 105 minutes.

Brother Carl. (1971). Written and directed by Sontag. Black and white, 97 minutes.

Promised Lands. (1974). Written and directed by Sontag. Color, 87 minutes.

Unguided Tour. (1983). Written and directed by Sontag. Color, 72 minutes.

EDITIONS

Artaud, Antonin. *Selected Writings*. Edited with an introduction by Susan Sontag. Translated by Helen Weaver. New York: Farrar, Straus, Giroux, 1976.

Barthes, Roland. *A Roland Barthes Reader*. Edited with an introduction by Susan Sontag. New York: Hill & Wang, 1981.

COLLECTED WORKS

A Susan Sontag Reader. With introduction by Elizabeth Hardwick. New York: Farrar, Straus, Giroux, 1982.

SECONDARY WORKS

Benedict, Helen. "The Passionate Mind." *New York Woman*, 3 (November 1988).

Bernstein, Richard. "Susan Sontag, as Image and as Herself." *New York Times*, January 26, 1989, p. C17.

Braudy, Leo. "A Genealogy of Mind." *New Republic*, 29 November 1980, pp. 43–46. Review of *Under the Sign of Saturn*.

Brooks, Peter, "Death of/as Metaphor." *Partisan Review*, 46:438–444 (1979).

Elliott, George P. "High Prophetess of High Fashion." *Times Literary Supplement*, March 17, 1978, p. 304. Review of *On Photography*.

Gilman, Richard. "Susan Sontag and the Question of the New." *New Republic*, May 3, 1969, pp. 23–26. Review of *Styles of Radical Will*.

Holdsworth, Elizabeth McCaffrey. "Susan Sontag: Writer–Filmmaker." Ph.D. diss., Ohio University, 1981.

Kendrick, Walter. "Eminent Victorian." *The Village Voice*, October 15–21, 1980, pp. 44–46. Review of *Under the Sign of Saturn*.

Lacayo, Richard. "Profile of Susan Sontag." *Time*, October 24, 1988, pp. 86–88.

Miller, D. A. "Sontag's Urbanity." *October*, 49:91–101 (Summer 1989).

Nelson, Cary. "Soliciting Self-Knowledge: The Rhetoric of Susan Sontag's Criticism." *Critical Inquiry*, 6:707–726 (Summer 1980).

Ostriker, Alicia. "Anti-Critic." *Commentary*, 41:83–84 (June 1966). Review of *Against Interpretation*.

Parini, Jay. "Reading the Readers: Barthes and Sontag." *The Hudson Review*, 36:411–410 (Summer 1983).

Rubin, Louis D., Jr. "Susan Sontag and the Camp Followers." *Sewanee Review*, 82:503–510 (Summer 1974).

Sayres, Sohnya. *Susan Sontag: The Elegiac Modernist*. New York: Routledge, 1990.

Wood, Michael. "'This Is Not the End of the World.' " *New York Review of Books*, January 25, 1979, pp. 28–31.

Young, Vernon. "Socialist Camp: A Style of Radical Wistfulness." *The Hudson Review*, 22:513–520 (Autumn 1969).

INTERVIEWS

Boyers, Robert, and Maxine Bernstein. "Women, the Arts, & the Politics of Culture. An Interview with Susan Sontag." *Salmagundi*, no. 31–32:29–48 (Fall 1975–Winter 1976).

Brennan, Paul. "Sontag in Greenwich Village: An Interview." *London Magazine*, 19:93–102 (April–May 1979).

Cott, Jonathan. "Susan Sontag: *The Rolling Stone* Interview." *Rolling Stone*, October 4, 1979, pp. 46–53.

Fries, Kenny. *"AIDS and Its Metaphors:* A Conversation with Susan Sontag." *Coming Up!,* March 1989.

Movius, Geoffrey, "Susan Sontag, an Interview with Geoffrey Movius." *New Boston Review,* 1:12–13 (June 1975).

Simmons, Charles. "Sontag Talking." *New York Times Book Review,* 18:7, 31, 33 (December 1977).

Toback, James. "Whatever You'd Like Susan Sontag to Think, She Doesn't." *Esquire,* July 1968, pp. 58–61, 114–116.

—CELESTE GOODRIDGE

Jean Toomer
1894–1967

IN 1923, JEAN TOOMER published *Cane,* an enigmatic, lyrical work that mixed prose with poetry and intertwined the African-American folk culture of the South with the bourgeois, urban rhythms of the North. Hailed as emblematic of the "New Negro" in America, *Cane* was the product of a generation that was, in the words of black scholar and critic Alain Locke, "vibrant with a new psychology" and interested in the "development of a more positive self-respect and self-reliance." As quoted in the Norton Critical Edition, Sherwood Anderson once told Toomer, "Your work is of special significance to me because it is the first negro work I have seen that strikes me as being really negro." Anderson wrote that he considered Toomer to be "the only negro . . . who seems really to have consciously the artist's impulse." In 1925, Locke listed Toomer among a "vivid galaxy of young Negro poets," writers who "have now stopped speaking for the Negro—they speak as Negroes," and William Stanley Braithwaite called Toomer "the very first artist of the race, who . . . can write about the Negro without the surrender or compromise of the artist's vision." With *Cane,* Toomer seemed to have gained a prominent position among those influential black writers who were a part of the phenomenon later known as the Harlem Renaissance.

Shortly after *Cane* was published, however, Toomer dropped out of the literary scene to become a disciple of the mystic G. I. Gurdjieff. More importantly, Toomer's own ambivalent attitude toward both his African-American heritage and the question of race in general separated him from that group of writers with whom he is most frequently linked—black writers like Countee Cullen, Alain Locke, Zora Neale Hurston, and Langston Hughes—who were all deeply involved in the expression of an African-American art. Toomer is quoted by Kerman and Eldridge (1987) as having said he considered himself "of no particular race. I am of the human race, a man at large in the human world, preparing a new race." As such, he was eager to distance himself from the New Negro movement, though he willingly allowed "racial factors" to be used in order to promote the publication of *Cane,* and he frequently stressed the vital part that black folk culture had played in creating a sense of spiritual wholeness within him during his stay in rural Georgia in the early 1920's.

But it is just this complex reaction to race that makes Toomer such an interesting and important figure in the history of American writing. Both Toomer's own attitude toward his mixed racial heritage and the ways in which race is represented in his works expose the complex, often contradictory, feelings and thoughts that make up an individual's racial consciousness. Even more importantly, the ways in which Toomer's work and career have been critically revised and reconstructed reflect the efforts of African-American critics to forge their own notions of racial tradition and identity. Toomer's career as a literary artist was a relatively short-lived one, though he continued to write philosophical, instructive tracts throughout most of his life. After *Cane* only "Blue Meridian" (1936) and a handful of other works merit serious critical attention. Still, the ways in which Toomer has figured in the development of an African-American literary tradition—from the work of the New Negro movement of the 1920's to the efforts of contemporary critics like Houston Baker, Nellie McKay, and Henry Louis Gates, Jr.—coupled with the delicacy, complexity, and force of his portrayals of African-American culture, have secured his position among the most influential writers of twentieth-century American literature.

The history of Jean Toomer's relationship to race begins with his maternal grandfather's place in the history of the United States as the first black governor of any state in the Union. Pinckney Benton Steward Pinchback was born in Macon, Georgia, in 1837, the free son of Major William Pinchback, a white plantation owner, and his mulatto former slave, Eliza Stewart. Stewart bore William ten children in all, though only two survived into adulthood. According to Toomer, Stewart was of English, Scotch, Welsh, German, African, and Indian descent, and she and her children were maintained separately from William Pinchback's legal wife and family. This support ended in 1848 with Major Pinchback's death, when the twelve-year-old Pinckney was forced to fend for himself, eventually working on cargo boats on the Mississippi and earning a reputation as a gambler.

In New Orleans, in 1860, Pinckney married Nina Emily Hethorn, whom Toomer describes as a "white Creole" with no Negro blood, though this description has been disputed by some of Toomer's biographers. At best, we can say that both Pinckney and Nina Pinchback could be considered black according to the definitions then prevalent in American society, though both were also sufficiently light-complected to allow them to "pass" in either black or white society. Kerman and Eldridge cite an 1863 letter—kept by Toomer in a tin box with other private possessions—Pinchback's sister Addie wrote to him saying, "If I were you Pink I would not let my ambition die. I would seek to rise and not in that class either but I would take my position in the world as a white man as you are and let the other go for be assured of this as the other you will *never* get your rights." Pinchback had been involved in recruiting blacks for the Union army in 1862 and had planned to see Lincoln for permission to raise black troops in Ohio and Indiana shortly before the war ended. By the time of Addie's letter, he had already appeared in public to speak out against the treatment the newly freed blacks were receiving in the South. Pinchback's ambition told him to stay with "that other class," and soon after Congress passed the Reconstruction Acts in 1867, Pinchback organized the Fourth Ward Republican Club in Louisiana.

P. B. S. Pinchback was a forceful, shrewd, domineering politician, and his fortunes, both political and monetary, rose quickly as he became a state senator, a commission merchant, the owner of a semi-weekly newspaper, and the director of the New Orleans schools. In 1871 he was narrowly elected lieutenant governor, replacing a reputedly incorruptible black man who had died unexpectedly. Pinchback battled openly with Governor Henry Clay Warmoth, each seeking greater control of the state senate, until Pinchback, as president of the senate, held a pre-dawn ceremony to swear in all of the newly elected Republican members, many of whose senate seats were contested by Democrats who supported the governor. The new senate quickly impeached Warmoth on charges of corruption and bribery, and Pinchback served as the governor of Louisiana for the remaining month and a half of Warmoth's term.

After his short term as governor, the legislature elected Pinchback a senator from Louisiana, but the seat was contested by, and ultimately lost to, a Democrat. Spending the next three years trying to regain his senate position, Pinchback spoke out against election fraud in Louisiana as well as in Cinncinnati, Indianapolis, and Memphis, earning the attention and support of Frederick Douglass. His rise to prominence and wealth continued during these years, as Pinchback served as a delegate to both the national and state Republican conventions, and he continued to receive a variety of political appointments, most notably as an internal revenue agent and a surveyor of customs for the Port of New Orleans. However, according to Arna Bontemps in *100 Years of Negro Freedom*, Pinchback felt betrayed by his own party "on account of his race," and with the sometimes violent return to power of white Democrats in the South, Pinchback's political career in Louisiana was effectively over by 1879.

Still, Pinchback's rise had been considerable, and he was described in a newspaper article in 1887, quoted in Kerman and Eldridge, as a "prudent economical financier" earning "about $10,000 a year from stocks and bonds." He raised his family as part of the southern aristocracy, owning a mansion staffed by servants in New Orleans and traveling often for speaking engagements and vacations in Washington, D.C., and Saratoga Springs. He left Louisiana in 1892, building a substantial, three-story house in a semirural section of Washington. Here Toomer's mother, Nina, and her two brothers (Pinchback's oldest son, Pinckney, was already on his own in Philadelphia) were raised in a style

befitting the man whom many still called "Governor." Lavish entertainers, the Pinchbacks lived in a swirl of social engagements, attending balls and playing host to the elite of Washington.

But Pinchback's control over his family was strict; he groomed all of his children as if, Toomer later wrote, they were part of a plan to establish some "new political dynasty." Pinckney, the oldest son, was a pharmacist who had studied at the College of Pharmacy in Philadelphia. Bismarck, the next oldest and an influential model for Toomer, was sent to Yale in order to become a doctor, but he never completed his study there. Nina was sent to finishing school in preparation for an appropriate match to be overseen by Pinchback, and Walter, the youngest, was sent to Andover Academy in order to study law in college, though he too returned to Washington before finishing his studies.

In fact, with the exception of Pinckney, all of his children were to defy their father's desires for them and disappoint their own best expectations in a way that was later to become the pattern of Toomer's life as well. Bismarck graduated from Howard University with an interest in the arts, an interest Pinchback strongly disapproved of. He sent his son to Mississippi to practice medicine, but Bismarck hated it there. He got his son a Civil Service appointment to an Indian reservation, but Bismarck once again returned unhappy. Finally, living at home in his thirties, Bismarck took a minor job in the government and spent his free time lounging in bed, reading, and writing. This literary life of leisure was a source of inspiration for the young Toomer and a constant irritant to Pinchback. The youngest, Walter, also disappointed his demanding father by abandoning his studies and ending up at home, working for the government and serving briefly in Cuba during the Spanish-American War.

Pinchback's sharpest disappointment, however, came from Toomer's mother, who, perhaps in defiance of Pinchback's strict management of her life, married the flamboyant Nathan Toomer —a man twenty-seven years older than she, who seemingly came out of nowhere onto the Washington social scene in 1894. Kerman and Eldridge cite Toomer's notebooks, which record that his father was of English, Dutch, and Spanish descent, the son of a wealthy Georgia planter. Nathan Toomer's mother was "of mixed blood, including Negro and Indian," but Nathan "lived with both white and colored people. The rigid division of white and Negro did not apply in his case." Both Nathan and Nina described themselves as "colored" on their marriage license.

In both background and style, as well as in age, Nathan Toomer was a great deal like Pinchback. He bought a house in Washington shortly after the marriage, paying for it in cash, and seemed to promise for Nina a continued life of elegance, flair, and protection. Three months after they were married, however, Nathan left her pregnant and with little support to run the house. Claiming that he had to return south to take care of his finances, Nathan left for Georgia, coming back to Washington only briefly to see the birth of his son, Nathan Pinchback Toomer, on December 26, 1894. He visited his wife and child sporadically during the course of the next year and abandoned the family completely in October of 1895.

Nina moved back in with her father in 1896 after having lived with a friend and rented out her house for a short time. Pinchback quickly demanded that the baby's name be changed if they were to live under his roof, and while she opposed any legal changes, Nina finally agreed informally to call her son Eugene Pinchback, though she continued to refer to him as Eugene Toomer. Toomer later remarked in *The Wayward and the Seeking: A Collection of Writings by Jean Toomer* (1980), that he found both names displeasing and that he thought "the names we human beings attach to ourselves are among the most ridiculous features of our existence." From

his notebooks we learn that he decided to call himself Jean Toomer at the age of twenty-five because it was a name that sounded more like "a poet, a man of letters, a philosopher," and at forty-five he called himself Nathan Jean Toomer in the hopes that his "final name till death" would mark "a radical sharp rise upwards into a new being, a new consciousness, a new birth." This shifting of names and identities, brought about by his father's deserting the family and his grandfather's need for strict control over his household, marked the beginnings of a personal and spiritual insecurity that haunted Toomer throughout his life. As Toomer's biographers, Cynthia Kerman and Richard Eldridge, point out, this insecurity is made clear in an undated poem found in the same tin box that contained his great-aunt Addie's letter to his grandfather:

Above my sleep
Tortured in deprival
Stripped of the warmth of a name
My life breaks madly. . . .
Breaks against the world
Like a pale moth breaking
Against sun.

This insecurity manifested itself in a pattern of behavior that Toomer followed throughout his life. Either Toomer had to be the acknowledged leader of whatever activity he was involved in, or he withdrew into his own private, inner world. In *The Wayward and the Seeking,* Toomer recalls that "I was a good fighter. In fact I was the leader of our, as it were, gang. I could lick any boy my size in the neighborhood." Toomer lived to be outdoors with his friends, running freely through the "glorious playground" of Washington at the turn of the century. But this happiness was relatively short-lived. In what Toomer called the "Dark Summer" of 1905, in his "Outline of an Autobiography," quoted in *The Wayward and the Seeking,* his mother became increasingly distant from the family, and when an illness confined him indoors for several months, he withdrew from his "gang," entering a stage where "inner things [were] more real and interesting than outer [things]." When his mother remarried in 1906, moving first to Brooklyn and then to New Rochelle, New York, Toomer found solace for his insecurity in Arthurian romances, calling himself "The Black Prince Toomer."

Nina's second marriage was little better than her first, and Toomer saw Archibald Combes, his white stepfather, as his mother's inferior in every regard. Then in 1909, Nina fell ill with appendicitis, and because of delays in getting an operation, she died unexpectedly that summer. Toomer wrote that he "came to meet life with [his] mind" and withdrew even further into his inner world, giving the impression of indifference to the devastating events around him. He moved back with his grandparents, who had moved to live with his Uncle Bismarck in Washington, and for the first time was immersed in a predominantly black culture.

In an essay called "On Being an American," collected in *The Wayward and the Seeking,* Toomer described these new conditions:

In the Washington of those days . . . there was a flowering of a natural but transient aristocracy, thrown up by the, for them, creative conditions of the post-war period. These people, whose racial strains were mixed and for the most part unknown, happened to find themselves in the colored group.

Like his grandfather, Toomer's ambition led him to desire a place among the "aristocracy," and he considered his new environment to be more vibrant and alive than the predominantly white neighborhoods he had lived in. Unlike Pinchback, however, Toomer was uncomfortable among the "colored group." He had wanted to attend prep school for a year before entering college in order to counter what he expected would be the detrimental effect of having at-

tended a black high school, but his grandfather's resources were severely reduced by this time. Instead, Toomer listed himself as white and was admitted to the agricultural program at the University of Wisconsin in 1914, envisioning himself as becoming part of the landed gentry—a role that combined his grandfather's early treatment of him as "the scion of some great family" and his father's supposed position as a wealthy Georgia planter.

For the first time, Toomer confronted the problem of his race in his own life and resolved that if he were forced to explain his background, he would represent himself as an American, a mixture of several bloodlines. Toomer felt that Pinchback had misrepresented his racial background in order to further his political career, and that as a category, race in America should be meaningless since all Americans, he argued, were a combination of a variety of backgrounds. His time at Wisconsin began well enough—he was extremely popular and decided to run for freshman class president—but when it became apparent that he would not win the election, he gradually lost interest in school and withdrew shortly after Christmas vacation.

Toomer tells us in *The Wayward and the Seeking* that during the next four years, he drifted from school to school, "unconsciously seeking—as all men must seek—an intelligible scheme of things, a sort of whole into which everything fits, or seems to fit, a body of ideals which holds a consistent view of life and which enables one to see and understand as one does when he sees a map." At first Toomer enrolled in the Massachusetts School of Agriculture in Amherst, but when troubles arose over the transfer of grades from Wisconsin, he left. Next, in 1916, Toomer sought this "consistent view of life" in a rigid, physical discipline, and he enrolled in the American College of Physical Training in Chicago, where he became an outstanding athlete and something of an expert in anatomy.

After attending public lectures on naturalism and atheism, however, he began reading widely in the literature of sociology and soon became an advocate of socialism. Toomer added Herbert Spencer, Ernst Haeckel, and Victor Hugo to his list of revered authors and began giving his own somewhat eclectic lectures on evolution, economics, philosophy, and the origins of the universe.

A disastrously condescending lecture on "The Intelligence of Women" ended Toomer's weekly talks, but not his enthusiasm. He left Chicago to take a summer course in sociology at New York University, now dreaming of a life in academics. He later enrolled in a history course at City College and began reading George Bernard Shaw and Henrik Ibsen. But Toomer soon grew dissatisfied with his studies, and after having been rejected as a volunteer for the army—he wrote that he was opposed to war but attracted to soldiering—he drifted back to Chicago and taught physical education for a short while in Milwaukee. From 1917 to 1919 he continued to "bum around" New York, Baltimore, and Washington, much to his grandfather's frustration, still sure that he was meant to fulfill some "superior destiny" but with no idea about the means by which he would reach it.

Working briefly as a fitter in the New Jersey shipyards toward the end of 1919, Toomer tried to win the workers over to socialism but found them only interested in "playing craps and sleeping with women." Socialism, he concluded was "a pipe dream possible only to those who had never really experienced the proletariat," and he returned to New York, where he discovered the work of Walt Whitman and, most importantly, Goethe's *Wilhelm Meister*. Toomer writes in *The Wayward and the Seeking:*

It seemed to gather all the scattered parts of myself. I was lifted into and shown my real world. It was the world of the aristocrat—but not the social aristocrat; the aristocrat of culture, of spirit and character, of ideas, of true nobility. . . . I resolved to devote myself to making of myself such a person as I caught glimpses of in the pages of *Wilhelm Meister*. For my specialized work, I would write.

Living in New York's Greenwich Village, Toomer quickly came into contact with several of the literary world's leading young figures, among them Lola Ridge, Edwin Arlington Robinson, Hart Crane, Van Wyck Brooks, and Waldo Frank. Frank and Toomer developed a close friendship, with the more experienced Frank drawing Toomer into his mystical vision of democratic America. Theodore Dreiser, Sinclair Lewis, and Sherwood Anderson were included with Leo Tolstoy, Fyodor Dostoyevsky, and Gustave Flaubert among his pantheon of revered writers, and he read heavily in Eastern mysticism, Buddhism, and theosophy. Toomer wrote "essays, articles, poems, short stories, reviews, and a long piece somewhere between a novel and a play . . . a trunk full of manuscripts," but he never attempted to publish any of them. Then, Toomer recalls in *The Wayward and the Seeking,* "after several years of work, suddenly, it was as if a door opened and I knew without a doubt that I was *inside.* I knew *literature!* And that was my joy!"

Despite this insight into literature, Toomer had yet to find a sense of internal harmony that would enable him to order his experience in a style and manner he could find acceptable. Continued conflicts with his grandfather, with whom he had returned to live in 1920 and whose failing health required constant attention, became "a struggle for life." He had written a long poem called "The First American" during the winter of 1920–1921, and the effort had left him exhausted. The following summer, however, Toomer was offered a position by the principal of a rural, black agricultural and industrial school near Sparta, Georgia, and, putting his grandfather in a hospital and hiring someone to look after his grandmother, Toomer sought an end to his frustrations by going South.

Toomer had long been curious abut the black folk culture and his own ties, through his father, to the rural experiences of African Americans. Living in a shack in the backwoods of Georgia, hearing folk songs and spirituals for the first time in his life, Toomer felt that sense of spiritual and emotional harmony that had eluded him for so long. In "Why I Entered the Gurdjieff Work," quoted in McKay, Toomer writes:

I had seen and met people of all kinds. I had never before met with a folk. I had never before lived in the midst of a people gathered together by a group spirit. Here they were. They worked and lived close to the earth, close to each other. They worked and loved and hated and got into trouble and felt a great weight on them. . . . And what I saw and felt and shared entered me, so that my people-life was uncased from the rest of myself. The roots of my people-life went out to those folk, and found purchase in them, and the people became people of beauty and sorrow.

But to Toomer, these folk songs were an elegy to a way of life that was already passing. As Toomer notes in *The Wayward and the Seeking,* despite the "rich and sad and joyous and beautiful" sounds of these spirituals, "the Negroes of the town objected to them. They called them 'shouting.' They had victrolas and player-pianos. . . . The folk-spirit was walking in to die on the modern desert. That spirit was so beautiful. Its death was so tragic." Still, Toomer identified with his folk spirit so intensely that he lost his own identity to it. Despite the lack of refinement, the oppressive poverty, and the stings of racial hatred, these people had a primal dignity about them that Toomer both admired and felt compelled to record. He sent off a poem, "Geor-

gia Night," to Claude McKay at the *Liberator* the day before he left Sparta, and on the train ride back to Washington he began to write the prose sections that would make up the first part of *Cane.*

In December of 1921, the month after Toomer returned, his grandfather died, and Toomer accompanied the body back to New Orleans for burial. With only his grandmother to look after, Toomer wrote clearly and quickly. "Kabnis," for example, "sprang up almost in a day," and "Fern" was composed with nearly no revisions. By April of 1922, he records, almost all of the pieces that made up *Cane* had been completed. He had reunited with Waldo Frank by this time and developed a close working relationship with him. Kerman and Eldridge note that Toomer found in Frank "a deeply intuitive and sympathetic mind," and the two traveled south together to Spartanburg, South Carolina, for a week in order to experience "the bite and crudity of pure Negro : White southern life." Instrumental in helping Toomer compile and revise his pieces into the coherent whole of *Cane,* Frank recommended the work to his own publisher, Boni and Liveright.

Toomer had also developed a correspondence with Sherwood Anderson at this time, and he had visited the home of Alain Locke—a Howard University professor who was soon to be a central figure in the New Negro movement—where he met, among others, Countee Cullen. He wrote again to Claude McKay, who this time published "Carma," "Reapers," and "Becky"—later collected in *Cane*—in the *Liberator.* He contacted Lola Ridge of *Broom,* and Jane Heap of the *Little Review.* He also wrote to DuBose Heyward, author of *Porgy,* in order to join the South Carolina poetry society that Heyward headed. In all of this correspondence, Toomer seems to have had two purposes: to promote himself as a new writer and to explain (often in contradictory ways) his treatment of race in *Cane.* As noted in the Norton Critical Edition of that novel, Toomer proposed with Sherwood Anderson, for example, the creation of a new magazine that would concentrate on the "contributions of the Negro to the western world" and wrote that he hoped that his own art would "aid in giving the Negro to himself." Kerman and Eldridge note that Toomer wrote to Hayward that "in no instance am I concerned primarily with race; always I drive straight for my own spiritual reality, and for the spiritual truth of the South." "The only time I think 'Negro,' " he wrote to Waldo Frank, "is when I want a particular emotion which is associated with his name."

Still, with the publication of *Cane* in 1923, Toomer was greeted by Locke as "a bright morning star of a new day of the race in literature." Kerman and Eldridge point out that Horace Liveright, his publisher, saw the opportunity to promote Toomer as part of an emerging scene of African-American literature and referred to him as "a colored genius," and leading black writers such as W. E. B. Du Bois, Countee Cullen, and William Stanley Braithwaite urged Toomer to continue in his "race contribution." *Cane* represented for these writers the voice of the African American made audible, an objective evocation of the black experience. "What stirs inarticulately in the masses is already vocal upon the lips of the talented few," Alain Locke wrote, "and the future listens, however the present may shut its ears."

Cane opens with this voice, taken from the oral tradition of spirituals and the blues, in a four-line hymn to his first female avatar of the South, Karintha:

Her skin is like dusk on the eastern horizon
O cant you see it, O cant you see it,
Her skin is like dusk on the eastern horizon
. . . When the sun goes down.

In the sixteen pieces that make up this first section, Toomer intertwines verse with narrative,

connecting brief prose sketches of six women with pairs of poems, blending poetry and prose in both the first and the last sketch. Toomer continues to experiment with form throughout *Cane*, unifying his work in both its focus on black experience and its movement from the folk culture of Georgia to the urban North, to return again to the South in a dramatic narrative that centers on the reconciliation of Ralph Kabnis—possibly the narrator of all three sections and a clear figure of Toomer himself—with his own southern heritage. In the original version of *Cane*, Toomer emphasized this continuity between sections by putting two rising arcs before each of the first two sections and beginning the third with two arcs mirroring each other.

Set in rural Georgia, the scene of the first section of *Cane* is the valley in Sparta that Toomer had lived in, "with smoke-wreaths during the day and mist at night." Impressionistic and, at times, even surreal, Toomer's narrative records the daily hardships, desires, and conflicts of a people oppressed by poverty and racial hatred. Privileging no single voice or perspective, Toomer moves from distanced narration to first-person retelling, mixing lyricism, sensuality, and innocence with harsh violence and numbing indifference. Throughout each of these pieces, however, there remains a sense of loss, a sense of falling off from the "race memories of king and caravan" to the sterile industrialization that is gradually invading the land. As Toomer writes in "Carma," "the Dixie Pike has grown from a goat path in Africa."

In "Song of the Son," a poem that appears midway in this first section, Toomer makes clear his elegiac purpose in this section:

In time, for though the sun is setting on
A song-lit race of slaves, it has not set;
Though late, O soil, it is not too late yet
To catch thy plaintive soul, leaving, soon gone,
Leaving, to catch thy plaintive soul soon gone.

Toomer exemplifies this fading spirit in the lives of the women he portrays and in his identification of them with the land they grew up on. Each of these six women, though in a sense indomitable, is worn down by prejudice and separation—they become desirable possessions whose spirituality is broken by racial and sexual domination. From Karintha—who carries "beauty, perfect as dusk when the sun goes down" and is made into a prostitute by men who "do not know that the soul of her was a growing thing ripened too soon"—to Carma—"in overalls, and strong as any man"—to Becky—"the white woman who had two Negro sons"—each of these women is alienated from both society and self, made victim by a violence beyond her control.

This violence is best expressed in the section's final vignette, "Blood-Burning Moon." Here Louisa, a young black woman, is the lover of both Bob Stone, the son of the white people she works for, and a black man named Tom Burwell, who refuses to share her with anyone. Allowing each character's consciousness to dominate the three parts that make up the story, Toomer begins with Louisa's dreamy thoughts of the two men who "had won her," as she sings "softly at the evil face of the full moon":

> Red nigger moon. Sinner!
> Blood-burning moon. Sinner!
> Come out that fact'ry door.

In Tom's section, Toomer records both Burwell's anger at the rumors about Louisa and Stone and his gentle helplessness in confronting Louisa about the rumors. "An next year if ole Stone'll trust me," he promises her, "I'll have a farm. My own. My bales will buy yo what y gets from white folks now."

Stone's section opens with his violent confusion over his attraction to Louisa and the need to sneak about in order to see her. "His family had lost ground." In the old days he would have "went in as a master should and [taken] her." Refusing to share "his girl" with a black man and ashamed that "Bob Stone, of the old Stone family" had to get "in a scrap with a nigger over a nigger girl," he confronts Burwell, pulls out a knife, and has his throat slashed by Burwell in a fight. Stone staggers into town, telling a group of white men Burwell's name, and in the story's final scene, Tom is burned alive at the old factory while Louisa sings insanely to the full moon.

"Blood-Burning Moon" brings to a fitting close the complex structure of feeling that makes up Toomer's Georgia. Ultimately helpless against the brutal forces of white, industrial society, the inhabitants of Toomer's fictitious town of Sempter maintain what dignity they can by clinging to the mysterious spirit of place that winds through these stories like the smell of boiling cane syrup. Alternately tough and lyrical, ironic and sentimental, humorous and violent, Toomer's narrative and poems pay an honest tribute to the fading folk culture of the South.

The second section of *Cane* opens with the jangling, jazz-like, urban rhythms of "Seventh Street" in Washington, D.C., in a song very different from the folk spirituals of Georgia:

Money burns the pocket, pocket hurts,
Bootleggers in silken shirts,
Ballooned, zooming Cadillacs,
Whizzing, whizzing down the street-car tracks.

The seven narratives and five poems that make up this middle section concentrate on the stifled lives of northern blacks, with only one poem, "Harvest Song," recalling the close relationship to the land that characterized the first part of the book. Middle-class respectability, the aftereffects of World War I and Prohibition, and the tensions between races alienate the figures here from their surroundings as well as from each other. The stories in this section are more closely autobiographical, combining incidents from Toomer's days at Wisconsin, his vacations at

Harper's Ferry, and his relationship with a young white woman in Chicago in 1916. Toomer focuses on both men and women in these narratives, showing how both have altered their behavior to fit a white world from which they are excluded.

The North had promised blacks economic opportunity and an escape from racial oppression, but as Dan Moore, the main character in "Box Seat," has learned, blacks are no more than "a baboon from the zoo" to most northerners, and the lack of jobs and continued oppression lead him to a maddening violence. Separated from the folk spirit of the South and of their past, the black people of Toomer's North lack those connections that can heal them. As Toomer writes in "Calling Jesus":

Her soul is like a little thrust-tailed dog, that follows her, whimpering. I've seen it tagging on behind her, up streets where chestnut trees flowered, where dusty asphalt had been freshly sprinkled with clean water. Up alleys where niggers sat on low door-steps before tumbled shanties and sang and loved. At night, when she comes home, the little dog is left in the vestibule, nosing the crack beneath the big storm door, filled with chills till morning. Some one . . . eoho Jesus . . . soft as the bare feet of Christ moving across bales of southern cotton, will steal in and cover it that it need not shiver, and carry it to where she sleeps: cradled in dream-fluted cane.

North and South combine in the book's final section, a six-part, dramatic narrative called "Kabnis." As Toomer wrote to Waldo Frank, "Kabnis is me," and with the figure of Ralph Kabnis, Toomer relates his teaching experience in the South and his desire to record the fading song he heard there. He also exposes the internal contradictions and sense of alienation that dominate the previous two sections. Kabnis' ancestors are "Southern blue bloods," but as he learns in Georgia, "Ain't much difference between blue

and black." Several characters here are of a mixed racial background, and the problems of reconciling their African-American heritage in a violent world of white, middle-class values provides the subject for most of the dialogue. "Nigger's a nigger down this way, Professor," one character tells Kabnis, "An only two dividins: good an bad. An even they aint permanent categories. They sometimes mixes um up when it comes to lynchin."

Kabnis dreams of being an orator and a poet, a prophet "shapin words after a design that branded . . . my soul." But no one character here occupies this privileged position. Instead, all of the characters in "Kabnis" merge to describe the "twisted awful thing" that Kabnis hopes to capture. Still, Kabnis does recognize that "th only sin is whats done against the soul. The whole world is a conspiracy to sin, especially in America, an against me. I'm the victim of their sin. I'm what sin is." Toomer's vision ends with Kabnis leaving Sempter in sunrise and "birth-song," leaving some hope for redemption in the life that *Cane* celebrates.

Between 1921 and 1923, Toomer also finished three other works focusing on black life that deserve some brief comment. *Balo* and *Natalie Mann* (published posthumously, in *The Wayward and the Seeking* [1980]), use widely differing styles to explore racial conditions in America. *Balo* was performed in 1923–1924 by the Howard University Players, and it was later anthologized by Alain Locke and Montgomery Gregory in *Plays of Negro Life* (1927). A realistic play that focuses on the strengths of the common black family, *Balo* presents both the black family and the black folk community as strong, viable, sustaining structures in its characters' lives. *Natalie Mann* is an expressionistic work in the vein of Eugene O'Neill that joins *Cane* in its condemnation of middle-class values and American materialism. Using a woman as the play's protagonist, Toomer explores the kinds of social, economic, and sexual pressures that destroy the human spirit. Through the sad, short life of his own mother and the submissive role his grandmother was forced to occupy, Toomer was intensely aware of the painful position women held in modern society, and this play, though never staged or published during Toomer's lifetime, is a testament to their strength.

Toomer also wrote the short story "Withered Skins of Berries" during this period. Here he examines the kinds of pressures and conflicts that lead someone to "pass" for white. The story combines the lyricism of *Cane* with the brutality of racial hatred, mixing images of "John Brown's body" an "African Guardian of Souls," and "the Georgia canefields" with a modern, northern office in downtown Washington. Toomer reveals the complex feelings of envy and self-loathing that motivate his protagonist, a mulatto secretary, to gain a position in the white world. The story was rejected by the *Little Review* in 1923, and its subject was to haunt Toomer throughout his life.

About the time that Toomer had finished *Cane,* he came across the work of P. D. Ouspensky, a disciple of the Greek-Armenian mystic George Ivanovich Gurdjieff. Along with Hart Crane, Gorham Munson, and Waldo Frank, Toomer shared an enthusiasm for Ouspensky's ideas about an invisible, "noumenal world" that could be apprehended through the development of a "cosmic consciousness." These ideas fit in well with the "organic, mystic Whole" that he and Frank had envisioned for the new American culture, and the teachings of Ouspensky and Gurdjieff represented a view of experience that unified the physical, spiritual, and emotional elements that Toomer had explored in *Cane.* As Cynthia Kerman and Richard Eldridge point out, "while others may have read *Cane* to see how a man could fit his human view into his blackness, [Toomer] was trying to fit the blackness that was

a part of him into a more comprehensive human view." In the writings of Gurdjieff, Toomer thought he had at last found that "intelligible scheme of things" that he had been looking for since he started college. Moreover, by attaining "higher consciousness," Toomer would become a true "aristocrat of the spirit," and he resolved to follow philosophy and become a teacher of Gurdjieff's system.

Gurdjieff had established the Institute for Harmonious Development of Man in Fontainebleau, near Paris, and in 1924 Toomer joined the flock of disciples who studied with him there. Gurdjieff's "Fourth Way" combined rigid discipline with hard physical labor in a series of exercises that were designed to break a person out of the mechanical behavior that warped his essential being. The goal was to reach a state of self-detachment by gradually learning to control the physical, spiritual, and emotional centers of one's being. Gurdjieff's system codified many of the beliefs and desires that Toomer had been developing since adolescence, and he verified in Toomer that sense that he was meant to fulfill some special destiny as a leader among men. Also, Gurdjieff's teachings affirmed Toomer's feelings, evident in his notes, that attributes such as race are merely "prejudices" and not "realities"—that "one should not be dependent upon externality for what happens to one, that this is shameful. And in this way [one] rubs against the Negro, his positions and attitudes, in a white world."

Toomer had fallen out with Waldo Frank over his relationship, probably romantic, with Frank's wife, Margaret Naumburg, and he gradually separated from the rest of the writers he knew in New York, especially those associated with the New Negro movement. His growing dissatisfaction with writing fiction led to an eventual break from the literary life and circles he had been a part of, though he continued to write. In 1925 he sent a manuscript entitled "Values and Fictions" to Liveright, but the work was very different from *Cane* and *Natalie Mann*. A long, introspective, psychological statement written in the second person, "Values and Fictions" was meant to document Toomer's own growth in Gurdjieff's teachings and help others on their own path to greater self-consciousness. Toomer expected it to be rejected, and it was. A short story called "Easter" appeared in the *Little Review* in the spring of 1925, and this work too reflected the Gurdjieffian belief that people exist as static "types" and that traditional religions hold no keys to enlightenment.

Studying the Gurdjieff system with A. R. Orage in New York, Toomer was asked to establish his own group, first in Harlem and later in Chicago. In Harlem, the changed author of *Cane* was greeted with some reserve. Langston Hughes, in his *Big Sea* (1940), describes Toomer as having "an evolved soul," one that "made him feel that nothing mattered, not even writing." The Harlem group initially attracted several members of the local intelligentsia, including Wallace Thurman, Dorothy Peterson, Aaron Douglas, Nella Larsen, and Harold Jackman. Toomer also became acquainted with Mabel Dodge Luhan, a wealthy patronness of the arts and political activist, while he was in Harlem, but his New York group eventually broke up because few of its members could afford the time or money needed to devote themselves to Gurdjieff's teachings.

In Chicago, however, Toomer met with some success as a group leader, and he taught there from 1926 to 1932. During this time he continued to write, though his work was designed almost exclusively to promote the ideas contained in Gurdjieff's teachings. In 1928, two short stories, "Mr. Costyve Duditch" and "Winter on Earth" were published, and the novella "York Beach" was published in *The Second American Caravan* the next year. All three works stress the mechanical nature of modern existence and the ways in which we separate ourselves from true spiritual being. Two other manuscripts completed in 1929—"Transatlantic" and "Essentials"—share in Toomer's representation of himself as "a member of a new race, produced from a blending of bloods which existed in recognized races," as he says in "Transatlantic." An essay entitled "Race Problems and Modern Society," published in 1929, similarly stressed that "problems of race . . . exist in the human psyche and nowhere else." The only worthwhile activity, Toomer exhorts, is the attainment of higher consciousness by waking out of our sleeping bodies and recognizing our collective identity both with and within the universe. *Essentials: A Philosophy of Life in Three Hundred Definitions and Aphorisms* was printed privately by a press that Toomer had established with Chaunce Dupee in 1931, and, as its title suggests, it too was marred by the dry, egocentric, philosophical pronouncements that had come to dominate Toomer's style—one that he had borrowed in imitation of Gurdjieff himself.

During this time, Toomer's personal relationship with the master had become severely strained over financial matters, and he began to think about forming his own institute, modeled after the one at Fontainebleau. In 1932, he led a group of his own in Portage, Wisconsin, where he met and later married Margery Latimer, a novelist and feminist who worshiped Toomer and eagerly sought his control and advice. Within a year, however, Latimer had died giving birth to a daughter, and Toomer spent the next two years in relative isolation, trying to organize and publish Latimer's letters. Toomer stayed briefly with Georgia O'Keefe at Alfred Stieglitz' family home in Lake George, New York, and he published an essay entitled "The Hill" in Waldo Frank's *America and Alfred Stieglitz* (1934), in which he praised Stieglitz and his work. Through O'Keefe, Toomer met Marjorie Content, a wealthy, artistic New Yorker who had earlier been married to Harold Loeb. The two fell in love immediately and were married in 1934, moving to a farm in Doylestown, Pennsylvania, where Toomer lived until his death in 1967.

Marjorie Content Toomer was a stabilizing force in Toomer's life, and her father, a successful financier, provided the couple with much of their income. Toomer was still writing daily and continued to teach according to the Gurdjieff method, though he had broken all ties with Gurdjieff himself in March of 1935. The symbols and ideas of the "Fourth Way" continued to dominate Toomer's writing throughout this time, and he focused his attention on writing long, autobiographical pieces designed to explain and illustrate his own growth in cosmic consciousness. Excerpts from these works were collected by Darwin Turner in 1980 and published under the title *The Wayward and the Seeking: A Collection of Writings by Jean Toomer.*

Turner's book takes its name from a collection of poems that Toomer had been writing throughout the 1930's, and the best work he produced at this time was a long poem entitled "Blue Meridian," which was published in *The New Caravan* in 1936. The work had its origins in the poem "The First American," written in 1920, and it represented a fusion of Toomer's own ideas about race with the mystical idealism of Gurdjieff in a project modeled after Waldo Frank's desire to revitalize and replace the myths and symbols of American culture: "a new America, / To be spiritualized by each new American." In a voice that borrows heavily from Whitman, Toomer sings the praises of an America where "Growth, Transformation, Love" will lead to the creation of a new brotherhood of man that will break through the boundaries of race to form a "human nation" made up of "the human race." Paralleling the Mississippi with the Ganges, Toomer mixes imagery and icons from Judaism, Christianity, Buddhism, African lore, and the teachings of Gurdjieff to celebrate his ideal of America in cosmic unity with the "Radiant Incorporeal."

The poem is a fitting culmination of much of Toomer's thought at the time, and it was his last "literary" work to be published. In 1938, Toomer began attending Quaker meetings in Doylestown, and after a disastrous trip to India in 1939 in search of spiritual harmony, Toomer became an active Quaker, writing several pamphlets and tracts for the church over the course of the next decade. One such work—taken from an address Toomer gave at the Yearly Meeting in Philadelphia in 1949 and published as *The Flavor of Man*—shows how Quaker thought blended with Toomer's earlier beliefs: "The primary ingredient of man's substance is love, love of God, love of man, and through love, a sense of unity with all creation. . . . The alternatives, I am convinced, are starkly these: Transcendence or extinction."

But Quakerism was not the last stop in Toomer's search for spiritual fulfillment. He studied the works of Carl Jung in the late 1940's and began Jungian analysis in 1949. The next year, according to Kerman and Eldridge, he read L. Ron Hubbard's *Dianetics,* and he entered into a course of study that he hoped would allow him both to "contact the painful root of my racial conflict" and to become a teacher of Scientology. But during this time, Toomer's health was failing rapidly. As early as the mid 1930's he had experienced pain and exhaustion, but he considered these ailments to be signs of his spiritual disabilities. In the 1940's he underwent surgery for a kidney ailment, and his eyesight began to fail him. Considering the importance that Toomer had attached to physical activity, this time of failing health only exacerbated his spiritual and emotional decay. Jean Toomer spent the final years of his life in a nursing home, where he died of arteriosclerosis on March 30, 1967.

Toomer's career was rescued from complete obscurity by Arna Bontemps, who had met Toomer in New York in the 1920's. An author in his own right, a compiler of anthologies of black literature, and a librarian at Fisk University, Bontemps contacted Toomer in 1960 after a fellow faculty member saw one of Toomer's Quaker pamphlets, and the wife of another member of the faculty said that she knew Toomer well through the Young Friends Society. Bontemps purchased over fifteen cartons of Toomer's papers for the Fisk collection, among them manuscripts of several unpublished poems, plays, short stories, and novels, and volumes of autobiographical pieces. Bontemps also resurrected interest in Toomer's work when he published "The Negro Renaissance: Jean Toomer and the Harlem Writers of the 1920's," an essay that was included in Herbert Hill's 1966 collection *Anger and Beyond: The Negro Writer in the United States*. The essay lauded Toomer for heralding "an awakening of artistic expression for Negroes," but criticized him for being a "voluntary Negro" in affirming his blackness when it suited his purposes but denying his heritage when it presented him with problems. As Bontemps writes:

The elusiveness of Jean Toomer in the face of complexities like these can well stand for the elusiveness of Negro writers from Charles W. Chesnutt to Frank Yerby. What Toomer was trying to indicate to us by the course he took still intrigues, but I suspect he realizes by now that there is no further need to *signify*. The secrets are out. As the song says, "There's no hiding place down here."

Alice Walker perhaps best sums up Toomer's situation regarding both *Cane* and his identity as an African American, when she writes in "The Divided Life of Jean Toomer" that Toomer meant *Cane* "to memorialize a culture he thought was dying, whose folk spirit he considered beautiful, but he was also saying good-bye to the 'Negro' he felt dying in himself." By turning away from the problems of race, even for his dream of a universal, American race of human beings, Toomer left the fertile soil that had produced his greatest work to explore the ideal realm of an inner, spiritual world. The drive to be like Goethe's Wilhelm Meister, the desire to be an aristocrat of the spirit, both commited Toomer to writing in the first place and frustrated the more democratic impulses of his life and fiction. A curious record of racial contradictions, Toomer remains an enigmatic, if not somewhat sad, figure in American literature.

Selected Bibliography

WORKS OF JEAN TOOMER

NOVEL

Cane. Foreword by Waldo Frank. New York: Boni and Liveright, 1923; University Place Press, 1967, introduction by Arna Bontemps; Harper and Row, 1969, introduction by Darwin T. Turner; Liveright, 1976; Norton, 1988.

PROSE

Essentials: A Philosophy of Life in Three Hundred Definitions and Aphorisms. Privately published. Chicago: H. Dupee, 1931.
The Flavor of Man. William Penn Lecture, 1949. Published as a pamphlet by Young Friends Meeting of Philadelphia, 1949, 1974, and 1979.

POETRY

"As the Eagle Soars." *Crisis*, 41:116 (April 1932).
"Banking Coal." *Crisis*, 24:65 (June 1922).
"Blue Meridian." In *The New Caravan*. Edited by Alfred Kreymborg, Lewis Mumford, and Paul Rosenfeld. New York: Norton, 1936. Pp. 633–654.

"Brown River Smile." *Pagany*, 3:29–33 (Winter 1932).

"White Arrow." *Dial*, 86:596 (July 1929).

PLAYS

Balo. In *Plays of Negro Life*. Edited by Alain Locke and Montgomery Gregory. New York: Harper and Brothers, 1927. Pp. 269–286.

Natalie Mann. In *The Wayward and the Seeking: A Collection of Writings by Jean Toomer*. Edited by Darwin T. Turner. Washington, D.C.: Howard University Press, 1980. Pp. 243–325.

The Sacred Factory. In *The Wayward and the Seeking: A Collection of Writings by Jean Toomer*. Edited by Darwin T. Turner. Washington, D.C.: Howard University Press, 1980. Pp. 327–410.

SHORT STORIES

"Easter." *Little Review*, 11:3–7 (Spring 1925).

"A Certain November." *Dubuque Dial*, 4:107–112 (November 1, 1935).

"Mr. Costyve Duditch." *Dial*, 85:460–476 (1928). Reprinted in *The Wayward and the Seeking: A Collection of Writings by Jean Toomer*. Edited by Darwin T. Turner. Washington, D.C.: Howard University Press, 1980.

"Winter on Earth." In *The Second American Caravan: A Yearbook of American Literature*. Edited by Alfred Kreymborg, Lewis Mumford, and Paul Rosenfeld. New York: Macaulay, 1928. Pp. 694–715. Reprinted in *The Wayward and the Seeking: A Collection of Writings by Jean Toomer*. Edited by Darwin T. Turner. Washington, D.C.: Howard University Press, 1980.

"York Beach." In *The New American Caravan*. Edited by Alfred Kreymborg, Lewis Mumford, and Paul Rosenfeld. New York: Macaulay, 1929. Pp. 12–83.

AUTOBIOGRAPHICAL WRITING

Chapters from "Earth-Being." *Black Scholar*, 2:3–14 (January 1971).

A Fiction and Some Facts. Privately published. Doylestown, Pa.: n.p., *ca.* 1937.

Selections from "Earth-Being," "Incredible Journey," "On Being an American," and "Outline of an Autobiography." In *The Wayward and the Seeking: A Collection of Writings by Jean Toomer*. Edited by Darwin T. Turner. Washington, D.C.: Howard University Press, 1980. Pp. 15–133.

ESSAYS

"The Hill." In *America and Alfred Stieglitz: A Collective Portrait*. Edited by Waldo Frank et al. Garden City, N.Y.: Doubleday 1934. Pp. 295–302.

"A New Force for Cooperation." *Adelphi*, 9:25–31 (October 1934).

"Oxen Cart and Warfare." *Little Review*, 10:44–48. (Autumn/Winter 1924–1925).

"Race Problems and Modern Society." In *Problems of Civilization*. Edited by Baker Brownell. New York: Van Nostrand, 1929. Pp. 67–111.

UNPUBLISHED NOVELS

"The Angel Begoria" (1940). Jean Toomer Papers. Collection of American Literature. The Beinecke Rare Book and Manuscript Library, Yale University, New Haven, Conn.

"Caromb" (1932). Jean Toomer Papers.

"The Gallonwerps" (1927; revised 1928). Originally written as a play, revised as a novel. Jean Toomer Papers.

"Transatlantic" (1929; revised as "Eight Day World," 1933; revised, 1934). Jean Toomer Papers.

UNPUBLISHED PLAYS

"A Drama of the Southwest" (unfinished, 1926). Jean Toomer Papers.

"The Gallonwerps" (1927). Jean Toomer Papers.

UNPUBLISHED STORIES

"Drachman" (1928).

"Fronts" (date uncertain).

"Love on a Train" (1928).

"Lump" (*ca.* 1936). Jean Toomer Papers.

"Mr. Limph Krok's Famous 'L' Ride" (1930).

"Pure Pleasure" (date uncertain).

"Two Professors" (1930).

COLLECTED WORKS

The Wayward and the Seeking: A Collection of Writings by Jean Toomer. Edited by Darwin T. Turner, Washington, D.C.: Howard University Press, 1980.

The Collected Poems of Jean Toomer. Edited by Robert B. Jones and Margery Toomer Latimer. Introduction and textual notes by Robert B. Jones. Chapel Hill: University of North Carolina Press, 1988.

MANUSCRIPTS AND PAPERS

The Armistad Research Collection. Will W. Alexander Library, Dillard University, New Orleans, La.

Jean Toomer Papers. Collection of American Literature. The Beinecke Rare Book and Manuscript Library, Yale University, New Haven, Conn.

Jean Toomer Special Collection. Cravath Memorial Library, Fisk University, Nashville, Tenn.

BIOGRAPHICAL AND CRITICAL STUDIES

Banc!, 2 (May 1972). Fisk University Library; Special Collections issue on Jean Toomer.

Baker, Houston. "Journey Toward Black Art: Jean Toomer's *Cane.*" In his *Singers of Daybreak: Studies in Black American Literature.* Washington, D.C.: Howard University Press, 1974. Pp. 53–80.

Bell, Bernard W. "Portrait of the Artist as High Priest of Soul: Jean Toomer's *Cane.*" *Black World,* 23:4–19, 92–97 (September 1974).

———. "Jean Toomer's 'Blue Meridian': The Poet as Prophet of a New Order Man." *Black American Literature Forum,* 14:77–80 (Summer 1980).

Benson, Brian Joseph, and Mabel Mayle Dillard. *Jean Toomer.* Boston: Twayne Publishers, 1980.

Bontemps, Arna. "The Harlem Renaissance." *Saturday Review,* 30:12–13, 44 (March 22, 1947).

———. "The Negro Renaissance: Jean Toomer and the Harlem Writers of the 1920s." In *Anger and Beyond: The Negro Writer in the United States.* Edited by Herbert Hill. New York: Harper and Row, 1966. Pp. 20–36.

———. *100 Years of Negro Freedom.* New York: Dodd, Mead Co., 1961.

———. Introduction to *Cane.* New York: Harper and Row, 1969.

Bowen, Barbara E. "Untroubled Voice: Call-and-Response in *Cane.*" *Black American Literature Forum,* 16:12–18 (Spring 1982).

Bradley, David. "Looking Behind *Cane.*" *The Southern Review,* 21:682–694 (Summer 1985).

Braithwaite, William Stanley. "The Negro in American Literature." *Crisis,* 28:204–210 (September 1924).

Bus, Heiner. "Jean Toomer and the Black Heritage." In *History and Tradition in Afro-American Culture.* Edited by Gunter H. Lenz. Frankfurt: Campus, 1984.

Byrd, Rudolf P. "Jean Toomer and the Afro-American Literary Tradition." *Callaloo,* 8:310–319 (Spring/Summer 1985).

Christensen, Peter. "Sexuality and Liberation in Jean Toomer's 'Withered Skin of Berries.' " *Callaloo,* 11:616–626 (Summer 1988).

DuBois, W. E. B., and Alain Locke, "The Younger Literary Movement." *Crisis,* 27:161–163 (1924).

Durham, Frank, ed. *Studies in "Cane."* Columbus: Merrill, 1971.

Frank, Waldo. Foreword to *Cane.* New York: Boni and Liveright, 1923.

Gates, Henry Louis, Jr. *The Signifying Monkey: A Theory of African-American Literary Criticism.* New York: Oxford University Press, 1988.

Hill, Herbert, ed. *Anger and Beyond: The Negro Writer in the United States.* New York: Harper and Row, 1966.

Huggins, Nathan Irvin. *Harlem Renaissance.* New York: Knopf, 1979.

Kerman, Cynthia Earl, and Richard Eldridge. *The Lives of Jean Toomer: A Hunger for Wholeness.* Baton Rouge: Louisiana State University Press, 1987. This work brings together much of Toomer's unpublished work and archival materials in an excellent study.

Locke, Alain, ed. *The New Negro: An Interpretation.* New York: Albert and Charles Boni, 1925.

McKay, Nellie Y. *Jean Toomer, Artist: A Study of His Literary Life and Work, 1894–1936.* Chapel Hill: University of North Carolina Press, 1984.

Munro, C. Lynn. "Jean Toomer: A Bibliography of Secondary Sources." In *Black American Literature Forum,* 21:275–287 (Fall 1987).

Rosenfeld, Paul. "Jean Toomer." In his *Men Seen.* New York: Dial Press, 1925. Pp. 227–236; Freeport, N.Y.: Books for Libraries Press, 1967.

Rusch, Frederik L. "Jean Toomer's Early Identification: The Two Black Plays." *MELUS,* 13:115–124 (Spring/Summer 1986).

Turner, Darwin T. "Jean Toomer: Exile." In his *In a Minor Chord: Three Afro-American Writers and Their Search for Identity.* Carbondale, Ill.: Southern Illinois University Press, 1971. Pp. 1–59.

———. "An Intersection of Paths: Correspondence between Jean Toomer and Sherwood Anderson." *College Language Association Journal*, 17:455–467 (June 1974).

———. Introduction to *Cane*. New York: Liveright, 1975.

Walker, Alice. "The Divided Life of Jean Toomer." In her *In Search of Our Mothers' Gardens: Womanist Prose*. San Diego: Harcourt Brace Jovanovich, 1983.

—BRIAN A. BREMEN

Lionel Trilling

1905–1975

By the time of his death on November 5, 1975, Lionel Trilling's preeminence as a critic and teacher of literature was undisputed. He had taught at Columbia University in New York City since 1932, ascending steadily through the various professional levels, from the instructorship he had held during his graduate student days through the stages of tenured and chaired professorships, capping his academic career with the University Professorship, Columbia's highest faculty distinction. He was the author of eight books and over 250 articles, as well as the editor of numerous other works. He had been the recipient of honorary degrees from a number of universities in the United States and Britain. He had been George Eastman Visiting Professor at Oxford, Charles Eliot Norton Professor of Poetry at Harvard, and a Visiting Fellow at All Souls College, Oxford. The National Endowment for the Humanities had chosen him to receive its first Thomas Jefferson Award in 1972.

No more central a figure in literary criticism or the academic study of the humanities can be imagined. Yet Trilling's attitude about professional literary criticism, scholarship, and instruction in general, and about his own position within the academic establishment, was never a wholly comfortable one. A repeated theme in his writings, particularly of the later years, is that the very institutional status accorded literary works when they are handled in an academic context and by academic methods tends to be acquired at the expense of the power of those works as direct experiences. And that literature should remain a powerful, emotional, heuristic *experience* Trilling always insisted. "There are moments," Trilling confessed in the introduction to his anthology *The Experience of Literature* (1967), "when it seems . . . that all the discourse that goes on in the classroom and in essays and books is beside the point, that all this secondary activity is obtruding itself upon the primary activity of reading literature. . . ." Looking back on his career in 1971 Trilling remarked in "Some Notes for an Autobiographical Lecture" (in *The Last Decade*) that "I am always surprised when I hear myself referred to as a critic. After some thirty years of having been called by that name, the role and function it designates seem odd to me."

If Trilling's view of himself as a professional literary critic and teacher was marked by ambivalence, so too was his perspective on himself as a Jewish intellectual. The product of a traditional Jewish household in New York and a resident of that city for all but a few years of his life, Trilling was ill at ease with the "positive" and pervasive Jewishness of the metropolis and much of its intellectual life. This unease was with him even during the period between 1925 and 1931 when he was associated with *The Menorah Journal*, a bimonthly devoted to Jewish-American social and cultural concerns. At the conclusion of an impatient review of what he referred to as "Another Jewish Problem Novel" (published in *The Menorah Journal* in 1929 and later collected in *Speaking of Literature and Society,* 1980), Trilling asserted that

only when the Jewish problem is included in a rich sweep of life, a life which would be important and momentous even without the problem of Jewishness, but a life to which the problem of Jewishness adds further import and moment, will a good Jewish novel have been written and something said about the problem.

Trilling's own "Jewish problems"—his Jewish identity problem—was subordinated to the "rich sweep" of the mainstream culture of Europe and America that he studied and mastered. Responding to a 1944 symposium on "American Literature and the Younger Generation of American Jews" (*Contemporary Jewish Record,* February 1944; reprinted as "Under Forty" in *Speaking of Literature and Society*), he was willing to admit that "my existence as a Jew is one of the shaping conditions of my temperament," but he then added that

I cannot discover anything in professional intellectual life which I can specifically trace back to my Jewish birth and rearing. I do not think of myself as a "Jewish writer." I do not have it in mind to serve by my writing any Jewish purpose. I should resent it if a critic of my work were to discover in it either faults or virtues which he called Jewish.

The acceptance of a specifically Jewish dimension or direction would have amounted, for Trilling, to the sin he laid at the doors of the leading Jewish writers of his youth: the sin of "a willingness to accept exclusion and even to intensify it, a willingness to be provincial and parochial." Trilling would never accept that fate. In the tra-

dition of the great nineteenth-century novels he so admired, he may have imagined himself as the young man from the provinces—the ethnic provinces—who would storm the cultural capital of the West, making himself its greatest authority. In the process, however, a minimal but intransigent Jewish identity would serve one vital, if negative, purpose: it would preserve the distance between Trilling and that great gentile culture he mastered, thus preserving the sense of the self's conquest over alien material. To perform that function, Jewish identity could boil down to no more than the "feeling that I would not, even if I could, deny or escape being Jewish. Surely it is at once clear how minimal such a position is—how much it hangs on only a resistance (and even only a passive one)."

To some extent bound up with this conflicted attitude about his Jewishness was Trilling's view of his political identity, which took shape in the 1930's and 1940's, the period during which he also came into his full powers as an intellectual. Here again one sees Trilling taking up a cautious stance both inside and outside of what he took to be established, organized positions. One such position for New York intellectuals was that offered by the American Communist Party and its affiliates. It was the period of the "fellow travelers"—liberal intellectuals drawn leftward into sympathy with Moscow by the economic depression in America and by the specter of fascism in Europe—and during those early depression years that saw growing support among American intellectuals for the policies and supposed moral leadership of the Soviet Union, Trilling identified himself with the radical cause, though his allegiance to Soviet-sponsored agencies was brief and he was never a member of a communist organization. In the years that followed, appalled by the treacheries of Stalin—the Moscow purge trails, the debacle of the Spanish Civil War, the crowning ignominy of the Nazi-Soviet pact—Trilling was yet more dismayed by the evident willingness of fellow travelers in the West to discount damning reports or to appeal to "exigencies" that justified Stalin's actions.

But Trilling's response was characteristic. He did not flee to the political right to seek a resting place for a troubled conscience: Whittaker Chambers, an old acquaintance, had done just that, and he furnished Trilling with a living example of the "tragic comedian" of twentieth-century politics—the man who exchanges one extreme political investment for its opposite; Trilling depicted Chambers' guilt-ridden political shift in his 1947 novel *The Middle of the Journey*. Neither did Trilling turn to embrace Trotskyism, as a significant number of disaffected American Communists were to do. Instead, he moved toward another ambivalence. Establishing himself within the great Western liberal humanist tradition, he defined himself throughout his works as a dogged internal opponent of liberalism's cherished complacencies. He was fond of repeating John Stuart Mill's exhortation to his fellow liberals that they should study the conservative Samuel Taylor Coleridge: with Mill, he argued (in the essay "Kipling" in *The Liberal Imagination,* 1950) that "we should pray to have enemies who make us worthy of ourselves" because they strengthen our resources, while unworthy allies tempt liberals "to be content with easy victories of right feeling and with moral self-congratulation." The title of Trilling's most influential book, *The Liberal Imagination,* serves to identify its author with that imagination, but the book's essays carry out a determined critique of liberal temptations and pieties.

Ambivalence, then, represented a key element in Trilling's sense of himself in his several defining relationships—with the academy and cultural life, with Jewishness, with liberal politics and culture. We are accustomed to regarding the trait as a weakness, an indecision, but it may actually account for Trilling's unique personal authority as a critic of culture and society for some thirty-five years. In both politics and aesthetics, Trilling's was a principled ambivalence, a resistance to system and theory in their tendencies to transcend the given reality. His writings have their distinctive themes and tones, but these have the merit of stemming from an apparent refusal to validate the claims of any movement or school for the sake of solidarity alone. Trilling is certainly open to many criticisms, but the response he made to one charge in particular should be kept in mind. Richard Sennett writes he once accused Trilling, "You have no position; you are always in between," and that the answer he received was "Between is the only honest place to be." Throughout his career, Trilling identified with figures (real or fictional) who had inhabited the force field of "dialectical tension" between the great contending pressures of their ages or between the great contending pressures of any age, those contrary pulls toward social stability and conformity on the one hand and self-realization on the other. His imagination responded to the "tragic" conviction that life in civilization is always conflicted, compromised, even painful for the selves who jostle against each other seeking fulfillment. His understanding of the relationship between culture and society, his notion of the role of art within social and individual life, always bore the marks of this commitment to tension. "A culture," he wrote in 1940 (see "Reality in America" in *The Liberal Imagination*), "is not a flow, nor even a confluence: the form of its existence is struggle, or at least debate—it is nothing if not a dialectic." And Trilling continued, speaking of nineteenth-century American writers in terms that apply equally well to himself:

And in any culture there are likely to be certain artists who contain a large part of the dialectic within themselves, their meaning and power lying in their contradictions; they contain within themselves, it may be said, the very essence of the culture, and the sign of this is that they do not submit to serve the ends of any one ideological group or tendency.

Some such perspective is required for an appreciation of Trilling's career, which is not to be summed up by reference to the narrow conventional meaning of "critic," let alone "literary critic." What "critic" came to mean through Trilling's performance of that role is much closer to the meaning given above to "artist," and many of Trilling's remarks about literary artists he favored resonate with self-defining reverberations. He sought to occupy a central place in the traditional literary culture of his country and Europe, and so made his field of study broad enough to encompass the "yes and no" of Western culture in their many avatars; at the same time he sought to remain independent of mind, nimble in judgment. A phrase he had come across while researching his doctoral dissertation on Matthew Arnold in the 1930's—a phrase Arnold himself had quoted from Michel de Montaigne—provided Trilling with a lasting intellectual ideal: the best critic and the best artist were to him *"ondoyant et divers"*—"undulating and diverse"; that phrase is especially applicable to the novel, the capacious and variegated genre which always formed a point of reference in his thinking. As a critic, Trilling sought to be what in his 1943 book on E. M. Forster he described the novelist as being: "the agent of a moral intention which can only be carried out by the mind *ondoyant et divers* of which Montaigne spoke."

Lionel Trilling was born in New York City on July 4, 1905, the only son of David and Fannie Cohen Trilling. His father had emigrated as a young man from Bialystok in Lithuania (now Poland); his mother had been born in London's East End. There she had acquired a lasting Anglophilia that was to have its effects on her son, as was her prodigious reading, particularly in nineteenth-century English and continental fic-

tion. Lionel was four or five years old when Fannie began reading Victorian novels to him, and she informed him at about the same time that she envisioned an Oxford doctorate for him in the future. These readings and goals made a foundation for the persona Trilling later exhibited at Columbia, both in his student and his teaching days. His evident fascination with the complex and nuanced pictures of society offered by the Victorian novel led Alfred Kazin to charge, in *New York Jew* (1978), that Trilling had made Victorian England his "intellectual motherland" and that the "extraordinarily accomplished son of an immigrant tailor was so passionate about England and the great world of the English nineteenth-century novel that his image of this literature turned England into a personal dream." In later years, Trilling's demeanor was often considered refined and mannerly, to the point that Irving Howe would remark of him (in an interview collected in French, *Three Honest Men*), "this extraordinarily suave, elegant, dapper man didn't look or behave quite as if he were descended from the Byalistok [*sic*] Trillings." Edward Shoben notes that the family name, though authentic, "suggests one conferred by immigration authorities . . . [at] Ellis Island"; Diana Trilling, Lionel's widow, writing in "A Jew at Columbia," an appendix to *Speaking of Literature,* doubts whether Trilling's freedom to build either his career or his public persona would have been the same "had his name been that of his maternal grandfather, Israel Cohen."

The Trilling household was conservative in its religious practices, though stress was laid on the cultural value of maintaining Jewish tradition rather than on devoutness. The family kept kosher at home, but ignored the guidelines outside the house—David was an aficionado of ham and shellfish. Lionel remembered a childhood free of conflicts between the Jewish circle clustered around the local synagogue and the groups he encountered through public school and the rest of the community. He studied for his bar mitzvah, which eventually took place at the Jewish Theological Seminary, but he was clearly uninspired by the entire process. He would later claim never to have mastered Hebrew.

David Trilling's work as a custom tailor earned a reasonably comfortable life for the family, but there was disappointment in his past and there would be more in later years. It was said that David had effectively been banished from Bialystok as a result of some obscure shame surrounding his bar mitzvah. When he decided to abandon tailoring for the wholesale fur business, he dreamed of great successes based on an unlikely scheme, which now seems sadly comic—for the production of winter fur coats for the chauffeurs of well-to-do families; but the day of the open car had already passed. David's failure in business placed an extra financial and emotional strain on Lionel during those early Depression years when he was beginning his academic career.

Graduating from a city high school in 1921, Trilling entered Columbia College at the age of sixteen, beginning an association with the school that would last, with only brief interruptions, until his death over fifty years later. His first years at Columbia were fitful and undistinguished, but once he entered the orbit of John Erskine's General Honors program he seemed to have found his place. Erskine was nothing less than a missionary in the cause of general humanistic education, and he had persuaded the skeptical college authorities that a curriculum of Western classics from Homer to the twentieth century would have the effect of rounding the student into the "whole man" which Matthew Arnold had described as the desired result of education and culture. Specialization and philological scholarship were to give way to a broad inquisitive intelligence; the students, who were given no secondary materials to aid them in their confrontation with the texts they read, were guided through small-group discussions that focused on the apparently universal questions of philosophy and morality raised by the texts.

Stemming from the ideals of Arnold, Erskine's courses are clearly the forerunners of the "Great Books" programs still thriving at Columbia, the University of Chicago, and St. John's College; and they had a decisive influence in shaping Lionel Trilling's goal of becoming a critic and teacher of literature. In "Some Notes for an Autobiographical Lecturer" (1971), Trilling spoke of Erskine's curriculum as an adaptation for democratic society of the Renaissance ideals of humanistic education: Erskine believed, as had Sir Philip Sidney,

that men who were in any degree responsible for the welfare of the polity and for the quality of life that characterized it must be large-minded men, committed to great ends, devoted to virtue, assured of the dignity of the human estate and dedicated to enhancing and preserving it; and that great works of the imagination could foster and even institute this large-mindedness, this *magnanimity*.

But to remember that by the early 1920's Erskine and Columbia were operating in a city that for several decades had been the beachhead for the great immigrant waves from Europe is to recognize the practical importance, the ideological character, of Columbia humanism. For first-generation Americans like Trilling, the value of the Erskine program was to be found in its attempt to bring students of different cultural backgrounds into one cultural fold,

showing young men how they might escape from the limitations of their middle-class or their lower-middle-class upbringings by putting before them great models of thought, feeling, and imagination, and great issues which suggested the close interrelation of the private and personal life with the public life, with life in society.

The Erskine courses were thus Trilling's road out of parochial or provincial life in America, and the focus on the relationship between personal and political concerns would become a distinctive feature of his own work.

The influences of the program and its projected aims can also be registered in other facets of Trilling's career. As a critic and teacher, Trilling remained decidedly a nonspecialist, ranging across the broad terrain of Western literary and philosophical works. He made no secret of his great preference for undergraduate teaching over the more technical instruction of graduate students. His own intransigent humanism militated against what he regarded as the various airless systems and methods that would have their day of fashion in academic circles—at the end of his career he was attacking structuralism as he had attacked New Criticism years earlier. To treat a work of literature in a *human* manner meant to Trilling to avoid treating it as primarily an affair of structure, as a piece of architecture, the delicate balances and tensions of which could be minutely examined and decorously appreciated; literature, he always insisted, dealt in *ideas,* by which he did not mean prefabricated "pellets of intellection" borrowed from philosophy or theology and given "treatment" in literary works. In "The Meaning of a Literary Idea," the final essay in *The Liberal Imagination,* Trilling suggest that great literature gave great ideas fully rounded life, brought them into living relationship with readers; it was "in competition with philosophy, theology, and science . . . [and sought] to match them in comprehensiveness and power and seriousness." And to Trilling's mind the literary masterpiece would usually win this contest by virtue of its fullness in bodying forth ideas and emotions together, for "the ultimate questions of conscious and rational thought about the nature of man and his destiny match easily in the literary mind with the dark *un*conscious and with the most primitive human relationships."

Trilling graduated from Columbia College in 1925 and took a master's degree in English the following year. During the 1926–1927 academic year he taught in the experimental college created by Alexander Meiklejohn at the University of Wisconsin at Madison. The vast American Midwest was both fascinating and troubling to the inveterate young New Yorker: the complacencies of a homogeneous Christian culture alarmed him and made him reconsider his status as a Jew. In a short story describing this period, "Notes on a Departure" (collected in *Of This Time, Of That Place*), Trilling indicated some of the anxiety he felt at the prospect of being absorbed into gentile American life and the urge toward that necessary distance that an acknowledgement of his Jewishness would procure. Of his protagonist, Trilling writes,

Once he had felt that the town was going to make him do things which he must not do. It sought to include him in a life into which he must not go. To prevent this he had made use of a hitherto useless fact. He had said, "I am a Jew," and immediately he was free.

Back in New York, Trilling put this hitherto useless aspect of himself to work as an editor and contributor to *The Menorah Journal,* to which he had been introduced as an undergraduate. The journal promoted a frank and informed acknowledgment of Jewish cultural identity, seeking to free modern American Jews of the habit of regarding their origins as a stigma or burden. Between 1925 and 1931, Trilling published twenty-five articles, reviews, and stories in the journal, but his critical distance from the program of advancing a specifically Jewish self-awareness should not be underestimated. Most of Trilling's contributions were reviews of current "Jewish fiction," which he was apt to judge according to the standards of the best British or continental novels. Elinor Joan Grumet argues that Trilling used these occasions "to exorcise his ethnic habits of mind, by making those reflexes the subject of literary contemplation.''

In 1929 Trilling married Diana Rubin and was teaching part-time at Hunter College while continuing to work on *The Menorah Journal* and studying at Columbia toward a Ph.D. The Wall Street crash meant that both Lionel's parents and the Rubins needed his assistance, so Trilling undertook a heavy burden of part-time teaching and book reviewing to make ends meet. The situation worsened when Diana became seriously ill with hyperthyroidism and required continual care and attention. In 1932 the English department at Columbia granted Trilling an instructorship paying $2,400—and entailing a considerable teaching load—but he still needed to supplement that income by what he could earn from his other labors. Not surprisingly, progress on his doctoral dissertation was slowed to a crawl, and Trilling's confidence, and the confidence of the department in him, waned. In 1936 he was informed that his instructorship would not be renewed.

The department's action has been the subject of much adverse comment, not only because of Trilling's subsequent reputation, but also because the action is embroiled in the issue of anti-Semitism in the American university system. Diana Trilling wrote in ''A Jew at Columbia,'' her appendix to *Speaking of Literature,* that ''the departmental spokesman said he would not be reappointed for a next year because 'as a Freudian, a Marxist, and a Jew' he was not happy there.'' There is little question that Columbia, like most major American universities, was just then accustoming itself to the idea of Jewish faculty members—they numbered a handful during Trilling's student days—and some disciplines were more resistant than others. English literature was one such field, as Trilling knew. Elliot Cohen, *The Menorah Journal*'s managing editor, had been a brilliant student of literature at Yale, but he had decided that, for Jews, the obstacles to an academic career in the field were

still too great. (Cohen is best known today as the founding editor of the journal *Commentary.*)

In retrospect, Trilling would write in ''A Novel of the Thirties'' (collected in *The Last Decade*) that ''when I decided to go into academic life, my friends thought me naive to the point of absurdity, nor were they wholly wrong. . . .'' His initial appointment had been something of a test case for the department, perhaps facilitated by his polished manner and the fact that his name did not sound ''too Jewish.'' His interests in Karl Marx and Sigmund Freud—and he was no doctrinaire Marxist or Freudian—were almost inevitable for up-to-date young intellectuals in the 1930's, but these were ''downtown,'' Greenwich Village interests that had no foothold in the conservative and gentlemanly corridors of the university; besides, Marx and Freud were considered ''Jewish'' thinkers whose theories aimed at the disintegration of traditional society.

Still, Trilling was unquestionably overextended in his commitments and had made no discernible progress on his dissertation. In any case, the incident somehow instilled in him the determination he had been lacking. He called on senior faculty members in the department and persuaded them to reverse their decision, arguing, according to Diana Trilling in ''A Jew at Columbia,'' that ''they were getting rid of a person who would one day bring great distinction to their department.'' His earnest appeal worked, and he progressed steadily on his dissertation from then on. After it was completed and published, Trilling was appointed Assistant Professor at Columbia, the first Jew to become a regular member of the English faculty. That priority is worth mentioning because Columbia President Nicholas Murray Butler had a direct hand in Trilling's hiring and a clear polemical point to make through his intervention. As part of a scholar-exchange program, Butler had proposed to send philosopher Felix Adler to Berlin

University—it was 1939—but the chancellor there had written back to protest the sending of a Jew. At a gathering where Trilling and the chairman of the English Department were present, Butler recounted the story and pointedly referred to his response—"At Columbia, sir, we recognize merit, not race." That summer Trilling had his assistant professorship.

The subject of Trilling's dissertation has to be seen as part of Trilling's problem in completing it. Trilling had decided on an intellectual biography of Matthew Arnold, a topic unlikely to inspire much enthusiasm among the orthodox scholars, especially since Trilling was determined to seek a wider audience, to de-emphasize archival scholarship in favor of a broad critical analysis of Victorian thought. To be sure, this commitment was not in Trilling's mind from the start. "It did not occur to me until I was pretty well into it," he later wrote in "Some Notes for an Autobiographical Lecture," "that I had chosen for my subject a man who touched almost every problematical aspect of a great and complex cultural epoch." Initially thinking of Arnold as an interesting but second-tier poet of melancholy temperament, Trilling discovered qualities in Arnold that were to serve as the basis for his own critical principles and style. Arnold, Trilling came to recognize, "had pitted himself against the culture, . . . had tried to understand the culture for the purpose of shaping it"; he was perhaps "the first literary intellectual in the English-speaking world." Not least among Arnold's attractions was that he shared the impulse to broaden the audience for cultural debate—he was the first Oxford Professor of Poetry to deliver his inaugural address in English, eschewing the dons' Latin.

Matthew Arnold, which was published in 1939, is an impressive debut, nothing less than a cultural and intellectual history of the nineteenth century with Arnold at its center, confronting the dialectical tensions of the age with his own "sub-tle critical dialectic." It is a long—by far the longest of Trilling's books—and occasionally digressive volume; one reviewer thought it was three aspiring books in one. It is also a constructive "misreading" of Arnold to the extent that it defines Arnold in such a way as to make him particularly of use to Trilling and his milieu. At the root of Arnold's shifting, often contradictory cultural thought, Trilling found a fundamental devotion to "ambivalence"—in the sense of undogmatic openmindedness—toward the rapidly changing society of his day; and Trilling recognized parallels between Arnold's England, with its obsessive concern over the effects of democratization and the waning of religious authority, and his own era, with its international spectacle of fascism and communism, warring ideologies that proclaimed the death of liberal democracy.

Arnold had sought a revision of liberalism in his day, recognizing that the liberating force of individualism in the Protestant Reformation had given way to utilitarian theories that seemed nothing more than rationalizations of the factory owners' economic interests. And in light of the broad political enfranchisement effected by the 1867 Reform Bill, liberal individualism needed a safeguard against the tyranny of the "unenlightened" majority. Arnold tried to find it in "culture," which he considered the nurturing of the "best self" within every individual, that part of the self not ruled by class interests but by humane reason. The problem for Arnold was that Englishmen of his day had not yet developed their best selves, so the state, the only presence in society in which Arnold could recognize impartiality, would remain in absolute authority as regent until that time. Arnold called himself "a liberal of the future" and took up the phrase "Force till right is ready" as a motto for his conviction that challenges to state authority could not be brooked, that they could justifiably be suppressed, because the state acted in the best interests of the entire nation and preserved the ideal of that future society in which men could truly choose the right.

Trilling's critics have been troubled by what they take to be his endorsement of Arnold's cultural politics, though in fact he is highly critical of many of Arnold's views. But it is clear that the several years' engagement with Arnold's thought during Trilling's apprenticeship had their decisive effects. One of the reasons the book took so long to write, it seems, is that it forced Trilling to reconsider the basis of his own early-1930's radicalism. The philosopher Sidney Hook, who informally supervised the project from 1931, recalled that Trilling's original purpose had been to subject Arnold to a rigorous Marxist-dialectical analysis; as Trilling worked, however, he established a more respectful critical relationship with Arnold, and the Marxist theoretical apparatus dropped out in favor of what Trilling perceived as Arnold's own version of the dialectic. In the context of the 1930's, this constituted a shift of allegiances from a rigid system—the Marxist—which claimed to possess the key to all history, to an ambivalent individualism capable of meeting distinct historical changes with different responses.

Trilling admired Arnold for his freedom from a party-line interpretation of events. For example, as Trilling poses in the introductory note, how did Arnold feel about the French Revolution?

Was he a partisan of the Revolution or its vigorous opponent? We might show by quotation that he was either or both, but actually he was neither; his feeling about the Revolution was determined, first, by his notion of the historical context in which it had occurred and, second, by the particular historical moment in which he was writing. What determined him to speak for or against the Revolution at any particular time was his conception of how much of the Revolutionary principle England at *that* time required.

A passage like this one obliges us to read it as also a statement about Trilling and his relations with Arnold and Marxism in the 1930's. Trilling's shift toward Arnold was a response to his conception of how much of the Arnoldian antidote American intellectuals at his time required. The move established Trilling as an heir to the nineteenth-century tradition of "anti-mechanical" social criticism, which objected to the unrestricted, machine-like operations of laissez-faire capitalism; Trilling's perception was that the monolithic Soviet Marxism of his time was functioning in just as mechanical a fashion to direct the political and cultural judgments of sympathizers in the West. Nor was Trilling alone in this view. In 1937 he had begun publishing pieces in the *Partisan Review,* a cultural journal newly reconstituted after a period spent following the lead of the Communist International; the editors, Philip Rahv and William Phillips, had broken with Stalinist communism and had taken up a Trotskyite position respecting the relative independence of art and literature from political exigencies. They were strong supporters of literary modernism, contrasting its radical styles and forms with the stodgy, narrow-minded socialist realism that had become the cultural policy of communism, adopted by the First Congress of Soviet Writers in 1934. In *Partisan Review* Trilling found a venue for many of the essays he would write over the next decades, the essays that were to be his primary form of expression and that were to establish his critical reputation.

The years from 1939 to 1950 make up the key decade in Trilling's development. During this period he articulated his insider's critique of modern liberalism in a book-length study of E. M. Forster, in a novel and several short stories, and in the essays that make up his 1950 volume, *The Liberal Imagination.* His position, insofar as a single one can be discerned, can be summed up in a description he applied to Nathaniel Hawthorne in 1940. Hawthorne, Trilling says, "could dissent from the orthodoxies of dissent"; Trilling considers this a stance on both literature and politics. The phrase appears in the opening essay of *The Liberal Imagination,* "Reality in America," a brilliant piece in which Trilling takes the liberal intellectuals to task for their addiction to a literary realism based on a simple-minded conception of "reality" as "always material reality, hard, resistant, unformed, impenetrable, and unpleasant." Reality thus conceived is numbingly simple, elemental, and impervious to the mind and will and the moral complexities in which they are entangled. Well-meaning liberals are swayed into dumb submission, into orthodoxy, claims Trilling, whenever they see signs that a writer has broken through to this level of "reality"; they suspect and stand aloof from actual moral intelligence; they prefer Theodore Dreiser to Henry James. In politics this means that they are in thrall to movements addressing the Common Man, the myth of the completely nonintellectual being who purportedly lives at a more authentic angle to "reality" than do intellectuals with their abstract ideas. But do intellect, perspicacity, subtlety, and the appreciation of complexity really have no place in reality, Trilling asks? Over against the crude literary and political materialism he diagnoses, Trilling establishes, in essays on James's *The Princess Casamassima* (1948) and on "Manners, Morals, and the Novel" (1948, in *The Liberal Imagination*), his conception of moral realism as the defining characteristic of the great, large-canvass nineteenth-century novels that embrace the societies they describe in their totality, dramatizing the prevailing conflicts and tensions in all their variousness.

Looking at the contemporary American cultural scene in the late 1940's, Trilling writes in "Manners, Morals, and the Novel,"

Perhaps at no other time has the enterprise of moral realism ever been so much needed, for at no other time have so many people committed themselves to moral righteousness. We have the books that point out the bad conditions, that praise us for taking progressive attitudes. We have no books that raise questions in our minds not only about conditions but about ourselves, that lead us to refine our motives and ask what might lie behind our good impulses.

Trilling understood that, for intellectuals, politics can be a means of expressing or compensating for hidden desires and frustrations. His customary manner of cultural analysis would become the investigation, mainly by means of literary-critical articles with their own local agendas, of the personal motivations behind the impulses of the American intellectuals. But personal motivation should not be given a narrow interpretation here. By considering what unstated fulfillments liberal intellectuals were seeking, Trilling was writing a psychological analysis of his culture, and, to that end, he employed the theories of Freud in an unprecedented and influential way. Several of Trilling's essays of the 1940's discuss the advantages and disadvantages, the strengths and weaknesses, of Freud's ideas for cultural analysis—the essays "Freud and Literature" (1940) and "Art and Neurosis" (1945) are classic accounts of Freud's shortcomings as an interpreter of literature and art, emphasizing instead the value of Freud's overall conception of mind for an appreciation of the place of art in psychic and public life. A major concern of Trilling's is to show that Freud's notions treat art as a "normal" function of mind theoretically open to everyone, not as the activity of specially endowed, "mad" artists as much of Western tradition conceives of them. Other essays, such as the one on James's *The Princess Casamassima* or that on Wordworth's "Immortality Ode" (1941), draw vital inspiration from specific Freudian insights and show the potential of a nonmechanical psychoanalytic criticism.

At a more basic level, Trilling's assumption,

shared with the Freud of *Civilization and Its Discontents,* was that the cost of life in civilization, in culture, was a restriction on the self's desire for absolute autonomy and gratification. In "The Princess Casamassima" Trilling argues that the protagonist of James's novel

recognizes what very few people wish to admit, that civilization has a price, and a high one. Civilizations differ from one another as much in what they give up as in what they acquire; but all civilizations are alike in that they renounce something for something else. We do right to protest this in any given case that comes under our notice and we do right to get as much as possible for as little as possible; but we can never get everything for nothing.

The Freudian idea informing this passage supplied Trilling with a lasting framework for his critique of the liberal imagination: it wants everything for nothing. In the fellow travelers and their descendents Trilling sees the intellectual sin of dreaming of a society without psychic restraint and conflict, along with the delusion of imagining such a society could be planned, once and for all, by rational intellect. Politics is not really politics for the intellectuals; it is self-hatred (in the idealization of the nonintellectual) and the will to power (in the desire to build society anew by rational intellect) projected onto external life. The attraction of Marx and the USSR was that they seemed to promise an end to all the conflict and frustration that make us hate the ordinary politics of continual struggle and inevitable compromise. In his essay "The Sense of the Past" (1942), included in *The Liberal Imagination,* Trilling claimed that Marx had given voice to

what has come to be a secret hope of our time, that man's life in politics, which is to say, man's life in history, shall come to an end. . . . With all the passion of a desire kept secret even from

ourselves, we yearn to elect a way of life which shall be satisfactory once and for all. . . .

Trilling's attack on the dream of an end to history, and his shift of allegiance from Marx to Freud, has made him, in turn, the subject of numerous attacks, at least some of which warrant serious consideration. By endorsing Freud's notion that some "renunciation" of psychic desire is always a precondition for life in society, Trilling often appears to suggest that *any* criticism of the status quo is a bad-faith manifestation of the self's desire for what he calls "unconditioned" or limitless being. Because his discussions remain so general, his occasional disclaimers do not dispel this overall appearance. On the other hand, it is certainly worth considering whether intellectual discourse about culture and politics really has cultural or political ends in view, or whether it is primarily a means of self-protection and self-congratulation, a way of demonstrating purity of intention, for those with little directly at risk in the results of the positions they take. Especially worthy of criticism is the intellectuals' tendency, in spite of their capacity to comprehend moral complexity, to treat political and cultural matters in terms of simple binary oppositions, with "good" on our side and "bad" on the other. This habit of thought, or of the appearance of thought, licenses the idea that all of our problems and sufferings are ascribable to power wielded against us from outside; this in turn leads us to believe that if we can cast down the holders of that power, we will live without problems or suffering.

In literature, such convictions, as Trilling saw it, had built the vogue of proletarian novels and all exposé fiction "that point[s] out the bad conditions, that praise[s] us for taking progressive attitudes" ("Manners, Morals, and the Novel," in *The Liberal Imagination*). In his 1943 book on E. M. Forster, Trilling used the English novelist's work as a counterexample to the bad realism he saw all around him in America. Trilling praised Forster's "unremitting concern with moral realism, . . . which is not the awareness of morality itself but of the contradictions, paradoxes and dangers of living the moral life"; rather than showing life as offering the simple alternatives of Good and Evil in his novels, Forster had a fundamental perception of "the inextricable tangle" of "good-and-evil." Not surprisingly, Trilling finds Forster's 1910 novel *Howards End,* with its story of the entangled involvement of the well-meaning, intellectual Schlegel sisters with the wealthy businessman Henry Wilcox and the lower-middle-class Leonard Bast, to be the novelist's masterpiece, for it eschews the temptation that is inherent in its *dramatis personae*—the temptation to vilify Wilcox and exalt Bast. The willingness to insist that life is morally complicated and is likely to remain so earns Forster Trilling's esteem as a liberal who is "at war with the liberal imagination."

Apart from its literary objective, to shame the American novel back toward moral realism, Trilling's *E. M. Forster* is a polemical act for other reasons as well. To celebrate complication, good and evil, and being at war with the liberal imagination in 1943, when the Western allies are themselves at war against an obvious external "evil," is to exhibit the depth of one's commitment to a morally complex universe. As Trilling was aware, Forster was engaged during the war in the effort to protect civil liberties against the repressive enforcement of the Defense of the Realm Act; without such vigilance on behalf of democratic freedoms, Forster would argue, the allied powers would reduce themselves to the level of the fascists. Trilling evinced a similar conviction in his work of the 1940's. "To the simple mind," he writes in *E. M. Forster,* "the mention of complication looks like a kind of malice, and to the mind under great stress the suggestion of something 'behind' the apparent fact looks like a call to quietism, like mere shilly-

shallying." But in the preface to *The Liberal Imagination* Trilling asserted that "a criticism which has at heart the interests of liberalism might find its most useful work not in confirming liberalism in its sense of general rightness but rather in putting under some degree of pressure the liberal ideas and assumptions of the present time."

Trilling's campaign to put the ideas and assumptions of liberalism under pressure was also carried out in works of fiction written in the 1940's. From the beginning of his career, Trilling had wanted to write fiction, and he had produced several short stories during the 1920's; in the 1950's he was still entertaining the idea of further projects, which he never completed. But in the 1940's Trilling published his one novel, *The Middle of the Journey,* as well as a few stories. The novel has some real power, and at least one of the stories ("Of This Time, Of That Place" [1943]) manages a delicate pathos, but the works are all limited by their author's apparent desire to produce a fiction of "ideas": characters tend to occupy fixed ideological positions, from which they perform fairly predictable actions and utter fairly predictable, all-too-polished platform statements. But the fictions are, at any rate, continuations of Trilling's cultural-political arguments by other means. The story "The Other Margaret" (1945; collected in *Of This Time, Of That Place*), for example, debunks the liberal assumption that all personal defects are the result of society: Margaret, the protagonist's thirteen-year-old daughter, excuses the repeated bad behavior of "the other Margaret," the family's maid, "because she's colored. She has to struggle so hard—against prejudice. It's so *hard* for her." But the first Margaret begins to learn a hard lesson of her own when the maid deliberately breaks a small sculpture the girl has made, forcing the realization that personal responsibility still exists, in spite of the convenient fiction that society is always to blame. "She *meant* to do it,'' the girl keeps repeating in amazement, when she sees the fragments of her sculpture. In *The Middle of the Journey,* the Crooms, an intellectual, fellow-traveling couple in the 1930's, similarly forgive the regular lapses of their hired man, Duck Caldwell, because Duck is ''so real,'' as Nancy Croom says, using ''reality'' in just the manner Trilling analyzed in his article ''Reality in America.'' The protagonist, John Laskell, is able to see that Duck is in fact a manipulative, self-indulgent, and violent man—his being a member of the working class is no excuse.

It is not only that personal responsibility is voided when the liberal holds society always to blame, according to Trilling. The acknowledgment of responsibility is the recognition that life—individual life—has real value, because actual consequences attend the decisions of a single person. It is a form of homage to personal existence; Marxism and the other great ideologies (including religion) negate the value of personal being by casting all action in terms of historical necessity or class consciousness or eschatology. And here we approach an important theme raised in the fiction of the 1940's, one that helps connect it to Trilling's work of the 1950's: the proper appreciation of living is bound up with a keen awareness of human mortality. A sentence Trilling was fond of quoting was E. M. Forster's statement (in *Howards End*) that ''Death destroys a man, but the idea of death saves him.'' In ''The Other Margaret,'' the protagonist, Stephen Elwin, arrives at the meaning of a random sentence he has been turning over in his mind all day: it is Hazlitt's claim that ''No young man believes he shall ever die.'' Listening to his daughter's rationalizations of the other Margaret's actions and recognizing that he has often committed similar liberal gestures, Elwin experiences a sudden enlightenment: it is the failure to believe in the reality of death that robs human beings of their reverence for personal life and responsibility. Conversely, the acceptance of the burden of responsibility entails an acceptance of the ultimate burden of death, but only by being thus burdened can one's life have any ''weight.''

John Laskell shares this perspective in *The Middle of the Journey.* Before the action of the novel opens, death has claimed the woman he loved, and Laskell has nearly died himself, suffering a dangerous case of scarlet fever. During the weeks of his convalescence, Laskell had found himself awestruck by the raw fact of ''being''—staring for hours at a rose, pondering the simple difference between what exists and what does not—and he has consequently acquired that reverence for life that is founded on a long, hard look at death. He longs to share his vision with others, but the forward-thinking Crooms show their unwillingness to dwell on such morbid subjects, as if they thought that death were ''a negation of the future and of the hope it holds out for a society of reason and virtue,'' as if death were ''reactionary.'' The novel works its way around to a denouement that forces the Crooms to acknowledge death, in a manner that cuts to the heart of their political illusions: Duck Caldwell, drunk, kills his daughter when he strikes her in raucous anger. In fact, Duck did not know that the girl's heart was weak, and the blows he administered were not hard, but they were sufficient to cause heart failure. At the end of the novel, when they have learned that Duck will be freed from jail because the death has been ruled accidental, Trilling's main characters debate the question of responsibility in the specific case. The Crooms are still fighting off the idea that Duck is to blame, speaking of ''social causes, environment, education or lack of education,'' and so forth; and yet Nancy Croom must admit that she does not want Duck to return to his job, for ''I can't stand the idea of having him around me.''

From this account of his novelistic assault on liberal pieties, it may seem that Trilling had indeed swung to the political right, but another major character in *The Middle of the Journey* is set in place to make us aware that John Laskell actually occupies that tense "in-between" position Trilling himself inhabited. Gifford Maxim, the character Trilling based on Whittaker Chambers, has changed from devoted communist to harshest Christian moralist almost overnight, and his argument about Duck is simply that the killer is "wholly responsible . . . for eternity, for everlasting." But Maxim, like the Crooms, is addicted to a future in which all will be made well—a future that, in Laskell's and Trilling's estimation, negates the present. Maxim thinks that there is divine judgment and mercy awaiting us all in that future, just as he had once believed in the eventual dictatorship of the proletariat leading to the withering away of the state. Only Laskell grasps what the novel presents as the lesson of "maturity," that "the future and the present were brought together, that you lived your life *now* instead of preparing and committing yourself to some better day to come."

To an extent, Trilling's developing theme of reverent acceptance of "being" and the present can be related to the existentialist movements of the 1940's and 1950's, although Trilling never addressed that affinity directly and had little of good to say about existentialists like Jean-Paul Sartre when they entered his purview. The foundation he would always return to was the "tragic humanism" of Freud, and in *The Opposing Self* (1955), his major essay-collection of the 1950's, Trilling rings the changes on the Freudian conclusion that an acceptance of human life entails an acceptance of limited or "conditioned" existence, a renunciation of the psyche's dreams of total gratification. But Trilling is deeply contradictory in the essays of this period, and it has been suggested that in the new conformity of the Cold War era, which saw the intellectuals' repudiation of Stalinism, he was for some time adrift, not yet sure of how to respond to the new conditions. And it is important to recognize, as Mark Krupnick has observed, that Trilling was operating in two very different modes in his writings of the decade. In the longer essays of *The Opposing Self,* Trilling figures *as* an opposing self, a voice in the wilderness, wandering through intricate loops of argument and association to carry out an obscure spiritual quest on behalf of American culture; but Trilling's other volume, *A Gathering of Fugitives* (1956), consisting mainly of short pieces written for two influential book clubs, presents an author who has made his peace with establishment culture, who adopts a calm, droll, confiding tone in order to introduce books of interest to his culturally ambitious middle-class readers.

Trilling's characteristic ambivalence begins to grow somewhat out of control in *The Opposing Self.* His Freudian and Arnoldian loyalties seem to come into conflict. The nineteenth-century English tradition to which Arnold contributed formulated "culture" as a compensatory field for the development of the self's emotional and imaginative capacities; material society organized according to utilitarian principles denied such development. But Freud had convinced Trilling that life in *any* form of civilization (and in this context "culture" is often used interchangeably with "civilization") imposed limits on the self, that the urge to seek compensatory fulfillment in dreams, in neuroses, and in art would be always with us. So Trilling is caught between two views of the "alienation" of the self, one specific to certain historical and political conditions, the other a supposed universal truth of the human condition. On the one hand, *The Opposing Self* announced itself in its preface as a book about "the *modern* self," the sense of selfhood dating from the late eighteenth century and identified by its "intense and adverse imagination of the culture in which it has its being." In "The Poet as Hero: Keats in His Letters," Trilling writes admiringly of the "heroism" of John Keats, who recognized that "Soul-making" or self-affirmation could proceed only in the face of a powerful, resisting, often painful external force. The modern self makes itself by its opposition to some self-denying power. Yet Keats's perception is presented as yielding a universal fact of life, not a new "modern" phenomenon; and it is never fully clear whether that self-denying power comes from the restrictions that civilization places on the self, or from the natural or "biological" truths of age and pain and mortality. Still, Trilling celebrates the boldness of Keats's will to maintain the self in spite of his deep vision of that-which-denies:

[Keats] canvasses the possibilities of amelioration of the human fate and concludes that our life even at its conceivable best can be nothing but tragic, the very elements and laws of nature being hostile to man. Then, having stated as extremely as this the case of human misery, he breaks out with sudden contempt for those who call the world a vale of tears.

The courage of this tragic affirmation is a dialectical courage: the self opposes what limits it, but acknowledges that limiting power as the necessary opposite against which the self constructs itself.

Essay after essay in *The Opposing Self* speaks of the need to attain a similar affirmation and of the quality in modern culture that militates against that effort. In our world and in our literature, Trilling argues, we have become so accustomed to the self-denying aspects of life—to "evil"—that our imagination succumbs to the temptation to imagine the self completely overcome by them, completely disintegrated; in the wake of Auschwitz, we are used to despair. Modern culture begins with the conviction that "we must, in our time, confront circumstances which are so terrible that the soul, far from being defined and developed by them, can only be destroyed by them." The danger is that we have come to valorize evil and terrible power, to make

the nihilistic assumption that only evil is real. Our culture has even come to confer what Trilling describes in "Wordsworth and the Rabbis" as "spiritual prestige" on whatever exhibits "some form of aggressive action directed outward upon the world, or inward upon ourselves." Trilling, who had tried to correct an earlier view of "reality in America," now tries to correct this other. We need, he believes, to recover a view of some resistant core of "being" on which to build such affirmations as Keats could manage. Writing on William Wordsworth, Leo Tolstoy, William Dean Howells, and George Orwell, Trilling repeatedly makes the point: we need to overcome our "hyperaesthesia" with an open appreciation of what Trilling variously calls "the elemental *given* of biology" or "the sentiment of Being," which is to say, the overwhelmingly simple fact of our, and others', existence as biological creatures. This appreciation was at the basis of Wordsworth's celebrations of common life in the figures of the Old Cumberland Beggar or the Leech-Gatherer of "Resolution and Independence"; looking at these isolated figures— poor, rootless, bearing almost no relationship to civilization—Wordsworth sees them as possessing that authentic kernel of being which is to be found and cherished in all humanity as the basis of the moral community of the world.

In similar fashion, Trilling argues, writers like Tolstoy, Howells, and Orwell offer their visions of the life-affirming value residing even, or especially, in the trivial details of bourgeois domestic life. Like the "common life" of Wordsworth's poetry, the unrefined, the undazzling, the mediocre is worthy of affectionate interest in the works of these authors. An aspidistra—"ugly, stubborn, organic emblem of survival"—is in one of Orwell's novels a symbol of the "biological-social heroism" of a man persisting with life at its most unpicturesque and finding a "stubborn joy" therein. Howells flies in the face of our yearning for the drama of unconditioned spirit with his insistence on the small "smiling aspects of life." In the essay *"Anna Karenina"* Tolstoy earns praise for perceiving that "to comprehend unconditioned spirit is not so very hard, but there is no knowledge rarer than the understanding of spirit as it exists in the inescapable conditions which the actual and the trivial make for it." Howells and Orwell are even prized for not being "geniuses," but rather common, honest men capable of loving the commonplace.

I have already noted the charge brought against Trilling for his tendency to elide what in human life is of natural cause and what is of social cause—the latter theoretically changeable by human effort, the former impervious to it; and his sympathy with those affirmations of what is "given" in life certainly seems liable to such a charge. But we should observe that Trilling's intention was to establish "biological faith" as a means by which the self can resist—oppose—the pressures brought to bear on it by culture or civilization or society. Indeed, in order to preserve this space "beyond culture," Trilling mounted a longstanding assault on post-Freudian analysts like Karen Horney, Erich Fromm, and Harry Stack Sullivan, who de-emphasized the biological or instinctual roots of behavior in favor of culturally specific sources like family structure. Trilling's argument here has clear affinities with his earlier opposition to Stalinism. As Trilling explained in "Freud: Within and Beyond Culture," a 1955 lecture delivered to the members of the new York Psychoanalytical Society (collected in *Beyond Culture,* 1965), biological fact has a fundamental place in Freud's thinking: over against the broad vistas of possible social-engineering "reforms" glimpsed by neo-Freudian theory, Freud demands that we recognize the human being's recalcitrance to plans to redesign society in hopes of eliminating psychic conflict. Trilling fears the hubris of the utopian social planners who may follow the neo-

Freudians; he believes that coerced conformity, not liberation, is likely to be the result of their blueprints for humanity. Regardless of whether Freud is wrong or right about the role of biology in human fate,

we must stop to consider whether this emphasis on biology . . . is not so far from being a reactionary idea that it is actually a liberating idea. It proposes to us that culture is not all-powerful. It suggests that there is a residue of human quality beyond the reach of cultural control, and that this residue of human quality, elemental as it may be, serves to bring culture itself under criticism and keeps it from being absolute.

Freud's and Trilling's "biologism" is usually offered as evidence of a reactionary view of human possibility, but Trilling's concern is that a theoretical limit be placed on the role of culture in *determining* individual life. Ironically, the argument bears a resemblance to those advanced by the Frankfurt-School Marxists Theodor Adorno and Max Horkheimer in the 1940's, in their attacks on the "totally administered society" of American consumer capitalism. Idiosyncratic dialecticians just as Trilling was, they too regarded the "totalizing" tendency of culture with suspicion and dread.

In the decade between 1955 and 1965 Trilling attempted to understand the relationship between the opposing selves he had described in his 1955 essay collection—Wordsworth, Keats, and others—and the conformist modern culture that now seemed to be closing in around the individual. Trilling was divided about the extent to which those original opposing selves represented the beginning of a continuous tradition of modern selfhood or a lost form of selfhood which we no longer apprehend. He often stressed the degree to which they stand apart from us—we who are the twentieth-century heirs to their tradition. In the back of Trilling's mind is Friedrich Nietzsche's famous distinction from *The Birth of*

Tragedy: they managed to maintain the balance and tension between Apollonian and Dionysian principles, while we hunger only for the terrible Dionysian aesthetics of self-disintegration. We scorn the simple idea of "pleasure" or "joy," with which the romantic poets were able to celebrate being. But there are also similarities. Modern literature, says Trilling—thinking of Feodor Dostoevsky, Franz Kafka, Thomas Mann, D. H. Lawrence, and others—is characterized by its

adversary intention, [its] actually subversive intention, . . . its clear purpose of detaching the reader from the habits of thought and feeling that the larger culture imposes, of giving him a ground and a vantage point from which to judge and condemn, and perhaps revise, the culture that produced him.

This is Trilling writing in 1965, in the preface to his collection *Beyond Culture.* As this passage suggests, modern literature does continue the "opposing self" tradition insofar as it seeks to counteract the conformist pressures of the civilization or "culture." Its ferocity of opposition is a new feature, but its main bearing toward culture is the same.

The real difference, then, between our forerunners and ourselves does not result from an essentially new quality in selfhood, but rather from the scale on which the model of the opposing self has been accepted within the culture at large. Through a variety of means, we have arrived at a very large scale of acceptance of that idea. From the opposing self, we have evolved the unprecedented phenomenon of what Trilling calls "the adversary culture." Since about the first quarter of the twentieth century, he argues, there has emerged in American society a substantial group that is attuned to the dynamics of oppositional selfhood and its demonstration in art; the group's development can be correlated to the growth of the American university as an arbiter of taste.

Trilling is responding, of course, to a shift that exactly correlates with his own career as well. When he first entered into the academic study of literature, he had been aware that the main body of intellectuals who commented on the general current or recent cultural scene was not affiliated with universities—Edmund Wilson, literary editor of *The New Republic,* may stand as the best example of the old breed. But by the 1950's and 1960's there were few "nonprofessionals" left. The professionalization of criticism also followed on and was facilitated by the efflorescence of modern literature from Dostoevsky to Joseph Conrad, William Butler Yeats, and Kafka. Academic literary study grew in absorbing and canonizing the modernist works. This has meant that the audience for modern literature has grown from the tiny readerships of the little magazines of the 1920's and 1930's to the burgeoning student body in the universities across America. At the same time, however, the canonization, the institutionalization of modern literature has put its adversary capacities very much in question. What happens when a large part of the establishment culture has learned to accept the subversive, opposing-self imagination of modern literature and art? Many of the essays in *Beyond Culture* try to address this question in the loosely-structured, associative manner increasingly characteristic of Trilling's later work.

Significantly, Trilling begins and ends the volume with essays on the teaching of literature in universities. The 1961 essay "On the Teaching of Modern Literature" is an extended rumination that reveals his frustrations in the attempt to make modern writing's subversive force hit home to the very college students who had requested that the course be offered. After detailing his carefully planned syllabus of challenging, provocative works, Trilling characterizes the students' habitual response to the "strong dose" he was offering them: they exhibit a baffling

readiness . . . to engage in the process that we might call the socialization of the anti-social, or the acculturation of the anti-cultural, or the legitimation of the subversive. When the term-essays come in, it is plain to me that almost none of the students have been taken aback by what they have read: they have wholly contained the attack.

The unshockability of his students amounts, for Trilling, to evidence that the modernists' oppositional stance—their spurning of the culture that surrounded them, their passionately spiritual rejection of the "specious goods" that bourgeois culture cast before them as objects of desire—has become part of an easily mimicked set of styles for conveying defiance of the general culture. The adversary culture is a parody of the original primal violence and power of literary modernism. We have evolved a conformity of nonconformity, or what Trilling refers to in "The Fate of Pleasure" as "an accredited subversiveness, an established moral radicalism, a respectable violence." The closing essay in *Beyond Culture* speaks in troubled tones of "The Two Environments" open to students of literature when they leave their universities: one is philistia, very much as it was in Matthew Arnold's time; the other the equally established adversary culture, which "shows the essential traits of any cultural environment: firm presuppositions, received ideas, approved attitudes, and a system of rewards and punishments." Like any culture, the adversary culture rewards conformist behavior: it delivers what Trilling calls "spiritual prestige" to those who can make the proper gestures betokening intransigence to cultural determination.

Beneath Trilling's provocative generalizations in *Beyond Culture* and his other late works was an awareness of what is usually called the "coun-

terculture" of the 1960's, and his apparent exposure of the inner mechanisms of the anticultural culture invites comparisons with his attacks on the bad faith of the 1930's fellow travelers. In the 1960's and 1970's, neoconservative disciples like Norman Podhoretz, exploiting this analogy, attempted to lure Trilling into alliance with their movement; in a 1974 *Commentary* discussion, Podhoretz urged Trilling to comply with his view that the cultural critic's best function ought then to be "to stand in an adversary relation to the adversary culture itself." It is true that Trilling had looked with little favor on the campus uprisings of the late 1960's, the most notorious of which occurred at Columbia; but it is also notable that he refused any such endorsements as Podhoretz urged him to make. And the idea of adversary culture surely contains its own measure of radical insight which we ought not overlook: it suggests the possibility that bourgeois society has protected itself by producing a safe alternative to itself within itself, where truly adversary sentiments may be purged away in symbolic, self-congratulatory actions.

Furthermore, in keeping with its highly general nature, Trilling's concept of the adversary culture has other objects in view than specific political alignments and events. It implicitly addresses itself to the large cultural phenomenon now commonly called postmodernism and raises new questions about the possible role of art in a society in which the adversary culture has become entrenched. In a note in his final book, *Sincerity and Authenticity* (1972), originally the Charles Eliot Norton Lectures at Harvard University, Trilling summed up the postmodern cultural scene as follows:

At the present moment, art cannot be said to make exigent demands upon the audience. That segment of our culture which is at all responsive to contemporary art is wholly permeable by it. The situation no longer obtains in which the experience of a contemporary work begins in resistance and proceeds by relatively slow stages to a comprehending or submissive admiration. The artist now can make scarcely anything which will . . . outrage [the audience's] habitual sensibility.

The postmodern is the vicious circle of consumer unshockability—since the consumer needs the prestige of demonstrated appreciation of the "adversarial"—and ever more futilely outrageous artistic attempts to shock. Trilling, having spent some forty years deeply involved with literature and art, is now posing the question whether they still have any capacity to contribute to the formation of actually autonomous individuals. He was forced to admit in the preface to *Beyond Culture* that "art does not always tell the truth or the best kind of truth and does not always point out the right way, that it can even generate falsehood and habituate us to it. . . ."

In one of the essays in *Beyond Culture,* Trilling reminds us that Dostoevsky's Underground Man, the classic example of the furious modern "opposing self," had hissed out his venom at the establishment with the words "I have more life in me than you have." It was an appeal to the biological again, the self-professedly "authentic" core of being that resists the encroachment of culture. In the rhetoric of the adversary culture, however, members construct a myth of their moral or spiritual superiority to the primary culture on the basis of such appeals to authenticity. Where was the self seeking actual, and not spurious, selfhood to go from here? Trilling had no prescriptive answer, but turned, in his final book, to an examination of what he now envisioned as the four-hundred-year history of modern selfhood. *Sincerity and Authenticity* begins by arguing that sincerity, the ideal of being "true to oneself" in order to uphold a communal standard of morality, emerged in Renaissance Europe as a response to the Machiavellian nature of court life; it is in Polonius' advice to Laertes, "to thine

own self be true," which we view as simplistic or platitudinous only because we are now so far from the ideal's original power. Implying a frank relationship between inner self and outer culture, sincerity was still viable in the Romantic period, when Wordsworth could describe the poet as simply "a man speaking to men." Eventually, however, sincerity lost its authority over us. Alongside it had grown, since the middle of the eighteenth century, the counterideal of authenticity, in which the self is conceived of as wholly private, resistant to culture's authority and resentful of it—the self of the Underground Man. By the latter part of the twentieth century, the ideal of authenticity has carried the day; it is clear that Trilling regards it as the driving force beneath the adversary culture.

Between those two poles Trilling hangs no conventional argument—though his sympathies plainly rest with the old, degraded sincerity—but rather an astonishing series of reflections on examples drawn from the literature, philosophy, and psychology of the past four centuries. The core of Trilling's contentions is familiar: the modern, post-sincerity self seeks its fulfillment, as G. W. F. Hegel had described, through the very alienation from its culture that would seem to negate it. Met with culture's limiting force, this self strives to be free of all limitation. But again, Trilling believes we are witnessing the institutionalization or domestication of such an alienated self: alienation from an "inauthentic" bourgeois culture is only indoctrination into adversary culture, where one learns what Theodor Adorno called "the jargon of authenticity" and competes for its peculiar rewards.

By turns brilliant and murky—*ondoyant et divers* to an almost maddening degree—*Sincerity and Authenticity* truly defies summary. Interpretations of Hegel, Freud, Denis Diderot, Johann Wolfgang von Goethe, Conrad, and Jean-Jacques Rousseau consort with references to Sartre, Jane Austen, Molière, Marx, Henry James,

Maximilien Robespierre, James Joyce, Herbert Marcuse, and many others. And because Trilling will allow himself neither hope nor nostalgia, sees no way forward or back, this plethora of references never fully coheres. But the force of Trilling's attack on the cult of authenticity commands respect. The book concludes with attacks on the contemporary psychologists, such as R. D. Laing and David Cooper, who had taken the ideal of authenticity to the point of asserting that insanity was a righteous and appropriate reponse to a false society. If society is nothing but corrupt power, they imagine, then what it defines as "rationality" is only another coercive, corrupting force; some protest this coercion by opting out of "reason" altogether. Trilling's rejoinder to the intellectual vogue that "madness is health, that madness is liberation and authenticity" is profound and stirring, a powerful blow struck in Trilling's longstanding war with the intellectuals. In "The Authentic Unconscious" Trilling writes,

many among us find it gratifying to entertain the thought that alienation is to be overcome only by the completeness of alienation, and that alienation completed is not a deprivation or deficiency but a potency. . . . The falsities of an alienated social reality are rejected in favour of an upward psychopathic mobility to the point of divinity, each one of us a Christ. . . .

The end result of our devotion to authenticity is the deification of psychosis and the spurning of all community; the adversary culture becomes an economy of its own, in which we may all strive for "upward psychopathic mobility" by showing how pure and how wronged we are.

There had been a large dialectic at work in Lionel Trilling's writings for many years; by the 1960's and 1970's Trilling was cutting back against the grain of his earlier thought. Nineteenth-century critics like Mill and Arnold had seen the arts as a necessary response to the

inhuman "rationality" of utilitarian capitalism, and for a time the effects of that response had been salutary. "The literature of the nineteenth century," Trilling wrote in "The Leavis–Snow Controversy" in *Beyond Culture*, "never wearied . . . of decrying the fatigue and dessication of spirit which results from an allegiance to mind that excludes impulse and will, desire and preference." But the valorization of the nonrational had gone to such extremes that a dose of "mind" or reason once again seemed in order. Trilling's last essays, including his 1973 Jefferson Award address, "Mind in the Modern World," repeatedly circled back to this point. To some extent it was an attempt to resuscitate a lost aspect of Matthew Arnold, the demand for "disinterest" and the "best self" that can rise above immediate self-interest; self-interest had proved itself capable of working irrationally. But the calls for a return of reason are tentative, as if Trilling were aware that his time for correcting the culture had already passed. And there is another Arnoldian aspect that had grown in Trilling's work in the later years: a willingness to take seriously Arnold's suggestion that culture could replace religion in guiding morality—though, as the case of the adversary culture made clear, culture might not always be guiding a form of morality we would welcome. For years, Trilling himself had clearly been engaged in a cultural-spiritual quest of his own. But he had nowhere he could honestly turn for "resolution"—not to the adversary culture, not to the cultural conservatives, not to religious faith—so he remained irresolute, ambivalent to the end.

He had made mistakes and was guilty of ambiguities. But as he had written years earlier about another critic, F. R. Leavis ("Dr. Leavis and the Moral Tradition," collected in *A Gathering of Fugitives*),

It isn't by his freedom from error that we properly judge a critic's value but by the integrity and point of his whole critical impulse, which, if it is personal and committed in the demands it makes upon life and literature, will be as instructive in its errors as in its correct judgments.

The passage gives us a standard of measurement well suited to its author. Trilling's works amount to an argument that criticism can be worldly and timely without being merely topical; they also combat the facile wish-fulfillment dream that each and every experience of conflict or pain in human beings can be attributed to—blamed on—wholly external factors.

While acknowledging the sometimes justified criticisms of Trilling that his writing lacked a sufficiently specific historical or political dimension, we should nevertheless give weight to Trilling's contention that it is the liberal fellow-traveler or the member of the adversary culture who seeks to do away with politics—politics, that is, as they actually exist in a contentious democracy—in order to arrive at a state of "unconditioned spirit" or "absolute authenticity." Trilling had indeed made great demands of life and literature: he had tried to make life honest by using literature as Matthew Arnold had said it should be used, as "a criticism of life." And Trilling had been committed to making his own work, his criticism, continually reach "beyond" mere literary criticism and beyond cultural criticism, to set literary and cultural observations in the fullest context of a criticism of life. If the broad scope of that commitment is the cause of his faults, it is also the cause of his strengths and the condition of his unique authority.

Selected Bibliography

WORKS OF LIONEL TRILLING

CRITICAL STUDIES
Matthew Arnold. New York: W. W. Norton, 1939.
E. M. Forster. New York: New Directions, 1943.

ESSAYS AND LECTURES
The Liberal Imagination: Essays on Literature and Society. New York: Viking, 1950.
The Opposing Self: Nine Essays in Criticism. New York: Viking, 1955.
Freud and the Crisis of Our Culture. Boston: Beacon, 1955.
A Gathering of Fugitives. Boston: Beacon, 1956.
Beyond Culture: Essays on Literature and Learning. New York: Viking, 1965.
Sincerity and Authenticity. Cambridge, Mass.: Harvard University Press, 1972.
Mind in the Modern World. New York: Viking, 1973.

NOVEL
The Middle of the Journey. New York: Viking, 1947.

COLLECTED WORKS
The Works of Lionel Trilling. Uniform Edition. 12 vols. New York: Harcourt Brace, 1978–1980. Includes *Matthew Arnold, E. M. Forster, The Middle of the Journey, The Liberal Imagination, The Opposing Self, A Gathering of Fugitives, Beyond Culture, Sincerity and Authenticity, Of This Time, Of That Place* (selected short stories, including "Of This Time, Of That Place" and "The Other Margaret"), *Prefaces to the Experience of Literature* (commentaries from Trilling's 1967 anthology), *Speaking of Literature and Society* (previously uncollected essays, 1924–1964), and *The Last Decade* (essays, 1965–1975).

MANUSCRIPTS
Archive in Rare Book and Manuscript Division of Columbia University Library, New York.

EDITED WORKS

The Portable Matthew Arnold. Edited and with an introduction by Lionel Trilling. New York: Viking, 1949.

The Selected Letters of John Keats. Edited and with an introduction by Lionel Trilling. New York: Farrar, Straus, and Young, 1951.

The Experience of Literature: A Reader with Commentaries. Edited and with commentaries by Lionel Trilling. Garden City, N. Y.: Doubleday, 1967. Anthology.

The Life and Work of Sigmund Freud. Edited by Lionel Trilling and Steven Marcus. With an introduction by Lionel Trilling. New York: Basic Books, 1970. A one-volume abridgment of Ernest Jones's three-volume biography.

Literary Criticism: An Introductory Reader. Edited and with an introduction by Lionel Trilling. New York: Holt, Rinehart, & Winston, 1970. Anthology.

The Oxford Anthology of English Literature. 2 vols. Coedited by Lionel Trilling. New York: Oxford University Press, 1973.

BIBLIOGRAPHIES

Barnaby, Marianne Gilbert. "Lionel Trilling: A Bibliography, 1926–1972." *Bulletin of Bibliography,* 31:37–44 (January–March 1974).

Robinson, Jeffrey. "Lionel Trilling: A Bibliographic Essay." *Resources for American Literary Study,* 8:131–156 (1987).

BIOGRAPHICAL AND CRITICAL STUDIES

Aaron, Daniel. *Writers on the Left: Episodes in American Literary Communism.* New York: Harcourt, Brace, & World, 1961.

Anderson, Quentin, Stephen Donadio, and Steven Marcus, ed. *Art, Politics, and Will: Essays in Honor of Lionel Trilling.* New York: Basic Books, 1977.

Barnaby, Marianne Gilbert. "Lionel Trilling: Modulations of Arnoldian Criticism at the Present Time." Ph.D. dissertation, University of Connecticut, 1975.

Barzun, Jacques. "Remembering Lionel Trilling." *Encounter,* 47:82–88 (September 1976).

Bloom, Alexander. *Prodigal Sons: The New York Intellectuals and Their World.* New York: Oxford University Press, 1986.

Boyers, Robert. *Lionel Trilling: Negative Capability and the Wisdom of Avoidance.* Columbia: University of Missouri Press, 1977.

Chace, William M. *Lionel Trilling: Criticism and Politics.* Stanford, Calif.: Stanford University Press, 1980.

Donoghue, Denis. "Trilling, Mind, and Society." *Sewanee Review,* 86:161–186 (1978).

Frank, Joseph. "Lionel Trilling and the Conservative Imagination." *Sewanee Review,* 64:296–309 (Spring 1956). Reprinted in Joseph Frank, *The Widening Gyre: Crisis and Mastery in Modern Literature.* New Brunswick, N.J.: Rutgers University Press, 1963. Reprinted with appendix in *Salmagundi,* 41:33–54 (Spring 1978).

French, Philip, ed. *Three Honest Men: A Critical Mosaic: Edmund Wilson, F. R. Leavis, Lionel Trilling.* Manchester, England: Carcanet New Press, 1980. Radio interviews about the three subjects.

Grumet, Elinor Joan. "The Menorah Idea and the Apprenticeship of Lionel Trilling." Ph.D. dissertation, University of Iowa, 1979.

Krupnick, Mark. *Lionel Trilling and the Fate of Cultural Criticism.* Evanston, Ill.: Northwestern University Press, 1986.

Kubal, David. "Lionel Trilling: The Mind and Its Discontents." *Hudson Review,* 31:279–295 (1978–1979).

Langbaum, Robert. "The Importance of *The Liberal Imagination.*" *Salmagundi,* 41:55–65 (Spring 1978).

O'Hara, Daniel T. *Lionel Trilling: The Work of Liberation.* Madison: University of Wisconsin Press, 1988.

Podhoretz, Norman. "Culture and the Present Moment: A Round-Table Discussion." *Commentary,* 58:41 (December, 1974).

Robinson, Jeffrey. "Lionel Trilling and the Romantic Tradition." *Massachusetts Review,* 20:211–236 (1979).

Samet, Tom. "The Modulated Vision: Lionel Trilling's 'Larger Naturalism.'" *Critical Inquiry,* 4:539–557 (1977–1978).

———. "Trilling, Arnold and the Anxieties of the Modern." *Southern Quarterly,* 16:191–209 (1977–1978).

————. "Lionel Trilling and the Social Imagination." *Centennial Review,* 23:159–184 (1979).

Scott, Nathan A., Jr. *Three American Moralists: Mailer, Bellow, Trilling.* Notre Dame, Ind.: University of Notre Dame Press, 1973.

Sennett, Richard. "On Lionel Trilling." *New Politics,* November 5, 1979, 209.

Shechner, Mark. "Psychoanalysis and Liberalism: The Case of Lionel Trilling." *Salmagundi,* 41:3–22 (Spring 1978).

Shoben, Edward Joseph, Jr. *Lionel Trilling: Mind and Character.* New York: Ungar, 1981.

Tanner, Stephen L. *Lionel Trilling.* Boston: Twayne, 1988.

Trilling, Diana. "Lionel Trilling: A Jew at Columbia." In Lionel Trilling, *Speaking of Literature and Society.* New York: Harcourt Brace, 1980.

Wald, Alan M. *The New York Intellectuals: The Rise and Decline of the Anti-Stalinist Left from the 1930s to the 1980s.* Chapel Hill, N.C.: University of North Carolina Press, 1987.

West, Cornel. "Lionel Trilling: Godfather of Neo-Conservatism." *New Politics,* n.s. 1, no. 1: 233–242 (Summer 1986).

—*JAMES BUZARD*

Alice Walker

1944–

"BLACK WOMEN SHOULD not be sacrificed for Black men's pride. Let the film roll.'' This was the edict of an African American viewer of *The Color Purple* when a *New York Times* reporter interviewed her in January 1986, shortly after the film's release. Alice Walker, on whose novel the film was based, had published two other novels, four books of poetry, two short-story collections, a biography of Langston Hughes for children, a book of essays, and an edition of Zora Neale Hurston's writing, and had frequently contributed to *Ms.* and other periodicals before the film was made. The novel *The Color Purple*, published in 1982, won both a Pulitzer Prize and an American Book Award in 1983. But it was the film version and the controversy it sparked that carried Walker's name far beyond literary circles to a mass audience unaware of her full career.

The most publicized aspect of the controversy concerned the film's representations of African American men. Faithful to the novel in its basic plot, the film covers forty years in the life of Celie, a woman in the rural South whose bonds with other women give her the sense of worth to survive her stepfather's and her husband's abuse and to transform her environment. A frequent and vehement criticism of the film was that the portrayal of Mister, Celie's husband, was unnec-

essarily harsh and brutal. To some critics Walker's extensive collaboration with the producers of the film represented an African American woman's collaboration with the white male establishment to perpetuate the racist stereotype of black men as dangerously violent. Novelist Ishmael Reed called both the film and the novel a "Nazi conspiracy." On his television show columnist Tony Brown hosted a largely hostile panel on *The Color Purple,* calling the program "Purple Rage." In print and on the "Donahue" show, Brown denounced the film as "the most racist depiction of black men since *The Birth of a Nation.*" Critical attacks by African American men on the film and on Walker proliferated in major newspapers and magazines in 1986, while African American women writers defended Walker and her novel—rather than the film—mainly in small journals.

The media's focus on the gender conflict that arose over *The Color Purple* tended to frame the controversy as a problem between African American men and women and to oversimplify the range of critical responses to the film. Actually, negative and positive evaluations were not split strictly along lines of either gender or race. The first reviews of the film in newspapers across the country were, with a few exceptions, overwhelmingly positive. Some critics objected to

Steven Spielberg's direction and pointed out problems that were later discussed in depth in intellectual journals. Leftist publications criticized the film for failing to examine social class and for misrepresenting the economic conditions of its characters. Walker contradicted this criticism, setting her own knowledge of the rural South in which she grew up against the critics' theoretical understanding of the economic conditions of the people she had written about: poor as they were, she insisted, they owned property and engaged in commerce. The most damning criticism was that the film stereotyped not just men but African American people generally, perpetuating the "exotic primitive" cliché, as old as colonialism, that the film industry had exploited in its representations of black people through decades of socially sanctioned racism. Some critics believed this image could be especially harmful during the Reagan era, when the legislative and economic gains African Americans had made during the civil rights struggle were being eroded.

Yet many black viewers, particularly black women, did not see the film this way. The woman interviewed by the *New York Times* had known "many Celies," she said; her female relatives had all been brutalized by their husbands. To two women in Tony Brown's studio audience, the film was not a commentary on the black race but on a "social reality." The one panelist who praised the film, Armand White, insisted: "It's a fable, it's a fantasy. . . . It is more about the oppression of black women than about black people."

How were African American women able to identify with a film that so many intellectual leaders deplored? Film scholar Jacqueline Bobo made this question the basis of a doctoral dissertation and several articles (to which the above paragraphs are indebted). Bobo analyzed the controversy according to several social theories and conducted interviews with African American

women viewers. The women she interviewed were deeply moved by Celie's triumph. "The lady was a strong lady," one interviewee said, "and she hung in there and she overcame." To say that black women's appreciation of the film represented a "false consciousness"—an unthinking cooperation with racist oppression—is too simple, Bobo argues, since black women are well aware of racism. Watching *The Color Purple,* they were also aware that the mainstream media had never before so nearly represented them; here were images of black women based on the constructions and experience of a black woman rather than of a white or a black man.

Bobo discusses the sources in film history—*The Birth of a Nation* (1915), *Hallelujah!* (1929), and *Cabin in the Sky* (1943)—from which Spielberg derived the "exotic primitive" stereotypes in *The Color Purple*. Nonwhite audiences are accustomed to the media's mythmaking about them, Bobo argues, and can choose either to avoid mass-media entertainment altogether or to watch resistantly, sorting through the images to derive meanings different from the message designed to produce a commercial success. Bobo concludes that viewers of *The Color Purple* who watched the film in this way found it progressive and useful.

For many, the film was an introduction not only to Alice Walker's writing but also to a whole cultural movement, a renaissance of African American women writers that began in the 1970's. As creative writers African American women had been producing fiction and poetry that attracted national attention more often than ever before; as scholars they were rediscovering a tradition of African American women writers dating back to the mid nineteenth century and earlier. To Bobo, the furor over *The Color Purple* should be understood as part of a much broader confrontation between this emergence of African American women as cultural workers and an older set of concepts associated with Black

Power. In the 1960's the Black Power movement gave unity among blacks against a racist society the highest priority on its political agenda, but that unity was achieved under male leadership, often at the cost of silencing women. The African American women's renaissance began as women artists broke this silence to criticize the relationships within black families and communities, to expose problems in African American life that needed change before African Americans could strengthen their social and political effectiveness. The stakes in this confrontation are extremely high: Can African American women have a distinct public voice? If the truths they tell and the fables they make out of their own experience are not valued and understood on their own terms, but are seen as merely serving white racism, the answer is ''no.''

Alice Malsenior Walker was born in Eatonton, Georgia, on February 9, 1944, the eighth and last child of Willie Lee and Minnie Tallulah Grant Walker. Among her ancestors she counts a woman born into slavery who lived over 120 years, a Cherokee great-grandmother, and a slave-owner who raped her great-great-grandmother when she was only eleven. Like most Southern rural African American families in the first half of this century, Walker's family was caught up in the sharecropping system, which strongly resembled its antecedent, slavery. Parents and children worked the fields or dairy of a white landlord in exchange for a portion of the crop (usually subsistence level), cramped and battered housing, a few hundred dollars a year. For the adults in the community where Walker grew up, education was a route of escape from poverty that they could provide for the next generation.

When Walker was eight years old, a pellet one of her brothers shot from a BB gun accidentally struck her in the right eye, blinding it and leaving a large white scar. Humiliated by other people's reactions to the disfigurement, Walker withdrew

into negative fantasies. Her school performance deteriorated, but on her own she read and wrote poems. At fourteen she spent the summer babysitting for a brother who lived in Boston. Understanding her feelings of shame, he and his wife paid for simple surgery that removed the scar, leaving only a small bluish crater. Her schoolwork immediately improved, and she graduated valedictorian of her high school class. With a rehabilitation scholarship for which her blind eye qualified her and seventy-five dollars collected by neighbors, she entered Spelman College in Atlanta at the age of seventeen.

Spelman, the country's oldest college for black women, devoted its educational program to refining the students according to traditional standards of Southern womanhood. During the years 1961–1963, when Walker attended Spelman, civil rights organizers worked hard in Atlanta, drawing Walker and other students into a kind of political activism that contrasted sharply with the college's conservative mission. Frustrated by Spelman's limitations, Walker transferred to Sarah Lawrence, an elite, mostly white women's college in Bronxville, New York. The summer before her senior year she visited Kenya and Uganda on an educational grant. She returned to college pregnant and suicidal. A friend arranged an abortion and, emerging from her despair, Walker wrote poems steadily for a week, slipping each finished poem under the door of the poet Muriel Rukeyser, then writer-in-residence at Sarah Lawrence. With Rukeyser's help, the poems were later published as Walker's first book, *Once*, in 1968.

After graduating in 1965, Walker briefly worked for the New York City Welfare Department. She had resolved to become a writer. Her first publication, an essay on the civil rights movement, won *The American Scholar*'s essay contest in 1966. That summer she attended the Bread Loaf Writers' Conference in Vermont, and in 1967 she received both a Merrill Writing Fellowship and a McDowell Colony Fellowship. She married Melvyn Leventhal, a civil rights attorney and conscientious objector to the Vietnam war, in 1967, and they moved to Mississippi. Walker worked on voter registration drives, taught black history to Head Start teachers, and served as writer-in-residence at Jackson State College (1968–1969) and Tougaloo College (1969–1970). A National Endowment for the Arts grant in 1969 supported her work on her first novel, *The Third Life of Grange Copeland,* into which she incorporated some aspects of her own family's history as sharecroppers. She finished writing the novel days before her daughter, Rebecca Grant Rosenthal, was born.

After the publication of her novel, Walker left the South with a Radcliffe Institute Fellowship to teach courses on black women writers—among the earliest such courses—at the University of Massachusetts at Boston (1971–1972) and Wellesley College (1972–1973). Her second collection of poems, *Revolutionary Petunias* (1973), received a National Book Award nomination and won the Lillian Smith Award of the Southern Regional Council. The following year her first collection of short stories, *In Love and Trouble* (1973), received the Rosenthal Foundation Award from the American Academy of Arts and Letters. Both volumes draw on Walker's years with the civil rights movement, taking a critical view of sexism within both conventional black communities and revolutionary groups, as well as of revolutionaries' contempt for people whose acts of resistance or strivings for fulfillment are theoretically incorrect. In 1974 her tribute to the poet Langston Hughes, a biography for children, was published.

Walker moved to Brooklyn, New York, in 1974, and became a contributing editor of *Ms.* the following year. In her second novel, *Meridian* (1976), she continued to weave the themes of revolution, sexism, and the traditions of black communities, using autobiographical material particularly in portraying a Southern black women's college and the civil rights movement's change into the militant Black Power movement. Told in patchworked episodes that double back in time, *Meridian* is the story of a woman who leaves her home in the rural South to join the civil rights movement and enter college. Meridian's guilt over rejecting the traditional values of motherhood and her ambivalence about revolutionary violence once the movement turns militant give her an almost mystical physical illness and a saintly dedication to advancing her people. Her methods are anachronistic; virtually alone, she carries out spontaneous nonviolent organizing efforts in a small community. Her eccentricity serves as a critique of the elitism, sexism, and militancy of the Black Power movement long after it has lost its strength, and she offers hope that nonviolent change is still possible.

She and Leventhal were divorced in 1977. A second McDowell Colony Fellowship and a Guggenheim grant supported her literary work from 1977 to 1978. Finding New York an unsuitably urban place to work on her next novel, which was to be set in the rural Georgia of her childhood, Walker moved to northern California in 1979. Before completing this novel, she published her edition of Zora Neale Hurston's writings (1979); her third book of poems, *Good Night, Willie Lee, I'll See You in the Morning* (1979); and her second collection of stories, *You Can't Keep a Good Woman Down* (1981).

The Color Purple was nominated for a National Book Critics Circle Award when it was published in 1982 and, the following year, received both the Pulitzer Prize and the American Book Award. Walker was named distinguished writer in Afro-American studies at the University of California, Berkeley, in the spring of 1982 and taught at Brandeis University as the Fannie Hurst Professor of Literature in the fall. Her important first collection of "womanist" essays, *In Search of Our Mothers' Gardens,* was published in 1983. Throughout the 1980's Walker traveled extensively, lecturing and reading her work at universities and conferences and joining delegations of writers to other countries. She also appeared and spoke at political gatherings, such as Nelson and Winnie Mandela's visit to San Francisco in 1990. Her fourth book of poems, *Horses Make a Landscape More Beautiful* (1984), and her second volume of essays, *Living by the Word* (1988), reflect the extension of her political commitments to the environment, animal rights, and antinuclear protest; the stretching of her self-definition as an African American to make interracial and international connections; and the sights, sounds, and smells of her rural home near Navarro, California. Her fourth novel, *The Temple of My Familiar* (1989), reaches far corners of the earth and weaves together the voices of characters of different cultures, economic classes, and historical eras.

While biographical information on living authors can be difficult to find, this is not true of Alice Walker. Most of the above information is available in numerous reference volumes; and her two collections of essays, a kind of patchwork autobiography, enrich the picture of the various parts of her life.

The common heritage of black Southern writers, Walker wrote in "The Black Writer and the Southern Experience" (1970, in *In Search of Our Mothers' Gardens*), is "a sense of *community*," of "solidarity and sharing," as well as

a compassion for the earth, a trust in humanity beyond our knowledge of evil, and an abiding love of justice. We inherit a great responsibility as well, for we must give voice to centuries not only of silent bitterness and hate but also of neighborly kindness and sustaining love.

Houses and churches in these communities were set back in woods and fields, invisible from the road. "The daily dramas that evolve in such a private world are pure gold," the stuff of storytelling, made more valuable as part of a writer's double vision of "a strictly private and hidden existence" and "the larger world that surrounds and suppresses" it.

Both of Walker's parents were superb storytellers. One of her mother's favorite stories recounted an experience of the Depression. On a day when Minnie Walker took government-issued vouchers to the Red Cross center in town to get a winter's supply of flour, she dressed in good used clothes that a sister in the North had sent to her. The white woman passing out flour angrily refused to give her any—judging that anyone who had the gall to dress better than she did not need assistance. Community and resourcefulness saw the family through the winter: they traded the corn they grew for flour. Walker's mother concluded the story with a moral about the workings of divine justice. In old age the white woman became senile and badly crippled. Turning the story to fiction in the early 1970's ("The Revenge of Hannah Kemhuff," in *In Love and Trouble*), Walker speculated: What if this woman's deterioration were a punishment willed by the recipient of her insensitivity and brought about by the folk craft of voodoo? Black folklore had been appropriated and distorted by a white resident of Eatonton, Joel Chandler Harris, and further alienated from its sources by Walt Disney in the film *Uncle Remus*. Looking for a black collector of folk culture, Walker discovered Zora Neale Hurston's *Mules and Men* (1935), "all the black folklore I could ever use."

Minnie Walker, though married at seventeen, as was expected, never pressured her daughters to marry. She and her sisters were strong, hardworking women who did not regard gender as a barrier to any kind of labor. "It is because of them, I know women can do anything," Walker has said. Slow to anger, Minnie Walker would explode at landlords who tried to persuade her to interrupt her children's education and send them into the fields full-time. "In Search of Our Mothers' Gardens" takes its title from Minnie Walker's artistry with flowers, her producing brilliant, original, life-filled gardens in "whatever rocky soil she landed on." Her gardens were also practical; she patched the walls of the family's cabins with sunflowers. By making creativity a part of their daily lives, Walker writes, women like her mother "handed down respect for the possibilities—and the will to grasp them." They exerted their resourcefulness to prepare their children for a world larger than they had known. She writes of them in the section "Women" of the poem "In These Dissenting Times" (in *Revolutionary Petunias*):

> They were women then
> My mama's generation
> Husky of voice—Stout of
> Step
> With fists as well as
> Hands
> How they battered down
> Doors
> And ironed
> Starched white
> Shirts
> How they led
> Armies
> Headragged Generals
> Across mined
> Fields
> Booby-trapped
> Ditches
> To discover books
> Desks
> A place for us
> How they knew what we
> *Must* know
> Without knowing a page
> Of it
> Themselves.

Walker's relationship with her father was more difficult, fraught with anger. A poem in *Once*

describes him beating her on Election Day. Writing about him in 1984, she remembered only one beating, probably not on Election Day, though the rage of the early poem accurately matched his unkindness to his child because of his political frustration. Walker's involvement in the black and women's movements gave her the ideological tools to understand her father's colorism and sexism as his absorption of the dominant white culture's values and to forgive him for his failures as an adult model. "Actually, my father was two fathers," Walker writes in "Father" (1985, in *Living by the Word*). His older children knew him when he was healthy and had faith in politics and education. In the 1930's he was one of the first black men to vote in their town, having organized a group of sharecroppers to exercise their rights. As his younger children knew him, he was " 'dragging-around' sick" with diabetes and high blood pressure, disillusioned, fearful, and resentful. Little had changed in the power structure of his world, and "education merely seemed to make his children more critical of him." But even in his last years, "he would come out with one of those startlingly intelligent comments about world affairs," reminding Walker of the father she did not know.

As a small child Alice was her father's favorite, a status she partly lost after her disfiguring eye injury and partly rejected to take sides with another daughter whom he mistreated because she resembled his mother, who had been killed by a lover when her son was young. Walker has images of a jolly, affectionate man that she thought were early memories of her father but learned were of a brother who left the South when she was very young. Her generation was raised to leave the South in search of better opportunities. Her five brothers moved to Boston, worked hard, and bought homes in pleasant neighborhoods. Her sisters, too, left the South, and she was expected to do likewise. She wrote in an essay in 1972 (collected in *In Search of Our Mothers' Gardens*): "It is part of the black Southern sensibility that we treasure memories;

for such a long time, that is all of our homeland those of us who at one time or another were forced away from it have been allowed to have.''

Walker's family and community took southern segregation for granted until civil rights activities began in the late 1950's. In 1960 her mother bought a television set, and after school Walker watched news reports of two black students integrating the University of Georgia with the support of the National Guard. Then Martin Luther King, Jr., appeared in the news, providing a charismatic focus for resistance to segregation. She writes in her tribute to King (1973, in *In Search of Our Mothers' Gardens*) that he, in urging African Americans to stay in the South and work to change it, ''gave us continuity of place, without which community is ephemeral. He gave us home.''

When Walker got on the bus to Atlanta and college at seventeen with a sewing machine, a typewriter, and a suitcase that her mother provided, a class barrier divided her from her roots. But the move also enabled her to join efforts to change the South, to connect the struggles of her community with worldwide struggles, and to tell the hidden stories of her forebears. There were civil rights demonstrations every Saturday morning in downtown Atlanta. Walker idolized the young members of the Student Nonviolent Coordinating Committee who led the movement. She wrote of this time (in an essay collected in *In Search of Our Mothers' Gardens*): ''We—young and bursting with fear and determination to change our world—thought beyond our fervid singing, of death.''

In the summer of 1962 Walker joined a group of Spelman students, funded by Atlanta churchwomen, who attended the World Youth Peace Festival in Helsinki, Finland. A member of the Cuban delegation gave Walker a copy of Fidel Castro's *History Will Absolve Me*, which Walker read, weeping as she recognized the familiar themes of oppression and resistance. For the rest of the summer she stayed with relatives in Boston and worked. The next summer she took a

train to join the March on Washington in August and heard Martin Luther King, Jr., deliver his great ''I Have a Dream'' speech.

Though racial issues permeated public life, few black authors were part of the academic curriculum at either of the colleges Walker attended. At Spelman in her sophomore year, Walker voraciously read Russian novels. The poets she read in college who influenced her style were Ovid, Catullus, Li Po, Emily Dickinson, William Carlos Williams, E. E. Cummings, and Robert Graves. During her senior year, she read Friedrich Nietzsche and Albert Camus, favorite philosophers of student activists dealing with the paradoxical isolation of working collectively for change. In the midst of the suicidal feelings she experienced that year, she learned that an elderly neighbor, Mr. Sweet, had died. Mr. Sweet played the guitar and sang the blues and was much beloved by children. Partly to celebrate her own survival of despair, Walker wrote a short story, ''To Hell With Dying,'' in which she fictionalized the love between Mr. Sweet and the children as a power that overcame death. Muriel Rukeyser sent the story to Langston Hughes, who published it in *Best Short Stories by Negro Writers: An Anthology from 1899 to the Present* (1967). When Walker met Hughes shortly before his death in 1967, she saw in him another Mr. Sweet:

Aging and battered, full of pain, but writing poetry, and laughing, too, and always making other people feel better. It was as if my love for one great old man down in the poor and beautiful and simple South had magically, in the new world of college and literature and poets and publishing and New York, led me to another.

Colorism marked Walker's social life at Sarah Lawrence; she and her African roommate dated white men, because black men preferred black women with lighter skin. She and Mel Leventhal lived together in New York while he was a law student, then married to legalize their bond before joining the civil rights struggle in Mississippi. Their interracial marriage was illegal in Mississippi, where miscegenation laws were still in place, and until their last year there, when integration had taken effect enough to reduce overt racial violence, Walker and Leventhal had to be careful where they appeared in public together. Black Power advocates, too, disapproved of mixed marriage, and Walker has said that during the 1960's black critics often judged her writing on the basis of her interracial "life-style" and not on its merits.

Leventhal handled school integration cases in Jackson and pressed suits against racist real estate agents. Walker went to Mississippi to "tirelessly observe it," to collect stories. As a technique for teaching black history to Head Start teachers with little education, Walker had the women write their autobiographies. Her search for black women writers arose from this experience. She had discovered the flaws in her Eurocentric college education and begun to fill in the gaps with the "college of reading," committed to preserving the heritage of black literature. Even in a course on black authors, taught by the poet Margaret Walker, that she audited at Jackson State, women authors were appended to the reading list like a footnote. But it was in this course that she learned of Zora Neale Hurston and set about correcting dismissive critical opinions of her.

In 1968 Walker and Leventhal marched at Martin Luther King's funeral. Shortly afterward Walker suffered a miscarriage. She became pregnant again the following year. Their reasons for wanting a child were not the best, Walker has written—partly curiosity, largely a wish to keep Leventhal from being drafted, since his draft board had rejected his application for conscientious objector status. Walker had written a preliminary version of her first novel in which the heroine, Ruth, was a civil rights lawyer. But while the civil rights movement was in the news every day, the lives of "ordinary" black people were still unobserved, and Walker shifted the focus of her novel to Ruth's forebears. Worried that motherhood would interfere with her writing, fearful for the safety of her husband, and anguished about the political worth of her writing and her pacifism, Walker again became depressed and suicidal. Her "salvation" during her last year in Jackson was a black woman psychiatrist, who helped her become aware "that I was holding myself responsible for the condition of black people in America" (*In Search of Our Mothers' Gardens*). Unable to act out violently, she wrote. Her art would probably change nothing, "And yet I felt it was the privilege of my life to observe and 'save' for the future some extraordinary lives."

Confronting the myths she had inherited about what motherhood should be, Walker worked through her guilt about leaving her small daughter in order to write, and came to celebrate motherhood. She began the five-year project of writing *Meridian,* in which maternal guilt is a major theme, along with pacifism and an overwhelming sense of responsibility for a community. In Boston, as a Radcliffe Institute Fellow, she shared an office with feminist scholar Patricia Meyer Spacks, who was researching women's creativity. Walker tried to make Spacks aware of black women writers, but Spacks's *The Female Imagination* (1975) dealt only with white writers.

Walker speculated in a 1979 essay that white feminists have difficulty thinking of black women as women because they prefer to avoid the guilt that accompanies an awareness of the racial barriers that grant their own children privileges denied to black women's children. Black women, on the other hand, were resisting feminism. At the Radcliffe Institute in 1973, Walker read her essay "In Search of Our Mothers' Gardens" and received a standing ovation. Later, at a panel discussion, she and June Jordan expressed their concern about the high rate of suicide among young women of color, who were under tremendous pressure to conform to different, conflicting social standards. One of the panelists insisted, "The responsibility of the black woman is to support the black man; *whatever* he does." Frustrated by the inadequacy of this response, Walker burst into tears. Though the Institute participants were not prepared to consider a feminist perspective on black women's lives, the experience confirmed Walker's commitment to recovering and interpreting the heritage of black women. In Zora Neale Hurston, Walker saw a woman whose nonconformity—her just being herself—was revolutionary, and whose work reflected racial health. Walker made a pilgrimage to Hurston's hometown, Eatonville, Florida, in 1973, found Hurston's unmarked grave in an overgrown field, and ordered an engraved tombstone commemorating "A Genius of the South."

Walker's father died in 1973. She wrote about standing aside, tearless, at his funeral while all but one of her siblings wept. Her relationship with her father improved spiritually after his death, she wrote in 1984, as her adult experiences helped her to understand him. One of these experiences was a trip to Cuba with a delegation of African American artists selected by the editors of *Black Scholar* and the Cuban Institute for Friendship Among People. There she met a man who reminded her of her father. Pablo Diaz, formerly a peasant, had become an official historian of the revolution, a change of social roles that was not possible for Willie Lee Walker despite his intelligence—but a transformation his daughter made, thereby placing a barrier between them.

Walker visited the South in 1976 to attend the March for Jobs in Atlanta. She had been living for two years in New York, where her husband continued to press civil rights suits against landlords and realtors. Since 1970, unemployment had led to the deterioration of black neighborhoods in Northern cities, and many people who had gone North in search of opportunities, including Walker's brothers and sisters, were mov-

ing back to the South. Though Walker enjoyed being close to "a multiethnic conglomerate of peacemakers" in New York, she admitted to her Southern friends that for the first time she feared other black people, whose communal bonds were shattered in Northern cities. There was a lull in political activism; the president and Congress seemed indifferent to the demands of poor and black people; and the FBI had revealed its extensive surveillance of the civil rights movement, which it was using to discredit Martin Luther King, Jr., years after his death. At the march, Walker's voice choked as she tried to sing the old rallying songs. The purest singing voice belonged to a young man who was obviously on drugs. She reflects in her essay "Lulls" (1977, in *In Search of Our Mothers' Gardens*): "What does this *mean,* I'd wondered, clutching my handbag tightly, annoyed at this reflex action even as I gazed with sorrow at his sensitive, though lost, dark face; aware it might not be long before I *knew.*"

Walker has written several essays about *The Color Purple.* In "Writing *The Color Purple*" (1982, in *In Search of Our Mothers' Gardens*) she remembers when the germ of the story came to her: she and her sister Ruth were discussing a love triangle. Ruth said, "And you know, one day The Wife asked The Other Woman for a pair of her drawers." This personal, sensual moment, rather than any grand public event, was to be the center of a historical novel. Obeying the demands of the characters that formed in her imagination, Walker moved west with her lover, Robert Allen (formerly an editor of *Black Scholar*), located a rustic house to rent, gave up travel engagements, and suspended her work for *Ms.* The sale of *You Can't Keep a Good Woman Down* provided enough money for her to live on for a year. When Walker's daughter, Rebecca, arrived after a stay with her father, "My characters adored her. They saw she spoke her mind in no uncertain terms and would fight back when attacked. . . . Celie . . . began to reappraise her own condition.

Rebecca gave her courage.'' Walker grieved for the characters on the day she finished the novel, but afterward she dreamed her ancestors visited her to thank her for writing it.

In 1984, when *The Color Purple* was selling rapidly, an Oakland mother asked the school system to ban it because she objected to her daughter's being exposed to it. Although she had not read the book, she believed that it was too sexually explicit and that it stereotyped blacks and degraded black people by using folk language. The integrated committee formed to study the book exonerated it, but the same questions arose again and again. A black women's magazine to which Walker had initially sent *The Color Purple* also objected to Celie's language. ''Black people don't talk like that,'' the editors insisted. In ''Coming in From the Cold'' (1984, in *Living by the Word*), a talk she presented to two writers' groups, Walker defended the realism of Celie's language and its importance to the raising up of the marginalized, almost lost histories of people like her.

For Celie's speech pattern and Celie's words reveal not only an intelligence that transforms illiterate speech into something that is, at times, very beautiful, as well as effective in conveying her sense of her world, but also what has been done to her by a racist and sexist system, and her intelligent blossoming as a human being despite her oppression demonstrates why her oppressors persist even today in trying to keep her down. For if and when Celie rises to her rightful, earned place in society across the planet, the world will be a different place, I can tell you.

The hostile reaction of some black men to the film *The Color Purple* saddened and disappointed Walker. Black men such as Malcolm X and Martin Luther King, Jr., had modeled the struggle for freedom, and yet many black men were unable to empathize with women's suffering under sexism. Celie's submissiveness is as much an illness as Mister's brutality, Walker wrote, and in the novel both are healed. The psychic illness of African Americans has to do with their inheriting attitudes and genes not only from black slaves but also from rapacious white slaveowners; Walker wrote of her efforts to come to terms with her own white great-great-grandfather. She charged critics of the film who attack its violent representations of black men with hypocrisy: What about films in which black people are CIA agents and spies, representatives of organizations that destabilize Third World countries? Of the critics' concern about what white people think of the film's representations of blacks, she writes in ''In the Closet of the Soul'' (1987, in *Living by the Word*): ''Since 'white people' are to a large extent responsible for so much of our worst behavior, which is really their behavior copied slavishly, it is an insult to black people's experience in America to make a pretense of caring what they think.''

Writing about her international travel during the 1980's, Walker drew connections between the themes of her work and social concerns elsewhere in the world. In 1983 she was part of a group of twelve American women writers who visited China. An editor in Shanghai told her *The Color Purple* was being translated into Chinese and remarked, ''It is a very *Chinese* story.'' Walker reflected:

What interests me is how many of the things I've written about women certainly do, in China, look Chinese: the impact of poverty, forced sex and childbearing, domination as a race *and* a caste . . . ; the struggle to affirm solidarity with women, as women, and the struggle to attain political, social, and economic equality with men.

In 1984, with Rebecca and Robert Allen, Walker visited Jamaica and made a pilgrimage to the memorial to Bob Marley in the tiny village of Nine Miles. She had discovered Marley's music while drafting the screenplay for the movie version of *The Color Purple* and considered him a brother. She writes in "Journey to Nine Miles" (1986, in *Living by the Word*): "Here was the radical peasant class, working-class consciousness that fearlessly denounced the Wasichus (the greedy and destructive) and did it with such grace you could dance to it." In 1987 they went to Bali. While noting in her journal the political violence in Bali's past, it was a Balinese chicken that became the subject of an essay, "Why Did the Balinese Chicken Cross the Road?" (1988, in *Living by the Word*), in which she considered vegetarianism and human kinship with animals. The Balinese chicken crossed the road, she wrote, "to get both of us to the other side"—to change human attitudes of domination over other creatures.

In the 1970's Walker had written to make white feminists aware of race and blacks aware of women's concerns; in the 1980's the crossovers among the political issues with which she dealt became yet more complex. Writing of nuclear proliferation in 1982, she quoted a long and thorough curse from the folklore Zora Neale Hurston collected. She speculated that at the heart of the resistance of people of color to the antinuclear movement is a desire for white men to be cosmically punished for their "crimes against humanity." Walker concludes her 1982 review of Helen Caldicott's book *Nuclear Madness* (in *In Search of Our Mothers' Gardens*): "The good news may be that Nature is phasing out the white man, but the bad news is that's who She thinks we all are." Walker's environmentalism converged with her interest in Native American folkways. In "Everything Is a Human Being" (1984, in *Living by the Word*), she wrote of the oppressed spirits of plants, animals, and the earth, using the Oglala Sioux word "Wasichu" to refer to their greedy exploiters. In a 1987 essay, "All the Bearded Irises of Life: Confessions of a Homospiritual" (in *Living by the Word*), Walker memorialized the spontaneity and outrageousness of the gay Castro district in San Francisco before the AIDS epidemic struck, drawing connections to other cultural losses: "So many cultures have died it is hard to contemplate the possible loss or dulling over of another one, or to accept the fact that once again those who can appreciate all the bearded irises of life will be visually, spiritually, and emotionally deprived."

In her notes for *The Temple of My Familiar* (the journal entry for June 17, 1987, in *Living by the Word*), Walker wrote of her sense of kinship, as an African American whose ancestors were slaves and peasants, with the poor of Latin America: *"I am Nicaraguan; I am Salvadorean; I am Grenadian; I am Caribbean; and I am Central American."* Introducing *Seeing Red*, a film on the history of the American Communist party in 1984 ("On Seeing Red," in *Living by the Word*), Walker spoke of "the parallel America we are constantly constructing alongside the one that is beginning to topple over, from its distortions and lies," revealing both Walker the Southern black writer and the great distance she has come. Her community is no longer an Eatonton, hidden off the roads, whose residents struggle against the boundaries of poverty and racism, but an interracial community of "alternative Americans" who share intimate journeys of self-discovery and global political concerns.

Walker's novels can be read as an ongoing narrative of an African American woman's emergence from the voiceless obscurity of poverty and racial and sexual victimization to become a reshaper of culture and tradition. It is a two-part narrative, with *The Color Purple* and *The Temple of My Familiar* revising the history told in *The Third Life of Grange Copeland* and *Meridian*.

In her first novel Walker adapted the realism and naturalism of such classic modern African American novels as Richard Wright's *Native Son*

(1940) and *Black Boy* (1945) in which a black man makes the northward flight that in slave narratives was a flight to freedom, only to find freedom elusive. Frustrated, disillusioned, and still powerless, he acts out violently. Walker turns this story inside out: the Northern sojourn is Grange Copeland's second life, the one about which we learn the least in her novel. While Grange, like Wright's Bigger Thomas, "kills" a white woman, Walker mitigates his responsibility for her death, in that he simply fails to help a distraught woman who rejects his help out of racism.

Thus Walker can treat this event not as an evil act on Grange's part but as a release of revolutionary anger enabling Grange to change. In his first life, trapped in poverty, he abuses his wife and son; in his third life, freed from self-loathing, he establishes a utopian community of two with his granddaughter, Ruth, which will release her from the cycle of violence and despair from which he came. Together, Grange and his son, Brownfield, Ruth's father, delineate a divided father figure much as Walker described her own father: one a nurturing enabler, the other lost to the values of the oppressive society. The cost to the older generation of black women of the events leading up to Ruth's emergence is enormous: her grandmother kills herself and her infant, her mother forsakes her education and career and is killed by Brownfield, and Grange can establish a haven for Ruth only by exploiting the "Blues woman," his second wife, Josie. Ruth will begin her new life in isolation, her "good father" Grange having sacrificed his life to save her from her "bad father."

By rejecting her first plan to make Ruth a civil rights attorney, Walker not only gained historical depth but also connected her first novel to the black fiction that was best known in the late 1960's, novels by men with male protagonists. Having reshaped the narrative she inherited to make room for a heroine, she continued the emergent woman's narrative with Meridian Hill. With a female protagonist, Walker had a new problem of literary revision to take up—What happens to a woman who bears a child? Traditional narratives of rape, seduction, or courtship silence their heroines through death or marriage. Meridian has a recurring dream: "She dreamed she was a character in a novel and that her existence presented an insoluble problem, one that would be solved only by her death at the end."

Walker avoids this end for Meridian by having her reject motherhood, stripping her femininity, and making her a worker for social change; but Meridian cannot unambivalently embrace the revolutionary violence that was healing to Grange Copeland. If the traditional female narrative is wrong for Meridian, the male-centered narrative Walker had devised is not a possibility either. Though Meridian emerges as an actor rather than a victim, she is isolated, like the young civil rights activists Walker recalls who favored Nietzschian and existentialist philosophy. *Meridian* critiques the relationships among black men and women but, as in *The Third Life of Grange Copeland*, the bonds between women are extremely troubled: sometimes sympathetic and supportive, often tortured with misunderstanding and harsh judgment. Meridian inherits her most cherished values—history and spirituality—from her father and refuses her mother's tradition.

By the time Walker wrote *The Color Purple*, the female communities to which she belonged had strengthened. Mainstream feminism was becoming increasingly aware of racial issues, and black women were creating feminist–womanist analyses of black literature and life that challenged the notion of uncritical loyalty to black men whatever the cost. Walker rewrote the history of obscure, "ordinary" black people during the time period covered in *The Third Life of Grange Copeland,* the era of her parents' generation. This time a female character was at the center, telling her own story, as if Walker were insisting that black women had always had a voice, one that only needed discovering by a sympathetic reader. The difficulty of making such a discovery, the risk that Celie's voice might have been lost forever, is structured into Walker's variation on the epistolary novel: most of the letters are addressed to God, not any person, and the ones addressed to people are long delayed from reaching their destinations.

Walker's solution to Celie's difficult early life is to create a female community for her, a fantasy solution through which Walker builds a utopia on contemporary feminist themes, affirming the folk traditions of black women while removing them from victimization. No longer the pathetic, exploited figure she was in *The Third Life of Grange Copeland*, the "Blues woman" has become the unconventional, "womanish" agent of other women's spiritual regeneration and self-fulfillment: Shug. While many critics have objected to this kind of fantasy solution, it seems entirely consistent with the practical artistry of a woman's everyday life that Walker describes in "In Search of Our Mothers' Gardens": intervening in history, she patches its broken walls with flowers.

This second version of Walker's narrative of the emergence of the African-American woman as a cultural maker is much more engaged with romance and less with realism than the first version. She describes *The Temple of My Familiar* as "a romance of the last 500,000 years." Like her earlier novels, it is episodic in structure, but it shows the new influence of such Latin American authors as Isabel Allende in its sprawling use of multiple narratives focused on personal lives with political events as a backdrop and its threading together of different systems of spiritual belief. The story of two couples saving their relationships by making unconventional adjustments serves as a frame for a collection of wondrous and exemplary tales that take place throughout the world, history, and prehistory. Among them are continuing news of the characters in *The Color Purple*. The greatest storyteller is Miss Lissie, an elderly black woman who dies in the course of the novel. Because she remembers all her past lives, Miss Lissie embodies the ancestry of the present generation. She even remembers being Adam—a memory that revises the creation myth, placing African women rather than white men at the center of cosmogony. Adam is the first white man, not the first human, and his matriarchal community expels him because of his mutated skin color.

Political action and social change for racial and sexual justice, important in Walker's first two novels, are insufficient alterations in the world, according to the later two novels. The very center and source of how we conceptualize humanity must be overturned. Immensely ambitious, *The Temple of My Familiar* has been regarded by reviewers as a mixed success. It will take time for critics to work out the elaborate literary issues that have been considered in relationship to Walker's earlier novels. For now, readers who value Walker as an author who created room in the traditions of narrative for voices unheard earlier because of sex, class, and race are likely to be disappointed by a novel near the end of which a sexual-spiritual breakthrough takes place in a San Francisco Bay area hot tub. But in the future, perhaps not.

The first African American woman to win a Pulitzer Prize, Alice Walker attracted the attention of high school and college curriculum planners. By 1984 *The Color Purple* was on required reading lists across the country. Students were enthusiastic about Walker's work but frustrated by the difficulty of finding secondary sources about her. Two academic teams of a librarian and a professor identified this problem at the same time, and each team assembled a book-length annotated bibliography on Walker. However, still many teachers are not aware that an extensive body of literary criticism has been written about Walker's work. The aim of this section is to direct teachers, librarians, and students to those resources and to give the reader an idea of the creative and scholarly context in which Walker has become recognized as a great American author.

For Walker's writing and the critical response up to early 1987, two bibliographies—Louis H. Pratt and Darnell D. Pratt's *Alice Malsenior Walker: An Annotated Bibliography* (1988) and Erma Davis Banks and Keith Byerman's *Alice Walker: An Annotated Bibliography, 1968–1986* (1989)—are equally useful research tools. The secondary history that they tell is a slice of the African American women's renaissance. It begins with a few positive reviews of Walker's first book, *Once,* a collection of poems she wrote during her last year in college. The reviewers note her sharp, minimalist style. More than a dozen popular and scholarly periodicals took note of Walker's first novel, *The Third Life of Grange Copeland.* The clear message of the novel is that African Americans must take responsibility for their own liberation. Walker's story concentrates on the torments her characters inflict on each other rather than the oppressiveness of white society; she focuses on the men's response to their powerlessness and despair by lashing out against their wives and children. The reviewers disagreed on whether the novel was true to life or bore "little resemblance to reality," and on whether political ideology impaired the book, but in 1971 critic Sam Cornish called it "one of the most important black novels we have." The first extensive interview with Walker appeared in *Publishers' Weekly* soon after the novel was published.

By 1972 Walker was one of very few African American women identified with women's liberation, and she took part in a forum on the women's movement published in *The American Scholar.* In 1973 her second volume of poetry, *Revolutionary Petunias,* was published. Reviewed less broadly than her novel, *Revolutionary Petunias* received more unqualified praise than *Once,* although one critic considered her poetry not as good as her fiction, a judgment that has been generally held. The simplicity and directness of Walker's poems do not inspire lengthy critical analysis, but many critics have used them to illuminate discussions of her themes. The poems in the second collection denounce black militancy and look to the past for a tradition of endurance and triumph. We remember our ancestors, the first poem's epigraph states, "because it is an easy thing to forget: that we are not the first to suffer, rebel, fight, love and die."

Biographical and bibliographical sketches of Walker began to appear in standard reference works in 1973, the year her first book of short stores, *In Love and Trouble: Stories of Black Women*, was published. The reviews show that both Walker's career and the literary renaissance of which she was a part were well under way. Two of the reviewers, Mary Helen Washington and Barbara Smith, are African American scholars who have since continued to write about Walker. In *Black World,* Washington associated Walker with other emerging African American women writers. Mel Watkins, a *New York Times* reviewer, connected Walker to Zora Neale Hurston, who became known as the precursor of current African American women writers. In *Ms.* (1974), Smith praised Walker's truth-telling about the inner lives of women for whom violence is an everyday occasion. Efforts to burst the myths surrounding black women's experience, Smith wrote, are "so pitifully rare in black, feminist, or American writing that each shred of truth about these experiences constitutes a breakthrough."

In 1974 and 1975 library and educational journals noted Walker's biography of Langston

Hughes for children. John O'Brien's *Interviews with Black Writers,* published in 1973, included a lengthy interview with Walker. Reconsiderations of Walker's work had begun to appear in academic books and journals. The first piece about Walker by Trudier Harris, another African American feminist scholar who would become one of her frequent critics, was a journal article on *The Third Life of Grange Copeland,* published in 1975. William Peden praised *In Love and Trouble* as a major collection in *The American Short Story: Continuity and Change, 1940–1975* (1975).

When Walker's second novel, *Meridian,* was published in 1976, it was reviewed in over two dozen major newspapers, magazines, and scholarly journals. Again, Walker's reviews were polarized. Some hailed the novel's power, while others criticized aspects of her technique: the uncentered episodic structure, the symbolism, the characterization, the ambiguous end. Two reviews noted a historical continuity between *The Third Life of Grange Copeland,* which closes with Grange's granddaughter, Ruth, escaping the cycle of poverty as the civil rights movement begins, and *Meridian.*

After *Meridian*'s publication several periodicals published interviews with Walker exploring the relationship between her writing and her life, and the reference series *Contemporary Literary Criticism* ran the first of many digests of the critical response to her work. In 1977 *Black American Literature Forum* published two scholarly essays on Walker, one by Trudier Harris exploring Walker's uses of folklore and one by Mary Helen Washington suggesting a thematic scheme for studying African American women writers along three historic dimensions: creative suspension, assimilation, and, since the late 1960's, emergence. Jeanne Noble contributed *Beautiful, Also, Are the Souls of My Black Sisters* (1978) to the project of creating a history of African American women. In the chapter on

"Black Women Writers of the New Renaissance," she identifies Walker's special contribution as exposing problems in male-female partnerships. Anne Z. Mickelson studied Walker's stories and *Meridian* in a cross-race context in her book *Reaching Out: Sensitivity and Order in Recent American Fiction by Women* (1979).

Walker published two books in 1979, an edition of Zora Neale Hurston's writings and a third collection of her own poetry, *Good Night, Willie Lee, I'll See You in the Morning.* Both were sparsely but appreciatively reviewed. In the *New York Times Book Review* Randall Kennedy noted that the Zora Neale Hurston edition marked the coincident emergence of feminist criticism and of sophisticated approaches to African American literature. The same convergence produced *Sturdy Black Bridges: Visions of Black Women in Literature* (1979), edited by Roseann P. Bell, Bettye J. Parker, and Beverly Guy-Sheftall, which includes two essays on Walker. In 1980 A. Robert Lee edited *Black Fiction: New Studies in the Afro-American Novel Since 1945,* with sections on *Meridian* and several of Walker's stories. That same year Barbara Christian, probably the first professor to teach a course solely on Alice Walker's writings, published *Black Women Novelists: The Development of a Tradition 1892–1976,* with a discussion of the movement from private experience to community in *The Third Life of Grange Copeland* and *Meridian.*

The second collection of Walker's short stories, *You Can't Keep a Good Woman Down,* was reviewed as widely as *Meridian* but with less enthusiasm. Some reviewers praised her use of fiction as social criticism while others disparaged her didacticism. To Barbara Christian the new stories represented black women's triumphant assertions, a positive complement to the despair of *In Love and Trouble.* More essays on Walker's earlier work appeared in 1981 and 1982 in academic periodicals and in books that added to the growing body of scholarly work on African

American literature, among them, Trudier Harris's *From Mammies to Militants: Domestics in Black American Literature* (1982), and *All the Women Are White, All the Blacks Are Men, but Some of Us Are Brave: Black Women's Studies,* edited by Gloria T. Hull, Patricia Bell Scott, and Barbara Smith (1982). Critics probed the philosophical issues in Walker's novels, the development of her characters in relationship to black folk tradition, and the remedies she saw for black women's victimization by black men. When *Black Scholar* surveyed African American writers in 1981, asking what the best books of the 1970's were, *The Third Life of Grange Copeland, Meridian, In Love and Trouble,* and *I Love Myself When I Am Laughing* . . . all appeared on the respondents' lists.

Several waves of newspaper and magazine coverage followed publication of *The Color Purple* in 1982: dozens of reviews, reports on Walker's winning several Georgia book prizes as well as the Pulitzer Prize and the American Book Award, and another round of considerations of the novel after the film was made. The reviewers generally agreed that Walker's greatest achievement in *The Color Purple* was creating Celie's voice—converting oral folk language into an expressive, poignant literary form that draws the reader into intimacy with Celie. Nettie's letters, written in standard English, provide parallels in colonialism and tribal tradition to the racism and sexism that oppress Celie, but many critics found Nettie's letters weak because of their less absorbing style.

A few criticisms of problems in structure and historical accuracy were raised even by enthusiastic reviewers. A small number of critics found fault with Walker again having given her fiction a clearly ideological orientation and with the lesbian relationship between Celie and Shug Avery, but far more praised the novel in the highest terms, finding in it a significance that made its stylistic flaws minor. Mel Watkins (1982) was one of several reviewers who saw Walker's previous theme of the estrangement and violence in the relationship between black men and women consolidated in *The Color Purple*. "No writer has made the intimate hurt of racism more palpable," Dinitia Smith wrote in *The Nation* (1982). In *The New York Review of Books* (1982), Robert Towers wrote that *The Color Purple* "exposes us to a way of life that for the most part existed beyond or below the reach of fiction, . . . the life of poor, rural Southern blacks as it was experienced by their womenfolk." To *Newsweek* reviewer Peter Prescott, *The Color Purple* was "an American novel of permanent importance" (1982).

In Search of Our Mothers' Gardens, published as reviews of *The Color Purple* continued to appear, gave critics new ways of discussing both Walker's writings and the literary movement of African American women. Many of the essays are about Walker's childhood and her development as an artist and activist. One reviewer characterized this book as an autobiography, and another pointed to its value in providing background for understanding *The Color Purple*. Reviewed almost as broadly as *The Color Purple, In Search of Our Mothers' Gardens* drew a similar mixed response, with some praising Walker's contribution to the uplifting of African American women and others criticizing her analysis of social issues as subjective and individualistic. The most influential parts of the book have been the title essay, first published in *Ms.* in 1974, and the opening epigraph, a definition of "womanist."

"In Search of Our Mothers' Gardens" finds a heritage of art, connected with everyday endurance and "a respect for the possibilities," in the quiltmaking and gardening of forebears whose creativity was otherwise suspended. The coined word "womanist" connects with this heritage. Walker defines the word first as "A black feminist or feminist of color," deriving it from "womanish," meaning willfully interested in knowing, taking charge, and acting beyond conventionally drawn boundaries. Second, Walker defines "womanish" as a woman who makes bonds, sexual or nonsexual, with other women but is "committed to survival and wholeness of entire people, male *and* female." Many critics quickly picked up the term "womanist," and Mary Helen Washington drew on *In Search of Our Mothers' Gardens* for an essay about African American women whose mothers nurtured their creativity that she published in *Mothering the Mind: Twelve Studies of Writers and Their Silent Partners* (1984), edited by Ruth Perry and Martine Watson Brownley.

Walker's third book of poems, *Horses Make the Landscape Look More Beautiful,* received only slight critical notice. Meanwhile, scholarly publications about Walker and mentions of her work proliferated as the attention *The Color Purple* was receiving stimulated broader interest in her earlier fiction, and as the body of African American literary criticism rapidly grew. Trudier Harris published another book in 1984, *Exorcising Blackness: Historical and Literary Lynching and Burning Rituals,* in which she placed *The Third Life of Grange Copeland* in the context of a tradition of black literature about the emasculating effects of racist exploitation. *Meridian's* themes were explored and connected to both feminist and African American themes: women's ambivalence about self-expression, complex relationships between mothers and daughters, the conflicting demands of radicalism and tradition, social action as a form of self-punishment, and a spirituality that transcends guilt and produces life-affirming political action.

Gloria Wade-Gayles wrote about character development in Walker's first two novels in *No Crystal Stair: Visions of Race and Sex in Black Women's Fiction* (1984). Thadious M. Davis traced a pattern linking contemporary intellectual concerns to the generationally structured experiences of rural, poor Southern blacks throughout Walker's writing in an essay included in *Women Writers of the Contemporary South* (1984), edited by Peggy Whitman Prenshaw. *Black Women Writers (1950–1980): A Critical Evaluation,* edited by Mari Evans, included essays on Walker by Bettye J. Parker-Smith and Barbara Christian. Claudia Tate published an interview with Walker among a series of interviews, *Black Women Writers at Work* (1983).

Review of *The Color Purple* continued to appear in 1984 as more in-depth essays explored the book's theology, its commonalities with the traditional American theme of the self's emergence from a dehumanized environment, and its introduction of healing through female bonding into the literature of domestic violence. Gloria Steinem included her 1982 profile of Walker for *Ms.* in her collected essays, *Outrageous Acts and Everyday Rebellions* (1984). Steinem's essay gives an overview of Walker's career and claims that her themes have universal significance, a level of meaning male critics deny to women and black writers alike. As if anticipating the public controversy that would erupt over the film of Walker's novel, Steinem writes that hurtful, negative reviews of Walker's work have come mostly from black men "reviewing their own conviction that black men should have everything white men have had, including dominance over women: or their fear that black women's truth-telling will be misused in a racist society."

Yet in 1984 a negative appraisal of *The Color Purple* came from a surprising source: Trudier Harris, one of the African American feminist critics most attentive to Walker's career. Harris found Steinem's article condescending and deplored the morality Steinem praised in Walker's novel: "What kind of morality is it that espouses that all human degradation is justified if the individual somehow survives all the tortures and ugliness heaped upon her?" The process of triumph depicted in the novel was unrealistic, resurrecting an old myth that black women survive by passive endurance, Harris wrote; and the novel's worst effect is that it gives fresh life to popular racist stereotypes of African American pathologies. Harris acknowledged that, because the book's unequaled popularity led to its being taken as the representative black woman's novel and Walker as a spokeswoman for all black women, "to complain about the novel is to commit treason against black women writers," but she believed that the uncritical reverence the novel received made complaint all the more necessary.

In 1985 and 1986 the popular media covered the filming of *The Color Purple,* its being nominated for eleven Oscars and winning none, and the recirculation of polarized opinions about both the novel and the film. At the same time new reviews of Walker's earlier books appeared and the scholarly literature grew. W. Lawrence Hogue included an essay on *The Third Life of Grange Copeland* as a feminist discourse in his book *Discourse and the Other: The Production of the African-American Text* (1986). *Black American Literature Forum* published articles on *The Third Life of Grange Copeland* and *Meridian.* Barbara Christian discussed *Meridian* and *In Love and Trouble* in her book *Black Feminist Criticism: Perspectives on Black Women Writers* (1985). Dozens of articles on *The Color Purple* appeared in scholarly books and journals, some taking up the public controversy, while others dealt with fictional technique and structure. A new journal, *Catalyst,* published three essays defending *The Color Purple* in its first issue (1986). Trudier Harris held to her opinion that Celie reincarnated old stereotypes in an essay for *Studies in American Fiction* (1986).

Philip M. Royster in *Black American Literature Forum* (1986), and George Stade in *Partisan Review* (1985), launched scathing attacks on Walker, while Richard Wesley wrote an article for *Ms.* (1986) objecting to "tribunals" against black women writers. In *English Journal* (1985)

Pepper Worthington offered high school English teachers answers they could give to parents who objected to the novel. In *Contemporary American Women Writers* (1985), edited by Catherine Rainwater and W. J. Scheick, Liz Fifer defended Nettie's letters by saying the contrast between Celie's and Nettie's diction increases the reader's appreciation of Celie's cultural predicament. In her book *Women Writing About Men* (1986), Jane Miller pointed out that *The Color Purple* offers men the possibility of redemption. Houston A. Baker, Jr., and Charlotte Pierce-Baker suggested in *Southern Review* that Walker's story about a family's quilts, "Everyday Use," could serve as an introduction to *The Color Purple:* Walker as a novelist worked like a quiltmaker, using scraps of marginal humanity in a process of "sacred creation" that gives function a higher value than art. Many critics discussed the novels' deconstruction of patriarchy and Walker's commitment to the cultural heritage of black women.

More books of scholarship and criticism drawing connections among the writings of African American women appeared in 1985 and 1986. Susan Willis discussed community, journey, and sensuality in the work of Walker and three other African American novelists in an essay for *Making a Difference: Feminist Literary Criticism* (1985), edited by Gayle Green and Coppelia Kahn. Keith E. Byerman discussed Walker's mixture of folklore and ideology in a chapter of his book *Fingering the Jagged Grain: Tradition and Form in Recent Black Fiction* (1985). Marjorie Pryse and Hortense J. Spillers included four essays that deal with Walker's work in an anthology of criticism, *Conjuring: Black Women, Fiction, and Literary Tradition* (1985).

The coverage of the bibliographic volumes on Walker by Pratt and Pratt and by Banks and Byerman ends in mid 1987, as African American scholarship and black feminist criticism increased in richness, sophistication, and productivity, having become established fields of study with their own sets of definitions and terms of discussion. At the same time scholars worked at rethinking the nature of the American tradition, integrating the study of American literature to include writers who had been omitted because of race and gender. In recent years those who have written about Walker have been black and white, female and male; the works of African American women writers are treated less and less as a special interest of African American critics and more as an important part of the diversity of contemporary culture.

Walker remains a controversial figure; but despite some critics' continuing objections to her portrayals of black men and other aspects of her writing, Walker's place as a central figure in American literature is secure. Much of the most complex and interesting criticism about her works has been written since 1987. She also has published two books since then, *Living by the Word* and *The Temple of My Familiar*. Little other than reviews has been written about these books; scholarly criticism will absorb them over the next few years.

J. Charles Washington helped to put to rest the controversy over Walker's portraits of black men with an essay on positive black male images in her short stories, published in *Obsidian* (1988). Washington recapitulates Trudier Harris's response to Gloria Steinem's essay and other objections to Walker's work, and says that the negative critics ignore positive images of men in her fiction. "Positive" should not mean "perfect" but "capable of growth and change," Washington insists, and such men exist throughout Walker's fiction. He points out that patriarchal definitions of gender roles limit both men and women in Walker's stories. Committed to a practical, politically functional art, Walker concentrates on the most oppressed group, African American women, which leaves her less time and energy for the common causes of men and women, Washington explains.

At the same time Washington's essay appeared, *Modern Fiction Studies* published a special issue on modern black fiction with essays on *Meridian* and *The Color Purple*, and *Black American Literature Forum* published essays on *The Third Life of Grange Copeland* and *The Color Purple*. In *The Hollins Critic* (October 1988) James Robert Saunders compared Zora Neale Hurston's *Their Eyes Were Watching God* and Walker's *The Color Purple*—a comparison critics have made again and again from various points of view, always with new insights. *Callaloo* published a special Alice Walker section in its second 1989 issue, with a selected bibliography following four essays, including one by Jacqueline Bobo on the controversy over the film, and one each on *The Third Life of Grange Copeland*, *Meridian*, and some of the stories.

The single most useful new book for those researching criticism on Walker is *Alice Walker*, published by Chelsea House in 1989. Edited by Harold Bloom, the selection emphasizes literary inheritance and family issues. Several of the essays have not been published elsewhere; among them is an assessment of *The Color Purple* by Bell Hooks. According to Hooks, the magic of the novel is that it fulfills important wishes of our time by skillfully combining fantasy and realism. Radical didacticism gives the book depth, but the fantasy resolutions arise from a conservative "narrative universe," shunting aside rather than resolving the contradictions between revolutionary change and middle-class values. Referring to *In Search of Our Mothers' Gardens*, Hooks points out that Walker has warned against fantasy resolutions but that she nevertheless grants them in her own fiction, desiring better conditions for her oppressed creations. "I liberated Celie from her own history," Walker says of the utopian aspects of *The Color Purple*; "I wanted her to be happy."

New books on African American women writers and black feminism are continually appearing. In *Specifying: Black Women Writing the American Experience* (1987), Susan Willis shows how several writers use black folk traditions of storytelling in their novels—for example, the brief anecdotes from which Walker's novels are built follow what Willis calls the "four-page formula," different from postmodern fragmentation in that each anecdote has its own closure. Specifying is a form of storytelling in which the speaker confronts and criticizes someone, calling him or her names as the community witnesses. To Willis, the confrontational approach to history taken by Walker and other black women novelists is a kind of specifying.

In *Black Feminist Criticism and Critical Theory* (1988), edited by Joe Weixlmann and Houston A. Baker, Jr., Missy Dehn Kubitschek gives *The Color Purple* as an example of an African American author's writing realistically about rape, whereas most Euro-American authors have used rape as a symbol. Abena P. B. Busia, writing about novels of the African diaspora, refers to "In Search of Our Mothers' Gardens" and *The Color Purple* in discussing the centrality of art of any kind to women's self-preservation under conditions of exile and obscurity. *Race, Gender, and Desire: Narrative Strategies in the Fiction of Toni Cade Bambara, Toni Morrison, and Alice Walker* (1989), by Elliott Butler-Evans, offers complex analysis of the ways Walker enters, displaces, and disrupts black history in order to create room for the empowerment of women in her first three novels. In *Inspiriting Influences: Tradition, Revision, and African-American Women's Novels* (1989), Michael Awkward describes "In Search of Our Mothers' Gardens" as the most influential early effort to connect pieces of African American women's expressive tradition. He emphasizes Zora Neale Hurston's importance as an "inspiriting" influence providing current black women authors with a sense of le-

gitimacy, and describes *The Color Purple* as Walker's repayment of a literary debt to Hurston.

Bernard W. Bell's *The Afro-American Novel and Its Tradition* (1987) is a comprehensive history and categorization of the types of novels that African American authors have written. Bell credits Walker with having spearheaded the reassessment of Zora Neale Hurston's literary significance and uses her term "womanism" in describing the primary concerns of black women novelists: the influences of racism, classism, and sexism on the development of love, power, autonomy, creativity, manhood, and womanhood in the black family and community. He classifies Walker as a neorealist, continuing the traditions of realism but displacing the individual ambivalence and the sense of social absurdity associated with realism to create a new order based on self-determination, community, and human rights. Summarizing *The Third Life of Grange Copeland, Meridian,* and *The Color Purple,* Bell points out that a new social order is achieved only in the last novel, where critical realism is tailored to folk romance in order to fit the themes of contemporary black feminism into a historical novel.

An essay on Walker and Hurston by Henry Louis Gates, Jr., is included in his *The Signifying Monkey* (1988). Gates's close analysis of the ways Walker adopted and revised Hurston's narrative technique leads him to describe the writing of *The Color Purple* as a loving act of "signifying" on Hurston, or of "literary bonding quite unlike anything that has ever happened within the Afro-American tradition." Shug Avery, the "blues woman" who helps Celie find sexual fulfillment as well as a religious faith free of a white male God, stands in for Hurston in Walker's novel, according to Gates. He sees *The Color Purple* as a breakthrough in contemporary African American fiction, in that Walker turns to black literature for a foundation of both form and content rather than putting black content into a form borrowed from white literary tradition.

Cushing Strout places a discussion of *Meridian* at the end of a book based on the reading lists he uses in teaching American literature, *Making American Tradition: Visions and Revisions from Ben Franklin to Alice Walker* (1990). Throughout the American tradition, the social condition of blacks is a test of the principles of freedom and equality, according to Strout, and he sees *Meridian*'s ending as reflecting the fear that those ideals will not be realized. Strout begins this essay with one of the first scholarly discussions of *Living by the Word*, which he uses to create a composite portrait of Walker—a portrait that might be largely unrecognizable to anyone who knew only her work up to *The Color Purple* and who categorized Walker strictly as a Southern rural black woman writer, though it is quite consistent with the many-sided point of view in *The Temple of My Familiar*. Besides her well-known feminism-womanism, Walker's current themes are environmentalism, socialism, counterculture, vegetarianism, and New Age occultism. Her politics are sometimes hyperbolic, sometimes sentimental, Strout says, but are strengthened by humor, self-irony, a willingness to notice contradictions inherent in being politically correct, and a deep feeling for tradition. Connecting the "new" Alice Walker with the author of *Meridian*, Strout points out that Walker has always shown more interest in black American than in black African cultural ancestry, and that this heritage is multiracial—including Native Americans, white slaveowners, and others, in addition to the African exiles.

Selected Bibliography

WORKS OF ALICE WALKER

POETRY

Once: Poems. New York: Harcourt, Brace & World. 1968.

Revolutionary Petunias and Other Poems. New York: Harcourt Brace Jovanovich, 1973.

Good Night, Willie Lee, I'll See You in the Morning. New York: Dial, 1979.

Horses Make a Landscape Look More Beautiful. San Diego: Harcourt Brace Jovanovich, 1984.

FICTION

The Third Life of Grange Copeland. New York: Harcourt Brace Jovanovich, 1970.

In Love and Trouble: Stories of Black Women. New York: Harcourt Brace Jovanovich, 1973.

Meridian. New York: Harcourt Brace Jovanovich, 1976.

Your Can't Keep a Good Woman Down: Stories. New York: Harcourt Brace Jovanovich, 1981.

The Color Purple. New York: Harcourt Brace Jovanovich, 1982.

The Temple of My Familiar. San Diego: Harcourt Brace Jovanovich, 1989.

CHILDREN'S LITERATURE

Langston Hughes, American Poet. Illustrated by Don Miller. New York: Crowell, 1974.

EDITED ANTHOLOGY

I Love Myself When I Am Laughing. . . . and Then Again When I Am Looking Mean and Impressive: A Zora Neale Hurston Reader. Old Westbury, N.Y.: Feminist Press, 1979.

ESSAYS

In Search of Our Mothers' Gardens: Womanist Prose. San Diego: Harcourt Brace Jovanovich, 1983.

Living by the Word: Selected Writings, 1973–1987. San Diego: Harcourt Brace Jovanovich, 1988.

BIOGRAPHICAL AND CRITICAL STUDIES

Allen, Robert. "Best Books of the '70s." *Black Scholar*, March–April 1981, p. 80.

Awkward, Michael. *Inspiriting Influences: Tradition, Revision, and African-American Women's Novels*. New York: Columbia University Press, 1989.

Babb, Valerie. *"The Color Purple:* Writing to Undo What Writing Has Done." *Phylon*, 47:107–116 (June 1986).

Baker, Houston A., Jr., and Charlotte Pierce-Baker. "Patches: Quilts and Community in Alice Walker's 'Everyday Use.' " *Southern Review*, n.s. 21:706–720 (Summer 1985).

Bannon, Barbara A. "Authors and Editors." *Publishers' Weekly*, August 31, 1970, pp. 195–197.

Bell, Bernard W. *The Afro-American Novel and Its Tradition*. Amherst: University of Massachusetts Press, 1987.

Bell, Roseann P., Bettye J. Parker, and Beverly Guy-Sheftall, eds. *Sturdy Black Bridges: Visions of Black Women in Literature*. Garden City, N.Y.: Anchor/Doubleday, 1979.

Berlant, Lauren. "Race, Gender, and Nation in *The Color Purple.*" *Critical Inquiry*, 14:831–859 (Summer 1988).

Bloom, Harold, Ed. *Alice Walker*. New York: Chelsea House, 1989. Includes essay by Bell Hooks.

Bobo, Jacqueline. *"The Color Purple:* Black Women as Cultural Readers." in *Female Spectators: Looking at Film and Television*. Edited by E. Deirdre Pribram. London and New York: Verso, 1988. Pp. 90–109.

———.*The Color Purple:* Black Women's Responses." *Jump Cut*, 33:43–51 (February 1988).

———. "Sifting Through the Controversy: Reading *The Color Purple.*" *Callaloo*, 12, no. 2:332–342 (1989).

Brown, Joseph A., S. J." 'All Saints Should Walk Away': The Mystical Pilgrimage of Meridian." *Callaloo*, 12, no. 2:310–320 (Spring 1989).

Burnett, Zaron W. *"The Color Purple:* Personal Reaction." *Catalyst*, 1:43–44 (Fall 1986).

Busia, Abena P. B. "Words Whispered over Voids: A Context for Black Women's Rebellious Voices in the Novel of the African Diaspora." In *Black Feminist Criticism and Critical Theory*. Edited by

Joe Weixlmann and Houston A. Baker, Jr. Greenwood, Fla.: Penkeville, 1988. Pp. 1–42.

Butler, Robert James. "Making a Way out of No Way: The Open Journey in Alice Walker's *The Third Life of Grange Copeland.*" *Black American Literature Forum*, 22:65–79 (Spring 1988).

Butler-Evans, Elliott. *Race, Gender, and Desire: Narrative Strategies in the Fiction of Toni Cade Bambara, Toni Morrison, and Alice Walker*. Philadelphia: Temple University Press, 1989.

Byerman, Keith, "Women's Blues: The Fiction of Toni Cade Bambara and Alice Walker." In his *Fingering the Jagged Grain: Tradition and Form in Recent Black Fiction*. Athens: University of Georgia Press, 1985. Pp.129–170.

Christian, Barbara. *Black Women Novelists: The Development of a Tradition, 1892–1976*. Westport, Conn.: Greenwood Press, 1980.

———. *Black Feminist Criticism: Perspectives on Black Women Writers*. New York: Pergamon Press, 1985.

Cornish, Sam. "Review of *The Third Life of Grange Copeland.*" *Essence*, April 1971, p. 2.

Davis, Thadious, "Alice Walker's Celebration of Self in Southern Generations." *Southern Quarterly*, 21:39–53 (Summer 1983).

Early, Gerald. *"The Color Purple* as Everybody's Protest Art." *Antioch Review*, 44:261–275 (Summer 1986).

Erickson, Peter. " 'Cast Out Alone/To Heal/And Recreate Ourselves.' " Family-Based Identity in the Work of Alice Walker." *CLA Journal*, 23:71–94 (September 1979).

Evans, Mari, ed. *Black Women Writers (1950–1980): A Critical Evaluation*. New York: Anchor/ Doubleday, 1984. Includes essays by Bettye J. Parker-Smith and Barbara Christian.

Fifer, Elizabeth, "Alice Walker: "The Dialect & Letters of *The Color Purple.*" In *Contemporary American Women Writers: Narrative Strategies*. Edited by Catherine Rainwater and William J. Scheick. Lexington: University Press of Kentucky, 1985. Pp. 155–171.

Gates, Henry Louis, Jr. "Color Me Zora: Alice Walker's (Re)Writing of the Speakerly Text." In his *The Signifying Monkey: A Theory of Afro-American Literary Criticism*. New York: Oxford University Press, 1988. Pp. 239–258.

Harris, Jessica, "An Interview with Alice Walker." *Essence*. July 1976, p. 33.

Harris, Trudier. "Violence in *The Third Life of Grange Copeland.*" *CLA Journal*, 19:238–247 (December 1975).

———. "Folklore in the Fiction of Alice Walker: A Perpetuation of Historical and Literary Traditions." *Black American Literature Forum*, 11:3–8 (Spring 1977).

———. *From Mammies to Militants: Domestics in Black American Literature*. Philadelphia: Temple University Press, 1982.

———. *Exorcising Blackness: Historical and Literary Lynching and Burning Rituals*. Bloomington: Indiana University Press, 1984.

———. "On *The Color Purple*, Stereotypes, and Silence." *Black American Literature Forum*, 18:155–161 (Winter 1984).

———. "From Victimization to Free Enterprise: Alice Walker's *The Color Purple.*" *Studies in American Fiction*, 14:1–17 (Spring 1986).

Hogue, W. Lawrence. "History, the Feminist Discourse, and Alice Walker's *The Third Life of Grange Copeland.*" *MELUS* 12:45–62 (Summer 1985).

Hull, Gloria T., Patricia Bell Scott, and Barbara Smith, eds. *All the Women Are White, All the Blacks Are Men, but Some of Us Are Brave: Black Women's Studies*. Old Westbury, N.Y.: Feminist Press, 1982.

Kennedy, Randall. "Looking for Zora." *New York Times Book Review*. December 30, 1979, pp. 8, 17.

Kubitschek, Missy Dehn. "Subjugated Knowledge: Toward a Feminist Exploration of Rape in African-American Fiction." In *Black Feminist Criticism and Critical Theory*. Edited by Joe Weixlmann and Houston A. Baker, Jr. Greenwood, Fla.: Penkeville, 1988. Pp. 43–56.

Lee, A. Robert, ed. *Black Fiction: New Studies in the Afro-American Novel Since 1945*. London: Vision, 1980.

McDowell, Deborah E. " 'The Changing Same': Generational Connections and Black Women Novelists." *New Literary History*, 18:281–302 (Winter 1987).

Mickelson, Anne Z. *Reaching Out: Sensitivity and Order in Recent American Fiction by Women*. Metuchen, N.J.: Scarecrow Press, 1979.

Miller, Jane. *Women Writing about Men*. London: Virago, 1986.

Mullen, Harryette. "Daughters in Search of Mothers or a Girl Child in a Family of Men." *Catalyst*, 1:45–49 (Fall 1986).

Noble, Jeanne. "Black Women Writers of the New Renaissance." In her *Beautiful, Also, Are the Souls of My Black Sisters: A History of the Black Woman in America*. Englewood Cliffs, N.J.: Prentice-Hall, 1978.

O'Brien, John. "Alice Walker." In *Interviews with Black Writers*. Edited by John O'Brien. New York: Liveright, 1973. Pp. 185–212. Reprinted in part as "From an Interview." In Alice Walker, *In Search of Our Mothers' Gardens*.

Peden, William. "The Black Explosion: 'I Mean, with All things Considered. The Field Is Opening up More and More. . . Ya Know—Bein' Black and Meanin' It. We're in Vogue These Days.' " In his *The American Short Story: Continuity and Change, 1940–1975*. Boston: Houghton Mifflin, 1975.

Prenshaw, Peggy Whitman, ed. *Women Writers of the Contemporary South*. Oxford: University Press of Mississippi, 1984.

Prescott, Peter S. "A Long Road to Liberation." *Newsweek*, June 21, 1982, pp. 67–68.

Pryse, Marjorie, and Hortense J. Spillers, eds. *Conjuring: Black Women, Fiction, and Literary Tradition*. Bloomington: Indiana University Press, 1985.

Ross, Daniel W. "Celie in the Looking Glass: The Desire for Selfhood in *The Color Purple.*" *Modern Fiction Studies*, 34:69–84 (Spring 1988).

Royster, Philip M. "In Search of Our Fathers' Arms: Alice Walker's Persona of the Alienated Darling." *Black American Literature Forum*, 20:347–370 (Winter 1986).

Sadoff, Diane F. "Black Matrilineage: The Case of Alice Walker and Zora Neale Hurston." *Signs*, 11:4–26 (Autumn 1985).

Saunders, James Robert. "Womanism as the Key to Understanding Zora Neale Hurston's *Their Eyes Were Watching God* and Alice Walker's *The Color Purple.*" *The Hollins Critic*, 25:1–11 (October 1988).

Smith, Barbara. "The Souls of Black Women." *Ms.*, February 1974, pp. 42–43, 78.

Smith, Dinitia. " 'Celie, You a Tree.' " *The Nation*. September 4, 1982, p. 181–183.

Stade, George. "Womanist Fiction and Male Characters." *Partisan Review*, 52, no. 3:264–270 (1985).

Steinem, Gloria. "Do You Know This Woman? She Knows You—A Profile of Alice Walker." *Ms.*,

June 1982, pp. 35, 37, 89–94. Reprinted in her *Outrageous Acts and Everyday Rebellions*. New York: Holt, Rinehart and Winston, 1983. p. 259–275.

Strout, Cushing. *Making American Tradition: Visions and Revisions from Ben Franklin To Alice Walker*. New Brunswick, N.J.: Rutgers University Press, 1990.

Tate, Claudia. "Alice Walker." In her *Black Women Writers at Work*. New York: Continuum, 1983. Pp. 175–187.

Towers, Robert. "Good Men Are Hard to Find." *New York Review of Books*. August 12, 1982, pp. 35–36.

Tucker, Lindsey. "Alice Walker's *The Color Purple:* Emergent Woman, Emergent Text." *Black American Literature Forum,* 22:81–95 (Spring 1988).

Wade-Gayles, Gloria. *No Crystal Stair: Visions of Race and Sex in Black Women's Fiction*. New York: Pilgrim Press, 1984. Pp. 102–114.

———. "Anatomy of an Error: *The Color Purple* Controversy." *Catalyst,* 1:50–53 (Fall 1986).

Washington, J. Charles. "Positive Black Male Images in Alice Walker's Fiction." *Obsidian II,* 3:23–48 (Spring 1988).

Washington, Mary Helen. "Teaching *Black-Eyed Susans:* An Approach to the Study of Black Women Writers." *Black American Literature Forum,* 11:20–24 (Spring 1977).

———. "An Essay on Alice Walker." In *Sturdy Black Bridges: Visions of Black Women in Literature*. Edited by Roseann P. Bell, Bettye J. Parker, and Beverly Guy-Sheftall. Garden City, N.Y.: Anchor/Doubleday, 1979. Pp. 133–149.

———. "I Sign My Mother's Name: Alice Walker, Dorothy West. Paule Marshall." In *Mothering the Mind: Twelve Studies of Writers and Their Silent Partners*. Edited by Ruth Perry and Martine Watson Brownley. New York: Holmes & Meier, 1984. Pp. 142–163.

Watkins, Mel. "In Love and Trouble." *New York times Book Review*. March 17, 1974, p. 40.

———. "Some Letters Went to God." *New York Times Book Review,* July 25, 1982, p. 7.

Wesley, Richard. *"The Color Purple* Debate: Reading Between the Lines." *Ms.,* September 1986, pp. 62, 90–92.

Weston, Ruth D. "Black Woman Writers: Taking a Critical Perspective." In *Making a Difference: Feminist Literary Criticism*. Edited by Gayle Greene and Coppelia Kahn. London and New York: Methuen, 1985. Pp. 211–231.

———. *Specifying: Black Women Writing the American Experience*. Madison: University of Wisconsin Press, 1987.

Worthington, Pepper. "Writing a Rationale for a Controversial Common Reading Book: Alice Walker's *The Color Purple*." *English Journal,* 74:48–52 (January 1985).

BIBLIOGRAPHIES

Banks, Erma Davis, and Keith Byerman. *Alice Walker, an Annotated Bibliography*. New York: Garland, 1989.

Byerman, Keith, and Erma Davis Banks. "Alice Walker: A Selected Bibliography, 1968–1988." *Callaloo,* 12, no. 2:343–345 (1989).

Kirschner, Susan. "Alice Walker's Nonfictional Prose: A Checklist, 1966–1984." *Black American Literature Forum,* 18:162–163 (Winter 1984).

Pratt, Louis H., and Darnell D. Pratt. *Alice Malsenior Walker: An Annotated Bibliography, 1968–1986*. Westport, Conn.: Meckler, 1988.

Werner, Craig. "Alice Walker." In *Black American Women Novelists: An Annotated Bibliography*. Pasadena, Calif.: Salem Press, 1989. Pp. 238–258.

—JANET GRAY

Richard Wilbur

1921–

Richard Wilbur's place among preeminent contemporary American poets is uncontested. And yet, despite broad confirmations (the poet laureateship, the Pulitzer and Bollingen prizes, among many other awards), this place has been somewhat more narrowly delimited than it should have been. This study will therefore attempt to augment the standard perception of Wilbur as the quintessentially refined New Critical poet whose musical and metaphorical wizardry has conjured some of the most dazzling yet suavely balanced and self-reconciliatory lyric poems of our time. During a mid century less given to contained forms of serious affirmation than to a barbarous history and its irregular songs of hurt or counterprovocation, Wilbur's art has been identified as fair-minded and masterful, a white magic devoted more to restorative and celebratory acts than to the darker perturbations of the agonized or the wild at heart. Wilbur has been regarded by some as lacking a "saving vulgarity"—too much Prospero, too little Caliban. While recognizing a degree of accuracy in that definition, one should also be alive to what challenges even the most admiring of its terms. Not only should one see how elements of Wilbur's later work have cracked the definition that had crystallized around his first two or three books; one should read the early work itself as having addressed more powerful incongruities than those which (primarily New Critical) readers saw as having been so gracefully resolved.

Slightly younger than the first generation of poets whose work began to be published during or after World War II—John Berryman, Randall Jarrell, Elizabeth Bishop, and Robert Lowell were born between 1911 and 1919—Wilbur is one of a larger group born during the 1920's: among them are Howard Nemerov, Anthony Hecht, Louis Simpson, Denise Levertov, James Dickey, Donald Justice, James Merrill, W. D. Snodgrass, Allen Ginsberg, A. R. Ammons, James Wright, John Ashbery, W. S. Merwin, Galway Kinnell, Philip Levine, John Hollander, and Adrienne Rich. Of all these postwar writers, he has hewn most closely and consistently to the grain of one of the most dominant kinds of poetry to emerge in the wake of the earlier modernists. Wilbur wrote in "On My Own Work" (1966, collected in *Responses: Prose Pieces 1953–1976*):

Most American poets of my generation were taught to admire the English Metaphysical poets of the seventeenth century and such contemporary masters of irony as John Crowe Ransom. We were led by our teachers and by the critics whom we read to feel that the most adequate and convincing poetry is that which accommodates mixed feelings, clashing ideas, and incongruous images. Poetry could not be honest, we thought, unless it began by acknowledging the full discordancy of modern life and consciousness. I still believe that to be a true view of poetry.

Wilbur was referring to the tenets of New Criticism, developed after T. S. Eliot by such theorists and practitioners as I. A. Richards, John Crowe Ransom, Alan Tate, Robert Penn Warren, and Cleanth Brooks. Less revolutionary than the modernists, the New Critics shrank from what they viewed as certain excesses in the ambitions of modernism, associated as these were with the harsh polarities of totalitarianism and chaos. More interested in forms of provisional restabilization rather than of further ground breaking or system building, New Critics also were initially skeptical about the modernist long poem, as well as about the poet's use of grand cultural or political designs. Hence they held a preference for brief, tense, formally balanced lyrics that stressed the artifice of textual autonomy and inner symmetries rather than overt biographical or historical referents. If the latter were evoked, they appeared less in their own "right" than as elements in a rhetorical composition; and if there were potentially dramatic or dynamic forces at work, these were carefully wrought into the counterpoise of art: Wilbur said in his "The Genie in the Bottle" (published in John Ciardi's *Mid-Century American Poets*):

The use of strict poetic forms, traditional or invented, is like the use of framing and composition in painting: both serve to limit the work of art, and to declare its artificiality: they say, "This is not the world, but a pattern imposed upon the world or found in it; this is a partial and provisional attempt to establish relations between things."

There had, of course, been other schools of postwar American poetry, one of the most notable being that derived from Ezra Pound, William Carlos Williams (whom Wilbur has consistently admired), and Charles Olson. And, following the late 1950's, most of Wilbur's initially likeminded contemporaries broke from the enclosures of New Criticism toward more open poetic forms, or toward the admission (in some cases confession) of apparently less artificial and less controllable material, whether autobiographical, historical, mythic, or surreal. Against these departures, Wilbur's career appears less volatile; and the equable tone of his work has reinforced the appearance of stable consistency, as if the entire oeuvre were itself a New Critical poem. Yet beneath its composed surfaces, Wilbur's poetry has, despite great coherence, developed and altered considerably. And in many respects these developments have underscored the least tractable (and most valuable) features of the earlier work—features that, like the subsequent developments, have seldom been fully measured either by Wilbur's few detractors or by many of his insightful admirers. By exploring the entire range of his work one can hope to gain a better sense not only of the superb array of "bottles," to use his metaphor for craft and container, but also of the often dark and uncanny genie moving within and between them.

Richard Wilbur was born in New York City on March 1, 1921. His mother, Helen Purdy Wilbur, "came of a Baltimore family with a tradition of newspaper-editing"—hence Wilbur's inherited commonsensical allegiance to pragmatic, communicative language, an allegiance that would long outlast his editorship of *The Amherst Student*; his father, Lawrence L. Wilbur, was a portrait painter—hence Wilbur's "busy eye" and painterly sense of composition. In an autobiographical sketch (1974, in *Conversations with Richard Wilbur*), Wilbur told his interviewer, Philip Dacey:

I am not yet feeble enough to be interested in genealogy, but it may as well be said that I am of the 11th generation from Samuel Wildbore, and am descended from settlers of Massachusetts and Rhode Island. The fact does not seem definitive to me. . . . In a time of ethnic and racial self-consciousness, it is of no particular advantage to a writer that he belongs to the Anglo-Saxon minority, which is now felt to lack decided characteristics, and about which, significantly, no jokes are told. Robert Lowell is the only writer of recent years to make much use of such ancestry, and it is by and large people of other provenance who now claim to represent some version of "the American experience."

Beyond Wilbur's blend of modesty and assurance, the statement points to his lack of the ancestral or ethnic agons by which many American poets most readily weld their private psyches to that of the nation. This accounts for the relative absence of inflation in Wilbur's work—the language and tone are those of a biographically reticent New Englander, whose half-rueful centrality neutralizes the means for various self-amplifications while also depriving him of the outsider's (or, in Lowell's case, rebellious insider's) leverage on which much poetry has depended for its contestatory weight or edge.

In addition, one may perceive an ancestral element in Wilbur's apparent impartiality and ethnically unburdened buoyancy as a poet, as well as in his uninflected access to the standard English that has flowed with deliberate clarity since Tudor times, passing through such poets as Robert Herrick and John Dryden, eventually to reach A. E. Housman and Philip Larkin. To this, Wilbur has brought his own exuberant inventiveness, as well as a leaven of American usage, cross-grained with the semantic wit of one who knows how to evoke the Latin or Romance echoes still layering so many English words:

> In those lapped roars
> And souring resonance he heard as well

> Hoarse trains that highball down the world's ravines . . . sick thrills
> Of transit and forsaking.

The result is a wide-ranging play of vocabulary, but one that seems to move outward from a core of plainness, just as many of Wilbur's lyrics themselves—for all the acts of persuasion in their rhetoric and form—seem to issue from a serenely centered voice, free of bias or special pleading. Indeed, the resulting freedom of the reader, the absence of obvious solicitations, may be the most difficult of gifts to receive. When reading lyric poems, we are more accustomed to being led by prosecution or defense than to hearing the more evenhanded accents of a judge or expert witness, seemingly impartial, however urgently engaged: while admiring its "brilliant negative," Wilbur's poem "Cottage Street, 1953" regards and, indeed, judges Sylvia Plath's work as "helpless and unjust." In a postwar culture unnerved by continuing abuses of power, we often withhold assent from poems that (however outraged) do not patently and with immediate pathos situate themselves in the unbalanced field of force where power, justice, or centrality itself is a matter of dispute.

Moving to what was still rural New Jersey in 1923, Wilbur's family settled "at modest rental in a pre-Revolutionary stone house on the estate of an English millionaire." (This and subsequent recollections can be found in *Conversations*.) On these "four-hundred-odd acres in North Caldwell . . . transformed into the Platonic idea of an English gentleman's farm," Wilbur absorbed the "decent, attractive, civilized" temper of this "spontaneous English colony": "all was tea, bowls, tennis, Episcopalianism, gardening, music, and bridge, with agriculture and commerce in the middle distance and background." There, invigorating this gently mocked gentility, he developed his abiding regard for the natural world—"it comes natural to me to use, in particular, botanical materials''—especially where a mild wildness abuts or partially submits to forms of cultivation. A similar, contrastive vigor characterized his ''riding the rails and hitchhiking all over America'' during vacations from Amherst; and it marks his poetry's sensitivity to what evades even the most ingenious of forms.

At Amherst (1938–1942) Wilbur found a ''superior English department,'' at that time riding the high tide of New Criticism. ''Converted . . . to disciplined reading,'' he became inclined toward what for some time promised to be a career as a literary scholar and critic. Although he had published a few poems while still an undergraduate, the jarring motive for becoming a poet in earnest came after graduation. Shortly after marrying Charlotte Hayes Ward in June 1942, Wilbur joined the 36th Infantry Division and served at Monte Cassino at Anzio, in the invasion of southern France, and on through the Siegfried Line. Wilbur has spoken (1975) of his wartime experience in ways that connect it directly to his writing:

I began to write rather constantly once I got abroad in the service. It was one of the few things one could do, under what were chiefly boring circumstances, to keep sane. . . . I think it was a question of confusion, or a desire to make order of confusion, to give words to one's fears and uncertainties and so tame them a little. . . . You have to have some experience of danger, lostness and mess. The bottom has to fall out of your thoughts periodically before you feel the need to be clear and orderly in words.

The above statement deepens our reading of Wilbur's early and subsequent work, as does his account of his reading experience during the war—especially his reading of Edgar Allan Poe (along with James Joyce, Dylan Thomas, Gerard Manley Hopkins, and Alfred Lord Tennyson):

I can remember that during one long week in which I scarcely got out of my foxhole at Monte Cassino, I read that whole paperback of Poe. For the first time I began to have a sense that there was something besides spookery in Poe, that there might be some kind of allegorical depth to his fiction. . . . Perhaps it was because under circumstances where one did very little save sleep and wake, one's attention was drawn to all of the semi-states which lie between full waking and deep slumber. I began to perceive that in Poe's fiction some effort was being made to represent the stages or stations of the mind.

We will soon measure the extent of Wilbur's self-described ''public quarrel with the aesthetics of Edgar Allan Poe.'' But it is worth recognizing how many of Wilbur's own poems cross and recross the semistates along the borders of sleep and wakefulness (among them ''Clearness,'' ''The Pardon,'' ''Merlin Enthralled,'' ''Marginalia,'' ''Love Calls Us to the Things of This World,'' ''Walking to Sleep,'' and ''In Limbo''), as well as how many of them take for their deeper subjects the ''stages or stations of the mind.''

In the light of these reflections on fear, boredom, and loss, as well as on the disorientation and attempted reordering of the world and the mind, we can now turn to Wilbur's first collection. While at war he was sending poems home to his wife and a few friends; after his return to graduate school at Harvard the poems were brought to the attention of the publishers Reynal & Hitchcock, who published them with some newer work as *The Beautiful Changes* (1947).

Several features of Wilbur's first book were immediately praised by Louise Bogan:

He has a remarkable variety of interest and mood, and he can contemplate his subjects without nervousness, explore them with care, and then let them drop at the exact moment that the organization of a poem is complete. This ease of pace, this seemingly effortless advance to a resolute conclusion, is rare at his age; the young usually yield to tempting inflation and elaboration.

Equally striking is the extraordinary freshness with which Wilbur re-perceives his world. This is partly a matter of tone and music, but for the moment let us notice the salient devices of simile and metaphor, and ask what makes Wilbur's use of them so distinctive. First, some early examples: Slicing open a potato is "like breaching a strangely refreshing tomb" ("Potato"); "The snow came down last night like moths / Burned on the moon" ("First Snow in Alsace"); ". . . twilight / Glides like a giant bass" ("The Peace of Cities"); "Then your love looked as simple and entire / As that picked pear you tossed me" ("June Light"). In each case the comparison creates something new, and the shock of that creation does much to provide the energy of Wilbur's poetry. But, unlike many metaphorists, Wilbur channels and ramifies that energy onward through the poem—by maintaining a modulated speaking voice and by integrating the comparison into larger currents of syntax, cadence, or stanzaic form. The effects and possible motives for this are several, and it is worth dwelling on them for a moment, because they lie near the heart of Wilbur's entire work.

Certainly the shock of refreshment is prolonged and shaped—becoming more a wave than an explosion; but beyond the pleasing athletic dexterity and vitality of this shaping, Wilbur is extending another effect of the metaphor itself: the sense of connectedness. Since one of his "motives for metaphor" is the creation of relatedness (Wilbur has spoken of the religious element in this enterprise), it is no coincidence that his comparisons are seldom left to shine alone but are invariably woven into a larger verbal scheme. This larger scheme is also that of a courteous conversationalist (perhaps a social analogue and instrument for the poem's creations of cooperative relatedness), whose interest is in keeping the discourse moving fluently along rather than stopping its flow with some arresting brilliance. In both these regards, Wilbur may be drawing on his admiration for seventeenth-century prose—and it is this, as much as his flair for compound description and allegory, that lies at the root of his early affinity with Marianne Moore. A virtuoso syntactician, careful to draw otherwise unassimilable curiosities of fact or figure into an unflappable conversational pursuit, Moore praised such authors as Donne, Francis Bacon, and Thomas Browne in the following terms: "Suggesting conversation and strengthened by etymology there is a kind of effortless compactness which precludes ornateness, a 'fearful felicity,' in which like the pig in the churn, imagination seems to provide its own propulsiveness."

The propulsiveness and fluency with which Wilbur integrates his metaphors may have yet further motives, at which the word "fearful" could hint. Indeed, the early poem "Objects" ends with the speaker self-described as "fearfully free." Bearing in mind that much of his early poetry emerged from the war, one notices that Wilbur's comparisons often register as estrangement that is as threatening as it is thrilling: the potato as tomb, the twilight as predator; even the lovely pear becomes "more fatal fleshed." In "First Snow in Alsace," the opening line ("The snow came down last night like moths") is pleasantly poetic; but the discomforting enjambment and extension of the simile to "Burned on the moon" brings an abrupt and mortal change. Characteristically, Wilbur moves beyond a possible fixation on this strangeness, pausing only for a caesural semicolon before calmly resuming, "it fell till dawn, / Covered the town with simple cloths." Like the syntax, the simplicity absorbs and recovers from the strangeness, even as the metaphoric play has now eased onward from burned moths to simple cloths. Similarly, the poetic form crystallizes quietly into the first of a series of interlaced stanzas of terza rima. In such ways the poem rehearses the experience of uncovering and recovering from the shock of estrangement.

Estrangement of a violent kind is clearly at the thematic core of the poem, which continues thus:

> shellbursts scattered and deranged,
> Entangled railings, crevassed lawn.
>
> As if it did not know they'd changed,
> Snow smoothly clasps the roofs of homes
> Fear-gutted, trustless and estranged.

"Deranged," "changed," "estranged": from the first, Wilbur's readers should have measured the toll in this persistant rhyme. (The later poem "Praise in Summer" again rhymes "derange" and "strange," and variants of "strange" recur in numerous others.) Clearly the brio of perceived resemblance has its disjunctive underside—comparison as crisis, not just delight—and the composures of phrasing and rhyme have compensatory as well as celebratory designs. Indeed, Wilbur's achievement makes these oppositions almost indistinguishable.

Continuing "First Snow in Alsace," one cannot think now of snow without also envisioning burned moths, wrecked homes, and such scenes of death as the poem goes on to describe: "beyond the town a mile / Or two, this snowfall fills the eyes / Of soldiers dead a little while." While calm, the hush is also that of desolation. And although the apparently amenable diction of "a mile / Or two" or "a little while" may lessen the horror, it renders such diction either limited or yet more menacing—as if a half-echo of Robert Frost's "Stopping by Woods on a Snowy Evening" were introduced only to make the familiar voice of Frost himself now seem either naively inadequate to this foreign enormity or still more disquieting from within its provinciality. Yes, "frost makes marvelous designs," as the poem goes on to concede; but Wilbur weighs

such marvels of natural design against the ghastly mess or yet more hideous design of war. Wilbur's line may thus evoke the darker and more pertinent Frost of "Design," which also rhymed "cloth" with a victim "moth" as part of its remorseless etching of "death and blight." However deftly en passant, Wilbur may thus have relayed both the genial and the vigilant nature of his inheritance from Frost—who has remained one of his principal influences.

In the same vein, Wilbur concludes by measuring the self-warming innocence of youth ("Ten first-snows back in thought . . . [the night guard] was the first to see the snow") against the chill of the dead, or of soldiers aged by the experience of last things. How much is a residual innocence now worth? The question has no obvious answer. On the one hand, boyish boastings of priority are ironized by subsequent warfare, and may even involve the competitive impulses that lead to war. On the other, such warmth and recollected freshness of perception, however marred, may revive an otherwise lethal freezing of the night guard's sensibility. Without it, the eyes of the survivors may be as snow-blinded as those of the dead.

"First Snow" ends, noteworthily, by representing the consciousness of a night guard. Having noticed that the refreshing power of Wilbur's similitudes is inseparable from a perception of threatening otherness and change, like that of war, we may now add that his alertness is likewise inextricable from a kind of vigilance. In fact, several poems in Wilbur's first book adopt overt or implied attitudes of guardedness. "Objects" enjoins us to "Guard and gild what's common," while the soldiers of "Mined Country" must unlearn their trust in the natural world so as to guard against concealed land mines. Like the homes in Alsace, "trustless and estranged," these pastures and woods, as well as the men "Stepping with care and listening / Hard for hid metal's cry," are

so mixed up
With earliest trusts, you have to pick back
Far past all you have learned, to go
Disinherit the dumb child.

Part of the trust fund lost to estrangement is thus an innocent infancy, as well as an early pastoral language. History's invasion of pastoral is an old story, going back past Edmund Spenser to Virgil; but the invasion and suffering are always renewed, as is the demand for an appropriate language to be used by those who guard the flocks: "Shepherds must learn a new language; this / Isn't going to be quickly solved." In many ways this threatening necessity, balanced by an implied originality, serves as a manifesto for a young poet breaking or guarding the ground of his own career. And while Wilbur's poetry will track man's historical or conceptual violations of the natural world, it will also guard against quick poetic solutions. Like many poems to come, "Mined Country" proposes a recovered wildness rather than an inner or outer region mined by our impositions:

Tell him to trust things alike and never to stop
Emptying things, but not let them lack
Love in some manner restored; to be
Sure the whole world's wild.

As "in some manner" betrays, however, the restoration of wildness is a paradoxical goal, compromised by the manners of language as much as by the necessary technology of a mine detector—a latter-day shepherd's crook. For Wilbur, whose brilliant mind and manners always shape the very wildness they would restore or praise, this further problem, too, will not be "quickly solved." It remains one of the most fascinating elements of his entire career.

This sensitivity to wildness suggests yet another motive for the distinctive fluency with which Wilbur tends to surpass even the most inspired of his comparisons. To the accommo-

dated recognition of strangeness, and to the ductility of civil address, we can add Wilbur's skepticism about imposing upon or deludedly trying to apprehend a "wild" reality that evades even the most ingenious of our figures. "Objects" speaks of "a net which catches nothing," and it urges us to "forget / Uses and prices and names; have objects speak." The net recurs in "An Event," where Wilbur supersedes one simile for flocking birds ("As if a cast of grain leapt back to the hand") with another ("They roll / Like a drunken fingerprint across the sky!")—only to reject that last superb comparison:

Or so I give their image to my soul
Until, as if refusing to be caught
In any singular vision of my eye
Or in the nets and cages of my thought,

They tower up, shatter, and madden space
With their divergences, are each alone
Swallowed from sight, and leave me in this place
Shaping images to make them stay: . . .

Even the refutation of his figures of speech requires yet further metaphors (nets, cages, tower, madden, swallowed), as if to confess that language itself, particularly its figurative element, is unavoidably mined with that which it would sweep clear. And so the vigilance spoken of earlier extends as much to Wilbur's craft and medium as to his subjects—even when the subject is that very need for vigilance. One way to measure the course of Wilbur's development—extending to as late a poem as "Lying"—is to follow the deepening skepticism of that vigilance, associated as it is with more than merely epistemological concerns.

Wilbur's "Praise in Summer" confronts the distortion that inheres in any refreshing use of metaphor—but here it suggests something like a compulsion in the poet's malpractice:

And then I wondered why this mad *instead*
Perverts our praise to uncreation, why

Such savor's in this wrenching things awry.
Does sense so stale that it must needs derange
The world to know it? . . .

The sonnet is bound by such urgent words as
"must needs," "mad," and "awry" ("Mined
Country" had worried that "Some scheme's
gone awry"); "perverts" and "wrenching" dramatize the turning of figuration. Clearly, such
rhetoric admits more than a decorative compunc-
tion for its abuses. But if we expect a purgative
return to literal truths, the poem concludes:

> To a praiseful eye
> Should it not be enough of fresh and strange
> That trees grow green, and moles can course in
>   clay,
> And sparrows sweep the ceiling of our day?

Not only is the question rhetorical, its rhetoricity
is stressed by the return to metaphoric play within
the final line. The question answers itself by the
very language with which it has been posed.

With a deepened sense of Wilbur's necessary
rather than merely willed estrangements, we
should turn back to several other early poems
that portray the estranger himself. "Water Walker" is the most remarkable of these. Here the
very means of self-portrayal is inherently metaphorical and estranging, since the speaker's self
is presented only via the multiple figures of the
caddis fly and of the apostle Saul/Paul—each of
which is subject to metamorphosis. Like the fly
and the convert, the poet may be condemned (by
a force somewhere between biological and spiritual necessity) to exist in a state of betweenness,
waterborne yet in flight, a convert Roman
preaching to Greeks, an uneasy foreigner who,
like metaphor or poetic language itself, keeps
crossing the borderline of his own otherness,
"Always alike and unlike." To the radically converted survivor of war, the world will obviously
seem other than what it was. To such a survivor
who is also a poet, a maker of metaphoric con-

versions, his own identity will have become that
of a "Stranger to both" sides of the several divisions between literal and figurative, or familiar
and unfamiliar, worlds. Unable to dwell in a
world whose otherness he has noted *and* aug-
mented, he discovers "Heaven and hell in the
poise / Betwixt 'inhabit' and 'know' "—a discovery that evokes ultimate judgment. And, as
the poem concludes, "justice" is somehow the
heart of the matter:

> Who learns
> How hid the trick is of justice, cannot go home,
>   nor can leave,
> But the dilemma, cherished, tyrannical,
> While he despairs and burns

> Da capo da capo returns.

Those lines serve a writ on Wilbur's entire
career—its musically recapitulated cherishing of
a need to do justice to the changing world. The
need is tyrannical, and the poet is its main victim
and disciple, repeatedly compelled to a task that
can have no resolution. The presence of tyranny
confirms that Wilbur's estrangements were suffered rather than merely administered, and it
sharpens the "dilemma" noticed in the poet's
testing of his own words. While such a perception moves beyond New Critical claims of poetic
resolution, it also points to how many of
Wilbur's other poems wrestle with the very matter of justice—a justice often directed beyond the
supposed limits of the poem. Thus "On the Eyes
of an SS Officer" both diagnoses the self-
blinding injustice of fanatics and calls down an
actual judgment on the worst of such would-be
purifiers: "I ask my makeshift God of this / My
opulent bric-a-brac earth to damn his eyes."

Similarly, other poems adjudicate between the
possessiveness of a collector and the work of a
painter like Pieter de Hooch, whose way of doing justice to "A Dutch Courtyard" makes the
scene immune to consumption; or between the

narrowly honor-bound Percy or Hal and the roundly life-affirming Falstaff ("Up, Jack"); or between the "small strict shape" of the costumed performing dancer and her unmeshed return to "a little wilderness of flesh" ("L'Etoile"). Meanwhile, to forestall his own errors of perceptual judgment, Wilbur conjures the baffling and fluent variegations of a sycamore so that his eye "will never know the dry disease / Of thinking things no more than what he sees" ("Poplar, Sycamore").

In each case, Wilbur's fidelity is to a world beyond strict apprehension or even comprehension. The book's first poem, "Cicadas" (called "Cigales" in *The Beautiful Changes*), celebrates a "thin uncomprehended song [that] springs healing questions into binding air." Like that song, although far from thin, Wilbur's own poems reserve a teasing element—either of incomprehensible music or of contradiction—that pledges the world which "darts without the word." As we now recognize, that pledge marks a restless fidelity to what changes. Like the visions of Paul, this "troubles" us by enforcing a loss of the familiar world or self, and by pointing to our own mortality. One cannot embrace change without also accepting mortal loss; and it is this mature renunciation, deeper than its aesthetic or conceptual counterparts, that gives Wilbur's work its early and lasting depth, as well as its unusual balance of calm and celebration. This is what allows him to "choose / To welcome love in the lively wasting sun" ("Sunlight Is Imagination"), and to write the extraordinary philosophical love poem that titles and concludes the book. "The Beautiful Changes" meditates on how beauty (and, by implication, poetic metaphor) alters, both reflexively and as an agent that quickens us to see things as yet more strangely other than they once appeared—less our own, and yet by loss released to that mysterious stirring beyond recognition or selfhood that lies at the heart of wonder:

One wading a Fall meadow finds on all sides
The Queen Anne's Lace lying like lilies
On water; it glides
So from the walker, it turns
Dry grass to a lake, as the slightest shade of you
Valleys my mind in fabulous blue Lucernes.

The beautiful changes as a forest is changed
By a chameleon's tuning his skin to it;
As a mantis, arranged
On a green leaf, grows
Into it, makes the leaf leafier, and proves
Any greenness is deeper than anyone knows.

Your hands hold roses always in a way that says
They are not only yours; the beautiful changes
In such kind ways,
Wishing ever to sunder
Things and things' selves for a second finding, to
    lose
For a moment all that it touches back to wonder.

The Beautiful Changes appeared while Wilbur was studying English literature at Harvard Graduate School. After studying for a year on the G.I. Bill, and receiving an M.A. degree (1947), he began three years as a junior fellow at Harvard's Society of Fellows. During this time he continued his study of Poe—a study that yielded ground-breaking essays and lectures on Poe's work. While marking the limits of Poe's exclusionary poetry ("with few exceptions . . . what brilliance they have is like that of a Fourth of July rocket destroying itself in the void"), Wilbur reveals the allegories of otherworldly disengagement that work like "undercurrents" through the fiction. A true poet–critic, he applies a far from disinterested edge to these studies of such works as "Ligeia," *The Narrative of Arthur Gordon Pym,* and the detective stories. As in a Poe narrative, where (according to Wilbur's insight) two characters may represent divergent parts of a single soul, Wilbur draws critically close to his subject in order to clarify and perhaps exorcise Poe's remorseless drive for dematerialization. Although fascinated by Poe's dream exploration of shifting borders of consciousness, and by his "estranging" spirituality, Wilbur makes of Poe a "road not taken"—one that covers similar psychic territory but leads in a direction whose very oppositeness dramatizes Wilbur's intended celebration of the "things of this world." That celebration becomes one of the main objects of Wilbur's second collection of poems, *Ceremony and Other Poems* (1950).

If Poe sought the absolute and the timeless, the poems of *Ceremony* necessarily embrace the temporal world. Even more intensely than had been true of his earlier registry of change, Wilbur's espousal of incarnate, material existence ("A World Without Objects Is a Sensible Emptiness") commits him to "a most material loss" and to a "lament for grace's early term" ("Lament"). And whereas a chief element and agent of estrangement in *The Beautiful Changes* had been war, it is not time and a more general sense of mortality that (in "The Beautiful Changes") "sunder[s] / Things and things' selves for a second finding"—if, indeed, such recoveries are possible.

This last doubt troubles such poems as "The Pardon" and "The Death of a Toad." In the former, the speaker is haunted by the dog whose death he had once evaded ("I could not forgive the sad or strange / In beast or man"). Now the dog returns, if not for redemption ("I dreamt the past was never past redeeming: / But whether this was false or honest dreaming"), then for an acknowledgment that would humbly extend the limits of kindness to encompass the strangeness of death ("I beg death's pardon now. And mourn the dead.") Similarly—as Randall Jarrell failed to see—"The Death of a Toad" incriminates its own idealizing compensations ("ebullient seas . . . Amphibia's emperies") with a final, unflinching regard for what is lost. If "A World Without Objects" deliberately blurs its poetic

lampshine in "the steam of beasts," these two poems about dead beasts modulate such "light incarnate" from the glowing "fierce and mortal green" of "The Pardon" to the "haggard daylight" of "The Death of a Toad."

Wilbur's prismatic images or phrases thus render something more than poetic luminosity itself. And the ceremonies suggested by the volume's title are often designed to humble the human and the poetic will—partly by urging it to tend the mortal rather than the mental flower ("La Rose des Vents"), and partly by warning it against solipsism ("The Terrace") or the infernal insistence on autonomy ("A Problem from Milton"). These and other poems caution against versions of a "Thüle of the mind's worst vanity" ("Clearness"); as in "Grasse: The Olive Trees," they point out the dangers and futilities of attempting to possess or to bring near any idealized state of paradise, be it Eden ("Castles and Distances"), or a purchased love ("Marché aux Oiseaux"), or a realized, rather than a projected, linguistic sufficiency ("Games Two").

It would be wrong, however, to suppose that Wilbur's sense of limits and of renunciations leads to an inertly resigned poetry. The opposite is true, for various reasons. By exploiting the genre of argument or meditational debate, several poems give free rein to an impulse of spirit, imagination, or desire before checking that impulse by exposing its futility or cost. The poems thus not only enjoy a measure of dramatic complexity and dynamism; they also actually exercise rather than suppress the drives they seek to curb. Or perhaps it would be more accurate to say that Wilbur's poems redirect their spiritual, questlike energies into their celebrations of the given world. This world is consequently perceived with an unusual vibrancy that inheres as much in the mobility and the textures of Wilbur's subjects as in the embodiments of such qualities in his craft. Both world and poem come to share an interanimating "scintillant embrace," in which the network of mind, senses, and language seems to mesh with the reticulated vitality of its objects. Three examples follow, from ''A Glance from the Bridge,'' ''Conjuration,'' and ''Part of a Letter'':

[Gulls] rise and braid their glidings, white and
    spare,
Or sweep the hemmed-in river up and down,
Making a litheness in the barriered air, . . .

Backtrack of sea, the baywater goes; flats
Bubble in sunlight, running with herringbone
    streams;
Sea-lettuce lies in oily mats
On sand mislaid; stranded
Are slug, stone, and shell, as dreams
Drain into morning shine, and the cheat is ended.

Easy as cove-water rustles its pebbles and shells
In the slosh, spread, seethe, and the backsliding
Wallop and tuck of the wave, and just that
        cheerful,
        Tables and earth were riding

Back and forth in the minting shades of the trees.

Such writing is clearly buoyed by an intense participatory relish; and despite Wilbur's caution that ''never noun / Found what it named,'' his poems constantly exceed mere acts of denomination. Perhaps not since Gerard Manley Hopkins (but here without a sacrificial drive) has a poet so brilliantly and empathetically deployed the more than denotative resources of lyric poetry to celebrate the ''ingenerate grain'' of the world.

In this participatory sense, whereby unnatural artifice accentuates the stress and play of natural energy, Wilbur's title poem declares that ''ceremony never did conceal, / Save to the silly eye, which all allows, / How much we are the woods we wander in.'' This poem (on a painting by Bazille) self-reflexively concludes:

What's lightly hid is deepest understood,
And when with social smile and formal dress

She teaches leaves to curtsy and quadrille,
I think there are most tigers in the wood.

Imagining tigers, the mind's eye recalls the ''striped blouse'' of the painted woman; but instead of assimilating the animals to artifice and fashion, it detects how artifice and fashion reveal their own and the woman's element of wildness. ''We are the woods we wander in'' recovers the old association of woods with wilds, and of ''wood'' with human wildness (the lovers in *A Midsummer Night's Dream* became ''wood within the wood'').

Thus, at the heart of human artifice Wilbur stresses a hunting restlessness, a quality that inhabits the sculptured figures in one of *Ceremony*'s finest poems, ''Giacometti.'' Rejecting inert stone statues that freeze the human image and the human will, Wilbur honors Giacometti's art for its mobility, its truth to moments when ''we ourselves are strange / To what we were,'' its portrayal of a stripped-down pilgrim, anonymous and ''unspeakably alone.'' This fully present but radically incomplete ''starless walker, who cannot guess / His will'' becomes Wilbur's Everyman, ''in whose guise we make / Our grim departures now, walking to find / What railleries of rock, what palisades?'' Like his wood wanderer of his earlier water walker or night guard, Wilbur's anonymous pilgrim may be one of the most uneasy but most authentic figures for his own poetic vocation and career. Beneath the ''formal dress'' of his work we may imagine ''the single form we can assume,'' a roughened, shuffling creature ''made / Of infinite farewells,'' a migrant figure ''pruned of every gesture, saving only / The habit of coming and going.''

The genie of Wilbur's career certainly seems to have been ''walking, walking'' during the years following the publication of *Ceremony*. Despite his position as Briggs-Copeland assistant professor of English composition at Harvard (1950–1955), Wilbur spent long periods away from Cambridge, first as a Guggenheim Fellow in New Mexico (1952–1953), then as a Prix de Rome Fellow in Italy (1954–1955), before accepting an appointment as associate professor at Wellesley College (1955–1957), from which he moved again to become a professor of English at Wesleyan University (1957–1977). These years also brought further departures as a writer—an early attempt to write a verse drama, a highly successful verse translation of Molière's *The Misanthrope,* the award-winning short story "A Game of Catch," the compilation *A Bestiary* (poems and prose, illustrated by Alexander Calder), and a sequence of lyrics for a Broadway version of Voltaire's *Candide* in collaboration with Lillian Hellman and Leonard Bernstein. At the same time, Wilbur continued to write lyric poetry, publishing his third collection, *Things of This World,* in 1956.

Although the poems of *Things of This World* have much in common with Wilbur's earlier work, they move with greater freedom and authority, and the elegant build of his poems now seems to have taken on further muscle and robustness. Certain themes have gained in cogency and range of application, while the manner of their presentation has become both more relaxed and more high-spirited. One such theme, emphasized by the title, is the poet's continuing devotion to "things of this world"; and the signature poem, "Love Calls Us to the Things of This World," suggests how strongly that devotion now defines the poet's very "calling":

The eyes open to a cry of pulleys,
And spirited from sleep, the astounded soul
Hangs for a moment bodiless and simple
As false dawn.
               Outside the open window
The morning air is all awash with angels.

Some are in bed-sheets, some are in
          blouses,
Some are in smocks: but truly there they are.
Now they are rising together in calm swells
Of halcyon feeling, filling whatever they wear
With the deep joy of their impersonal breathing;

Now they are flying in place, conveying
The terrible speed of their omnipresence,
          moving
And staying like white water; and now of a
          sudden
They swoon down into so rapt a quiet
That nobody seems to be there.
                         The soul shrinks

From all that it is about to remember,
From the punctual rape of every blessed day,
And cries,
          "Oh, let there be nothing on earth but
               laundry,
Nothing but rosy hands in the rising steam
And clear dances done in the sight of heaven."

Yet, as the sun acknowledges
With a warm look the world's hunks and colors,
The soul descends once more in bitter love
To accept the waking body, saying now
In a changed voice as the man yawns and rises,

"Bring them down from their ruddy
          gallows;
Let there be clean linen for the backs of thieves;
Let lovers go fresh and sweet to be undone,
And the heaviest nuns walk in a pure floating
Of dark habits,
               keeping their difficult balance."

With an exuberant play of high and low diction, direct speech, and variously indented lines of differing length, Wilbur gives fresh, accessible force to the old debate of body and soul—here capturing the moments of transition through which the soul chooses to acknowledge both the waking body and the world. Crossing Poe's territory in reverse, the poem turns from sleep and the shapings of pure spirit, to embrace the "hunks and colors" of daily life; but even its initial phantasm of angels inhabits such ordinary stuff as laundry—indeed, depends on laundry for its manifestation. Wilbur himself admits, "I don't really want to have much truck with angels who aren't in the laundry, who aren't involved in the everyday world. It's a poem against dissociated and abstracted spirituality."

While the intention of the poem is clearly expressed, its theme is not merely argued in the abstract but, rather, exemplified by its own "embodiment" within both a narrated action (the story of an awakening) and a dramatized turn of direct speech. Whereas the beautifully entranced fantasia of angels ends with the suspicion that "nobody seems to be there," the poem itself ends within the presence of a direct speaker: the embodied soul, whose "changed voice" marks its journey from a momentary shrinkage to a full acceptance of incarnation. The laundry may now serve as a garment for the body, rather than only as a fabric for angels or the "angelic imagination." And the final stanza ("Bring them down . . . Let there be . . .") leads the descendental impulse home with nothing less than a redemptive and creative authority. Saving the laundry (and angels) from the gallows, and hence rejecting any notion that martyrdom must be the price of spirituality, the soul also uses the language of divine creative fiat as it brings a world into being—a balanced world occupied not only by thieves and heavy nuns but also by the continuing possibility of finding angels in the wash.

A descendental impulse invigorates many other poems in *Things of This World*. Most literally, there is the slow downward dance of "Piazza de Spagna, Early Morning"—a poem that moves from a "sleepy pirouette" to a "called-for falling glide and whirl," as if this were again a figure of vocation; or the "down again" speaker in "A Voice from Under the Table"; or the brilliantly registered descents of water in "A Baroque Wall-Fountain in the Villa Sciarra." Blending description and debate, this last poem sets the "saecular ecstasy" of an earthly "faun-menage" against the vertical "water-saints" outside St. Peter's. The poem's life is in the engaged virtuosity of its water portraits:

Sweet water brims a cockle and braids down

  Past spattered mosses, breaks
On the tipped edge of a second shell, and fills
  The massive third below. It spills
In threads then from the scalloped rim, and
    makes

  A scrim or summery tent
For a faun-menage and their familiar goose.
  Happy in all that ragged, loose
Collapse of water, its effortless descent

. . . .

  Before St. Peter's—the main jet
Struggling aloft until it seems at rest

  In the act of rising, until
The very wish of water is reversed,
  That heaviness borne up to burst
In a clear, high, cavorting head, to fill

  With blaze, and then in gauze
Delays, in a gnatlike shimmering, in a fine
  Illumined version of itself, decline,
And patter on the stones its own applause?

Although Wilbur prefers the fauns "at rest in fullness of desire / For what is given," his conclusion points to the residual spirituality of this preference; for the baroque sculpture figures a perfectly fulfilled unfulfillment from which we ourselves remain separate, and to which we can at best aspire with Franciscan devotion—a "dreamt land / Toward which all hungers leap, all pleasures pass."

In addition to being called down to the things of this world, we are thus committed to a "humble insatiety,'' a state explored with growing frequency in Wilbur's work. Whether in the drunken phrases of ''A Voice from Under the Table'' (''The end of thirst exceeds experience . . . Well I am down again, but not yet out. / O sweet frustrations, I shall be back for more''), or in the thoughtful essay on Emily Dickinson's ''Sumptuous Destitution'' (1959), Wilbur urges that privation may be our paradoxically enriching fate.

The creature of appetite (whether insect or human) pursues satisfaction, and strives to possess the object in itself; it cannot imagine the vaster economy of desire, in which the pain of abstinence is justified by moments of infinite joy, and the object is spiritually possessed, not merely for itself, but more truly as an index of the All.

Wilbur's metaphorical unifications may thus be not only an imitation of the world's own single braid but also an expressive procedure and product of ''the vaster economy of desire'' that unifies things by virtue of its ''profound perspective.'' Perhaps another name for this is love—the love that calls us to the things of this world, that relishes the light incarnate or the play of falling water, that moves Bruna Sandoval ''For love and in all weathers'' to keep the church of San Ysidro (''A Plain Song for Comadre''), and that enables the poet's eye to perceive angel feathers in the stained suds of Bruna's scrub water. Such love is at the far-from-complacent center of Wilbur's work, whose very intricate craft, no less than its metaphorical leaps, may well be the sign of its strenuous desire.

Desire can be kept sharp only by its perpetual defeat. Hence a deepening of Wilbur's early stress on the related insufficiency of language itself. Even metaphor must fail to apprehend its object, as in ''Mind'' or ''An Event''—the challenge being to keep that failure a ''graceful error.'' So, too, the mind should never relinquish its own dreaming, for it is precisely the ''vain attempt'' of imagination and metaphor that provides one of the ''cross-purposes'' by which ''the world is dreamt.'' The cautionary fable ''Merlin Enthralled'' exposes the impoverished world of fact that survives after the enchanter's power is gone; and it is from ''the blue unbroken reveries / Of the building dead'' that even such an admittedly pragmatic structure as a railway station may arise (''For the New Railway Station in Rome''). Clearly, if love calls us to the things of this world, the answer to that call is what we make of such things—and therefore what we add to them:

''What is our praise or pride
But to imagine excellence, and try to make it?
What does it say over the door of Heaven
But *homo fecit?*''

It is at this high pitch of wit and confidence, with a strongly reinforced faith in the purpose and craft of his vocation—even to the point of supposing the fabrication of heaven—that Wilbur concludes his third book.

Things of This World received the National Book Award, the Pulitzer Prize, and the Edna St. Vincent Millay Memorial Prize. In 1957, *Poems 1943–1956* was published in London by Faber and Faber, and Wilbur was elected to the National Institute of Arts and Letters. While a professor of English at Wesleyan, he became general editor of the Laurel Poetry Series, was elected chancellor of the Academy of American Poets, and visited the Soviet Union as a cultural representative of the United States. In short, the years between Wilbur's third and fourth books of poetry—*Advice to a Prophet and Other Poems* appeared in 1961—brought not only great recognition but also a broadening of Wilbur's cultural presence as a poet. And the effects of this appear in the new poems. Almost half of them are spoken by a communal ''we,'' and many of them assume the authority of deliberate instruction (as ''advice'' suggests). In some respects, Wilbur's poetic stance has thus widened to include a more social basis while also moving from states of responsiveness to exercises of responsibility. To be sure, Wilbur remains very much a lyric poet; but it is worth noticing his achievement of a socially tempered lyricism (marked by a more direct conversational style, greatly reinforced by his work in verse drama), and his unusual reclamation of the lyric's potential for a discreet and valuable didacticism.

These achievements were especially rare in American poetry after the late 1950's. Just as the descendental impulse in *Things of This World* (an impulse shared by many writers of the time, particularly after Lowell's *Life Studies*) was unfashionably braced by Wilbur's dramatic spiritual impulse and affirmative demeanor, so the personal accents of Wilbur's lyric speech paradoxically stand out through their supple inclusions of social address and by their potentially communal as well as communicable nature. During a decade in which lyric poetry became either increasingly introverted and private, on the one hand, or asocially oriented toward objectivism, myth, or "deep image," on the other, Wilbur's work thus attained a distinction that should not be overlooked. This socially tempered (often first person plural) lyricism, and a regained capacity for lyric didacticism, should be counted among Wilbur's contributions to the poetry of his time.

Confirming the importance of verse drama to Wilbur's development of a more immediate conversational address, *Advice to a Prophet* includes an excerpt from Molière's *Tartuffe* (a segment that nicely negotiates the demands of rhymed couplets and of rapid dialogue). The volume opens with a debate in direct speech, "Two Voices in a Meadow," matched later by "The Aspen and the Stream." In the former, an apparent divergence between the floating milkweed and the unmoving stone is mediated by their shared (and symmetrically phrased) submission to their own natures, and thereby to their place in a shared scheme both of nature and of divinity. Emblematic of Wilbur's

new work, this debate both sharpens dramatically assertive individual voices ("As casual as cowdung / Under the crib of God, / I lie where chance would have me, / Up to the ears in sod''), *and* sketches the "yield[ing]" of such voices to a greater common design.

"Advice to a Prophet" focuses precisely on communicative strategy, here the attuning of prophetic utterance to its audience. Maintaining a dramatic intensity, the poem is spoken not by the isolated prophet but, rather, by one of the civic community ("When you come, as you soon must, to the streets of our city"). This crucial strategic move suggests an important element of Wilbur's own evolving stance—here designed to mediate, as if from within the social sphere, between the isolated knowledge or sensibility of the prophet and the communal need of a society.

The need for this kind of mediating (rather than "mad-eyed") speaker is urgently historical—as is the content of his speech, which is also personal, since it focuses on how we may affectively (hence effectively) be made to experience the abstract threat of nuclear war. This public lyric is therefore designed to enhance our fear and our belief, to make our emotions capable of registering what otherwise leaves us dangerously numb. And the emphasis pursues a distinctly lyric turn from the obvious facts to a more subjective, indeed poetic, truth regarding our dependence on the natural world for images of our best selves. To threaten nature is to threaten the mirror and language by which we figure forth our courage, our love, and our spiritual identity:

Ask us, prophet, how we shall call
Our natures forth when that live tongue is all
Dispelled, that glass obscured or broken

In which we have said the rose of our love and
    the clean
Horse of our courage, in which beheld
The singing locust of the soul unshelled,
And all we mean or wish to mean.

Countering several forms of dangerous isolation, "Advice to a Prophet" thus reforges links between the citizen and the prophet, the human and the natural world, as well as between a personal and a historical domain. It is an integrative poem against selfishness—or, rather, a poem that reveals how even self-interest requires the safeguarding of otherness. In this respect the poem advances Wilbur's thematic and stylistic concerns; and several other poems in *Advice to a Prophet* similarly set examples of interdependence and cooperation against kinds of blind selfishness.

"The Undead" is one such poem, a portrait of demonic vampires whose possessive fear of life and loss has dispossessed them of both selfhood and vitality, leaving them in the condition of mere predators forever isolated from their prey. But the poem's didactic intent, well balanced by the vivid and amusing gothicism of its vampire lore, goes beyond condemnation. By calling on our sympathy, it seeks to avoid our potentially self-isolating or predatory attitude toward the undead. We must go beyond merely using them for our own edification:

Nevertheless, their pain is real,
And requires our pity. Think how sad it must be
　　To thirst always for a scorned elixir,
　　　The salt quotidian blood

Which, if mistrusted, has no savor;
To prey on life forever and not possess it,
　　As rock-hollows, tide after tide,
　　　Glassily strand the sea.

The sympathy of this appeal is intriguing, particularly when viewed alongside other poems in which Wilbur points to the inherent "insatiety" of both language and human desire—their inability to possess their objects. ("The Undead" appeared in *The New Yorker* just two months after "Ballade for the Duke of Orléans," whose refrain varies the line "*I die of thirst,*

here at the fountain-side.") Perhaps the demons of "The Undead" are uneasily close to those of poetry itself, even while the poem explores the very danger that Wilbur's current development seeks to avoid. Not unlike earlier rebuttals of abstract spirituality, "The Undead" summons in order to acknowledge as well as to exorcise. If its stylizations, rhetoric, and voice make a dominant element of the lyric poem inherently self-isolating and self-regarding (whether as New Critical icon or as confessional cry), Wilbur's strength is to point the lyric away from the dangers of "utter self-concern."

Once noticed, the positive motif of self-yielding emerges in such diverse poems as "October Maples, Portland," "A Fire-Truck," "The Aspen and the Stream," the inventively parabolic "Shame," and the haunting "Fall in Corrales." The communal speaker of the last comes to "Stand in the wind and, bowing to this time, / Practise the candor of our bones." Beyond the play of bone whiteness and truth, Wilbur speaks of a more-than-intellectual practice—a submission not just to forces beyond us but also to other than merely rational powers or susceptibilities within the self. This may lead to the uncanny or surreal underworlds glimpsed in "Stop," "Junk," and "A Hole in the Floor" (the last quoted below):

For God's sake, what am I after?
Some treasure, or tiny garden?
Or that untrodden place,
The house's very soul,
Where time has stored our footbeats
And the long skein of our voices?

Not these, but the buried strangeness
Which nourishes the known:
That spring from which the floor-lamp
Drinks now a wilder bloom,
Inflaming the damask love-seat
And the whole dangerous room.

Here Wilbur returns to that domain of estrangement noticed since his earliest work. This is the idiosyncratic vision, however adjusted between the singular "I" and the "long skein of our voices," that lurks as a crucial presence below what might otherwise have been the too secure floorboards of Wilbur's poetry. Beneath either domesticity or sociability, this nourishing genie also bewilders, inflames, and endangers. In its curious light, we may now recognize how even the carefully public "Advice to a Prophet" depends on reckoning the right degree of strangeness in order to conjure "an undreamt thing." And (despite the book's conclusion with the communal and reconciliatory "A Christmas Hymn") no reading of *Advice to a Prophet,* or of Wilbur's increasingly complex work at large, can afford to slight this haunting and nearly unassimilable element—hushed and resistant in "Another Voice," hideously threatening in "Someone Talking to Himself":

> Off in the fathomless dark
> Beyond the verge of love
> I saw blind fishes move,
> And under a stone shelf
> Rode the recusant shark—
> Cold, waiting, himself.

The commingling of a direct, instructive address with an element of strangeness or psychological exploration marks the title poem and several others in *Walking to Sleep* (1969). And Wilbur's experimental widening of his own repertoire beyond the New Critical lyric argument-poem now extends to several narrative works, including "The Agent," a disturbing story in blank verse. So, too, he further diversifies his own voice by means of almost a dozen translations, each of which displays Wilbur's characteristic humility, fidelity, and virtuosity as a translator while also allowing him to write in a manner sometimes very different from his own.

Clearly, Wilbur's talent is restlessly continu-

ing to test and extend itself. Matching or driving these changes, there is also a deepening of vision. *Walking to Sleep* not only ranges more widely to encompass the perspectives of geology, astronomy, and myth; such rangings frequently respond to various intensified states of alarm—fear, insomnia, anxiety. Although still generally affirmative, this is a more troubled book, and Wilbur's capacity for cheer or comfort preserves itself only by the most arduous endeavor.

The opening poem, "The Lilacs," warns of what will come. Set in the insistent, alliterative pattern of Old English verse, but with the lines broken, like the lilacs,

> . . . stark, spindly,
>   and in staggered file,
> Like walking wounded
>   from the dead of winter

the poem dwells with great violence on the lilacs' return to blossom:

> Out of present pain
>   and from past terror
> Their bullet-shaped buds
>   came quick and bursting,
> As if they aimed
>   to be open with us!

What is fascinating here is not only the emphatic torment and near-military threat but also the gathering focus on the act of disclosure. As the poem continues, it suggests a reference both to a return to poetry (underscored by the poem's placement) and to the way Wilbur's poems themselves may ask to be read. In this regard, "Lilacs" may be both an act of reopening and a manifesto, especially to those readers whose superficial response to Wilbur's elegance or reticence has prevented them from recognizing how such effects not only may derive from but also may essentialize or transfigure states of unease, silence, or perceived mortality:

These lacquered leaves
                    where the light paddles
And the big blooms
                    buzzing among them
Have kept their counsel,
                    conveying nothing
Of their mortal message,
                    unless one should measure
The depth and dumbness
                    of death's kingdom
By the pure power
                    of this perfume.

We may ask why Wilbur's admission of torment or threat has deepened in this new book. The second poem, "On the Marginal Way," offers one significant answer: It is "the time's fright within me which distracts / Least fancies into violence." Accounting for a sudden fall into fantasies of holocaustal violence (he is viewing boulders strewn along a beach), the speaker implies an era of both nuclear threat and intensifying conventional warfare that must have revived his own memories of mass violence ("The Agent" returns to World War II). This is the decade of Hecht's *The Hard Hours* and Lowell's *For the Union Dead;* and Wilbur soon wrote "A Miltonic Sonnet" to castigate President Lyndon Johnson for the crassness and brutal imperialism that were imposing their "cattle-brand" on the American psyche as much as upon the victimized small nations.

As one might expect, Wilbur attempts to press back against "the time's fright within me." Apart from the rather uncharacteristic political satire of "A Miltonic Sonnet," his strategy involves a vigorous turn to a world beyond either the individual self or the human domain. Thus "On the Marginal Way" moves to "take cover in the facts," although this means turning away from a fantasy based on historical fact ("Auschwitz' final kill") to a different order of fact—the actual rocks on the beach, and their geological history. By a dramatic lengthening of perspective beyond that of human

history, Wilbur reaches a vision of creation by which to offset the nightmare of human destruction, and in which to resituate and renew our human origins. The strewn boulders now seem "Comely as Eve and Adam, near a sea / Transfigured by the sun's return"; and this regenerative news may now counterpoise the "tidings of some dirty war." Pointedly, this perspective requires the kind of imaginative self-yielding noticed in *Advice to a Prophet*. Now the intent has become more purgatorial, and its earnest perfection and joy are carefully framed by prayer:

Though, high above the shore
On someone's porch, spread wings of
     newsprint flap
The tidings of some dirty war,
It is a perfect day: the waters clap
Their hands and kindle, and the gull in flight
Loses himself at moments, white in white,

And like a breaking thought
Joy for a moment floods into the mind,
     Blurting that all things shall be brought
To the full state and stature of their kind,
By what has found the manhood of this
     stone.
May that vast motive wash and wash our
     own.

In addition to internalized historical fear, there is an increasingly intimate attention in Wilbur's new work to threats of aging and death, on both a personal and a planetary scale. And here again, Wilbur's resistant equilibrium depends on a depth of perspective that "takes cover" in the facts of botanical or astronomical time. In this way his work expands to the far-reaching movements of "Fern-Beds in Hampshire Country," "In the Field," "Seed Leaves," and "Under Cygnus" while also doing justice to the intimate losses and fears of "For Dudley" and "Running."

"I am part of that great going, / Though I stroll now, and am watchful." These lines, from the third section of "Running" ("Dodwells Road"), with their echo of Hardy's "The Going" and their matured version of Wilbur's own original vigilance, characterize much of Wilbur's work from this time forward. They introduce a somber meditation on inevitable exhaustions and losses, from which Wilbur shakes free only by turning once again with a benedictory offering to the world beyond him and to the generation that will survive him. The direct, colloquial language—Wilbur now grafting his dramatic skills onto the heart of the lyric—is part of that urgent breakthrough:

> But why in the hell spoil it?
> I make a clean gift of my young running
> To the two boys who break into view. . . .

"Walking to Sleep" is by no means directly autobiographical. Instructing an insomniac on the art of falling asleep, the speaker refers more to his addressee than to himself; and his own position is the purportedly impersonal and controlled stance of the teacher. Yet the poem's psychological focus gives it an introverted cast, while the speaker's generously elaborated knowledge—complete with the kinds of fear and watchfulness found in adjacent poems—does seem to derive from personal experience. The instructional stance, like the poem's wit and expatiatory largess, may itself be a compensation, a version and attempted self-application of the suggested cure. Perhaps this instructor is speaking to himself.

The lesson is couched in a suave and ample blank verse, which promotes the careful relaxation, the fluent transitions, and the sense of surfeit conducive to sleep. And yet, despite its humor, the poem is shot through with images of violence and horror, sleep being at one point wooed as the "kind assassin [who] will draw a bead / And blow your brains out." We are still within the region of "On the Marginal Way," but the angle of presentation has grown more inwardly acute and the fears more persecutory—to the point of near-paranoia. One is trapped in the remorseless self-gaze of the insomniac; there is no easy access to the "cover" of external fact. Rather, the path to sleep must lead to an uncovering of "your dearest horror," for only by bringing such horrors to consciousness can the mind undo the defensiveness that keeps it awake. The poem cannot end without leading its supposed addressee to the "crossroads and its laden gallows tree," where he must "lift your gaze and stare your brother down, / Though the swart crows have pecked his sockets hollow." Though he craves sleep, perhaps this is what the insomniac most fears: to hang suspended, eyeless, dead to the world.

For a poet as wakeful and visually observant as Wilbur (we may think back to the night guard of "First Snow in Alsace," whose open eyes oppose the snow-filled eyes of the dead), this figure might be especially haunting. Horribly twinned to the insomniac, he might indeed be a demon relative of the dark genie that haunts and perhaps even motivates Wilbur's generally bright work. Inseparable from Wilbur's celebratory "wit and wakefulness," the unease of this far-from-calm agent may thus be fathomed moving not only throughout "Walking to Sleep" but also beneath the composed surface of the poem's destination—"a pool / On whose calm face all images whatever / Lay clear, unfathomed, taken as they came."

In another formal departure, "The Agent" extends Wilbur's mastery of blank verse to a narrative about an American agent dropped behind enemy lines during World War II. Sent to prepare the destruction of a European town, he carries out his mission with deft professionalism. The story is told with unfussed and vivid detail; but what gives the poem its luster, and its menace, is the complex way in which the apparent detachment of the third-person narrative nevertheless allows the entire event to unfold from the agent's point of view. Hence the distance between agent and narrator is reduced—a reduction intensified by the portrait of the agent's near-poetic gifts: his linguistic skill attuned to dialectal nuance, his finely honed senses, his creative ability to forge a self (as Wilbur now forges the identity of the agent). This is not to suggest that the poem is a self-portrait but, rather, to explore what investment Wilbur might have had in writing this unique narrative.

In a crucial phrase, the agent is said to "savor and betray." Since few would question Wilbur's savoring fidelities, perhaps the agent fascinates by his antithetical nature—he is the faithful poet's nightmare. But what if there were a yet more intimate fascination? What if Wilbur were still haunted by his early insight that even the most faithful celebration, if cast in a poetry as rich in metaphor as his own, betrays its literal subject? "Praise in Summer" had asked "why this mad *instead* / Perverts our praise to uncreation, why / Such savor's in this wrenching things awry." How is that "uncreation" different from destruction?—a question Wallace Stevens also faced. Is Wilbur wrestling, however obliquely, with the demon that accuses those writers who most strongly savor this world, but who have nevertheless crossed what Seamus Heaney has called "the frontier of writing"? In a similar vein, we may read more intimately into the poem's final portrait not only betrayal ("a pure impostor / Faithless to everything") but also the agent's irremediable exile between worlds (recall the early "Water Walker") and his self-punitive fantasy of execution by his own side. However literally remote from Wilbur, the agent's work and fate thus take on a minatory fascination—one that marks "The Mind-Reader," just as versions of its enmeshments exercise the canny and uncanny "Lying."

Walking to Sleep includes a section of translations; and while the task of translation may provoke its own anxieties about fidelity and betrayal, Wilbur's versions of poems by Jorge Luis Borges, Andrei Voznesensky, François Villon, and others are scrupulously faithful without sacrificing an equivalent fluency or formal rigor within his own language. Unlike Lowell's "Imitations," Wilbur's translations follow his preference elsewhere for honoring a world beyond the ego, as well as for tempering his private voice to accommodate a shareable speech. Still, his selections are motivated; and it is probably that the feverish surreality of Voznesensky and the earthy valedictions of Villon will allow Wilbur both to speak in ways that his own more equable and decorous temperament seldom allows, and to continue to stretch the limits of his own work.

Wilbur has said of his translations of Molière and Racine, "It can help you to broaden your expressive range. . . . Translating drama involves impersonation, the imitation of attitudes and emotions. There's undoubtedly some transference from such practice to one's own work; more of oneself becomes articulate." Broadening his expressive range, Wilbur's continuing translations of Molière have further sharpened the dramatic as well as the social edge of his own lyrics, while also providing a vehicle for his comedic war against rigidities of all kinds. These prize-winning and popular works (*The Misanthrope, Tartuffe, Candide, The Learned Ladies*) are among the few successful verse dramas to be performed in our time. Accompanied by Wilbur's illuminating prefaces, they have much to tell us of both the original dramatist and the translator.

The 1970's brought Wilbur further acclaim: several poetry awards, honorary degrees, the presidency and then successive chancellorships of the American Academy of Arts and Letters. Such recognition increased through the 1980's, culminating in his appointment as second poet laureate of the United States. Yet his work shows no sign of resting on such laurels, either in theme or in method. On the contrary, *The Mind-Reader*

(1976) includes the unprecedented long dramatic monologue of the title poem, as well as several works of a newly autobiographical nature—the mordant narrative in quatrains ("Piccola Commedia"), poems addressed to members of his family ("The Writer" and "A Wedding Toast"), a haiku on sleeplessness ("Sleepless at Crown Point"), and the poem "In Limbo," which brings a more private urgency to Wilbur's fascination with states of disorientation, self-loss, imposture, homeless borderings between the worlds of sleeping and waking, spirit and flesh. With such innovations, Wilbur follows the example of the trees in "A Black Birch in Winter":

New wood, new life, new compass, greater girth,
And this is all their wisdom and their art—
To grow, stretch, crack, and not yet come apart.

No matter how autobiographical, Wilbur's poems never approximate the confessional verse of many of his contemporaries. Avoiding the unprotected immediacies of Lowell, Berryman, or Plath (he explicitly distances himself from Plath, however sympathetically, in "Cottage Street, 1953"), he joins such masters of oblique or mediated disclosure as Elizabeth Bishop, James Merrill, and Anthony Hecht. While poems like "Walking to Sleep," "The Agent," and "The Mind-Reader" objectify certain issues that interest him, the exact nature and degree of that interest cannot be narrowly specified. At least three advantages result: a rewarding complexity, a portrayal of traits or dilemmas shared by persons other than the poet, and a certain largess and buoyancy in the independent detailing and mood of the work. Even when penetrating psychological depths, Wilbur's commitment is always to a world "Not governed by me only."

"The Mind-Reader" is one of Wilbur's most suave and beguiling works—although such qualities, associated with his own charms as a poet, are now ironically displayed as part of the dubious wares of a somewhat seedy and perhaps alcoholic telepathist. In an effortlessly sinuous blank verse, so caressing and flexible that it seems to be telepathically attuned to the listener's mind, the speaker confesses the origins and practice of his work. He opens with a mesmerizing fugue on the subject of loss:

Some things are truly lost. Think of a sun-hat
Laid for the moment on a parapet
While three young women—one, perhaps, in mourning—
Talk in the crenellate shade. A slight wind plucks
And budges it; it scuffs to the edge and cartwheels
Into a giant view of some description:
Haggard escarpments, if you like, plunge down
Through mica shimmer to a moss of pines
Amidst which, here or there, a half-seen river
Lobs up a blink of light. The sun-hat falls,
With what free flirts and stoops you can imagine,
Down through that reeling vista or another,
Unseen by any, even by you or me.
It is as when a pipe-wrench, catapulted
From the jounced back of a pick-up truck, dives headlong
Into a bushy culvert; or a book
Whose reader is asleep, garbling the story,
Glides from beneath a steamer chair and yields
Its flurried pages to the printless sea.

This luxuriously ravishing passage, whose every amenability is a carefully manipulated solicitation, binds the listener to a doubly motivated account: the speaker is in love with such losses, and these "truly lost" objects contrastively introduce those which his powers *can* retrieve. By an irony that is surely relevant to the poet, the most uncanny and, hence, powerful aspect of the mind reader's gift is precisely what disempowers and entraps him. It is this terrible dispossession, even more than the subsequent confessions of occasional charlatanism, that make Wilbur's poem one of the most arresting among other typ-

ically postmodern ironizations of the ancient to-
pos of inspiration:

    I tell you this
Because you know that I have the gift, the
        burden.
Whether or not I put my mind to it,
The world usurps me ceaselessly; my sixth
And never-resting sense is a cheap room
Black with the anger of insomnia,
Whose wall-boards vibrate with the mutters,
        plaints,
And flushings of the race.

"Black with the anger of insomnia." Hence,
as in "Walking to Sleep," a longing for
release—figured as the place where "the book is
drowned." And, like Prospero requesting that
his audience's "indulgence set me free," the
speaker solicits (telepathically of course—"Ah,
you have read my mind") another mezzo-litro to
bring him closer to oblivion. This last ploy
shrewdly extends the speaker's self-subversions
to the reader: if the mind reader is the victim of
his compulsions, are we (who have now come to
share a version of his gift: to obey his solicitations, and to support his habit) any less addicted
in our listenings? If the mind reader is a figure
for the tyrannical aspects of a poet's genie, what
kind of grip does he have on our own need for
uncanny retrievals and prophecies? If habitual
readers of poetry are any less addicted than the
poets, it may be only a matter of degree. The
closing words of this "studious" drinker are
"Grazie, professore."

"The Writer" also attends to a painfully compelled travail; and by a characteristic self-
revision (itself evincing the kind of work he
describes), Wilbur surpasses his metaphor-wish
that his daughter have a "lucky passage" in the
craft of her art. Recalling a trapped starling that
had battered itself "humped and bloody" before
managing to escape through a window, he acknowledges, "It is always a matter, my darling, /

Of life or death, as I had forgotten. I wish /
What I wished you before, but harder." The
blend of tact, patience, and passion is typically
Wilbur's, as is the arduously engaged spiritual
dimension of the poem, linked as it is to the
writer's quest: "our spirits rose" on seeing the
bird "clearing the sill of the world."

New and Collected Poems (1988) breaks yet
further ground. It does so in at least three directions. First, there is the adventurous experiment
"On Freedom's Ground," a cantata in celebration of the Statue of Liberty. Here Wilbur's gift
for writing a communal lyric utterance tests itself
against the challenges of a musical setting and
the hazards of potential simplicity or sentimen-
tality. The poem succeeds by its formal versatility, its graceful (and democratic) interweaving of
ceremonial and colloquial language, and its related modulations among retrospect, praise, critique, mourning, and continuing aspiration.

A second departure, "Lying," takes Wilbur's
blank verse into the realm of the meditative essay
while furthering his long and frank exploration
of some of the more troubling motives and prem-
ises of poetry's ineradicably fictive nature. Since
the early "Praise in Summer," the issue has
teased or haunted a number of poems; now it
reaches its most rewarding trial, crossed as it is
with Wilbur's equally challenging fascination
with fidelity. The poem ends with the paradoxical proof that even the great images of fidelity,
like that of Roland, are the work of fiction, or
have been shaped by the benign infidelity of the
image maker. Whether lying to enliven a dead
party—a resurrective act, depending on its own
genetic fiat (of an unseen bird)—or resorting to
lies about art's tempering of brutality (Chiron
teaching Achilles the art of the lyre), or fabricat-
ing the scene of our own origins and fall, poetry
has always been an uncanny and ungrounded
trick of deception. At times the duplicity of
words, exaggerated as it is by the medium of
poetry itself, would seem to be the original dou-

ble agent, the liar in the lyre, the faker in the inscription *homo fecit* over the door of heaven.

Finally, Wilbur broaches a new response to the pressures of time and mortality. Several new poems continue to celebrate acts of self-yielding, but do so now with a consistent stress on the generative nature of such acts. The figures of the milkweed and the aspen had offered early versions of this; but now—as if against the threat or limit of individual mortality—Wilbur offers images of finite creatures giving up their bound identities, thereby prolonging or transforming their life force into further incarnations. A dominant new figure is that of dissemination. In "All That Is":

Under some clipped euonymus, a mushroom,
Bred of an old and deep mycelium
As hidden as the webwork of the world,
Strews on the shift night-wind, rising now,
A cast of spores as many as the stars.

Hence a different mode of release: instead of the escape into oblivion, an invigorating dispersal toward new life and to a renewed weaving of the webs of creation and of language—this poem is largely an ode to crossword puzzles, which, like poems, provide a "rite of finitude" by which to conjure and braid a world beyond the puzzle.

The disseminative image of strewn spores matches that of the "loose change" in "Icarium Mare," or the "sifting" of the fire bush in "Alatus," or of the shadblow in "Shad-Time," where once again the links are made to the mind and to an art associated with poetry:

The shadblow's white racemes
Burst here or there at random, scaled with red,
　As when the spitting fuse of dreams
　　Lights in a vacant head,

　Or as the Thracian strings,
Descending past the bedrock's muted staves,
　Picked out the signatures of things
　　Even in death's own caves.

"Rites of finitude" would be a good term for Wilbur's poems, provided that one recognizes both their air of spontaneous improvisation and their homage to what lies infinitely beyond them. Despite their maturity, these late poems are in many ways his most youthful, charged with the joyful and rejuvenating participation in a more-than-finite life force. With an astonishing litheness that marks their "wide-deploying motives of delight," these poems seem to imitate the transformative fluencies of a subject that "Instant by instant chooses to / Affirm itself and flow."

Just as such affirmations go beyond the finite self, so they require a more than cognitive or merely aesthetic faculty and motive. Wilbur seems to have found a way to suggest a combination of physical thrust and intuitive surmise. In the brilliant, death-tinged "Alatus," he writes:

　　See how the fire-bush, circled
　　By a crimson verge

　　Of its own sifting,
　　Bristles aloft its every
　　Naked stem, lifting

　　Beyond the faint sun,
　　Toward the hid pulse of things, its
　　Winged skeleton.

Such resurrective bristling thus comes as much from the bone as from the mind. Or from the deepest region of the mind, beneath intellection. Giving up certainty, being caught into a more than individual identity—this is the "rite / Or masque, or long charade / Where we, like these, / Had blundered into grand / Identities" ("Leaving"). Just as it is the true catch in "Trolling for Blues," where the bluefish breaks free from its first metaphoric identity to pull the fisherman toward a revision of his own:

　He is a type of coolest intellect,

　Or is so to the mind's blue eye until
　He strikes and runs unseen beneath the rip,

Yanking imagination back and down
Past recognition to the unlit deep
Of the glass sponges, of chiasmodon,

Of the old darkness of Devonian dream,
Phase of a meditation not our own,
That long mêlée where selves were not, that life
Merciless, painless, sleepless, unaware,
From which, in time, unthinkably we rose.

In their own striking and running to the long melee past recognition, and in their bringing of language itself into a disseminating flow of vitality—as if the words themselves were racemes, spores, or strewn stars—Wilbur's most recent poems thus seem to challenge any confident definition of the limits and artificiality of poetry. They may be rites of finitude, but the enactment of their rituals summons or joins for a moment something unlimited and wild. And if there must remain a border between their closed (because manifest) identities and the unassimilable multiplicity of life beyond them, that border works more as a lure than as an aesthetic device. Along with his darker genie, it is this bright margin and lure that will no doubt keep drawing Wilbur to his remarkably joyful and unappeased pursuit. As he asks in ''Hamlen Brook'':

> How shall I drink all this?
>
> Joy's trick is to supply
> Dry lips with what can cool and slake,
> Leaving them dumbstruck also with an ache
> Nothing can satisfy.

Selected Bibliography

WORKS OF RICHARD WILBUR

POETRY

The Beautiful Changes and Other Poems. New York: Reynal & Hitchcock, 1947.

Ceremony and Other Poems. New York: Harcourt, Brace, 1950.

Things of This World. New York: Harcourt, Brace, 1956.

Poems 1943–1956. London: Faber & Faber, 1957.

Advice to a Prophet and Other Poems. New York: Harcourt, Brace & World, 1961.

Loudmouse. New York: Crowell-Collier, 1963.

The Poems of Richard Wilbur. New York: Harcourt, Brace & World, 1963.

Walking to Sleep: New Poems and Translations. New York: Harcourt Brace Jovanovich, 1969.

Digging for China: A Poem. Garden City, N.Y.: Doubleday, 1970.

Opposites. New York: Harcourt Brace Jovanovich, 1973.

Seed Leaves: Homage to R. F. Boston: David Godine, 1974.

The Mind-Reader: New Poems. New York: Harcourt Brace Jovanovich, 1976.

Seven Poems. Omaha: Abattoir Editions, 1981.

New and Collected Poems. San Diego: Harcourt Brace Jovanovich, 1988.

PROSE

Responses: Prose Pieces 1953–1976. New York: Harcourt Brace Jovanovich, 1976.

Elizabeth Bishop: A Memorial Tribute. New York: Albondocani Press, 1982.

''Advice from the Muse.'' Deerfield, Conn.: The Deerfield Press, 1981.

TRANSLATED WORKS

The Misanthrope, by Molière. New York: Harcourt, Brace, 1955.

Candide, by Voltaire. Translated with others. New York: Random House, 1957.

Tartuffe, by Molière. New York: Harcourt, Brace and World, 1963.

The School for Wives, by Molière. New York: Harcourt Brace Jovanovich, 1971.

The Learned Ladies, by Molière. New York: Harcourt Brace Jovanovich, 1978.

Molière: Four Comedies. New York: Harcourt Brace Jovanovich, 1982.

The Whale and Other Uncollected Translations. Brockport, N.Y.: BOA Editions, 1982.

Phaedra, by Racine. San Diego: Harcourt Brace Jovanovich, 1986.

MANUSCRIPT PAPERS

Apart from some early manuscripts in the Poetry Collection, Lockwood Memorial Library, State University of New York at Buffalo, the primary archive of Wilbur's papers is in the Robert Frost Library, Amherst College. This extensive collection includes poetry, translations and adaptations, and miscellaneous papers.

BIBLIOGRAPHY

Field, John P. *Richard Wilbur: A Bibliographical Checklist.* Kent, Ohio: Kent State University Press, 1971. Lists both primary and secondary works.

BIOGRAPHICAL AND CRITICAL STUDIES:

BOOKS

Butts, William, ed. *Conversations with Richard Wilbur.* Jackson: University Press of Mississippi, 1990. An indispensable collection of interviews (1962–1988) with a biographical chronology.

Hill, Donald L. *Richard Wilbur.* New York: Twayne, 1967.

Poulin, A., Jr., ed. *Contemporary American Poetry.* 2nd ed. Boston: Houghton Mifflin, 1975. Pp. 391–405.

Salinger, Wendy, ed. *Richard Wilbur's Creation.* Ann Arbor: University of Michigan Press, 1983. A collection of reviews and essays that includes a bibliography of secondary works.

Wallace, Robert. *Writing Poems.* Boston: Little, Brown, 1982. Pp. 302–309.

ARTICLES

Bogan, Louise. "Verse." *The New Yorker,* November 15, 1947, pp. 130, 133–134.

Ciardi, John. "Our Most Melodic Poet." *The Saturday Review,* August 18, 1956, pp. 18–19.

Farrell, John P. "The Beautiful Changes in Richard Wilbur's Poetry." *Contemporary Literature* 12:74–87 (Winter 1971).

Hall, Donald. "Claims on the Poet." *Poetry* 88:398–403 (September 1956).

Hecht, Anthony. "The Motions of the Mind." *Times Literary Supplement* no. 3923:602 (May 20, 1977).

———. "Master of Metaphor." *The New Republic,* May 16, 1988, pp. 25, 27–30, 32.

Jarrell, Randall. "A View of Three Poets." *Partisan Review* 18:691–700 (November/December 1951).

———. "Fifty Years of American Poetry." *Prairie Schooner* 37:1–27 (Spring 1963).

Jensen, Ejner J. "Encounters with Experience: The Poems of Richard Wilbur." *New England Review* 2:594–613 (Summer 1980).

Leithauser, Brad. "Reconsideration: Richard Wilbur. America's Master of Formal Verse." *The New Republic,* March 24, 1982, pp. 28–31.

McClatchy, J. D. "Dialects of the Tribe." *Poetry* 130:41–53 (April 1977). Includes a review of Wilbur's *Mind-Reader.*

Mills, Ralph J., Jr. "The Lyricism of Richard Wilbur." *Modern Age* 6:436–440 (Fall 1962).

Nemerov, Howard. "What Was Modern Poetry? Three Lectures." In his *Figures of Thought: Speculations on the Meaning of Poetry and Other Essays.* Boston: David Godine, 1978. See Lecture 3, "What Will Suffice," pp. 183–198.

Oliver, Raymond. "Verse Translation and Richard Wilbur." *The Southern Review* (Baton Rouge) 11:318–330 (April 1975).

Sayre, Robert F. "A Case for Richard Wilbur as a Nature Poet." *Moderna Spraak* 61:114–122 (1967).

Taylor, Henry. "Two Worlds Taken as They Come: Richard Wilbur's 'Walking to Sleep.' " *The Hollins Critic* 6:1–12 (July 1969).

Weatherhead, A. K. "Richard Wilbur: Poetry of Things." *ELH* 35:606–617 (1968).

—PETER SACKS

Tom Wolfe

1931–

*I*N THE WORLD of American letters in the late twentieth century, there have been few more colorful and controversial figures than Tom Wolfe. Emerging in the mid 1960's from the milieu of newspaper Sunday supplements and glossy general-interest magazines, he became a prominent practitioner and spokesman for the New Journalism, a hybrid form of nonfiction in which novelistic techniques were applied to factual material. He has fashioned himself into a complex, paradoxical persona—a kind of icon for the times in which he lives. Dressed in hand-tailored white suits with functioning buttons at the cuffs, wearing shirts with high starched white collars, he has immersed himself in the lives of stock-car racers, New York social climbers, striptease artists, astronauts, and gamblers in Las Vegas, reporting on even the least dandified areas of popular culture in a style that simultaneously celebrates and satirizes its subjects. In addition to his work in nonfiction, Wolfe has published fiction and numerous satirical drawings. He has attacked what he characterizes as the pretensions of the literary establishment, and in return has sometimes been labeled a relentless self-promoter whose works have no intellectual and very little literary merit. Yet Wolfe's groundbreaking works of nonfiction have been extremely influential, both in affecting the practices of newspaper and magazine journalism and in making nonfiction a significant literary form of the time.

Thomas Kennerly Wolfe, Jr., was born in Richmond, Virginia, on March 2,1931, to Helen Hughes and Thomas Kennerly Wolfe. His father was a professor of agronomy at Virginia Polytechnic University and the editor of the journal *Southern Planter*. Wolfe's childhood, which seems to have been comfortable and fairly uneventful, was spent entirely in Richmond, where he attended a private school, St. Christopher's. From an early age, he demonstrated an interest in writing. At St. Christopher's, he was the coeditor of the school newspaper; at home, he entertained himself by composing new versions of Arthurian legends. On one occasion, inspired by having read a book about Napoleon, he composed his own "biography" of the emperor. As a teenager, he read widely in American literature, progressing from the popular novels of James T. Farrell and James M. Cain to works by Ernest Hemingway, William Faulkner, John Steinbeck, and Thomas Wolfe (to whom he was not related).

By the time he matriculated at Washington and Lee University in 1947, Wolfe had decided to become a writer. He majored in English, took creative-writing classes, and was one of the three founding editors of *Shenandoah,* a literary magazine with national circulation. He contributed short stories to the magazine's first two issues, which were published in 1950. He dressed somewhat eccentrically, often wearing dark shirts with his suits and never failing to go out without a hat and an umbrella. He also participated in a number of less writerly extracurricular activities, serving as sports editor of the college newspaper and pitching on the varsity baseball team.

Wolfe had ability enough as a pitcher that when he graduated from college, he played semiprofessional baseball and tried out for the major leagues. He quickly found out that he was not talented enough to become a professional ballplayer, and he decided instead to go to graduate school. He entered the American Studies program at Yale University and spent the next five years reading widely. He delved into Elizabethan rhetoric and studied the sociology of religion. He also discovered the works of some Russian avant-garde writers—the Serapion Brothers group, Yevgeni Zamyatin, Boris Pilnyak, Aleksei Remizov, and Andrei Sobol—who had used symbolist techniques to write fiction about the Russian Revolution. Acknowledging that human thought often lacked the finish attributed to it in the conventions of nineteenth-century novels, they broke up their representations of characters' thoughts with odd punctuation. When Wolfe later began to write experimental journalism, he borrowed these techniques, and he has often claimed that the Serapion group, Zamyatin, and their postrevolutionary cohorts were more influential on his writing than anything else that he encountered in graduate school.

Ultimately, Wolfe wrote a dissertation titled ''The League of American Writers: Communist Organizational Activity Among American Writers 1929–1942'' and received a doctorate. Despite his Ph.D., he did not pursue an academic career. Instead, he decided to try to find work on a newspaper. His decision was self-consciously literary. The pantheon of American literature seemed to consist of men who had apprenticed themselves to the art of fiction by working first as reporters. By going to work for a paper, Wolfe determined to place himself squarely within a tradition of great American novelists that included Herman Melville, Mark Twain, Stephen Crane, and Ernest Hemingway.

Wolfe traveled to New York City, hoping to find a job. After four months there, he still had received no offers of employment, and he decided to look for work in other parts of the country. Eventually, he took the only job that was offered to him—on the Springfield *Union,* in Massachusetts. He remained there from 1956 until 1959, when he was hired by the *Washington Post.*

At the *Post,* Wolfe's first assignment was to cover local news of the District of Columbia, a beat that he found more interesting than one as a political correspondent on Capitol Hill. Soon, however, he was given the more important job of Latin-American correspondent, and his coverage of Cuba in 1960 won a Washington Newspaper Guild Award. Nevertheless, he felt limited by the rigid stylistic requirement of the straight news reporting that he was doing for the *Post,* so he sent a portfolio of his clips to the New York *Herald Tribune,* a paper that he felt would be more sympathetic to his talents and disposition as a writer.

Wolfe went to work for the *Herald Tribune* early in 1962. The *Herald Tribune* was a venerable American paper, having been founded by Horace Greeley in the nineteenth century. For almost twenty-five years, however, the publication had suffered financial difficulties. In an effort to save the paper from bankruptcy, its editors were experimenting with both its format and its news style. The *Herald Tribune* placed a greater emphasis on feature reporting than did *The New York Times,* for example, and writers were instructed to bring out the emotional truth—the human interest—of events in as many stories as they could. Headlines were short and to some degree sensationalistic. The result was a journalism that was usually livelier than stories published in *The New York Times,* but that was sometimes thought to be biased and irresponsible.

Wolfe was assigned to the city desk, where he functioned essentially as a feature writer. He reported on such topics as a rent strike staged by students at New York University and the disappearance of a reputed Mafia boss from Fort Lee, New Jersey. He filled his articles with minute, atmospheric details that would have seemed irrelevant in more conventional journalism.

By the end of the year, New York City newspapers had been shut down by a printers' strike; the *Herald Tribune* did not go to press again for 114 days. During the break in the newspaper's publication, Wolfe approached the editors of *Esquire* magazine and proposed several articles to them, including one on the world of custom cars, a subject that he had treated, but in his opinion not done justice to, in an article for the *Herald Tribune. Esquire* sent him to the West Coast, where he gathered information about a subculture that was foreign to sophisticated East Coast readers. When Wolfe returned to New York, he found himself unable to write the article. He felt stymied in his efforts to organize and interpret the material, which seemed to lie outside the bounds of subject matter considered appropriate for cultural analysis. The editors of *Esquire* had reserved space for the article in an issue that would soon be going to press. They had also locked a two-page color illustration onto the printing press. The cost of canceling Wolfe's piece would be enormous, but Wolfe continued to be blocked. Finally, in exasperation, the magazine's editor, Byron Dobell, asked Wolfe simply to submit his typed notes to the magazine, so that a staff member could patch them together into an article.

Wolfe went home and began to type: "Dear Byron, The first good look I had at customized cars was at an event called a 'Teen Fair,' held in Burbank, a suburb of Los Angeles beyond Hollywood. . . ." As he typed, his thoughts began to flow freely into prose. By the middle of the night, Wolfe found himself writing furiously; by morning, his memo to Dobell had ballooned to forty-nine pages. He delivered the manuscript to *Esquire* at 9:30 A.M., and by 4 P.M., Dobell had called to say that the magazine would run the memo as Wolfe had submitted it, simply striking out the words "Dear Byron." The piece appeared in the November 1963 issue under the title "There Goes (Varoom! Varoom!) That Kandy-Kolored Tangerine-Flake Streamline Baby."

Wolfe later described the drafting of the memo to Dobell as a kind of epiphany—a moment when he both saw his subject matter clearly for the first time and realized ways to break free of the standardized formulas of newspaper writing, to go beyond conventional journalism to a form that more fully captured the reality he observed. His subject was the creation of style by members of the American middle class, particularly teenagers, as the result of the money poured into the American economy after World War II. In the introduction to his 1965 collection *The Kandy-Kolored Tangerine-Flake Streamline Baby,* he writes,

Suddenly classes of people whose styles of life had been practically invisible had the money to build monuments to their own styles. Among teen-agers, this took the form of custom cars, the twist, the jerk, the monkey, the shake, rock music generally, stretch pants, decal eyes—and all these things, these teen-age styles of life, like Inigo Jones' classicism, have started having an influence on the life of the whole country.

"There Goes (Varoom! Varoom!) That Kandy-Kolored Tangerine-Flake Streamline

Baby'' was a loosely structured, somewhat rambling account of Wolfe's visit to the Teen Fair and his subsequent investigation of the subculture of custom-car builders. Its tone was casual, and Wolfe thrust himself as first-person narrator right into the middle of the action as a participating observer with some admitted weaknesses. He acknowledged his capacity to become distracted, admitted possible engagement in ''inchoate leching'' at the sight of teenage girls, and said that he had harbored prejudiced or stereotypical notions of what the owners of custom cars are like: ''probably skinny little hoods who wear T shirts and carry their cigarette packs by winding them around in the T shirt up near the shoulder.'' Unlike the standard newspaper story, which uses a pyramidal structure to arrange facts in descending order of importance, ''The Kandy-Kolored Tangerine Flake Streamline Baby'' proceeded almost by free association, mixing description of the car show and biographical treatments of two customizers with frequent digressions to discuss the relationship of the custom-car subculture to the history of Western art. The piece treated a number of themes that became central to the bulk of Wolfe's work. He portrayed the young men's fascination with their fast machines both as a way of defining social status and as a kind of substitute religion. He also articulated a thesis that would prove to be recurrent: despite the cultural establishment's consensus that custom cars were tacky, there was no intrinsic difference between them and great modern art. He thus implied that the determination of artistic gestures has more to do with social fashion than with intrinsic beauty and worth.

Although the stylistic innovations of ''There Goes (Varoom! Varoom!) That Kandy-Kolored Tangerine-Flake Streamline Baby'' were striking, they were nothing compared to what soon followed. Wolfe's trip to California to cover the custom-car show initiated a period of intense journalistic activity. When the printers' strike ended in April 1963, he returned to the city desk at the *Herald Tribune,* and his stories began to be displayed more prominently. The strike, however, had left the paper in the worst financial condition it had yet experienced, and the *Herald Tribune*'s future seemed imperiled. As part of a final effort to save the paper, its editors started a new Sunday supplement, called *New York,* which contained stylishly written stories of life in the city. The magazine made its debut in September 1963, and Wolfe was assigned to write a weekly article for it. Although each of these weekly pieces was supposed to be 1,500 words long, Wolfe's stories usually ran from twice to four times that length.

During the nine succeeding months, Wolfe published twenty articles in *New York.* He also contributed three more stories to *Esquire.* He wrote about demolition derbies on Long Island, stock-car racing in North Carolina, rock-music impresarios, and the Women's House of Detention in Greenwich Village. He composed character sketches of Cassius Clay, Cary Grant, and Huntington Hartford, the heir to the A&P tea company fortune. He described the comings and goings of the wealthy New Yorkers who spent their Saturdays shopping for fine art in the expensive galleries of Manhattan's Upper East Side. He revealed the tyranny that nannies exerted over the families for whom they worked, intimidating their employers into buying expensive British prams and serving champagne at children's birthday parties. The assignments almost blurred into one another. In the introductory essay to his *The New Journalism* (1973), Wolfe described the experience in characteristically vivid terms:

I can remember flying to Las Vegas on my two regular days off from the *Herald Tribune* to do a story for *Esquire*—''Las Vegas!!!!''—and winding up sitting on the edge of a white satin bed in a Hog-Stomping Baroque suite in a hotel on the

Strip—in the decor known as Hog-Stomping Baroque there are 400-pound cut-glass chandeliers in the bathrooms—and picking up the phone and dictating to the stenograhic battery on the *Trib* city desk the last third of a story on demolition derbies in Long Island for *New York*—"Clean Fun at Riverhead"—hoping to finish in time to meet a psychiatrist in a black silk mohair suit with brass buttons and a shawl collar, no lapels, one of the only two psychiatrists in Las Vegas County at that time, to take me to see the casualties of the Strip in the state mental ward out Charleston Boulevard.

Wolfe's style developed rapidly. He elaborated on the techniques of "There Goes (Varoom! Varoom!) That Kandy-Kolored Tangerine-Flake Streamline Baby," creating an exuberant and copious style. He embraced the brand names and jargon of a burgeoning consumer culture and celebrated them in a breathless, syncopated prose. He pursued specificity relentlessly, multiplying details far beyond both necessity and the previous limits of journalistic decorum. He cannibalized his own metaphors, and with each rearticulation, his tropes seemed pushed to further expenses of factual and imagined detail. In "There Goes (Varoom! Varoom!) That Kandy-Kolored Tangerine Flake Streamline Baby," for example, he had described the skin-tight pants then fashionable among teenage girls by writing that "well, skin-tight does not get the idea across; it's more the conformation than how tight the slacks are. It's as if some lecherous old tailor with a gluteus-maximus fixation designed them, striation by striation." In "The Peppermint Lounge Revisited," which he wrote for *New York* in December 1963, he described the same kind of pants again. That piece begins:

All right, girls, into your stretch nylon denims! You know the ones—the ones that look like they were designed by some leering, knuckle-rubbing old tailor with a case of workbench back who

spent five years, like Da Vinci, studying nothing but the ischia, the gemelli and the glutei maximi.

Wolfe exploited newfound freedom in the relationship between author and journalistic material, developing a series of techniques to radically dislocate the journalistic narrator from his conventionally neutral, objective stance. He began "The Voices of Village Square," a story written for *New York* about the Women's House of Detention in Greenwich Village, by writing

Hai-ai-ai-ai-ai-ai-ai-ai-ai-ai-ai-ai-ai-ai-ai-ai-ai-ai-ai-ai-ai-ai-ai-ai-ai-ai-ai-ai-ai-ai-ai-ai-ai-ai-ai-ai-ai-ai-ai-ai-ai-ai-ai-ai-ai-reeeeeeeeeeeeeeeeeeee!

O, dear sweet, Harry, with your French gangster-movie bangs, your Ski Shop turtleneck sweater and your Army-Navy Store blue denim shirt over it, with your Bloombury corduroy pants you saw in the *Manchester Guardian* airmail edition and sent away for and your sly intellectual pigeon-toed libido roaming in Greenwich Village—that siren call really for you? Hai-ai-ai-ai-ai-ai-ai-ai-ai-ai-ai-ai-ai-aireeeeeeeeeee!

Obviously Harry thinks so.

The most immediately surprising thing about the passage, of course, is its typographic and onomatopoeic extravagance—the repetition of "ai-" forty-eight times in the first paragraph and twelve in the third to create the illusion of a manic female prisoner calling the name "Harry" at the top of her lungs. Beyond its immediate visual eccentricity, the piece makes an even more radical departure from standard journalistic practice. As Wolfe puts it in his essay "The New Journalism," he as narrator here "hectors" his subject—directly addressing him in a sarcastic tone, making fun of his clothes, his haircut, his quasi-intellectual attitude, his awkward sexuality. By the beginning of the fourth paragraph, the narrator has shifted direction and is addressing the reader in an intimate, confiding tone, suggesting by the phrase "Obviously Harry thinks so" that the truth of his judgments of Harry are also obvious to the reader.

As often as Wolfe adopted an adversarial stance toward his subject, he merged the subject's voice with his own, creating a version of *style indirect libre* that he later called "the downstage voice." Often his modulation into the perspective of one of his characters was only fleeting and momentary, but occasionally he based entire passages on it. For example, he began "The First Tycoon of Teen," a piece for *New York* about the rock-music impresario Phil Spector, by entering Spector's mind as he sat in a plane awaiting takeoff:

All these raindrops are *high* or something. They don't roll down the window, they come straight back, toward the tail, wobbling, like all those Mr. Cool snow heads walking on mattresses. The plane is taxiing out toward the runway to take off, and this stupid infarcted water wobbles, sideways, across the window. Phil Spector, twenty-three years old, the rock and roll magnate, producer of Philles Records, America's first teen-age tycoon watches . . . this watery pathology. . . . It is *sick, fatal.*

While not as flamboyant as the "hectoring narrator" that began "The Voices of Village Square," passages such as this one, which verges on stream of consciousness, were in many ways more revolutionary and problematic. Wolfe claimed that the passage described what actually went on in the mind of Phil Spector as he sat in the plane just before take-off. He argued that his stream-of-consciousness technique made it possible to record this truth—a higher truth than either conventional reporting or fiction could do. Yet no matter how thorough and accurate Wolfe's reporting, or how detailed Spector's description of what he was thinking at a particular time, it was impossible for Wolfe ever really to know

what was going on inside the mind of another person. To write from a perspective within the subjective experience of another person thus required an epistemological leap more comfortably undertaken by a writer of fiction than of fact. Wolfe's arguments for the higher-truth content of his writing were belied somewhat by the tendency of his stream-of-consciousness passages to all sound fairly similar to one another, no matter which subject's voice was being adopted.

Wolfe's stance toward his subjects was consistently irreverent, even satiric. He made fun of the people he wrote about by giving tremendous importance to the trivial details of their lives, revealing, through this breach of journalistic decorum, that both his subjects and his readers were enraptured by triviality. His satire had a conventional, even puritanical aspect. Wolfe frequently implied that the neon lights, capri pants, decal eyes, and other accoutrements of life in the 1960's were but a thin veneer applied to cover up inexorably rotting flesh, particularly female flesh. In the *Esquire* piece "Las Vegas (What?) Las Vegas (Can't Hear You! Too Noisy) Las Vegas!!!!" for example, he balanced his descriptions of the "buttocks décolletage" pants that prostitutes and other young women wore with the image of four old people from Albuquerque, New Mexico, "up all night, squinting at the sun, belching from a surfeit of tall drinks at eight o'clock Sunday morning and—marvelous!—there is no one around to snigger at what an old babe with decaying haunches looks like in Capri pants with her heels jocked up on decorated wedgies."

By 1965, Wolfe had become a much-discussed figure on the literary scene. His prose had seized the public's attention, and the satirical drawings that he had been producing since his days on the Springfield *Union* had become well enough regarded to be given an exhibition at a New York gallery. Wolfe had also acquired the reputation of a dandy, notorious for the white suit that he seemed always to wear. He had had the suit made in 1962, his first year in New York. It was made of silk tweed. He had intended to wear it during the summer, as men in his native Virginia did, but he found that the material he had chosen was too heavy to wear in hot weather. So he wore the suit in the fall and winter, and quickly found that that gesture infuriated people. This encouraged him to wear the suit all the more. He maintained that his bizarre outfit distanced him from the people whom he interviewed and thus freed him to ask naive questions. He also admitted that he enjoyed the notoriety that his costume brought him.

Early in 1965, Wolfe became the center of a literary scandal resulting from the publication in *New York* on April 11 and 18 of a two-part series of articles about *The New Yorker* magazine. *The New Yorker* was the most respected general-circulation magazine in America, and its reputation was almost sacred. Over its forty-year history, it had regularly published the writing of James Thurber, E. B. White, and Edmund Wilson, among others, and had become famous for publishing long, ground-breaking works of non-fiction. Nevertheless, to Wolfe and to his editor at *New York,* Clay Felker, *The New Yorker* seemed to have grown long-winded and dull—a fair target for critical attack. In addition, the editorial staff of *The New Yorker* were notoriously reticent, even secretive, about the place where they worked, thus making the magazine an alluring subject for a reporter. Wolfe set out to write a profile of the magazine and its editor, William Shawn, but Shawn and most of his staff refused interviews. Wolfe wrote and published the two articles anyway. The first of these he titled "Tiny Mummies! The True Story of the Ruler of 43rd Street's Land of the Walking Dead!" In the article Wolfe, using many of his newly developed techniques, painted a withering portrait of Shawn as a pathologically shy pre-server of the legacy left by Harold Ross, the magazine's founding editor. He argued that

Shawn's obsessively curatorial attitude toward Ross's magazine extended as far as not allowing anyone who came to work at the magazine after Ross's death to put pictures on the walls of their offices. In the second of the two articles, "Lost in the Whichy Thicket," Wolfe made even more damning charges. *The New Yorker*'s prose, he argued, was enervated by a bevy of editors and fact checkers who, acting without the knowledge or consent of the writers themselves, riddled originally taut prose with scores of long and tedious subordinate clauses.

The response was as immediate as it was outraged. Shawn approached the *Herald Tribune*'s owner and asked that the pieces not be published. After his plea went unheeded and the pieces appeared in print, a number of *New Yorker* writers wrote letters to the editor of the newspaper, condemning Wolfe for his malicious attack and pointing out that the pieces were riddled with factual inaccuracies.

Wolfe later argued that the articles were misconstrued. He claimed that he had intended them as a *jeu d'esprit*—a kind of parody that, while based on some facts, ought to have been recognized as obvious fantasy. To most of his readers, however, the parody was not recognizable. The piece, from its title on, claimed that it was the *true* story of *The New Yorker*. And furthermore, the piece by implication argued that these "true" facts about Shawn and the magazine's editorial offices somehow invalidated the journalism that was being produced there, a journalism that was renowned for its factual accuracy.

The scandal created by Wolfe's articles about *The New Yorker* remained very much on the public's mind several weeks later, in June 1965, when a collection of many of the pieces that Wolfe had written for *Esquire* and *New York* was published as *The Kandy-Kolored Tangerine-Flake Streamline Baby*. The book became an immediate best-seller and received generally favorable reviews. The most influential review of the collection, however, was overwhelmingly negative. Dwight Macdonald, a renowned commentator on culture and a frequent contributor to *The New Yorker,* wrote two articles for *The New York Review of Books* in which he eviscerated Wolfe's style in both *The Kandy-Kolored Tangerine-Flake Streamline Baby* and the articles about *The New Yorker.* Macdonald derisively described Wolfe's brand of writing as "parajournalism": "a bastard form, having it both ways, exploiting the factual authority of journalism and the atmospheric license of fiction." Macdonald charged Wolfe with abandoning the traditional mission of the journalist—to convey information—and replacing it with a baser goal—the creation of entertainment. He further argued that Wolfe filled his pieces with both factual inaccuracies and uncheckable facts, and that the distortions created by his radical style prevented the reader from knowing anything about the reality that Wolfe was purporting to describe. Although it was possible to construe these quasi-factual statements as versions of the "knowing details" that fiction writers used to give their works verisimilitude, Macdonald argued, Wolfe's details were not arranged into a meaningful fictional pattern. His pieces themselves were uninteresting unless the facts were really true. And if *The New Yorker* articles were any indications, Wolfe's facts tended not to be. In the second of his two articles, Macdonald painstakingly went through Wolfe's send-up of *The New Yorker* and picked it apart factual inaccuracy by factual inaccuracy.

Although part of Macdonald's animus against Wolfe undoubtedly resulted from anger on behalf of a magazine that employed him, some of his aggressiveness in attacking Wolfe's writing also came from his belief that "parajournalism" had become a widespread and pernicious form of writing. And indeed, by 1965, people had begun to talk about a "new journalism," in which reporters approached their material as writers of fiction would, using novelistic techniques to reveal the inner experiences of their subjects and a deeper truth than the objectively verifiable one typical of most journalistic articles. This talk took place amid a growing sense that the novel had died—that novelists, having run up such blind alleys as metafiction and fabulism, had in fact killed the genre by exhausting its power to describe life. If the novel did not continue to serve its traditional role as the chronicler of society's manners and morals, then the New Journalism would.

Within the next several years, a number of important book-length works of literary nonfiction were published. Truman Capote's *In Cold Blood* was published in 1966 as a book after having been serialized in *The New Yorker,* and Capote claimed that the work initiated a new genre, the "nonfiction novel." Whether or not his claim was true, *In Cold Blood* was soon followed by other works, such as Norman Mailer's *The Armies of the Night* (1968), which staked similarly ambitious claims for the literary importance of nonfiction. Meanwhile, the ranks of journalists who applied fictional techniques to the pieces they wrote for newspapers and magazines continued to grow. They soon included writers such as Hunter Thompson and Joan Didion.

Wolfe continued to write short articles similar to those in *The Kandy-Kolored Tangerine-Flake Streamline Baby,* primarily for *New York.* He returned to California, where he chronicled the lives of surfers and stripteasers. He profiled celebrities as diverse as Hugh Hefner and Marshall McLuhan. He saw, however, that literary nonfiction was becoming a prominent and prestigious form of writing, and he began to search for a topic for a more ambitious piece of writing. Henry Robbins, Wolfe's editor at the publishing house of Farrar, Straus and Giroux, showed Wolfe copies of some letters that the novelist Ken Kesey had written to Larry McMurtry, another novelist, from Mexico, where he was in hiding as a fugitive from drug charges in the United States. Wolfe found the letters intriguing and decided to fly to Mexico to interview Kesey and write a story about the life of a fugitive. Before he could get there, however, Kesey had reentered the United States and been arrested by the FBI. Wolfe flew instead to San Francisco, where Kesey was in jail. He talked to Kesey and met his followers, a group of oddly dressed men and women who referred to themselves as the Merry Pranksters.

Wolfe remained in California interviewing his subjects for a month. His story of Kesey, the Pranksters, and their experiments with LSD first appeared as a three-part series in *New York*. Originally, Wolfe intended to edit the three articles into a single, fairly short piece that he would include in his next anthology. But as he revised the articles, the subject grew to such an extent that he decided to write a book instead. On a single day in 1968, Wolfe staked his claim to importance in the new literary tradition that had so recently and quickly emerged. He published two books: *The Pump House Gang,* a collection of short pieces similar in subject and style to those that had been collected in *The Kandy-Kolored Tangerine-Flake Streamline Baby* and composed during the ten months following the publication of that volume, and *The Electric Kool-Aid Acid Test,* Wolfe's book-length, novelistic account of Kesey and his followers.

The Electric Kool-Aid Acid Test staked Wolfe's claim to the generic importance of literary nonfiction. In both *The Kandy-Kolored Tangerine-Flake Streamline Baby* and *The Pump House Gang,* Wolfe had shied away from the major events of the 1960s—the war in Vietnam, the Kennedy assassination, the civil rights movement—in favor of the description of what were coming to be known as "life-styles"—the ways in which people defined themselves through their pursuit of leisure and their disposal of discretion-ary income. In *The Electric Kool-Aid Acid Test,* he took on one of the major developments of the decade—the emergence of the drug culture and the "hippie" movement—and treated it in a way that resonated with the classic themes of American literature. *The Electric Kool-Aid Acid Test* is in many ways a tale of the frontier. Kesey is a "horny-nailed son of the Western sod," a native of Oregon, the son of a man who moved West in order to seek his fortune. The West in which Kesey grows up, however, is a tamed one—territory swept by "the incredible postwar American electro-pastel surge into the suburbs." This closed, commercialized frontier is the setting for the exploration of the psychological wilderness created by hallucinogenic drugs, particularly LSD.

The structure of *The Electric Kool-Aid Acid Test* is punctuated by two journeys. In the first of these, Kesey and the Pranksters drive a converted school bus painted in psychedelic colors to the New York World's Fair. The journey is aimless and fitful, full of stops and starts. Although the Pranksters ultimately reach New York, they never seem to get to the World's Fair. The goal of the journey becomes simply, as a sign on the front of the bus reads, Furthur. The Pranksters drop acid and make movies of themselves, hoping to achieve a breakthrough in spontaneous communication. They invert the classic pattern of a pattern voyage, substituting a psychological and cognitive frontier for a geographic one as they travel back toward the region from which the pioneers originally came. They also parody the "journey to the East" that often symbolizes the path toward mystical enlightenment. Despite the claims attached to the taking of LSD, the experimentation with drugs on the trip brings dissension, paranoia, and in some cases, insanity, rather than heightened awareness.

The second significant journey of the book, Kesey's flight into Mexico to avoid arrest on drug charges, describes, much more straightforwardly, travel through an actual physical wilderness. The Mexico of his exile is a land of "scrub cactus, brown dung dust and bloated corpses, dogs, coyotes, armadillos, a cow, all gas-bellied and dead, swollen and dead." Kesey lapses into paranoia; his presence in the landscape, which results from the souring of the LSD experience, comes to symbolize psychedelic consciousness gone bad. The story of Kesey in Mexico bears a striking resemblance to the tales of desperadoes that filled volumes of pulp fiction—a similarity that Wolfe said attracted him to the story.

In *The Electric Kool-Aid Acid Test,* Wolfe pushed the shifting points of view and typographical approximations of thought that he had begun to use in *The Kandy-Kolored Tangerine-Flake Streamline Baby* even further than he had in that book. At times, he advanced the narrative through doggerel poetry, and he made more extensive use of stream of consciousness than he had previously. He opens his account of Kesey in Mexico, for example, by entering Kesey's mind as he imagines the police breaking into his hideout to arrest him:

Haul ass, Kesey. Move. *Scram. Split flee hide vanish disintegrate.* Like *run.*

Rrrrrrrrrrrrrrrrrrrrrrrrrev revrevrevrevrevrevrevrevrevrev or are we gonna have just a late Mexican re-run of the scene on the rooftop in San Francisco and sit here with the motor spinning and watch with fascination while the cops they climb up once again to *come git you—*

THEY JUST OPENED THE DOOR DOWN BELOW. ROTOR ROOTER, SO YOU HAVE MAYBE 45 SECONDS ASSUMING THEY BE SLOW AND SNEAKY AND SURE ABOUT IT.

It was more difficult in *The Electric Kool-Aid Acid Test* than in his previous writing for Wolfe to penetrate to the subjective reality of his characters. The passage quoted above is atypical in that Kesey's thoughts, although paranoid and de-

luded, are at least coherent. In contrast the Pranksters' experience is generally ecstatic, irrational, essentially resistant to language. They fill the audio and video tapes that they constantly make with rhyming, playful, but ultimately nonsensical language. This language surrounds them, pouring forth from the sound equipment that they bring with them everywhere. When Wolfe meets Kesey at the Pranksters' warehouse after Kesey's release from jail, for example, his observations are accompanied by the sound of an enigmatic message being played on a tape recorder: "the blissful counterstroke . . . through workhorse and intercourse . . . the blood that was available to him in intercourse . . . made us believe he was in the apple sauce for twenty years."

The Pranksters develop a kind of theoretical justification for their babbling talk. They divide subjective reality neatly into two categories—the enlightenment of the drug experience and the proliferating viewpoints that dominate at other times. Only the enlightened can create and interpret Prankster language; others remain bound by what Kesey refers to as "fantasies." Wolfe borrows vocabulary from the sociology of religion to describe the Pranksters' view of the world. He writes, "The world was simply and sheerly divided into 'the aware,' those who had had the experience of being vessels of the divine, and a great mass of 'the unaware,' 'the unmusical,' 'the unattuned.' " More than had any essay in *The Kandy-Kolored Tangerine-Flake Streamline Baby, The Electric Kool-Aid Acid Test* raises the epistemological issue of whether any writer can enter the mind of his characters in prose and claim that the resulting work is nonfiction. In the author's note to the book, Wolfe presents his sources as evidence that his recreation of the Prankster's "mental atmosphere" was solidly based in fact: "All the events, details and dialogue I have recorded are either what I saw and heard myself or were told to me by people who were there themselves or were recorded on tapes or film or in writing.'' He credits the articulateness of Kesey, who had not only talked to him but allowed him access to letters written from Mexico. He also cites the abundance of tapes, letters, diaries, photographs, and film in the Prankster archives. The text, however, disputes the author's implicit claim that these materials embody an unmediated and fully describable reality. Wolfe repeatedly shows the Pranksters jockeying for control over editing the tapes, resisting what some of them consider Kesey's attempts to manipulate both the events that they record and their own recording of them. The ''documentary'' archives that Wolfe celebrates, in other words, are themselves shaped by minds battling toward power rather than knowledge; they are testaments primarily to the evasiveness of truth and the limitations of individual human perspective.

Despite its claims to capture reality more truly and fully than conventional journalism, even New Journalism is at two removes from subjective experience. The subject chooses what to tell the reporter, and a complex of motives both conscious and unconscious determines that choice. The reporter then selects out material from what the subject has told him, and shapes it. In an ideal world the reporter would shape this material in such a way as to reveal the truth beneath what the subject has presented, but in the real world of journalistic transactions, the reporter's own limited consciousness simply rearranges the utterances of his subjects. The style of *The Electric Kool-Aid Acid Test* is in many ways an acknowledgement of this epistemological problem. Although Wolfe goes further toward stream of consciousness than he had in *The Kandy-Kolored Tangerine-Flake Streamline Baby*, his style—with its turns into narrative poetry, its repetitions, its typographic renderings—seems even more obviously imposed upon the subject than it had in the first book.

With the publication of *The Electric Kool-Aid Acid Test*, Wolfe's interests seemed to shift toward what others considered the central issues of the 1960s. His next book, *Radical Chic & Mau-mauing the Flak Catchers*, appeared in 1970 and deals with manifestations of the racial unrest then besetting the United States. *Radical Chic & Mau-mauing the Flak Catchers* is a more blatantly political book than Wolfe had written previously. The book pairs two pieces: ''Radical Chic'' is an account of a party given by Felicia Bernstein and her husband, New York Philharmonic conductor Leonard Bernstein, to benefit two members of the Black Panther party who had been charged with attempting to blow up the Bronx Botanical Garden. ''Mau-mauing the Flak Catchers'' describes poor blacks and ethnic minorities in Oakland manipulating the welfare bureaucracy.

''Radical Chic'' contains perhaps the most acute social satire that Wolfe ever wrote. After discovering an invitation to the party on another reporter's desk, Wolfe went to the Bernstein's with a notebook in hand. He thought that he was taking notes for a novel that he hoped to write about New York society. He recorded conversations and noted the minute details of both the Bernsteins' apartment and the clothing worn by those in attendance. When he had gathered his material, he decided that it was too good not to publish immediately, so he wrote an article for *New York*. *Radical Chic & Mau-mauing the Flak Catchers* contains a revised version of this article.

The piece casts doubts on the guests' motives for attending the benefit and mocks them brilliantly for being unable to break out of their socially privileged frame of reference. Wolfe adopts the voice of a posited guest:

Mmmmmmmmmmmmmmmm. These are nice. Little Roquefort cheese morsels rolled in crushed nuts. Very tasty. Very subtle. It's the way the dry sackiness of the nuts tiptoes up against the dour savor of the cheese that is so nice, so subtle. Wonder what the Black Panthers eat here on the hors d'oeuvre trail? Do the Panthers like little Roquefort cheese morsels rolled in crushed nuts this way, and asparagus tips in mayonnaise dabs, and *meatballs petites au Coq Hardi,* all of which are at this very moment being offered to them on gadrooned silver platters by maids in black uniforms with hand-ironed white aprons . . . The butler will bring them their drinks . . . Deny it if you wish to, but such are the *pensées métaphysiques* that rush through one's head on these Radical Chic evenings just now in New York.

The passage, with its excessive musing on the quality of the hors d'oeuvres, accentuated by the repetition of "little Roquefort cheese morsels," seems to represent the skewed and inappropriate priorities brought to the party by those who attended.

Wolfe dismissed the party as an example of *nostalgie de la boue,* or "nostalgia for the mud"—the tendency of members of an aristocracy to imitate the manners of the peasant class in order to avoid being confused with the bourgeoisie—which, being only one step removed from the lower classes, cannot afford to imitate peasants, even if only for fun.

The theme was a favorite of his. He had treated it earlier in "Tom Wolfe's Guide to Etiquette," which had appeared in *The Pump House Gang,* and he had mentioned the phrase in passing in several other of his works, but in "Radical Chic" he gives the concept its fullest analysis. He makes fun of the damning paradox implicit in giving a benefit party for the Black Panthers while employing retinues of servants. He also establishes ironic parallels between the "sincere concern" that the partygoers had for the blacks, and their equally deep concern "for maintaining a proper East Side life-style in New York Society"—for having a summer home to which one can escape from "daddies from Long Island

in balloon-seat Bermuda shorts bought at the Times Square Store in Oceanside and fat mommies with white belled pants stretching over their lower bellies and crinkling up in the crotch like some kind of Dacron-polyester labia."

But departing from his strategy in most of his earlier work, in "Radical Chic," Wolfe does not let the satiric narrative speak for itself. He supports his description of the party at the Bernsteins' with lengthy passages of fairly straightforward sociological analysis and exposition of the historical context, occasionally allowing a "downstage voice" to comment on the commentary. The tension between sharp, satirical narrative and nonsatirical analysis ultimately weakens "Radical Chic." Wolfe seems unable to bridge these two modes, and the piece trails off at its end into a discussion of how *The New York Times* reported on the party and a description of developing tensions between blacks and the Jewish Defense League over the issue of black anti-Semitism.

Whatever the weaknesses of "Radical Chic," the title phrase quickly became a byword. The piece also thrust Wolfe into the center of another literary furor. The critical debate surrounding the article centered primarily not on how well Wolfe had satirized the Bernsteins and their guests, but on whether he had any right to satirize such an event at all. Even this far into Wolfe's career, some major critics, most notably Jason Epstein in *The New York Review of Books,* identified the voice of the article with the political opinions of Wolfe himself. Epstein argued that Wolfe had not given the partygoers enough credit for being serious in their political commitments. He pointed out that it was in fact impossible for Wolfe to know just what "*pensées métaphysiques*" might have been running through the minds of the Bernsteins and their guests, and he charged that Wolfe's supposed satire was in fact a projection of his own resentment of the wealthy and powerful onto a set of admirable, if slightly naive, white liberals.

During the early 1970's, Wolfe made use of his ever-growing notoriety to advance the cause of the New Journalism. Wearing his white suit, he traveled the lecture circuit, describing and advocating the techniques that he and other practitioners of the form used. He seemed like a post-psychedelic Mark Twain. At the same time, Wolfe wrote articles about the New Journalism and the death of the novel for *New York* and *Esquire*. He also joined with E. W. Johnson to edit an anthology of the new writing. The book, published in 1973, was titled simply, *The New Journalism*.

In his introduction to *The New Journalism,* Wolfe sketches out the historical and theoretical contexts for the literary nonfiction writing of the 1960's. He places the development of that kind of journalistic writing among a group of newspaper writers who, like Wolfe, had become journalists as a way of biding time until they could "work the fat off their writing" and "escape" to life as novelists. He describes the life of a newspaper reporter in romantic terms that resemble stereotypes from the movies more than they do reality.

Wolfe locates the birth of the New Journalism in the literary milieu of the mid 1960's, when writers began to realize that they could apply many of the techniques of realistic fiction to nonfiction writing—that there was, in other words, no need to "escape" into fiction from a career as a newspaper reporter. He describes how this realization came at a time in which writers and critics were debating the death of the novel and important novelists, among them John Barth, Donald Barthelme, and Thomas Pynchon, were choosing not to write social realism just when society had seemed to become more interesting and problematic than it had been in years.

Wolfe describes the history of the New Journalism with metaphors that cast journalists such as himself into the role of barbarians at the gate, storming the "civilized" empires of conventional journalism and fiction writing. He describes such journalists as unschooled and to a large extent unintellectual, stumbling across the techniques of realism instinctively and accidentally rather than learning them through the study of past masters. "For the gluttonous Goths there is still only the outlaw's rule regarding technique," he writes. "Take, use, improvise."

These metaphors, however, exist in tension with the bulk of the essay's argument and with the learning that Wolfe brings to bear on that argument. Wolfe stakes out elaborate claims for the "new" literary nonfiction as a genre. He traces out a number of historical parallels between the development of the novel and the development of the New Journalism, citing the works of Henry Fielding, Tobias Smollett Honoré de Balzac, Charles Dickens, and Nikolay Gogol as models of realistic writing.

The most important and revolutionary aspect of the New Journalism, he says, was the way in which its practitioners realized the "aesthetic dimension" of reporting and found ways to ferret out the real story behind the official version of any event. In Wolfe's view, the New Journalists were a kind of epistemological elite, perceiving and representing truths that most other reporters missed. Once they had obtained this "real story," the New Journalists shaped it by applying what Wolfe describes as the four standard techniques of realistic fiction: scene-by-scene construction, full recording of dialogue, third-person point of view, and the copious use of details that reveal what he calls the "status life" of the subject being written about.

The result of this hybridization, Wolfe writes, is

a form that is not merely *like a novel*. It consumes devices that happen to have originated with the novel and mixes them with every other device known to prose. And all the while, quite beyond matters of technique, it enjoys an advantage so obvious, so built-in, one almost forgets what a power it has: the simple fact that the reader knows *all this actually happened*. The disclaimers have been erased. The screen is gone. The writer is one step closer to the absolute involvement of the reader that Henry James and James Joyce dreamed of and never achieved.

Wolfe rests his argument on the presupposition that realism was not just a technique but a sine qua non of modern literature, a technological advance analogous to the development of electric power. Without realism, he claims, no literary genius can express itself. He overstates his claims for realism, perhaps deliberately. His celebration of the New Journalism's verisimilitude masks the fact that turning to factual writing had been as much an abandonment of realistic fiction as the move to fabulist novels had been. He leaves unacknowledged his own borrowings from the techniques of the avant-garde. Despite the broad opposition that Wolfe draws between his own work and the experimental fiction of the 1960's, the two forms of writing share a common epistemological stance, both emphasizing, as John Hellman has pointed out, the ways in which human consciousness alters the reality it perceives.

It has been argued that by thus overstating his case, Wolfe hoped to create outrage and thereby publicize his own work. Whatever the reasons for the particular shape of the argument, Wolfe's position was not a fleeting one. During the years following the publication of *The New Journalism,* Wolfe continued his attack on modernism, extending it to the realms of the visual arts and architecture. He published two books, *The Painted Word* (1975) and *From Bauhaus to Our House* (1981), both of which lambasted the avant-garde and held up earlier styles as appropriate models for modern art.

Wolfe had written about the art world since the beginning of his career. In essays such as "The Saturday Route" and "The New Art Gallery Society," which were published in *The Kandy-Kolored Tangerine-Flake Streamline Baby* and "Bob and Spike," which had appeared in *The Pump House Gang,* he had satirized the tendency of wealthy New Yorkers to view modern art as "the center of social rectitude"—as a necessary taste for those wishing to climb the social ladder. His success in these early pieces had resulted from the keenness with which he had observed and recorded the pretensions of living, breathing art patrons.

In *The Painted Word,* Wolfe gives a synoptic history of modern art, structured according to the socioeconomic paradigm that had been implicit in his earlier, shorter essays. He argues that avant-garde artists live and work with a divided sensibility. They owe half their allegiance to the Romantic notion of the artist as rebel, producing works that shock the bourgeoisie; the other half they owe to the prevailing aristocracy, with whom they live in a kind of symbiosis. From the aristocracy, the artist receives his money, his prestige, his fame; from the avant-garde artist, the member of high society receives what Wolfe refers to as

a peculiarly modern reward . . . namely, . . . the feeling that he may be *from* the middle class but he is no longer *in* it . . . the feeling that he is a fellow soldier, or at least an aide-de-camp or an honorary cong guerilla in the vanguard march through the land of the philistines.

Collecting modern art, like supporting the Black Panthers, is no more and no less than a strategic maneuver in a class war.

The result of this sociological arrangement, according to Wolfe, is an art that does not present any obvious visual rewards. It thus gives rise to the secondary institution of art theory, which becomes necessary in order to bestow at least an intellectual interest on works that are not intrinsically appealing. To illustrate this theory, he discussed the writings of three art critics who championed the various movements of modern art—Clement Greenberg, Harold Rosenberg, and Leo Steinberg.

Although *The Painted Word* was the first book that Wolfe published after *The New Journalism,* in it he used fewer of the techniques of the New Journalism than at any other time in his career. Despite his celebration of the art of reporting, *The Painted Word* and *From Bauhaus to Our House* are more essayistic than reportorial. This seeming paradox has several possible explanations. Both pieces were written for *Harper's,* a magazine that nurtured the essay much more than did either *New York* or *Esquire.* The change in style may also have resulted from a desire on Wolfe's part to develop from a journalist into a man of letters. Critics generally agreed that Wolfe's ideas were thin and trivial, and that they could not stand up without the reportage that had enlivened his earlier work. *The Painted Word* and *From Bauhaus to Our House* revealed that Wolfe's aesthetic tastes, like his political tastes, were reactionary.

At the same time that Wolfe was publishing *The Painted Word* and receiving criticism such as this, he was involved in the most sustained work of reporting in his career. Throughout most of the 1970's, he was involved in the research that would lead to his writing *The Right Stuff* (1979), arguably his greatest work. *The Right Stuff* began in January 1973 as a four-part series in *Rolling Stone* magazine on the occasion of the launch of the Apollo 17—the last flight to the moon. Wolfe delivered a chatty, ultimately unsuccessful history of the U.S. space program, written in the putative voice of the "astronauts' collective unspoken." He seemed to delight in his creation of the raunchy, chummy, macho style that he used to express this voice, and his pursuit of this style interfered with the construction of a successful narrative.

Originally, Wolfe intended quickly to rewrite the four articles and publish them in book form in 1973. He soon discovered, however, that he in fact knew very little about the space program, and he spent the following six years traveling across the country, interviewing the astronauts and other participants in the American exploration of space. Some of his subjects were recalcitrant: a few of the astronauts, notably Alan Shepard and Neil Armstrong, refused to be interviewed, and others were either reluctant or unable to describe their emotional states at important historical moments. Wolfe's reporting was also impeded by historical distance: some of the events he described took place as early as 1959, and his subjects simply could not remember what they had said or thought at particular times. To supplement his interviews, Wolfe studied NASA's archives of the program, which had recently been declassified. He made particularly heavy use of the agency's postflight debriefings of the astronauts, during which the astronauts had been asked to describe the particulars of their flights in minute detail.

During the six years that he spent researching *The Right Stuff,* Wolfe continued to write and publish short magazine articles. Some of these were published in *Mauve Gloves & Madmen, Clutter & Vine* (1976), a collection of pieces and drawings dating from as early as 1967. Most of the pieces are in the same mode as the essays in *The Kandy-Kolored Tangerine-Flake Streamline Baby* and *The Pump House Gang.* They include "The Me Decade and the Third Great Awakening," in which Wolfe wrote about the growing trend toward self-actualization movements, programs in which bored and anxious members of the middle class tried to discover and come to terms with their "real" selves. His phrase "the Me Decade" gained wide currency and came to be a kind of tag that defined the 1970's.

"The Truest Sport: Jousting with Sam and Charlie," another of the essays in *Mauve Gloves & Madmen, Clutter & Vine,* was Wolfe's first and only treatment of the Vietnam war, published after the United States had withdrawn its troops. Wolfe celebrated, in strikingly apolitical terms, the bravery of two particular Navy fighter pilots flying missions over North Vietnam from the aircraft carrier *Coral Sea.* The pilots, John Dowd and Garth Flint, are celebrated as heroes not because they endured the suffering imposed on soldiers by politicians carrying out an unjust war, nor because they were brave protectors of Americans from the Communist threat, but because they had the grace to operate complicated, dangerous machinery under the pressure of battle.

"The Truest Sport: Jousting With Sam and Charlie" was in many ways a sketch for *The Right Stuff.* In his foreword to the 1983 paperback edition of that book, Wolfe wrote that, following his *Rolling Stone* articles on the space program, he became fascinated by "the psychological mystery" of why military pilots were willing to take the enormous risks they did in "an era literary people had long since characterized as the age of the anti-hero." He located his topic within a specific literary tradition, contrasting his treatment of pilots' work with novels such as Erich Maria Remarque's *All Quiet on the Western Front* (1929) and Louis-Ferdinand Céline's *Journey to the End of the Night* (1934), in which the main character was the lowly foot soldier, portrayed as a victim rather than a hero of war. Instead of following his antiheroic convention, Wolfe wrote a traditional heroic tale of daring exploits. He argued that he was therein resuscitating a genre that had been relegated to pulp magazines.

In the course of reworking his articles from *Rolling Stone,* Wolfe narrowed the scope of his coverage: instead of writing about the entire space program, he concentrated on the seven Mercury astronauts, the first Americans to be launched into orbit around the Earth. Of all those who participated in the space program, the Mercury astronauts were perhaps the purest versions of the American hero. Viewed as enormously

brave men who had risked their lives in order to help the United States catch up to and then surpass the Soviet Union in space, they had been lionized by the American public—made the recipients of ticker-tape parades and the subjects of frequent, adulatory articles in the press, particularly in *Life* magazine, which had exclusive rights to the personal histories of the astronauts and which cast them into the one-dimensional role of apple-pie, all-American heroes.

In *The Right Stuff,* Wolfe refutes this popular conception of the astronauts' heroism. Once again, as he had in *The Electric Kool-Aid Acid Test,* he fits his story into the pattern of the frontier narrative. Unlike the psychological territories that he had described in *The Electric Kool-Aid Acid Test,* however, space is a literal wilderness, and its exploration yielded at least superficially a tale of conventional heroism, of men risking great physical danger to explore the unknown for the sake of their country. This heroism, which the astronauts themselves were loath to describe, Wolfe refers to simply as "the Right Stuff," the idea that more than simply being willing to die,

a man should have the ability to go up in a hurtling piece of machinery and put his hide on the line and then have the moxie, the reflexes, the experience, the coolness, to pull it back in the last yawning moment—and then to go up *the next day,* and the next day, and every next day, even if the series should prove infinite—and, ultimately, in its best expression, do so in a cause that means something to thousands, to a people, a nation, to humanity, to God.

Yet as it is described in Wolfe's narrative, the astronauts' heroism is something considerably more complex. Inevitably, perhaps, Wolfe places the story of the astronauts' accomplishments within the context of a struggle for status. The status system governing the astronauts' conduct is defined by the exploits of test pilots, who routinely risk death in order to push airplanes through the sound barrier and out of the earth's atmosphere. By repeated demonstrations of daring and mastery of complicated machinery, pilots separate themselves from the ranks of the less expert and join ever-smaller confraternities of pilots with the Right Stuff. Wolfe refers to this process as "climbing the ziggurat." The goal of every pilot is to reside alone at the top of that imaginary pyramid.

Near the opening of *The Right Stuff*, Wolfe draws a portrait of the man who rested atop the pyramid in the days just before the beginning of the space program. Chuck Yeager, the first pilot to break the sound barrier, presides over the fraternity of fliers. Tight-lipped and toughened, he builds feats of heroism out of recklessly daring pranks. He breaks the sound barrier, for example, two days after cracking several of his ribs in a drunken midnight horseback ride across the desert.

For the astronauts to define their heroism against these standards proves problematic. As Yeager himself is quick to point out, the astronauts serve as passengers rather than pilots of their spacecraft and seem to have been chosen for their ability to stay calm in situations that force the relinquishing of control. They are subjected to degrading medical examinations and forced to perform dull, repetitive tasks. The running joke among the astronauts is that they are being trained for a job that could just as easily be accomplished by a chimpanzee.

The astronauts achieve the top of the pyramid in two ways: by gradually asserting their power and prowess, taking control within the bounds of the program, and by having the title of hero bestowed on them from without, by an adoring American public. *The Right Stuff* examines both these aspects of their success, and it becomes as much a study of how Americans form their cultural icons as a description of how individuals rise to the top of whatever status system they

belong to. Wolfe satirizes the wholesome image in which *Life* cloaks the astronauts and shows that the status system defining the world of the pilots and astronauts bears only the slenderest relationship to the status system prevailing in the United States at large. He plays upon the disharmony between the astronauts' successful ascent of the ziggurat and their almost aggressive tackiness—their Ban-lon shirts, their relish of such "low rent" pastimes as hard drinking, drag racing, and womanizing. For Wolfe, this dissonance is the defining characteristic of the astronauts' lives, but it is covered up by a press "determined that in all matters of national importance the *proper emotion,* the *seemly sentiment,* the *fitting moral tone* should be established and should prevail; and all information that muddied the tone and weakened the feeling should simply be thrown down the memory hole." Wolfe refers to this press as "the consummate hypocritical Victorian gent."

Wolfe's own style in *The Right Stuff* is simpler and perhaps closer to the fictional models he espoused in *The New Journalism* than it had been previously in his career. The language is freer of experimental techniques than it had been, for example, in *The Electric Kool-Aid Acid Test*. Wolfe used an omniscient point of view to narrate the book, frequently modulating into a downstage voice that was considerably more restrained than it had been in the *Rolling Stone* articles. The characters are presented almost as caricatures, flattened into assemblages of a few salient characteristics that are then repeated almost as epic epithets. John Glenn is the "good Presbyterian," the one astronaut who turned his back on the rowdy behavior of his colleagues and "seemed to enjoy shocking people with his clean living." Alan Shepard switches between two personas— that of the "Icy Commander," a stern and correct career Navy officer, and "Smilin' Al of the Cape," whose eyes glow at the sight of Corvettes and nubile young women. Phrases such as these delimit Wolfe's characterization of the astronauts, defining their conflicts with each other and their grappling with the demands of the Mercury program. Through this flattened style, Wolfe mimicked the form of *Life* magazine's pop heroism while undermining its presuppositions.

The cartoonlike quality of his characterizations is a response to the epistemological issues raised by the book's subject. As Chris Anderson has pointed out, *The Right Stuff*, like *The Electric Kool-Aid Acid Test*, ultimately concerns itself with the difficulty, if not the impossibility, of capturing reality in words. Reticence is central to the code of pilot conduct. As Wolfe puts it, "The very words *death, danger, bravery, fear* were not to be uttered except in the occasional specific instance or for ironic effect." Instead, the subjects of bravery and death were to be "adumbrated in *code* or *by example*." The reticence that governs the pilots' conduct also dictates Wolfe's flattened style. To violate that reticence with complex explications of psychology and motive would have been to falsify the nature of the astronauts' experience.

The Right Stuff was the most critically and commercially successful book that Wolfe had yet published. It won both the American Book Award and the National Book Critics Circle Award for nonfiction in 1980, and it was later made into a Hollywood film. During the years immediately following the publication of the book, Wolfe maintained a steady literary output, but his reportorial activity once again seemed to slow. In 1979 and 1980, he published a series of satiric cartoons with text in *Harper's*, under the title "In Our Time." The pieces, although amusing, were frivolous, taking on the all-too-familiar questions of status and style without further developing his ideas on those subjects. Wolfe nevertheless republished the series in 1980, along with some other fugitive magazine pieces, as a book which also bore the title *In Our Time*. In 1981, he published *From Bauhaus to Our House*,

his sequel, as it were, to *The Painted Word*. The following year, *The Purple Decades*, an anthology of his best and best-known pieces, was released.

From very early in his career, Wolfe had publicly announced his intention to write a novel. On several occasions, Wolfe had even said that he was currently at work on one. His descriptions of this work varied somewhat in their particulars. At some times, he announced that he was writing a novel about teenagers. At others, he claimed to be writing a book called "Vanity Fair" which he said would describe all of life in New York. He vacillated on the question of whether that book was fiction or nonfiction. He said, however, that he wanted to write a book that was about New York City in the same way that Balzac's and Zola's works had been about Paris and Dickens' and Thackeray's had been about London. "Radical Chic" had started out as a kind of working paper for this enterprise.

For years, nothing materialized. But in the summer of 1984, *Rolling Stone* magazine published the first installment of a serialized novel by Wolfe, called *The Bonfire of the Vanities*. The enterprise seemed perhaps more appropriate to Victorian England than to an American rock-and-roll magazine in the 1980's. It was, however, in keeping with the pattern of *The Electric Kool-Aid Acid Test* and *The Right Stuff*, each of which was first published serially in a magazine and then, significantly revised, published as books.

Wolfe wrote to deadline each week, publishing each chapter or group of chapters before the following ones were written. His topic, as he had promised, was New York City, and he "reported" the story in much the same manner and to much the same extent as he had reported his works of nonfiction. The plot centered on the downfall of Sherman McCoy, a wealthy white Manhattanite who, while driving with his mistress, gets lost in the South Bronx and mortally injures a poor black teenager named Henry Lamb in a hit-and-run automobile accident. To write the story, Wolfe rode the subways back and forth to the Bronx, making detailed observations of the other passengers. He investigated the Bronx criminal court system. And he drew upon his long exposure to the life of wealthy New Yorkers—the world he had described in such pieces as "Radical Chic"—to fashion the character and the environment of McCoy.

The serialization of Wolfe's novel proved to be something of an education in fiction writing carried out in public. Between the time that *The Bonfire of the Vanities* appeared in *Rolling Stone* and its publication as a book in 1987, Wolfe made significant revisions to the text. He renamed some of his characters, altered significant details of the plot, tightened the dialogue and description, and redrew the character of Sherman McCoy. In the *Rolling Stone* series, Wolfe had cast McCoy as a best-selling author and self-made man, the son of a very middle-class "quality-control engineer" for a General Electric plant in Springfield, Massachusetts. In the story's serial version, McCoy lives in an enormous Park Avenue apartment with a marble foyer, and he frequents the dinner parties of the *haut monde*. While the McCoy of the final version lives in the same apartment and goes to the same dinner parties, his profession and family background have been changed, so that the faintly autobiographical but unconvincing portrait of the magazine series has been revised into a coherent and convincing character. The revised Sherman McCoy is a Yale-educated millionaire bond trader on Wall Street, the son of a blue-blooded WASP lawyer.

McCoy is ultimately brought down not by his own moral flaw but by the coincidence of other people's ambitions, charted through the conventionally intricate plotting of a Victorian novel. McCoy's accident becomes a cause célèbre for each member of an enormous cast of characters, including a militant black minister from Harlem,

a Bronx district attorney running for reelection in a racially troubled city, and a dissipated British reporter for a tabloid newspaper, who hopes to resuscitate a dying career by covering the scandalous crime. Each of these characters cynically adopts the comatose Henry Lamb as an emblem of industrious black youth trying to escape a life of crime in the ghetto. Each likewise makes McCoy a scapegoat for all the crimes that powerful white New York has ever inflicted on the black underclass.

Wolfe's revision of the character of McCoy gives a topical edge to the satire, anchoring the fiction more firmly in the apocalyptically greedy New York of the 1980's. It also allows Wolfe to draw an extensive allusion to *The Great Gatsby*, as Nicholas Lemann pointed out in his review of the novel in *The Atlantic* magazine. In both novels, an automobile accident in which a rich man, accompanied by his mistress, kills someone who is economically and socially downtrodden leads to the wealthy man's downfall. Wolfe inverts the socioeconomic pattern of F. Scott Fitzgerald's novel: whereas Jay Gatsby is a member of the nouveau riche who is betrayed by his aristocratic friends Daisy and Tom Buchanan, in Wolfe's novel, it is McCoy the blueblood who is done in by the treachery of the new rich.

For all its narrative sweep and its resonance with classic American literature, *The Bonfire of the Vanities* is not without its flaws. No one character, not even McCoy, is sufficiently rounded to elicit much sympathy from the reader. As Lemann argued, for all the novel's resemblance to *The Great Gatsby*, it lacks that work's elegiac tone and ultimately seems rather hollow.

The Bonfire of the Vanities nevertheless enjoyed enormous popular success. Because of its stylistic conservatism, some critics dismissed it as simply a popular novel. It is too soon to know whether the novel, despite its flaws, will come to be viewed as a serious work of literature, but since the publication of the book, Wolfe has created another literary uproar by attempting to formulate a theoretical justification for the kind of conventional fiction that he wrote. In an essay for *Harper's* titled "Stalking the Billion-Footed Beast: A Literary Manifesto for the New Social Novel," Wolfe returns to the territory that he had last explored in his introduction to *The New Journalism*. He approaches the question of realism in literature from the perspective of a fiction writer rather than a journalist, in some sense fulfilling the prediction that he had made in the essay opening the 1973 book that "there is a tremendous future for a sort of novel that will be called the journalist novel or perhaps documentary novel, novels of intense social realism based upon the same painstaking reporting that goes into the New Journalism." Once again, he takes issue with the absurdist, magical realist, and neofabulist writers of the 1960's and 1970's, arguing that realism is not simply one of a large variety of stylistic devices available to the writer, but a kind of technological advance, "like the introduction of electricity into engineering." And once again, he claims that "the *petis faits vrais* that create verisimilitude and make a novel gripping or absorbing . . . are essential for the very greatest effects literature can achieve."

In the early 1990's, Tom Wolfe was at work on another novel. Regardless of the directions his career takes, his journalistic work and his interpretations of that work have deeply influenced the writing of nonfiction and helped to accord a literary status to that kind of writing. Whatever the merits and defects of his work, his career seems a testament to a prescription that he himself issued in "Stalking the Billion-Footed Beast": "America today, in a headlong rush of her own, may or may not truly need a literature worthy of her vastness. But American novelists, without any doubt, truly need, in this neurasthenic hour, the spirit to go along for that wild ride."

Selected Bibliography

WORKS OF TOM WOLFE

The Kandy-Kolored Tangerine-Flake Streamline Baby. New York: Farrar, Straus and Giroux, 1965.

"Lost in the Whichy Thicket: *The New Yorker*—II." *New York*, April 18, 1965, pp. 16–24, 44.

"Tiny Mummies! The True Story of the Ruler of 43rd Street's Land of the Walking Dead!" *New York*, April 11, 1965, pp. 7–9, 24–27.

"How You Can Be As Well-Informed As Tom Wolfe." *Esquire*, November 1967, pp. 138, 212.

"The Author's Story." *The New York Times Book Review*, August 18, 1968, pp. 2, 40–41.

The Electric Kool-Aid Acid Test. New York: Farrar, Straus and Giroux, 1968.

The Pump House Gang. New York: Farrar, Straus and Giroux, 1968.

Radical Chic & Mau-mauing the Flak Catchers. New York: Farrar, Straus and Giroux, 1970.

"The Birth of the New Journalism: Eyewitness Report by Tom Wolfe." *New York*, February 14, 1972, pp. 30–45.

"The New Journalism: A la Recherche des Whichy Thickets." *New York*, February 21, 1972, pp. 39–48.

"Why They Aren't Writing the Great American Novel Anymore." *Esquire*, December 1972.

The New Journalism. New York: Harper & Row, 1973. With an anthology edited by Tom Wolfe and E. W. Johnson.

The Painted Word. New York: Farrar, Straus and Giroux, 1975.

Mauve Gloves & Madmen, Clutter & Vine. New York: Farrar, Straus and Giroux, 1976.

The Right Stuff. New York: Farrar, Straus and Giroux, 1979; Bantam, 1983.

In Our Time. New York: Farrar, Straus and Giroux, 1980.

From Bauhaus to Our House. New York: Farrar, Straus and Giroux, 1981.

The Purple Decades. New York: Farrar, Straus and Giroux, 1982.

The Bonfire of the Vanities. New York: Farrar, Straus and Giroux, 1987.

"Stalking the Billion-Footed Beast: A Literary Manifesto for the New Social Novel." *Harper's*, November 1989, pp. 45–56.

INTERVIEWS

Bellamy, Joe David. "Tom Wolfe." In his *The New Fiction: Interviews with Innovative American Writers*. Urbana, Ill.: University of Illinois Press, 1974. Pp. 75–96.

Hayman, Ronald. "Tom Wolfe in Interview." *Books and Bookmen*. 25:29–31 (November 1979).

Monaghan, Charles. "Portrait of a Man Reading." *Washington Post Book World*, September 1, 1968, p. 2.

Scura, Dorothy M., ed. *Conversations with Tom Wolfe*. Jackson, Miss., and London: University Press of Mississippi, 1990.

BIOGRAPHICAL AND CRITICAL STUDIES

Anderson, Chris. *Style As Argument: Contemporary American Nonfiction*. Carbondale, Ill., and Edwardsville, Ill.: Southern Illinois University Press, 1987.

Booker, Christopher. "Inside the Bubble: Re-reading Tom Wolfe." *Encounter*, September 1977, pp. 72–77.

Bredahl, A. Carl. "An Exploration of Power: Tom Wolfe's Acid Test." *Critique*, 23:67–84 (Winter 1981–1982).

Buckley, William F., Jr. "Mau-mauing Wolfe." *National Review*, January 12, 1971, p. 51.

Cohen, Ed. "Tom Wolfe and the Truth Monitors: A Historical Fable." *Clio*, 16:1–11 (Fall 1986).

Compton, Neil. "Hijinks Journalism." *Commentary*, 47:76–78 (February 1969).

Coyne, John R., Jr. "Sketchbook of Snobs." *National Review*, January 26, 1971, pp. 90–91.

Dickstein, Morris. "The Working Press, the Literary Culture, and the New Journalism." *Georgia Review*, 30:855–877 (Winter 1976).

Dunne, John Gregory. "Hog Heaven." *The New York Review of Books*, November 8, 1979, pp. 9–12.

Eason, David L. "Telling Stories and Making Sense." *Journal of Popular Culture* 15:125–129 (Fall, 1981).

———. "New Journalism, Metaphor, and Culture." *Journal of Popular Culture*, 15:142–149 (Spring 1982).

Edwards, Thomas R. "The Electric Indian." *Partisan Review*, 36:535–544 (1969).

———. "Low Expectations." *The New York Review of Books*. February 4,1988, pp. 8–9.

Epstein, Jason. "Journal du Voyeur." *The New York Review of Books*, December 17, 1970, pp. 3–6.

Epstein, Joseph. "Tom Wolfe's Vanities." *New Criterion*. 6:5–16 (February 1988).

Fishwick, Marshall, ed. "The New Journalism." *Journal of Popular Culture*, 9:95–249 (Summer 1975).

Gareffa, Peter M., and Mary V. McLeod. "Wolfe, Thomas Kennerly, Jr." In *Contemporary Authors*. New Revision Series. Detroit, Mich.: Gale Research Company, 1983.

Garrett, George. "Ladies in Boston *Have* Their Hats: Notes on WASP Humor." In *Comic Relief: Humor in Contemporary American Literature*. Edited by Sarah Blacher Cohen. Urbana, Ill.: University of Illinois Press, 1978.

Hartshorne, Thomas L. "Tom Wolfe on the 1960's." *Midwest Quarterly*, 23:144–163 (1982).

Hellman, John. *Fables of Fact: The New Journalism as New Fiction*. Urbana, Ill.: University of Illinois Press, 1981.

Hersey, John. "The Legend on the License." *Yale Review*, 70:1–25 (1980).

Hollowell, John. *Fact and Fiction: The New Journalism and the Nonfiction Novel*. Chapel Hill, N.C.: University of North Carolina Press, 1977.

Ivester, Stan. "The Latest from the Human Lapsometer." *Chicago Review*, 31:39–45 (Spring 1980).

Johnson, Michael L. *The New Journalism: The Underground Press, the Artists of Nonfiction, and Changes in the Established Media*. Lawrence, Kans.: University Press of Kansas, 1971.

Johnston, George Sim. "Manhattan Cut in Slices." *The American Spectator*, March 1985, pp. 25–27.

Kallan, Richard A. "Style and the New Journalism: A Rhetorical Analysis of Tom Wolfe." *Communication Monographs*, 46:52–62 (March 1979).

Kluger, Richard. *The Paper: The Life and Death of the New York "Herald Tribune."* New York: Alfred A. Knopf, 1986.

Lemann, Nicholas. "New York in the Eighties." *The Atlantic Monthly*, December 1987, pp. 104–107.

Letters to the Editor. *Harper's*, February 1990, 4–13.

Lewin, Leonard C. "Is Fact Necessary?" *Columbia Journalism Review,* Winter 1966, pp. 29–34.

Lounsberry, Barbara. "Tom Wolfe's Negative Vision." *South Dakota Review* 20:15–31 (Summer 1982).

Macdonald, Dwight. "Parajournalism, or Tom Wolfe and his Magic Writing Machine." *The New York Review of Books,* August 26, 1965, pp. 3–5.

———. "Parajournalism II: Wolfe and The New Yorker." *The New York Review of Books,* February 3, 1966, pp. 18–24.

Powers, Thomas. "The Lives of Writers." *Commonweal,* March 3, 1978, pp. 142–143, 147–148.

———. "Wolfe in Orbit: Our Mercurial Interests." *Commonweal,* October 12, 1979, pp. 551–552.

Rafferty, Terrence. "The Man Who Knew Too Much." *The New Yorker,* February 1, 1988, pp. 88–92.

Richardson, Jack. "New Fundamentalist Movement." *The New Republic,* September 28, 1968, pp. 30–35.

Rose, Barbara. "Wolfeburg." *The New York Review of Books,* June 26, 1975, pp. 26–8.

Ross, Charles S. "The Rhetoric of the Right Stuff." *The Journal of General Education,* 33:113–122 (1981).

Sheed, Wilfrid. "A Fun-House Mirror." *The New York Times Book Review,* December 3, 1972, pp. 2, 10–12.

Sommer, Robert. "Tom Wolfe on Modern Architecture: Further Comparisons of New Journalism and Social Science." *Journal of Popular Culture* 18:111–115 (Fall 1984).

Stone, Laurie. "Spaced Out." *The Village Voice,* September 10, 1979, pp. 71, 73, 76.

Tanner, Tony. *City of Words: American Fiction 1950–1970.* New York: Harper & Row, 1971.

Trachtenberg, Alan. "What's New?" *Partisan Review,* 41:296–302 (1974).

Tuchman, Mitch. "The Writings of Tom Wolfe: The Manchurian Candidate." *The New Republic,* October 25, 1975, pp. 21–24.

Vigilante, Richard. "The Truth About Tom Wolfe." *National Review,* December 18, 1987, pp. 46, 48–49.

Weber, Ronald, ed. *The Reporter as Artist: A Look at the New Journalism Controversy.* New York: Hastings House, 1974.

Weber, Ronald. "Tom Wolfe's Happiness Explosion." *Journal of Popular Culture,* 8:71–79 (Summer 1974).

———. *The Literature of Fact: Literary Nonfiction in American Writings.* Athens, Ohio: University of Ohio Press, 1980.

———. "Staying Power." *Virginia Quarterly Review,* 59:548–552 (1983).

Wills, Garry. "Imprisoned in the Sixties." *The New York Review of Books,* January 20, 1977, pp. 22–23.

Yagoda, Ben. "Astronauts and Other Icons of Pop Culture." *Books and Arts,* September 28, 1979, pp. 14–15.

Zavarzadeh, Mas'ud. *The Mythopoetic Reality: The Postwar American Nonfiction Novel.* Urbana, Ill.: University of Illinois Press, 1976.

—MICHELLE PRESTON

James Wright

1927–1980

"**I** HAVE WASTED my life," James Wright confesses in the last line of his best-known poem, "Lying in a Hammock at William Duffy's Farm in Pine Island, Minnesota." At once imperative and despairing, Wright's confession seems a plea that life be taken on its own terms; that life is more than the sum of days. A later prose poem, "Honey" (collected in *Above the River*), returns to similar emotional terrain. "My father died a good death," Wright concludes. "To die a good death means to live one's life. I don't say a good life. I say a life." It is Wright's contention that a good life would be somewhat limiting. Where would we be without loss, without even a brief acquaintance with despair? James Wright's is a poetry that cannot answer such a question. It takes a long, hard look at loss, finding among such pains some few rewards, and the occasional epiphany that life is worth living.

Born December 13, 1927, James Arlington Wright was the middle son of Dudley and Jesse Lyons Wright. That he was born in Martins Ferry, Ohio, in an area of the United States known for its mills and factories, for the frequent poverty of its citizens, is perhaps a fact more significant to Wright's work than the date of his birth. The poetry of place, of remembered or newly encountered towns and cities, would become in many ways Wright's stock-in-trade. In a brief essay titled "Childhood Sketch" he writes:

I was born . . . on Union Street. I don't know why I should cling to that particular useless detail. It may have something to do with the frequency of my family's moving. By the time I was ten years old we had lived in at least half a dozen houses, which were scattered apart from one another about as widely as possible in a small town of 16,000 inhabitants. . . . I love the variety of Martins Ferry, a skinny place stretched out along the river between the railroad and the abrupt hills.

Dudley and Jesse Wright were members of the working class. "My father worked as a die-setter at the Hazel-Atlas Glass Company. . . . He was a handsome man of great physical strength and the greatest human strength of all, an enduring gentleness in the presence of the hardship that the Great Depression brought to everyone," Wright remembered in "Childhood Sketch." "My mother's family came from West Virginia, and they were honest-to-God hillbillies to fare-thee-well." Theirs was an impoverished dignity. It is not hard to imagine the Wrights deeply and profoundly affected by the Depression, to imagine the young boy and his mother walking the nearby railroad tracks looking for stray lumps of coal fallen from passing trains. Although we cannot say with any certainty that such an incident ever happened, Wright's early childhood, its commonplace disadvantages, were a continual influence upon his life and his work. His parents, his native Ohio, the mills and factories comprising his first neighborhoods, the Ohio River: all recur throughout the body of his poetry.

Educated in public schools, James Wright began to write at an early age, his first inspirations the poems of James Whitcomb Riley and Lord Byron. Those early poems that survive seem at once sentimental and bitter, without the benefit of experience. His biographer Peter Stitt does however inform us that Wright "suffered a nervous breakdown" in his sixteenth year, a fact that might account for the somewhat maudlin tone of his early lyrics. A selection of these poems, published in the *Gettysburg Review* in 1990, reveals an adolescent's fascination with the self, and with romantic notions of art. In "To Justify My Singing," for example, the youthful Wright asserts:

> I am in love with poetry
> And she my love has been,
> For she has let me revel free
> In the sea of things unseen.

However naive, these early poems are technically sophisticated, employing a knowledge of form and meter well advanced for a young man. Nor does their relative immaturity belie a certain wit. The lines above are little if not filled with assonance ("poetry," "she," "me," "free"); yet, this heavy-handedness leads naturally into the wordplay of "sea" and "unseen."

After high school, Wright joined the army. The year was 1946: World War II had recently ended, and Wright found himself stationed in Occupied Japan, where he worked as a typist and continued to write poems. One ("Poem," reprinted in Stitt's selection in the *Gettysburg Review*) reveals a greater sense of emotional as well as technical control:

> . . .tonight I heard the whirring
> Of crickets that disturbs your pompom
>   whores
> Stirring in their beds on barren floors,
> And I could smell, not see, a stink stirring
>
> Through the night air; and suddenly I knew
>   I was not dreaming of Japan, I was alive
>   Hearing and smelling what the Japanese
>   poets could not give.
> I sat amazed, while the nightwind blew.

Wright goes on to exclaim, "To hell with poetry." Here, in some sense, are the beginnings of his attraction to harsher realities. "A human whore is a human whore / With a human face and a living, beating heart." His refusal, though, to indulge in "abstraction" is less an acceptance, an embracing of life's difficult truths, than it is a refusal of metaphor. "I knew her," he writes, "and no more." It is a youthful denial of poetry's transformative powers, powers that characterize Wright's mature work.

Shortly after his discharge from the army, Wright entered Kenyon College on the G. I. Bill. Because of his military enlistment after high school, Wright was older and more experienced than most other incoming freshman. Among his classmates was E. L. Doctorow, who enrolled at Kenyon fresh from the Bronx High School of Science. In a memoir of their years at Kenyon, Doctorow describes Wright as he appeared when they first met.

He was a hulking fellow, not particularly tall but built like a wrestler, with sloping shoulders and a size eighteen neck. . . . He had a round face with particularly small features—small mouth, and small eyes encircled with a pair of colorless plastic G.I. glasses which he regularly adjusted because his small nose had not a sufficient bridge to keep them up where they belonged.

Doctorow recalls Wright's appearance as seeming at odds with his intellectual capabilities, his talent for recitation of poems from memory. The novelist also notes Wright's "cultivation and celebration of the outcasts and pariahs of the college." It is clear that, from early on, Wright's intellectual allegiances lay with the high and the classical, and his emotional allegiances with the low, with the offbeat and the dispirited.

He was carrying within him such enormous contradictions—this dirt poor Ohioan set down in the intellectual park of an historic, private college, this poet alive in the constitution of a football lineman, this irremediably Midwestern American in unslakeable thirst for the language and culture of Europe.

Among Wright's teachers was the poet John Crowe Ransom, who had joined the faculty of Kenyon College in 1937. Ransom, an influential member of the Agrarians, a proponent of New Criticism, and the founder of the literary quarterly *Kenyon Review,* had earlier taught Kenyon graduates Robert Lowell and Peter Taylor. In an interview with Dave Smith, Wright credited Ransom with having taught him of "the Horatian ideal" in poetry: "the attempt finally to write a poem that will be put together so carefully that it . . . produce[s] a single unifying effect." Wright's poems first appeared nationally in the *Kenyon Review,* and Ransom was primarily responsible for Wright's receiving that magazine's poetry fellowship some years later, in 1958.

During his senior year at Kenyon, Wright completed an honors thesis on Thomas Hardy, and he graduated in the winter of 1952. Shortly after graduation, he married his high-school sweetheart, Liberty Kardules. The couple traveled the states from Ohio to Texas, and when Wright received a Fulbright fellowship to the University of Vienna, they went abroad to Austria. From Vienna, the Wrights returned to the United States, their newborn son Franz in tow. Wright then en-

rolled in the master's program at the University of Washington in Seattle, where he studied with Theodore Roethke and Stanley Kuntiz. After completing his master's degree, Wright entered the school's Ph.D. program, which he completed in 1959 with a dissertation titled "The Comic Imagination of the Young Dickens."

Wright's first book of poems, *The Green Wall,* was selected by W. H. Auden for the Yale Series of Younger Poets and published in 1957. In his foreword, Auden notes a theme that became a characteristic of Wright's work as a whole: a celebration of the outcast, to paraphrase E. L. Doctorow: "aside from love poems and poems addressed to relatives, the persons who have stimulated Mr. Wright's imagination include a lunatic, a man who has failed to rescue a boy from drowning, a murderer, a lesbian, a prostitute, a police informer, and some children, one of them dead."

The Green Wall comprises five sections: "Scenes and Laments," "To Troubled Friends," "Loves," "Stories and Voices," and an untitled final section. It opens with the poem "A Fit Against the Country," from which the volume takes its title. The wall, which appears in the poem's final stanza, seems an ivied partition (or fence), or a verdant hedge separating one weather, one season from another. To climb over "the green wall" is to leave behind a "vacant paradise" in which nature's usual suspects appear "bright" but somehow menacing. The first three stanzas of "A Fit Against the Country" (octaves ending in off-rhymed couplets) meld present description with past memory, the tense changing in the final lines. Here is the first stanza:

> The stone turns over slowly,
> Under the side one sees
> The pale flint covered wholly
> With whorls and prints of leaf.
> After the moss rubs off
> It gleams beneath the trees,

Till all the birds lie down.
Hand, you have held that stone.

The birds occupying the second and third stanzas, sparrow and tanager, become in their respective final lines remembered song and color: "Ear, you have heard that song" and "Eye, you have seen that bright color." Hand, ear, eye, give way to nose and mouth, which have known "the dark tang of earth." The "watered mouth," acquainted with soil, seems almost sexual, if not vaguely Freudian: the son who tastes his mother's flesh. In the last stanza, the body made whole again is advised to "hold [its] humor / Away from the tempting tree." The only tree mentioned in the poem so far is an apple, and it is the fruit and not the tree itself to which Wright alludes. "Odor of fallen apple / Met you across the air," he writes. The "fallen apple," the knowledge already won (at what cost?), signifies Wright's awareness of exile. The apple is the remembered fruit of a paradise ("the tempting tree, / The grass, the luring summer / That summon the flesh to fall") vacated not by nature but by man and woman. The fall to which the flesh is summoned is the loss of a prelapsarian innocence, though innocence seems ultimately too coy a word for Wright's well-honed sensibilities. We would do better to speak of a nostalgia, an affection, gone sour.

The weight of biblical allusion might seem heavy if a reader considers such reference an invocation of Judeo-Christian religion. But an expression of religious faith, questioned or unquestioned, is not Wright's aim. Wright's poetry seems almost decidedly agnostic. (He was raised a nonpracticing Protestant.) Rather, such allusions seem references to a common history, a shared mythology, sometimes subtle (as in "A Fit Against the Country") and sometimes overt. The epigram to "The Horse" (". . . the glory of his nostrils is terrible") is taken from Job 39:20.

19. Hast thou given the horse strength? hast thou clothed his neck with thunder?
20. Canst thou make him afraid as a grasshopper? the glory of his nostrils is terrible.

The horse's temerity is thrown into relief by the grasshopper's uncourageousness, as is the rider ("some young foolhardy dweller of the barrows") by the thrown (the wife, "whose saddle rocked her as a cradled child"). The wife is thrown, resuscitated, made to rise again. What Wright asks us to believe is that he "knew she would never rest again." The statement seems overly portentous, unlikely if considered as the result of this one accident. The failure to "rest again" thus becomes a more universalized injury to "the cradled child." It is another fall, of sorts, that threatens irrevocable exile from experience.

I knew that she would never rest again,
For the colts of the dusk rear back their hooves
And paw us down, the mares of dawn stampede
Across the cobbled hills till the lights are dead.

Though the poet is not Job, the final lines echo Job's acquiescence, his repentance in dust and ashes:

Run to the rocks where horses cannot climb,
Stable the daemon back to shaken earth,
Warm your hands at the comfortable fire,
Cough in a dish beside a wrinkled bed.

Neither faith nor reward results from the poet's accident-won humility. The fire might comfort, the bed offer welcome, safety; still, the cough, the sputum-filled dish, remind us of our human frailty, our grasshopper-like limitations.

Much has been made of Wright's intention to "write poems [that] say something humanly important instead of just showing off in language" and of his claim that Robert Frost and Edwin Arlington Robinson were important early influences on his work. (Both remarks appear on the dustjacket of *The Green Wall*.) In retrospect, these claims seem shortsighted: Wright would try to escape their reverberations for the rest of his career. Of the first, he would later say in an interview with the *Southern Humanities Review*, ''That was a sort of Puritanical statement, wasn't it? There's a certain pompousness about it. . . . Like beating against the sand, or being virtuous.''

Much has been made of Frost himself, while Robinson has become a largely neglected figure on the literary landscape. Robinson's life and career, which spanned the years following the Civil War to the years just prior to World War II, were marked by great success, including three Pulitzer Prizes. His work is populated with character studies (''Miniver Cheevy,'' ''Richard Cory,'' ''Captain Craig'') and descended from nineteenth-century transcendentalism, though a particularly individual, often dark, brand of that philosophy. Here is section 15 from Robinson's ''Octaves,'' an early poem:

> We lack the courage to be where we are:
> We love too much to travel on old roads,
> To triumph on old fields; we love too much
> To consecrate the magic of dead things,
> And yieldingly to linger by long walls
> Of ruin, where the ruinous moonlight
> That sheds a lying glory on old stones
> Befriends us with a wizard's enmity.

Except for the fanciful wizard of the final image, these lines might have been written by Wright himself; fancy was not a quality to which Wright was predisposed at this stage in his literary development. Rather, he absorbed Robinson's often acrimonious views of human nature and of the world. The world is often cruel, men and women its unwitting victims. Violence destroys what it cannot control: the beautiful, the feminine, the other.

In Wright's vision, animals, too, are subject to the world's malevolence. In ''On the Skeleton of a Hound,'' the poet circles the bones of a dead animal.

> Flies would love to leap
> Between his eyes and hum away the space
> Between the ears, the hollow where a hare
> Could hide

The skeleton prompts Wright to conjure an almost pagan image of women dancing around a fire. The idyll is interrupted when the poet ''scatter[s] this hulk about the dampened ground'' and ''throw[s]'' / The ribs and spine out of their perfect shape.'' What prompts an act that seems, at first, disrespectful? The poet's belief that earth, not man, should care for the dead; that moles, earthworms, ''honest bees,'' are better keepers of their own. They transform bone and flesh into usefulness again. The bees make of the hound's skull a hive: an image initially repulsive, then oddly comforting. Aware that he has little use for the hound anymore, the poet hastens the skeleton's return to earth. He hopes, we can imagine, that someone will one day do the same for his own remains. The hope is reinforced in ''Three Steps to the Graveyard,'' at the end of which ''a skinny old woman'' is scrubbing a tombstone, an image of human grief, and human folly.

Folly gives way to grief in the volume's next half-dozen or so poems. Wright mourns friends, laments a younger brother's wasted life, bemoans a ''defeated savior.'' It has been remarked that *The Green Wall* is filled with women and men who would save one another, but cannot. ''To a Defeated Savior'' is concerned with the death by drowning of a ''skinny swimmer'' and how that death haunts the sleep of the one who tried to save him. Wright's brother, Ted, once watched helplessly from a small boat on the Ohio River as another boy drowned nearby. ''He held his fishing pole out to the kid,'' Wright remembered, discussing the poem with *Southern Humanities Review,* ''and the kid tried to get hold of it but missed it, and sank.'' The haunting, the memory itself, becomes an end to life. Wright consoles, or means to console, his brother—though all that he can do is gently to echo his brother's failure.

> You would have raised him, flesh and soul,
> Had you been strong enough to dare;
> You would have lifted him to breathe,
> Believing your good hands would keep
> His body clear of your own death:
> This dream, this drowning in your sleep.

Dragging rivers and lakes for the drowned is a particularly American literary motif, one that Wright makes his own. The drowned appear throughout Wright's poetry, as though water itself were murderous. In "To a Defeated Savior," what seems peculiar to Wright is the poem's focus not on the dead swimmer but on the troubled sleep of his would-be rescuer.

Sleep takes on the strains of defeat and resignation in "A Song for the Middle of the Night," Wright's explanation to his son of a curse by Eustace Deschamps: "Happy is he who has no children; for babies bring nothing but crying and stench." The poem, however, is less an explanation of Deschamps' curse than it is a nursery rhyme of child abuse (in the guise of discipline) over generations:

> . . . my father once
> Laid me across his knee
> And solved the trouble when he beat
> The yowling out of me.
> He rocked me on his shoulder
> Where razor straps were vain:
> Legs up, la la, legs down, la la,
> Back to sleep again.
>
> So roll upon your belly, boy
> And bother being cursed.
> You turn the household upside down,
> But you are not the first.

Wright's love poems are frequently tales of violence, as though love were some misguided action. "A Poem About George Doty in the Death House" is based on an incident in which, Wright explained to Dave Smith, "a taxi driver named George Doty from Bellaire [Ohio] drove a girl out in the country and made a pass at her, which she resisted, so he banged her in the head with a tree branch and killed her." While the poem is concerned with violence, it is an emotional violence, not the murder itself, that the poem takes as its subject. It *is* a poem "about George Doty" and only tangentially about his victim. Written in relaxed though formal octaves, the poem succeeds—until its hyperbolic final stanza—because its form carries and plays against its subject matter. The dark sweetness of Wright's language means to instruct.

> Beside his cell, I am told,
> Hardy perennial bums
> Complain till twilight comes
> For hunger and for cold.
> They hardly know of a day
> That saw their hunger pass.
> Bred to the dark, their flesh
> Peacefully withers away.

The lesson to be learned from the bums, from Doty as he stares into "the shaving mirror / Pinned to the barren wall," is "simple, easy terror." This very simplicity, however, is made to seem grandiose at the poem's conclusion. The ease of terror, its common quality, is transformed by Wright into a weight that "no man ever bore." The singularity of Doty's burden, exaggerated or real, rings false—but leads us to accept Wright's explanation of his subversive interest in the murderer.

> Now, as he grips the chain
> And holds the wall, to bear
> What no man ever bore,
> He hears the bums complain;
> But I mourn no soul but his,
> Not even the bums who die,

Nor the homely girl whose cry
Crumbled his pleading kiss.

Wright understands, as well as anyone might, the nature of crime, explaining in the Smith interview: "[Doty] stumbled into something evil. . . . He was just a dumb guy who was suddenly thrust into the middle of the problem of evil and was not able to handle it." Wright returned to Doty for another poem, "At the Executed Murderer's Grave," which became the watershed of his 1959 collection, *Saint Judas*.

In "Sappho," Wright adopts the voice of a lesbian who briefly comforts a married woman. We assume that it is Sappho who speaks, though it is the felicity of her voice and not the details of her tale which convince us so. The love Wright's speaker describes is gentle but, not unlike Doty's violent attraction to his victim, ends in retribution and solitude. "Her husband came to pluck her like an apple," the voice of the poem remembers, as she remembers the cruel graffiti that neighborhood children "chalk / Against my house and down the garden walls." Still, from out of solitude, she asserts:

They cannot tear the garden out of me,
Nor smear my love with names. Love is a cliff,
A clear, cold curve of stone, mottled by stars,
Smirched by the morning, carved by the dark sea
Till stars and dawn and waves can slash no more,
Till the rock's heart is found and shaped again.

The poem's final image is that of the phoenix rising from ashes and flame. Sappho refuses the world's incendiary judgments of her love for other women: "There is a fire that burns beyond the names / Of sludge and filth of which this world is made." Sappho's transcendence is accomplished through a steadfast refusal to become like those who "sow the world with child." Hers is not a transcendence *of* the body but *through* the body, an idea to which Wright would eventually return.

Many of the poems that Auden suggested Wright omit from *The Green Wall* found their way into his second volume, *Saint Judas* (1959), which Wright once called his favorite book. Similar to its predecessor in form, though darker in tone, *Saint Judas*—despite its retrieval of poems intended for the first collection—seems more of a whole than *The Green Wall* and is ultimately the more mature work. Divided into three sections ("Lunar Changes," "A Sequence of Love Poems," and "The Part Nearest Home"), it too sheds light on outcasts and misfits. That they are now seen at less of a remove from the speaker allows for a greater depth of human feeling: pity, remorse, terror, complicity, love. In an interview with the *Paris Review*, Wright explained the collection as an attempt "to come to terms . . . with what I felt to be the truth of my own life, which is that of a man who wants very much to be happy, but who is not happy. I do not have the talent for happiness."

Unhappy living and teaching in Minnesota, unhappier still with the growing dissolution of his marriage, Wright transformed his unhappiness into poetry in which the most common refrain is a fear of growing old. He describes watching his subject in "Old Man Drunk," "I will see him sit / Under the vacant clock, till I grow old," observes flatly in "The Accusation," "Now you are dead, and I grow old," and says in "But Only Mine," "I knew / Somewhere above me boughs were burning gold, / And women's frocks were loose, and men grew old." Although Wright was only in his early thirties when *Saint Judas* appeared, this sense of impending age (and so death) suggests less of a physical deterioration than it does an emotional fatigue: a fatigue with his life and his work. It was about this time that Wright began a long struggle with alcohol. Although Wright was by no means the notorious drinker that his colleague and fellow poet, John Berryman, was known to be, his alcoholism, nonetheless, contributed to his sense of defeat.

Berryman once visited Wright in the hospital, where he had been admitted after suffering a nervous breakdown, with an offer to teach Wright's classes until he got well again.

The most telling, though discreet, prose account of Wright's addiction appears in the short memoir, "On the Occasion of a Poem: Richard Hugo," in his *Collected Prose,* which recounts a number of fishing trips the two poets took together. "Serious fishermen who stay overnight always run out of beer," Wright observes. Hugo's memoir of Wright records their mutual alcoholism in greater, less jovial, detail. Overall, little has been written of Wright's alcoholism, and perhaps rightly so. Despite such poems as "Two Hangovers" (in the 1963 volume *The Branch Will Not Break*), alcoholism bore only an indirect influence upon his poetry.

One exception to Wright's complaints of age in *Saint Judas* is "An Offering for Mr. Bluehart." The poet remembers an orchard, Mr. Bluehart's, from which he and "two or three good friends" stole the old man's apples. Characteristically, the foolish and the mean figures in Wright's poetry are often thin, or "skinny" (as in "Three Steps to the Graveyard" and "To a Defeated Savior"), and here Mr. Bluehart, whose name may be read as a pun, is described as "lean" and "satanic."

> Behind the orchard, past one hill
> The lean satanic owner lay
> And threatened us with murder till
> We stole his riches all away.
> He caught us in the act one day
> And damned us to the laughing bone,
> And fired his gun across the gray
> Autumn where now his life is done.

The apples are a temptation for the boys to commit theft, as the threat of gunfire is an invitation for them to risk their not yet embittered lives. The boys' daring stands in direct contrast to the old man's rancor, which the poet only later comes to understand. The poet's own rancor is suggested subtly in the tense change, from past to present, at the end of the first stanza. The "angry" sparrows that once chided the youthful thieves now "limp along the wind and die." The apples "are all eaten now." The final stanza is an attempt at reparation:

> Sorry for him, or any man
> Who lost his labored wealth to thieves,
> Today I mourn him, as I can,
> By leaving in their golden leaves
> Some luscious apples overhead.
> Now may my abstinence restore
> Peace to the orchard and the dead.
> We shall not nag them anymore.

"If old Mr. Bluehart is listening," Wright once prefaced a reading of the poem, "I enjoyed those apples very much."

Coherence and lucidity are the subjects of "The Morality of Poetry." "What I meant [by that title] was that there are different kinds of forms in poetry which are possible and to try to write any of them well is a good thing," Wright once explained. The poem begins with an epigraph from Walt Whitman: *"Would you the undulation of one wave, its trick to me transfer."* Like Whitman, Wright stands before the "complicated sea." From a flock of gulls, "a single naked gull" captures his eye, and so his imagination. The gull calls to mind "a single human word for love of air" (inspiration?), which "gathers the tangled discords up to song." The bones of a poem, like the bones of the gull, are "clean and spare." They must be "starve[d] . . . in darkness." Then the moon appears, a feminine muse, dashing the poet's "careful rules of song":

> Openly she soars,
> A miracle out of all gray sounds, the moon,
> Deepening and rifting swell and formal sky.
> Woman or bird, she plumes the ashening sound,
> Flaunting to nothingness the rules I made.

The sea, the gull, the moon, the poet: all these combine and recombine to fashion and undo the poem. All that remains, all that Wright can offer to replace his "careful rules," are forms that convey the morality, the good, of any poem. That good is not the starved lesson of the gull nor the opulent lesson of the moon. Rather, "the morality" of any poem is its singularity, its uniqueness, its representations of exterior and interior worlds.

If in "The Morality of Poetry" Wright made of the sea a discordant music, in "At the Slackening of the Tide" and "All the Beautiful Are Blameless" discord and song seem to exist as one another's natural opposites. A mother watches "her child . . . floating in oil" in "At the Slackening of the Tide"; while two men, "two stupid harley-charlies," take a young girl out on a lake to rape and murder her in "All the Beautiful Are Blameless." Ultimately, the former is the more successful poem, not for what Wright records of the scene, but for what the scene provokes in him. Here are the fourth and the seventh stanzas:

I would so anything to drag myself
Out of this place:
Root up a seaweed from the water,
To stuff it in my mouth, or deafen me,
Free me from all the force of human speech;
Go drown, almost.

Abstract with terror of the shell, I stared
Over the waters where
God brooded for the living all one day.
Lonely for weeping, starved for a sound of
    mourning,
I bowed my head, and heard the sea far off
Washing its hands.

In lines such as these, Wright's poetry begins to come into its own. They are once concerned with the violence of the world and the difficult redemption of the self.

The self Wright presents in "At the Executed Murderer's Grave" is outwardly less observant and certainly less compassionate than the self he had presented in "A Poem About George Doty in the Death House." Impatient with the sympathies Doty's case continues to provoke in him, Wright pleads to be let alone. Impatient with the artifice of the earlier poem, Wright's voice breaks. "Doty, you make me sick," he writes. "I am not dead. / I croon my tears at fifty cents per line." A price is paid for poems: the emotional expense of the poet, and the price "per line" offered by the magazines and journals to which the poems are sold. The poet's defense, his attempt to assuage the pain of empathizing with the lost and the damned, is mercenary, at best.

Wright described to Dave Smith how the poem came to be written: "The previous version . . . was very, very overblown and rhetorical. . . . When I came to try and put it into *Saint Judas* I was completely dissatisfied with it, so I sent it to [James] Dickey. He and I had had a misunderstanding and a disagreement earlier, followed very rapidly by an exchange of letters. . . . [The poem] was a mess, full of mythological and biblical references and . . . very Victorian." The disagreement arose from Dickey's criticism that Wright's work was "ploddingly 'sincere' " and "difficult to care about." Angered at first, Wright eventually came to see that Dickey's reaction held some validity. On a train ride from Seattle (where Wright had gone to defend his dissertation) to Minneapolis, he found himself without Dickey's comments and rewrote the poem from scratch. "[I] rewrote it as straight and direct and Robinsonian as I could make it." Earlier drafts of the poem center on Wright's complicity with his subject.

Father and citizen, I killed this man,
This man who killed another who might kill
Another who might slay another still.

The poem's final version opens with an epigraph from Freud, which some critics have perceived as a condemnation of capital punishment. *"Why should we do this? What good is this to us? Above all, how can we do such a thing? How can it possibly be done?"* The questions are taken from *The Future of an Illusion.* "He is referring," Wright once explained, "to the idea we call The Golden Rule," the idea that a man should behave toward others as he would have them behave toward himself (Matthew 7:12). In this light, the epigraph is a threefold judgement: of Doty for the murder, of Ohio for its sanctioned though no less brutal justice, and of Wright himself. It is of Wright's self-judgment, by and large, that the poem is fashioned. "My name is James A. Wright," the poem begins, "and I was born / Twenty-five miles from this infected grave." The statement establishes a shared sense of place for both the poet and his subject; it establishes as well the divergent paths each followed from their common beginnings. Wright ran "away before [his] time," while "Ohio caught George Doty." Rather, Wright believes that he has escaped his past, its landscapes, only to realize just how much a part of him Ohio, and George Doty, have become. "I pity myself, because a man is dead," he writes. "If Belmont County killed him, what of me?" That Wright repeats and repeats his own name (as well as Doty's) seems a sort of futile whistling in the dark. He longs to separate himself from the violence the grave suggests, as keenly as he longs to separate himself from the "quicklime hole of . . . defeat and shame" that is death.

> I hear the last sea in the Ohio grass,
> Heaving a tide of gray disastrousness.
> Wrinkles of winter ditch the rotted face
> Of Doty, killer, imbecile, and thief:
> Dirt of my flesh, defeated, underground.

It is a separation that can never be ("dirt of my flesh") wholly accomplished.

In "Saint Judas," the title poem, Wright provides an apocryphal tale of Christ's betrayer. Having marked Christ for capture by the Romans, Judas flees in order to kill himself. "I've always been strongly moved by his hanging himself," Wright observed in the interview with *Southern Humanities Review.* "Why did he do it? You would think he'd be a completely cold person. And yet, he couldn't have been to experience such complete despair." The theological definition of despair is the state of living without hope of redemption; certainly, Judas' act would bring him to such a state. Yet, Wright offers him one final chance.

> When I went out to kill myself, I caught
> A pack of hoodlums beating up a man.
> Running to spare his suffering, I forgot
> My name, my number, how my day began.

A sonnet, "Saint Judas" succeeds not because it focuses on the betrayal—his despair, and our knowledge of his actions, are givens—but rather because it focuses on Judas being moved to intervene and save the beaten man. That the man's assailants are dressed in uniforms suggests that they are Romans. Judas now ignores such men, with whom he had earlier bargained for blood money. "Flayed without hope," he confesses, "I held the man for nothing in my arms." Some critics have read (or misread) this line as ambiguous; they infer that Judas held the man for no obvious reason. A stronger argument can be made that Judas went to the man and held him without hope of recompense. No silver rewards this act. His only hope is clearly stated, three lines into the poem: to spare the man's suffering. That redemption seems possible, even for Judas, is Wright's vision of the damned finding if not salvation then some sort of peace. Closing a book that has all along argued "the desolation of the spirit," Wright tells us finally that the spirit might be healed.

Wright's next collection, *The Branch Will Not*

Break, was not published until 1963. In the years following the publication of *Saint Judas,* Wright's personal life suffered continued upheavals. He was divorced in 1962. The University of Minnesota denied him tenure in 1963. And, as numerous interviews reveal, he felt that he had arrived at the end of where his earlier poetic style might lead him. "After I finished [*Saint Judas*] I had finished with poetry forever," he told the *Paris Review.* "I truly believed that I had said what I had to say as clearly and directly as I could, and that I had no more to do with this art." In a letter to his editor at Wesleyan University Press, Wright vowed that he was "finished with what [he] was doing in that book"—both formally and thematically. Wright's spiritual desolation had, for the time being, silenced him.

The story of how Wright met the poet Robert Bly during this period is a famous one. Having read in the *Fifties,* a journal for which Bly served as coeditor, a translation from Georg Trakl, Wright wrote a letter ("sixteen pages long and single spaced") to which Bly responded succinctly, "Come on out to the farm." The two poets began work together on translations of the works of such poets as Jorge Guillén, Pablo Neruda, and César Vallejo, among others. "[Bly] reminded me that poetry is a possibility, that, although all poetry is formal, there are many forms, just as there are many forms of feeling."

The Branch Will Not Break reflects the changes, the difficulties and rewards, of the preceding years. Largely gone are the mannered stanzaic forms of Wright's earlier work, replaced by free-verse experiments with image and form. The poem "Goodbye to the Poetry of Calcium," its title referring to the hardened element whose name derives from the Latin *calx,* meaning "limestone," is a farewell to the poetry that Auden once favored. Other poets—Robert Lowell, Adrienne Rich, and Anne Sexton among them—

had undergone similar formal changes, but to call Wright's new poetry free verse should not imply the loose carelessness too often wrongly associated with that genre, especially with the poetry of that time, the 1960's. Wright's new poems are carefully formed, not by received ideas of meter and structure, but by the logic of thought, by the constantly expanding education of the heart. "The writer's real enemy," he remarked to Dave Smith,

is his own glibness, his own facility; the writer constantly should try to discover what difficulties there truly are inherent in a subject or in his own language and come to terms with these difficulties. If he does that, then he might be able to discover something in his own mind or in the language which is imaginative.

The poems are as firmly rooted to place, to Wright's native Ohio, as are his earlier poems. Frequently, their titles are their most visible roots. Now longer and more explicit, the titles provide the reader with not place alone but often time and circumstance as well. "Autumn Begins in Martins Ferry, Ohio" (a meditation on football and the violence of pride) and "Lying in a Hammock at William Duffy's Farm in Pine Island, Minnesota" are two examples. The titles thus grounded, Wright allows the poems themselves a greater fluency of thought. They are at once wholly concerned with both exterior and interior worlds. The "I" of these poems seems less forced, less of a poetic construct than, say, the "I" employed in "The Morality of Poetry."

Wright's poetic metamorphoses, like Rich's and Lowell's before him, was widely though not universally praised. Sexton, with whom Wright has more in common, bore the brunt of a criticism that was often mean-spirited and based upon the fact that she was a woman. Wright's poems from this period frequently have been labeled "surrealistic," a charge that he actively disputed, emphasizing the humor of true surrealism and the essential seriousness of his own work. The most dramatic case in point is "Lying in a Hammock at William Duffy's Farm in Pine Island, Minnesota":

Over my head, I see a bronze butterfly,
Asleep on the black trunk,
Blowing like a life in green shadow.
Down to the ravine behind the empty house,
The cowbells follow one another
Into the distances of the afternoon.
To my right,
In a field of sunlight between two pines,
the droppings of last year's horses
Blaze up into golden stones.
I lean back, as the evening darkens and comes
   on.
A chicken hawk floats over, looking for home.
I have wasted my life.

The final line enraged some critics, who felt that its assertion of a wasted life was unfounded, unsupported by anything preceding it. Wright argued that the line was not intended to act as a moral (though it does have some of the moral's quality of summation), that it was instead merely a statement of feeling—a "spot of time," as Wordsworth might have observed. The poem seems to skirt the edges of a criticism of poetry: that poetry is sometimes neither sustenance nor protection against life—which is also the subject of "Depressed by a Book of Bad Poetry, I Walk Toward an Unused Pasture and Invite the Insects to Join Me." Wright, in *Southern Humanities Review,* describes its genesis: "Someone asked me to review a certain anthology and the poems in it seemed to me to be so bad, so trite in their hysteria that I just got sick of them. I didn't want to expose my mind to those bone-crushing banalities anymore. I wanted to hear the cricket." The insects become the poet's muse, the grasshoppers' "burdened" thighs the music of the

pasture. "I want to hear them," he writes, "they have clear sounds to make."

Wright appears in many of these poems as a solitary figure, the word "alone" almost a refrain. In one poem, "Having Lost My Sons, I Confront the Wreckage of the Moon: Christmas, 1960," he is alone "after dark, / near the South Dakota Border." (Wright "lost" his sons—Marshall was born in 1958—while separated from his wife and permanently when they divorced.) From image to image, the poem proceeds, guided by moonlight:

The moon is out hunting, everywhere,
Delivering fire,
And walking down hallways
Of a diamond.

Behind a tree,
It lights on the ruins
Of a white city:
Frost, frost.

The moon delivers "inhuman fire," traversing ice, then settles on a city in which everything is frozen—as Christmas at the South Dakota border would be snow-covered. Note the wordplay of "lights": the moon both illuminates and lands upon the ruins. The landscape seems lunar. From warmth to cold, the progression is reminiscent of Emily Dickinson's poem #341, in which "freezing persons recollect the snow." Unlike Dickinson's speaker, who ends her poem by "letting go," Wright goes on "living, alone, alone." He passes the graves of natives (Chippewas) and immigrants (Norwegians), as if to say that everyone in this country is doomed. The graves are hidden, the headstone-like silos nearby are "charred." (By the moon's "fire"?) In the end, everything is dead ("dead riches, dead hands"), even the country itself ("the beautiful white ruins / Of America").

In direct contrast to such despair stands "A Blessing," a poem that Wright has somewhat disingenuously called "just a description." The poem is his return to the idea of a transcendence through the body. With "A Fit Against the Country" and "An Offering for Mr. Bluehart," "A Blessing" joins Wright's poems in which to cross a wall or boundary leads to some lesson. Again, Wright stands before a midwestern landscape. He and an unnamed friend are welcomed into a pasture by two horses, their guides toward "happiness." The horses "love each other," and yet, "there is no loneliness like theirs." That loneliness and love might coexist moves Wright to tenderness.

I would like to hold the slenderer one in my
  arms,
For she has walked over to me
And nuzzled my left hand.

The horse, a symbol of power and violence in "The Horse," is here an image of gentle acceptance. The mare's gesture, returned by Wright in kind, seems the "blessing" that allows him a transcendence, a release into nature:

Suddenly I realize
That if I stepped out of my body I would break
Into blossom.

Having been denied tenure at the University of Minnesota, Wright spent two years teaching at Macalester College in St. Paul. He received a Guggenheim fellowship in 1965 and then, in 1966, moved to New York City, where he took a position at Hunter College. The move to New York proved to be a renewal of sorts. He met and married his second wife, Anne, not long afterward. Yet the poems of this period—which were collected in the 1968 volume *Shall We Gather at the River*—seem obsessed with the past; with the landscapes of Ohio and Minnesota; with death-tinged rivers and memories of Jenny, an early love to whom the book is dedicated. "I was trying to move from death to resurrection and death again. . . . I was trying to write about a girl I

was in love with who [had] been dead for a long time," he told the *Paris Review*. "I tried to sing with her in that book. Not to recreate her; you can't recreate anybody, at least I can't." The river of the book's title is not Jordan but the river of memory and death; it is not Lethe but Styx, as in "To the Muse":

> Come up to me, love,
> Out of the river, or I will
> Come down to you.

The book opens with "A Christmas Greeting," a poem in heroic couplets (Wright never completely abandoned traditional forms) about an antihero: a drunk named Charlie "who died because [he] could not bear to live." This is the book's first death, which Wright seems both to fear and to long for:

> *I'm afraid to die,*
> *It hurts to die, although the lucky do.*
> *Charlie, I don't know what to say to you*
> *Except Good Evening, Greetings, and Good*
> * Night,*
> *God Bless Us Everyone.*

The line borrowed from *A Christmas Carol* reminds the reader of Wright's early affection for Charles Dickens, for whom he held a lifelong reverence, and also of that story's trinity of ghosts: past, present, and future. We might say that the same ghosts haunt Wright in this and the next poem, "The Minneapolis Poem."

Comprising seven sections, "The Minneapolis Poem" allows Wright's freer, more discursive style both room enough and opportunity to become more than epigrammatic. Here again is his cast of characters: murderous Native Americans, "split-lipped homosexuals," river suicides, "Negro girls" who work Chicago streets as prostitutes. The landscape is no more inviting:

The legless beggars are gone, carried away
By white birds.

The Artificial Limbs Exchange is gutted
And sown with lime.

Even the maimed have nowhere to go, now that
Minneapolis has become a city of "men . . .
who labor dawn after dawn" selling death.

I want to be lifted up
By some great white bird unknown to the police,
And soar for a thousand miles and be carefully
    hidden
Modest and golden as one last corn grain,
Stored with the secrets of the wheat and the mys-
    terious lives
Of the unnamed poor.

"In Response to a Rumor that the Oldest Whorehouse in Wheeling, West Virginia, Has Been Condemned" returns Wright to the banks of the Ohio River—"by the vinegar works"— where he recalls a vision of women walking headlong into the water. The women repeat this ritual nightly. They seem descendants of Mary Magdalene, sinners searching for grace. They must be searching for grace, Wright concludes, not because they have sinned but because the landscape has sinned against them:

For the river at Wheeling, West Virginia,
Has only two shores:
The one in hell, the other
In Bridgeport, Ohio.

And nobody would commit suicide, only
To find beyond death
Bridgeport, Ohio.

Though Wright declaims with his usual seriousness, there is something of the punch line in the final lines off this poem. He acts as both straight man and comic, setting the scene, the joke, and then revealing the deadpan absurdity of it all. Comedy, or black comedy, proves in Wright's hands to be tragedy, his heroines' tragic flaw the fact of their birthplace.

Over the next few years, Wright received a number of awards: a grant from the Rockefeller Foundation and a fellowship from the Ingram Merrill Foundation, both in 1969; the Brandeis University Creative Arts Citation in Poetry, the fellowship of The Academy of American Poets, and the Pulitzer Prize, all in 1972. Although the critical response to *Collected Poems* (1971) was largely favorable, the section titled "New Poems" presaged a temporary slackening of Wright's powers. A notable exception is "Many of Our Waters: Variations on a Poem by a Black Child," a long poem in seven sections that was delivered as the Phi Beta Kappa poem at the College of William and Mary in December 1969. Like Wright's other work from this period, "Many of Our Waters" is more discursive than not. Constructed around a remark made to Wright by a young black boy named Garnie, the poem touches upon the urban desolation of New York City and the rural desolation of the Ohio River valley; it also speaks to Wright's beliefs about the nature of poetry. "The kind of poetry I want to write," he says, "is / The poetry of a grown man." Wright's portrait of a grown man is typically bleak: "He shuts up. / He dies. / He grows." But he is redeemed by the "pure clear word" and by "the beautiful language of my friends." True poetry, Wright seems to believe, is born of union, of woman and man, of man and child.

In the early 1970's, the Wrights began to spend extended periods of time abroad, traveling through Europe for months at a time. These travels make up a large part of *Two Citizens* (1973) and *To a Blossoming Pear Tree* (1977). Wright's European poems, including a chapbook of prose poems, *Moments of the Italian Summer* (1976), stand in direct contrast to his poems of this period from America. The European poems seem light-filled, finding the poet at peace with himself, while the American poems are often filled with despair and can be painful, at times, to read.

Romantic love and bitter disappointment are his themes in these books, although Wright finds occasional consolation in poetry and art—not so much "the poetry of a grown man," but the classical, Horatian poetry praised in *Two Citizens* as "Prayer to the Good Poet." Perhaps they are one and the same. Wright's "Good Poet" is Quintus Horatius Flaccus, to whom the prayer is addressed, but the subject of the poem is Wright's relationship to his father (who died in 1973, while Wright was traveling through Italy) and to his son Franz. Wright finds himself at the apex of this family continuum, and discovers that he "can go on living." There is a gentle loneliness about the poem and its "quick and lonely / Metrical crystals of February," which are "just snow."

As with much of Wright's work from this period, the strongest, most resonant poems are those informed by thought, are those poems more introspective than declarative. In too many others, naked feeling falls unmitigated across the page. The poems generally are also more discursive than ever before. "Hell, I ain't got nothing," he writes in "Ars Poetica: Some Recent Criticism." "Ah, you bastards, / / How I hate you." The bastards are a gang of boys who once tried to stone a goat to death; but they are also made to serve as symbols for other dissatisfactions with "America, / Which I loved when I was young." As such, the boys' actions do not justify the poet's anger; the occasion cannot bear the weight Wright lays across its shoulders. Some years after its publication, Wright admitted that he found *Two Citizens* "badly written." "Obscure and self-indulgent," he went on to remark, "it talks around subjects rather than coming to terms with them."

Many of the poems in *Two Citizens* are addressed by the speaker to an unnamed other, a "you" who would appear to be Anne Wright, who seems a better muse for the poet than his long-dead Jenny. On the dustjacket, he commented that the book was "most of all a book of love poems. The two citizens are Annie and I." The two women, Anne and Jenny, stand at opposite ends of Wright's emotional spectrum, which was deteriorating from alcohol and renewed hospitalizations. Some months after Wright's father died, his mother passed away. Shortly thereafter, Wright joined Alcoholics Anonymous (in the spring of 1975), surely prompted to do so by John Berryman's well-publicized membership with that group. Joining AA led Wright for a short while back to health, a move that is reflected in *To a Blossoming Pear Tree*.

The collection opens with "Redwings," a meditation on the harsh and transitory nature of our lives. "Somebody is on the wing, somebody / Is wondering right at this moment / How to get rid of us." Birds and women may be killed, the earth made absolutely clean, but there are often small acts of human decency that raise us from the muck of our lives. The poem ends with the memory of having received "a nickel and a potato" from one of the hoboes by the Ohio. The act is quietly set down, allowed to speak for itself. The detail of many of these new poems allows Wright's more visionary poems a stronger grasp on reality, as in "One Last Look at the Adige: Verona in the Rain." The poem is largely a prayer against death:

> In the middle of my own life
> I woke up and found myself
> Dying, fair enough, still
> Alive in the friendly city
> Of my body, my secret Verona,
> Milky and green,
> My moving jewel, the last
> Pure vein left to me.

The poems go back and forth between Europe and America, between free verse and prose poems, between the past and the present. One poem remembers W. H. Auden as "kind." Indeed, Wright seems kinder himself, no longer quite so inclined to sweeping damnations of others and of America. The obsessive "I" that flawed much of *Two Citizens* is here less self-absorbed and more representative. Not changed is Wright's affection for stories from his past. "Hook" tells of a winter encounter between the speaker and a young Sioux at a bus shelter in Minneapolis. The Sioux, whose hand has been replaced by a hook, asks Wright if he has "enough money / To get home on" and then hands him sixty-five cents. Startled into acceptance by the fact that the coins were so freely given, Wright wonders:

> Did you ever feel a man hold
> Sixty-five cents
> In a hook,
> And place it
> Gently
> In your freezing hand?

With the hobo's gift of a potato and a nickel, the Sioux's gift frames (coming as it does near the book's end) the rest of the poems in *To a Blossoming Pear Tree*.

With the title poem, Wright achieves a kind of balance between the vehemence and cruelty of human emotion and the "unburdened" beauty of the natural world. The poem opens with an address to the pear tree. From a distance, the pear blossoms move Wright to envy, precisely because they hang beyond his reach. To have beauty within reach is to risk the knowledge that men and women are often less than beautiful, the realization that there is almost always an element of pain in even the most fleeting of unions. Wright illustrates this hard truth with a homosexual vignette, curiously free of prejudice or blame, the emotion too raw for such easy reprisals:

> An old man
> Appeared to me once

> In the unendurable snow.
> He had a singe of white
> Beard on his face.
> He paused on a street in Minneapolis
> And stroked my face.
> Give it to me, he begged.
> I'll pay you anything.

> I flinched. Both terrified,
> We slunk away,
> Each of us in his own way dodging
> The cruel darts of cold.

Wright's understanding of human sexuality, in poetry that reaches all the way back to "Sappho," is harsh and yet not harsh at all. He recognizes all too well the drives that bring bodies together, the urgencies of carnal need. He recognizes, too, that the act itself is often less violent than are the emotions the act both creates and destroys. The desperation of a man who would pay another man "anything" for sex, that he would beg, is what causes Wright to flinch—not that the meeting should have homosexual overtones. The speaker, having silently refused the man's plea, is nonetheless pained by the sight of a man "so near death / He was willing to take / Any love he could get." The "singed" remains of his passion play themselves out against the frigid and "unendurable" landscape, while Wright wonders how the pear tree "could . . . possibly / Worry or bother or care" for the players in such a misalliance. It cannot; it is made of blossoms and dew only. But Wright finds that he cares; he knows well the other's despair.

Placed side by side, "Hook" and "To a Blossoming Pear Tree" form a diptych. The Sioux's gift of sixty-five cents and the old man's offer to pay anything, both acts that disguise emotion as commercial exchange, are two halves of the portrait that is human loneliness. "I was trying to say that I am committed to the beauty of nature which I love very much," Wright remarked in an interview with Bruce Henricksen, "but that commitment . . . has to be qualified by my returning to my own responsibility as a human being. And the life of a human being is more complicated than the blossoming of a pear tree. It's full of pain.''

In 1978, after the publication of *To a Blossoming Pear Tree,* Wright received a second Guggenheim fellowship and returned with his wife to Europe, where he wrote many of the poems that would make up his final collection, *This Journey,* published posthumously in 1982. Like its predecessor, *This Journey* comprises equal parts free-verse and prose poems, memories of Ohio and Minneapolis, and travelogues from Italy and France. In addition, a handful of poems are set on the Atlantic in Rhode Island and on the Pacific in Hawaii. Also like its predecessor, it continues Wright's move away from the bitterness that marred the poems of the early 1970's. It would seem that he was finally more at peace with himself. The peace would not last long. While traveling in Europe, Wright's health began to fail, and, shortly after his return to New York, he was diagnosed with cancer of the tongue. A course of surgery and radiation therapy was planned. ''I will emerge from the surgery,'' he wrote to Leslie Marmon Silko, a poet and writer with whom he had recently established a correspondence, ''with diminished capacity to speak, and this will create a problem, since I make my living by speaking. But there is a good chance that I will continue teaching.''

In the hospital, Wright made a preliminary attempt to construct a new manuscript from his recent poems. A week or so before he died, he prepared a copy of the manuscript for his friend the poet Galway Kinnell, with a note reading, ''I think the book is more or less done.'' He died on March 25, 1980. *This Journey* did not appear until two years later, after a number of his fellow poets, at the request of Anne Wright, edited the volume for publication.

Wright's travels, and the love he felt for his wife and for Europe, helped to assuage many of his long-standing angers; they also helped to lessen his bonds to Martins Ferry. ''Wherever Home Is,'' a poem that appears early in *This Journey,* takes for its point of departure a statue of Leonardo da Vinci, ''haggard in basalt stone,'' his sculpted face covered by dying wisteria blossoms. Suddenly, a lizard appears ''between Leonardo's thumb and his palette,'' bestowing on both the statue and the poet ''the whole spring.'' Even amid the decaying stone and the ''gray'' blossoms, Wright finds an occasion to celebrate life—and to wonder that home is less geography than it is desire, the need to place oneself wherever one finds peace or happiness. To find such a place requires that one let go of the past.

> Goodbye to Leonardo, good riddance
> To decaying madmen who cannot keep alive
> The wanderers among trees.
> I am going home with the lizard,
> Wherever home is,
> And lie beside him unguarded
> In the clear sunlight.
> We will lift our faces even if it rains.
> We will both turn green.

One must let go of the past to embrace the present, and, to embrace the present, one must remain ''unguarded'' against its chameleon-like changes. Both the poet and the lizard-muse will ''turn green'': the color of spring and of life, of the wanderers' trees, but also the color of stone corrupted by air and vegetation.

The acceptance of life and death, the idea that a good death requires us to live our lives fully, runs like a thread throughout the collection. ''The Journey,'' from which the book's title derives, finds Wright in the Italian hill town of Anghiari, washing the dust of roads from his face. Although Wright had not yet been diagnosed with cancer, there is a strong sense of impending death in the poem, in the spider's nest he finds heavy with "mounds and cemeteries" of dust. As with the lizard of "Wherever Home Is," and the horses of "A Blessing," the poet is led to a sort of epiphany through his confrontations with animals and the natural world—but an epiphany that has less to do with nature itself than with the lives of men and women.

> The secret
> Of this journey is to let the wind
> Blow its dust all over your body,
> To let it go on blowing, to step lightly, lightly
> All the way through your ruins, and not to lose
> Any sleep over the dead, who surely
> Will bury their own, don't worry.

Though Wright's poetry as a whole suffers from periods of slackened control, his work includes individual poems and groups of poems that stand among the finest lyric poetry of the second half of the twentieth century. Certainly, among his contemporaries—Bly, Sexton, Kinnell, John Logan, and others—Wright stands out for the singularity of his vision, his ambitious pursuit of the Horatian ideal. It is still too soon to assess fully his impact on future generations of American poets, let alone his achievement. The 1990 edition of his "complete" poems, *Above the River,* lets the leader follow Wright along on his sometimes uneven, uneasy journey from apprenticeship to mastery. Given time, the weaker poems will fall away and the stronger remain. Only then will we clearly see how this midcentury man with no "talent for happiness" made of his private sorrows a poetry that demands its readers not waste their lives.

Selected Bibliography

WORKS OF JAMES WRIGHT

POETRY
The Green Wall. New Haven, Conn.: Yale University Press, 1957.
Saint Judas. Middletown, Conn.: Wesleyan University Press, 1959.
The Branch Will Not Break. Middletown, Conn.: Welseyan University Press, 1963.
Shall We Gather at the River. Middletown, Conn.: Wesleyan University Press, 1968.
Collected Poems. Middletown, Conn.: Wesleyan University Press, 1971.
Two Citizens. New York: Farrar, Straus, and Giroux, 1973.
Moments of the Italian Summer. Washington, D.C.: Dryad Press, 1976.
To a Blossoming Pear Tree. New York: Farrar, Straus and Giroux, 1977.
This Journey. New York: Random House, 1982.
Above the River: The Complete Poems. New York: Farrar, Straus and Giroux, 1990.

PROSE
Collected Prose. Edited by Anne Wright. Ann Arbor, Mich.: University of Michigan Press, 1983. Includes "Childhood Sketch."
The Delicacy and Strength of Lace: Letters. Edited and with an introduction by Anne Wright. Saint Paul, Minn.; Graywolf Press, 1986. Correspondence with Leslie Marmon Silko.

TRANSLATED WORKS
Twenty Poems of Georg Trakl. With Robert Bly. Madison, Minn.: Sixties Press, 1961.
Twenty Poems of César Vallejo. With John Knoepfle and Robert Bly. Madison, Minn.: Sixties Press, 1962.
The Rider on the White Horse. By Theodor Storm. New York: Signet, 1964.
Twenty Poems of Pablo Neruda. With Robert Bly. Madison, Minn.: Sixties Press, 1968.
Poems. By Hermann Hesse. New York: Farrar, Straus, and Giroux, 1970.

Wandering: Notes and Sketches. By Hermann Hesse. New York: Farrar, Straus, and Giroux, 1972.

BIOGRAPHICAL AND CRITICAL STUDIES

Bly, Carol. "James Wright's Visits to Odin House." *Ironwood,* 10:33–37 (1977).

Butscher, Edward. "The Rise and Fall of James Wright." *Georgia Review,* 28:257–268 (1974).

Costello, Bonnie, "James Wright: Returning to the Heartland." *New Boston Review,* 5:12–14 (August–September 1980).

Crunk [Robert Bly]. "The Work of James Wright." *The Sixties,* no. 8:52–78 (1966).

Doctorow, E. L. "James Wright at Kenyon." *Gettysburg Review,* 3, No. 1 (Winter 1990).

Hass, Robert, "James Wright." *Ironwood,* 10:74–96 (1977).

Hugo, Richard, "James Wright." In his *The Real West Marginal Way: A Poet's Autobiography.* (New York: Norton, 1986).

Matthews, William. "The Continuity of James Wright's Poems." *Ohio Review,* 18:44–57 (Spring–Summer 1977).

Smith, Dave, ed. *The Pure Clear Word: Essays on the Poetry of James Wright.* Urbana, Ill.: University of Illinois Press, 1982.

Stitt, Peter. "The Poetry of James Wright." *Minnesota Review,* 12:13–32 (Winter 1972).

———. "James Wright: The Quest Motif in *The Branch Will Not Break.*" In *The Pure Clear Word: Essays on the Poetry of James Wright.* Edited by Dave Smith. Urbana, Ill.: University of Illinois Press, 1982.

———. "An Introduction to the Poet James Wright." *Gettysburg Review,* 3, no. 1 (Winter 1990).

———. "James Wright's Earliest Poems: A Selection." *Gettysburg Review,* 3, no. 1 (Winter 1990).

Stitt, Peter, and Frank Graziano, eds. *James Wright: The Heart of the Light.* Ann Arbor: University of Michigan Press, 1990.

Wright, Anne. "A Horse Grazes in My Long Shadow: A Short Biography of James Wright." *Envoy,* Spring–Summer 1981, 1–5.

Wright, Franz. "Some Thoughts on My Father." *Poets and Writers,* 15:20–21 (January–February 1987).

Yenser, Stephen. "Open Secrets." *Parnassus,* 6:125–142 (1978).

Zweig, Paul. "Making and Unmaking." *Partisan Review,* 40:268–279 (1973).

BIBLIOGRAPHIES

McMaster, Belle M. "James Arlington Wright: A Checklist." *Bulletin of Bibliography,* 31:71–82 (1974).

Smith, Dave, "Selected Bibliography." In his *The Pure Clear Word: Essays on the Poetry of James Wright.* Urbana, Ill.: University of Illinois Press, 1982.

INTERVIEWS

André, Michael. "An Interview with James Wright." *Unmuzzled Ox,* 1:3–18 (February 1972). Included in Wright's *Collected Prose.*

Henricksen, Bruce. "Poetry Must Think." *New Orleans Review,* 6:201–207 (1978). Included in Wright's *Collected Prose.*

Heyen, William, and Jerome Mazzaro. "Something to Be Said for the Light." Edited by Joseph R. McElrath, Jr. *Southern Humanities Review,* 6:134–153 (Spring 1972). Included in Wright's *Collected Prose.*

Smith, Dave. "The Pure Clear Word." *American Poetry Review,* 9:19–30 (1980). Reprinted in his *The Pure Clear Word.*

Stitt, Peter. "The Art of Poetry XIX." *Paris Review,* 62:34–61 (Summer 1975).

—DAVID CRAIG AUSTIN

Louis Zukofsky
1904–1978

AFTER THE DEATH of Ezra Pound, so the story goes, a young journalist wished to find out who was the greatest living American poet. She made preliminary inquiries and contacted the leading candidates, asking their opinion. For the most part each one replied, in various ways, "I am." Seeing that she was getting nowhere, she took another approach. "Who," she asked, "is the second-greatest living American poet?" They all replied, "Zukofsky."

Whatever reputation the poet Louis Zukofsky continues to enjoy comes from the undeniable fact that three generations of poets have found his work to have compelling force. His "Objectivists" movement of the early 1930's, his intensely concentrated shorter poetry, and his life's work, the long poem "*A*," have all compelled the admiration of other poets. But for sixty years he labored at his craft in almost complete obscurity, and he has yet to attract a significant readership among academics, let alone among a larger public.

Louis' father, Pinchos Zukofsky, and his mother, Chana Pruss, were from a town called Most in the province of Kovna in what later was Lithuania. Chana and Pinchos were married in 1887 and had five children in Most, of whom three survived infancy: two daughters, born in 1888 and 1890, and a son born in 1892.

Like many in search of a better life, Pinchos came to the United States in 1898. He worked as a night watchman and as a pants presser in a men's clothing factory, and by 1903 he was able to send back enough money to bring his family to the United States. Pinchos and Chana's youngest child, Louis, was born on Chrystie Street in New York City on January 23, 1904.

Since his parents spoke only Yiddish, young Louis Zukofsky learned English on the streets of the Lower East Side, among the tenements where English was no one's native language, but the only language the various immigrant groups had in common. The conditions were squalid and crowded, but people were friendly. One of his earliest memories, from when he was about five years old, was of the "wealthy" Karchemsky family next door, from Odessa, where a visitor could get tea and matzos all year round. Pinchos was no less hospitable: he pressed visitors to stay to dinner, whether or not Chana had bought enough food for company.

Zukofsky was a precocious child, learning a Yiddish translation of Henry Wadsworth Longfellow's "Hiawatha" by heart when he was five. The neighborhood Italian children would corner him until he agreed to recite it, whereupon they would toss him pennies. He went to public elementary school and to Stuyvesant High School, at that time a school for students wanting to become engineers. An excellent student, he received all A's, but since his parents could not read the English of his report card it did not seem to make much difference. He signed the card for them.

Zukofsky was a gifted student. His family had moved to East 111th Street in East Harlem when he was ten or eleven, so that when Zukofsky entered Columbia at the age of fifteen, he could walk to the university. His closest friend there was Whittaker Chambers, who once took him to a Communist Party meeting. Whittaker's brother, Richard Chambers, later committed suicide (''Ricky'' 's death is movingly recounted in ''A''-3). Zukofsky finished at Columbia in 1923, shortly after his nineteenth birthday.

Zukofsky started writing poetry seriously when he was at Columbia. Some of early poems, never reprinted, were published in the Columbia College magazine the *Morningside*. In 1920 he was reading Hilda Doolittle (H.D.) and the Imagists. His first submission to *Poetry* magazine in Chicago was, appropriately enough, a translation of a poem by ''Yehoash,'' Solomon Bloomgarden, the Yiddish poet who had translated (and ''improved'') such poems as ''Hiawatha'' and Edward FitzGerald's ''The Rubaiyat of Omar Khayam.'' Harriet Monroe, though she knew no Yiddish, knew poetry and penciled ''poor translation'' on the letter Zukofsky sent accompanying the poems, sending him a polite letter of rejection. He persevered, and *Poetry* published his work, a sonnet entitled ''Of Dying Beauty,'' for the first time in January of 1924, just before his twentieth birthday. Containing lines such as ''Where fading splendor grays to powdered earth,'' the sonnet mercifully was never reprinted. Zukofsky may have read the Imagists, but their lessons had not yet registered. *Poetry* identified the new contributor only as ''from New York City.''

Pinchos Zukofsky was a pious Jew who attended Tifereth Jerusalem Synagogue on East Broadway in Manhattan, a few blocks south of Houston Street. Louis Zukofsky's wife later told Carroll Terrell that Zukofsky barely knew his father, who worked until close to midnight at a men's clothing factory, where he was the presser, and then got up early in the morning to go to synagogue for morning prayers. Thus Zukofsky's mother was the chief influence on him as a young man. His family was close-knit; only his brother spoke English.

Zukofsky had ambitions to become an engineer, but a philosophy instructor at Columbia interested him in the humanities, which seemed less demanding. Later in life, he would occasionally regret his decision. He also had an early and abiding interest in music.

Despite his father's piety, by the time he was twelve years old Zukofsky had abandoned his family's Judaism, although he did undergo a perfunctory bar mitzvah. He had a part-time job at the post office but was fired for refusing to come to work on Yom Kippur, though he had no intention of going to synagogue. Zukofsky also worked for a time as a part-time soda jerk at Nedicker's. His first job after leaving Columbia was as a private tutor of English as a second language. If a student did not show up, Louis did not get paid.

Like many great twentieth-century writers, Zukofsky came to the attention of Ezra Pound, then living in the Italian village of Rapallo and editing the *Exile*. In 1926 Zukofsky had written ''Poem Beginning 'The,' '' the first clear evidence he gave of having an important talent. He sent the piece to Pound who agreed to publish it in *Exile*'s spring 1928 issue. Pound wrote to Zukofsky on March 5, 1928, insisting that the young poet go down to Rutherford, New Jersey, to look up an old friend: ''Do go down an' stir up ole Bill Willyums . . . and tell him I tole you so. He is still the best human value on my murkn. visiting list.'' Zukofsky visited William Carlos Williams one Sunday and returned many, many times; they became lifelong friends.

"The" shows that Zukofsky had rapidly absorbed the Modernist revolution in literature taking place in Europe among English-speaking writers. The poem is most remarkable for its range of tone, though a self-ironic voice prevails, and for its quick uptake of (and take-off on) the art of obscure allusion being foisted on an unsuspecting public by James Joyce, Pound, and T. S. Eliot. "The" even has a modernist pseudo-apparatus, identifying the sources of some of the lines in unhelpful notes preceding the poem. In the "Fifth Movement: *Autobiography*" Zukofsky speaks of his situation as a first-generation American:

251 Assimilation is not hard,
252 And once the Faith's askew
253 I might as well look Shagetz just as much as
     Jew.
254 I'll read their Donne as mine,
255 And leopard in their spots
256 I'll do what says their Coleridge,
257 Twist red hot pokers into knots.
258 The villainy they teach me I will execute
259 And it shall go hard with them,
260 For I'll better the instruction,
261 Having learned, so to speak, in their colleges.

Apart from its frequent satiric, ironic, and comic episodes, "The" contains many heartfelt passages about his parents' early life in Russia, along with beautiful sections adapted from Yehoash.

Publication of "The" was not the only help Pound gave to the young poet. Zukofsky sent him a group of earlier poems, asking if they were of any value. Without seeking further permission, Pound wrote to Harriet Monroe, enclosing them and urging her to use them. Pound also suggested she use Zukofsky as a reviewer for *Poetry*. Hearing of Zukofsky's impecunious state, Pound sent him a check for five dollars (five times the cost of a very good meal in New York in those days), but Zukofsky, as ever correct, sent it back with thanks. Harriet Monroe valued Pound's advice, and she published Zukofsky's poems, seven separate lyrical sections titled "Siren and Signal," in *Poetry* for June 1929. Zukofsky later reprinted two of them in the 1941 volume *55 Poems*. This time *Poetry*'s "News Notes" took more notice: "Louis Zukofsky's work has appeared in *The New Criterion, Exile, Transition,* and *The Dial.*" Apart from promoting Zukofsky's work, Pound was also practical. He wrote to Harriet on November 1, 1928, even before the work appeared: "Do sent Zukofsky his chq. as soon as convenient. I think he can use it."

In fact, he could. He was without a job. Hearing that the editorship of *Connecticut Industry* was open, Zukofsky traveled to Hartford to interview for the position, but without result. While in Hartford he tried to see Wallace Stevens, but Stevens was away on business. For a time Zukofsky worked for the National Industrial Conference Board, writing and editing reports on such topics as industrial cafeterias and employee savings plans. He was grateful to receive a check for twenty-five dollars from Harriet Monroe in advance of publication of the poems she had accepted. Thanking her, he sent along some more, which she refused.

In 1928 he finished the first four movements of "*A*," a poem whose outline he had already sketched out in twenty-four movements. "*A*"-1 has as its occasion a performance of Johann Sebastian Bach's *St. Matthew Passion* that Zukofsky attended that year, and shows the influence of both Dante and Pound. Bach, who recurs throughout "*A*," appears again in "*A*"-2 in which the young poet clarifies his aesthetic principles in a dialogue with a disagreeing "Kay." "*A*"-3 is an elegy for "Ricky" Chambers, while "*A*"-4 treats the conflict between Zukofsky's Jewish ancestry and his American upbringing.

The poetry, which seems accessible now, was

at the time very avant-garde. Zukofsky sent the first two movements to Marianne Moore at the *Dial*; she found them interesting but inappropriate. Still, with Pound's backing, Zukofsky's life was becoming more exciting and his vocation as poet seemed more possible. Pound's father invited Zukofsky to visit him in Wyncote, Pennsylvania; visitors from Europe started to look him up, saying that Ezra Pound told them that he was the only intelligent man in the country. The first section of "Siren and Signal" (not one he reprinted), "He Came Also Still," was awarded honorable mention by the editors in the November issue of *Poetry*. Zukofsky reciprocated Pound's attention, and wrote a long and perceptive essay in 1929 titled "Ezra Pound: His Cantos," praising Pound's work. Edmund Wilson liked the essay, but rejected it as being too specialized for his magazine, the *New Republic*. The essay was later published in 1930 in the short-lived French literary journal *Échanges*.

Zukofsky was still casting about for a job. With Pound's support, he applied for a Guggenheim Fellowship but was turned down. He also applied for a teaching assistantship at the University of Wisconsin. H. B. Lathrop of the university wrote to Pound for an estimate of the young poet's abilities; on the basis of Pound's enthusiastic recommendation, Zukofsky was given an assistant's position in English and comparative literature at Madison for the academic year 1930–1931. Lathrop wrote to Pound on June 17, 1930:

I feel sorry and rather ashamed that a man of his evident talent should be willing to take such an unimportant place and work for so little money, but he thinks he is coming away from the tumult and anxiety of the metropolis to a place of quiet.

Madison was quiet indeed compared to New York City, but with the economic situation of the nation steadily worsening since the stock market crash of 1929, a secure job of any kind must have seemed desirable.

In 1930 he also finished "A"-5, -6, and -7. "A"-5 continues the dialogue with Kay, which resolves itself:

"You write a strange speech." "This."
One song
Of many voices.

"A"-5 is an amalgam of Bach, New York City, self-reflection, and imagist precision, still under the influence of Eliot

For I have seen self-taunt
tracked down in the mirror,
And besides it, asleep, the face open,
Edges of no one like it: Everlasting.

and Pound

And one afternoon: a field,
Two windows spacing a wall,
A heavy bulk move back of the windows

In "A"-6 Zukofsky comes into his own voice. As long as all of "A"-1–5 put together, it is a record of a trip across the United States, which concludes the first quarter of the poem in twenty-four movements by returning to many of "A"'s earlier subjects: Bach, Kay, and Ricky. It exhibits the strong interest in politics and a sympathy for workers that became Zukofsky's focus during his leftist years in the 1930's. Louis "modernizes / His lute" by quoting Henry Ford at the outset of the Great Depression: "'Many people are too busy to be unemployed,' says Henry. / (Especially those who have their own factories to take care of.)"

"A"-7 is the first of Zukofsky's bravura technical performances (which have no equal in twentieth-century English-language poetry), a series of seven sonnets in which the last (or penultimate) word in four of the sonnets is included in the first line of the subsequent sonnet. He limits himself to repeating the same words a number of times throughout the sequence; this remarkably restrained use of vocabulary gives "A"-7 the feel of a closely interwoven musical composition. While skillfully executed, these formal devices draw readers' attention to the artifice of the poetry, at the expense of its meaning, a move that was increasingly characteristic of Zukofsky's poetry for the rest of his career. This move was intentional; Zukofsky's exploration of every dimension of language except the referential came to dominate his poetic practice. Zukofsky chose only "A"-7 for inclusion in the "Objectivists" issue of *Poetry* he later edited, describing it to Harriet Monroe as "a rondeau or a fugue within the fugue of the entire poem." The other six movements appeared in the *New Review, Pagany*, and *An "Objectivists" Anthology*; ten years later, Zukofsky revised them all.

Pound continued to hector Harriet Monroe (and seemingly everyone else) on Zukofsky's behalf. Recognizing the young man's genius, Pound promoted his poetry and his criticism with friends at the *Criterion* and the *Hound and Horn*. The latter serialized Zukofsky's essay on Henry Adams, a revision of his thesis at Columbia. Zukofsky, Pound wrote to Monroe on September 26, 1930, was "one of the very few people making any advance in criticism. He *ought to* appear regularly in 'Poetry.'" Drawing on an almost twenty-year friendship, Pound pulled out all stops in the letter:

Hang it all.—you printed my "Don'ts" & Ford's essay in Poetry in 1913 etc. & they set a *date*. you ought not to let the magazine drift into being a mere passive spectator of undefined & undefinable events. . . .

You could get back in the ring. if you wd. print a number containing only people McKenzie believes in & that Zukofsky is ready to treat with serious criticism.

Must make *one no*. of *Poet*. different from another if you want to preserve *life* as distinct from mere *continuity*. C'mon you ain't ossified yet.

Zukofsky was fortunate to have found such an ally. When he wrote again to Harriet Monroe, he asked if he could trouble her to write a letter of recommendation for him for a Guggenheim Fellowship. His project, he wrote on the application form, was to write a long poem and develop a poetics. Yes, she wrote back, she would be glad to recommend him, and, by the way, would he care to edit a special number of *Poetry*, to be devoted to those poets whom members of his generation respected and read?

Such an opportunity comes rarely. He responded with alacrity, but also with his characteristic modesty: he had no group to put across, just work that he would like to see in print, William Carlos Williams for one. He was unsure about suggesting his own poetry for inclusion, although perhaps "A"-7, a crown of sonnets, would be appropriate—he would let Harriet Monroe be the judge.

When Pound heard the news from Monroe, he wrote back immediately: "in a few days it wd. have been a birfday present. . . . waal waaal my deah Harriet, I sho iz glad you let these young scrubs have the show to thei selves, and ah does hope they dust out your office." His only reservation, Pound said in the letter of October 24, 1930, was that Zukofsky "will be just too Goddam prewdent."

Zukofsky, in Madison, residing at the University Club, threw himself into the project. He had new responsibilities as a graduate student and two-thirds teaching assistant. His modest salary of one thousand dollars for the nine-month academic year was quickly depleted. He sent twenty-five dollars home each month, twenty-four dollars a month went to his rent, ten dollars for a weekly meal ticket, and four dollars and forty cents for club dues. Only about fifteen dollars remained each month for miscellaneous expenses such as laundry, postage, and books.

Zukofsky taught seven hours a week: one section of advanced first-year English, and two sections of a survey of English literature. Later, one of those sections was replaced by another class, "Introduction to English Literature," in which he taught poetics. He declared his intention of pursuing graduate work toward a Ph.D. thesis. He took graduate courses: a tutorial on Thomas Jefferson and a course on Provençal, undoubtedly on the recommendation of Pound.

Zukofsky was hard at work on his issue of *Poetry*. He asked for contributions from Robert McAlmon, S. Theodore Hecht, George Oppen, William Carlos Williams, and Carl Rakosi, a poet whom he thought possessed genius, though Rakosi had stopped writing in 1925. He also planned to include some of his own work. During this same busy period he prepared two critical essays on the poetry of William Carlos Williams that appeared in the January 1931 issues of *Symposium* and *Hound and Horn*.

Zukofsky was unhappy in the small city of Madison, so different from his beloved New York. The closest large city was Chicago, and his connection with *Poetry* gave him the excuse he was looking for to go there. He took the bus down to Chicago for the weekend of November 22 and 23, 1930, and met with Harriet Monroe and her assistant editor Morton Zabel. He showed them his "find," the poems of Rakosi, and took time to see the display of Impressionist paintings at the Art Institute.

He and Rakosi had developed a warm friendship through their correspondence. Rakosi, admiring "The" and the beginning of "*A*," invited his correspondent to visit New Orleans over his Christmas break, but Zukofsky was scheduled to visit his family in New York. In his letters, Zukofsky reported his height as 5 feet 10 inches and weight at 125 pounds (close to a lifetime high), his favorite poet as John Donne, and his

character as sane. He also registered a growing dissatisfaction with life in the Midwest, though he found a friend in one of his female students.

Zukofsky was unhappy with his lodgings at the University Club with its strict rules about female visitors, so he prepared to move to the scandalous (by the standards of the time) Irving Apartments. He signed a lease in late October for one room with a private bath and, all-important, a private entrance. He borrowed the first month's rent, $32.50, from René Taupin.

Zukofsky knew that depression-era America was not conducive to literary experimentation. He considered quitting writing and learning to drive a car instead. His strong left-wing tendencies were appropriate for the difficult times; the country seemed on the verge of a left-wing revolution. Despite misgivings, he did manage to articulate a common program for the contributors to his issue of *Poetry*. It was a combination of propaganda and criticism; it had both rhetorical intent and personal despair built in. He realized that by being daring, he might arouse the curiosity of both critics and the sedate audience of *Poetry*.

The February "Objectivists" issue of *Poetry* stirred up some controversy, as he had imagined it might. It represented the birth of a genuine American avant-garde artistic movement, but at a time little favorable for such a development. Although some critics have disputed whether or not the "Objectivists" were a genuine poetic movement at all, at the very least it gathered, in Harriet Monroe's words, "a group of writers interested in experiment in poetic form and method," a group that was filtered through the discerning critical intelligence of one individual.

Reaction to the "Objectivists" issue was mixed. Horace Gregory sent a letter to *Poetry* congratulating everyone concerned but warning that the " 'Objectivists' will die for lack of oxygen if they ignore the panorama of strictly American life, including the class struggle."

Gregory objected to the difficult style of the group and their apparent unconcern for the pressing social issues of the day. Stanley Burnshaw sent a long letter to *Poetry* about the lack of precision in the stated aims of the movement, to which Zukofsky replied at length.

Pound was delighted with the issue and wrote on February 12, 1931, to order four more copies, telling Harriet Monroe: "This is a number I can show my friends. If you can do another eleven as lively you will put the mag. on its feet." Both Pound and Williams thought Zukofsky's editing distinguished and his essay on Charles Reznikoff outstanding. Pound wrote: "The same authors badly edited wd. not have the same effect." Wrote Williams: "The boy has a flair for knowing what he wants."

Monroe had her doubts, and Pound wrote to bolster her again on March 27, 1931:

Although most of the contents was average, the MODE of presentation was good editing. The zoning of different states of mind so that one can see what they are, is good editing. . . . there has been a development in American verse during 20 years and the messy britons have not kept up with it.

Zukofsky continued to be disappointed with life in Madison. He applied for another Guggenheim; with the twenty-five hundred dollars he planned on going to Europe. His senior colleagues mistook his shy silence for arrogance. Although his move to the Irving Apartments meant he could entertain female visitors undisturbed, mostly he found little to do except work. Sometimes he would walk to the square or into the black section of town to eat at cheap restaurants where the food always upset his stomach; occasionally he bought a bottle of illegal whiskey at four dollars for a pint. He thought of going to Mexico over the summer with René Taupin; if he did not get the Guggenheim (he did not) he was going to move back East, unless the school

promoted him to instructor at five hundred dollars more per year.

His assistantship was renewed at the University of Wisconsin, but he determined not to accept it and planned on returning to New York when the school year ended. By mid June he had found a room at 50 Morton Street in New York City, but work was scarce and job hunting difficult; he went out every day with only spare carfare in his pocket. He still wrote, though poverty made it difficult.

Zukofsky and Williams considered a volume in homage to Pound, and Samuel Putnam was interested in publishing it, but the project was changed to an anthology of the "Objectivists." Zukofsky did receive some recognition; in mid August he lectured at the Gotham Book Mart on "Recencies in Poetry" (reprinted in 1932 in *An "Objectivists" Anthology*). He thought to make his new movement comprehensible, but felt that the audience did not understand him.

His disappointment regarding the unsympathetic reception to his new movement in poetry, combined with his continuing depression over his lack of financial prospects, did not prevent him from keeping up an energetic correspondence nor from continuing his efforts on behalf of his contemporaries. Zukofsky was a truly brilliant and generous critic of other poets, going over material sent to him word by word and giving very specific advice. In a letter to Rakosi on October 19, 1931, he observed that his own work was too far in advance of its time to gain a wide audience. Putnam dropped the Objectivist's project, but it was taken up by another publisher.

The new publisher was called TO Publishers; it was owned by George Oppen, and Zukofsky served as its editor. The two poets planned to issue six books a year in a six-by-eight-inch paperback format of 125 to 150 pages each. The first books were projected to be: (1) a novelette and other prose by William Carlos Williams; (2) "Prolegomena, Section 1" by Ezra Pound (the collected prose); (3) *Tre croce* (Three Crosses), by Tozzi, translated by Basil Bunting; (4) prose or poetry by Zukofsky; (5) "My country 'Tis of Thee," or other prose or poetry by Charles Reznikoff; (6) "Prolegomena, Section 2" by Pound. These books were to be called the "Discrete Series," and were to be priced at seventy-five cents each. To save costs, they were to be published in France. The enigmatic name of the new publisher was meant to suggest a noun in the dative case, to TO or for TO; although the word was treated as a noun, it was pronounced just like the preposition.

Zukofsky was paid for his work as editor by George Oppen. He had another source of revenue as well. Early in 1932, Taupin arranged to pay him fifty dollars a month for six months to collaborate on a book about Guillaume Apollinaire. Taupin taught at Columbia and had received a leave of absence and full pay from the university to do the book but was occupied with other things. Zukofsky wrote the entire book, which he finished in 1932 and titled "The Writing of Apollinaire." Taupin's translation of it appeared in France in 1934 as *Le style Apollinaire*. Zukofsky's connection to the experimental French poet is an important reason for the later interest of the "L=A=N=G=U=A=G=E" poets in his work.

In March the Guggenheim Foundation turned him down again. Taupin was in Europe but was due back by April 5, when he and Zukofsky were scheduled to take a trip to the West Coast. Zukofsky left for San Francisco on April 21, taking a southern route that led him through Juárez, Mexico, and Phoenix, Arizona. He apparently also went up to Canada, because he wrote to Harriet Monroe on May 2, 1932, from San Francisco that he was deported from Canada when he told them that his job was editor for TO Publishers. He was back in New York on June 21, 1932.

About this time he was editing an issue of *Contempo* about the "Objectivist" poets, but its editor, Milton Abernethy, later canceled his plans for it. TO published the *"Objectivists" Anthology* in September 1932 and then suspended publishing indefinitely, leaving Zukofsky again unemployed. He found a new apartment, at 39 Sidney Place in Brooklyn, and by collecting money that people owed him was able to afford the twenty-dollars-per-month rent, subsisting on fifteen-cent breakfasts and twenty-cent lunches. However, as he wrote to Carl Rakosi on October 13, 1932, he was not so completely desperate about employment that he would consider teaching in the public high schools. In early November 1932 he again wrote to Rakosi, taking the fact that William Carlos Williams was preparing to vote for Roosevelt as evidence of an imminent left-wing revolution. Zukofsky stayed afloat financially, in part, by selling his personal library book by book.

Zukofsky could not even afford *Poetry* and offered a poem to pay for a subscription. Kind Harriet Monroe returned the poem but gave him a subscription anyway. In correspondence with Pound, discussing whether to have him return as foreign editor of *Poetry*, she expressed doubts about Zukofsky's ability as a poet (and Pound's ability as a critic): "You think a lot of Zukofsky, for example, while I think he is no poet at all, his 'objectivist' theories seem to be absurd, and his prose style abominable." Zukofsky's mood, like that of the nation, was at an all-time low. The year 1933 was his least productive, although he did begin what would become his most extensive correspondence: on March 21, 1933, he wrote to the poet Lorine Niedecker, a close friend from his Madison days, about his disenchantment with objectivism.

In response to the economic situation, Zukofsky was promoting the formation of a writers' union to publish the work of deserving younger writers. He wrote to Rakosi on April 18, 1933, that he had secured the cooperation of Pound,

Williams, and Reznikoff, and that he was working through them to recruit Joyce, Ford Madox Ford, T. S. Eliot, Wyndham Lewis, Hemingway, and Yeats. He was also looking for financial backers and had secured pledges for two hundred dollars each from Tibor Serly and René Taupin.

The union, at first called "Writers Extant," became the Objectivist Press. Zukofsky did make some money from the *Apollinaire*; he also received some money from the inclusion of some of his poetry in Pound's *Active Anthology*. Pound, ever generous, was promoting a Zukofsky trip to Europe. He gave Zukofsky one thousand francs; another friend, the violist and composer Tibor Serly, apparently lent or gave Zukofsky the remaining money necessary, since by June the trip had been entirely arranged.

Zukofsky left New York on the *Majestic* on June 30, 1933, arriving in Cherbourg on July 6. He stayed for a couple of weeks in Paris, at the Hotel du Perigord. While there he saw Hilaire Hiler, Fernand Léger, Constantin Brancusi, and De Massot, all, it seems, at Pound's recommendation. Zukofsky left Paris to spend some time in Budapest, arriving on July 29, and then he went on to Rapallo, arriving on August 12. In Rapallo, he stayed with Ezra Pound's parents, Homer and Isabel Pound (in William Butler Yeats's old apartment), taking his meals with Ezra and Dorothy Shakespear Pound, and attending the "Ezuversity." Zukofsky later recalled Homer Pound's hospitality fondly; Homer, familiar with the impecunious condition of young poets, would force Zukofsky to take tea with them each day, saying that out West, people who turned down an invitation were shot as strangers. He left Rapallo at the beginning of September, and by the 15th, he was back in New York, living at 151 Remsen Street in Brooklyn, and again looking for a job to pay his fourteen-dollars-per-month rent.

The Objectivist Press was soon under way,

with plans to start with the collected poems of William Carlos Williams followed by a volume of work by Charles Reznikoff. Williams and Reznikoff were each to contribute financially to the publication of their volumes, Williams $100 and Reznikoff the $147 it would cost to cover all printing and some overhead costs.

Pound's "Ezuversity" clearly had some influence on Zukofsky, since he began to talk about economics and credit in some of his correspondence. He wrote to Carl Rakosi on November 9, 1933, of his intent to write a canzone with economics as its principal theme. He later accomplished his goal with the first half of "A"-9. The influence of his Italian sojourn would also show in his adoption of the sestina form for his brilliant poem "Mantis," written the following year.

"Mantis" and its companion poem " 'Mantis,' An Interpretation" are together an extended consideration of the plight of the poor in the distressed economic times of the Great Depression. The poem was occasioned by Zukofsky's observation of a praying mantis lost, imploring, and helpless in a New York subway. The poet's own inability to help the insect to recover its place in the natural green world reinforces his sense of powerlessness in the face of the hardships and indignities suffered by the "armies of the poor." He implores the mantis to take flight, to stir up the poor "like leaves." The poem ends with the moving, half-strangled cry to the mantis to "build the new world in your eyes, Save it!"

The companion poem explains the incident in the subway that provided the initial inspiration for the sestina. It records the first, false steps in its writing, and Zukofsky's search for the proper form in which to capture his emotion, not just at seeing the insect, but at all the thoughts that it awakes:

That this thoughts' torsion
Is really a sestina

Carrying subconsciously
Many intellectual and sensual properties of the
    forgetting and remembering Head
One human's intuitive Head.

Alluding to Dante Alighieri's discovery of his love for Beatrice, "Incipit vita nova" (the new life begins), Zukofsky combines a discussion about the genesis of an appropriate poetic form from the felt emotion (instead of a form imposed, "a Victorian / Stuffing like upholstery," upon material unsuited for it) with his personal and political concern for the poor in the United States:

The mantis, then,
Is a small incident of one's physical vision
Which is the poor's helplessness
The poor's separateness
Bringing self disgust.

The two poems are among Zukofsky's most successful work, combining genuine emotion, powerful imagery, and both experimental and traditional verse forms into a moving personal and political vision of a man aware of the causes of great injustice yet powerless to do anything to remedy them.

Like so many of his generation, Louis survived for the next eight years by working for the Works Progress Administration at jobs created by Franklin Delano Roosevelt's New Deal. He started on January 19, 1934, at a Columbia University project, taking exams to verify the results of an adult education program, studying Russian as part of the same program, preparing a series of poetry exams, and selecting quotations from world poetry that would serve as touchstones for study and comparison (this work was expanded and published by Zukofsky in 1948 as *A Test of Poetry*). He was later transferred to another Columbia project (and promised a three-dollar-per-week raise) that involved rewriting and editing a study of children's socially useful work. He

worked there until March 1935, when he began work for the New York City Arts Project, another WPA program, in support of WNYC public radio.

In January 1936 he transferred to the Federal Arts Project, supervising a group working on the Index of American Design. That work, involving a comprehensive survey of the history of American arts and crafts, continued until July 1939. From September 1939 until April 1942, except for a brief hiatus working for *La France en Liberté*, he again worked for the New York City Arts Project, producing radio scripts.

By April 1935 he had moved to 149 East 37th Street in Manhattan. He was bothered by an attack on him that appeared in the Stalinist review, *The New Masses*. The attack, by a writer identified as "Mr. Macleod," was apparently motivated by Zukofsky's association with Pound, who was vocal in his support of Benito Mussolini. He protested the attack in a letter to Carl Rakosi on April 17, 1935, pointing out that although he was not a member of the Communist Party, his poetry had expressed political awareness for a decade, and that in fact his work approached communist thought more closely than the work of the young English leftist poets Auden and Spender. The attack so incensed him that on April 6, 1935, he had written to the editors of the *New Masses*, complaining that Macleod's comments were filled with the same nazism that he was accusing Zukofsky of harboring. One of Macleod's statements in particular caused exasperation: "The Jews are a fact. Mr. Zukofsky has not emphasized the phenomenon." Zukofsky could only complain, justifiably, that Macleod showed no knowledge of "The" or of the fourth, fifth, and sixth movements of "A."

In 1935 Zukofsky and Jerry Reisman wrote a 132-page screenplay based on James Joyce's *Ulysses*, which they hoped to sell to Hollywood. On July 18, 1935, Zukofsky wrote to Joyce in Paris, offering the screenplay for sale. Joyce liked the screenplay and, knowing the film *The Informer*, hoped that John Ford might direct. A few years later, on February 17, 1941, when the Modern Library edition of *Ulysses* appeared, Zukofsky wrote to John Ford, trying to interest him in the screenplay, but to no avail.

Zukofsky had read *Ulysses* in Madison, word for word, aloud in his room with one of his pupils, Frank Heineman, and greatly admired it. His interest in film came from Charlie Chaplin, whose work he greatly prized, especially *Modern Times*. He would later admire the films of Jean Cocteau.

Zukofsky had first met the woman he would later marry, a young musician and composer named Celia Thaew, in 1934, when he supervised a WPA project on which she worked. By 1936 or 1937 they had become steady companions. Their first date was to hear Leonard Bernstein play a piano piece by Aaron Copland at Town Hall. He introduced her to Tibor Serly, a former student of Bartók who at the time played in the Philadelphia Symphony Orchestra, commuting from Manhattan. Zukofsky was passionate about music, particularly the music of Bach. He believed that in previous lives, if such existed, he had been a seventeenth century poet and a student of Bach.

In 1936, Zukofsky wrote *Arise, Arise*, a short play in two acts. It was based on his mother's death, after a lengthy bout with a lung infection, on his birthday in 1927. The title is from John Donne's "Holy Sonnet VII," which the character of the son reads at the play's beginning:

At the round earth's imagined corners, blow
Your trumpets, angels, and arise, arise
From death, you numberless infinities
Of souls, and to your scattered bodies go.

Although it was not published until 1962, it is an excellent first play, containing elements of both naturalistic and expressionistic drama, and Zukofsky would have had a promising career as a playwright had anyone taken notice. He exhibits a good ear for dialogue and a remarkably contemporary sensibility in his use of a second, "Dream" curtain behind the regular theater curtain, in his careful directions for a sparse set, and in his insistence that the actors should all be dancers. The play's only weakness is that it does not sufficiently establish audience sympathy for the characters: Zukofsky, personally close to the dramatic situation, assumes that his audience is too.

In 1937 he completed "A"-8. A very long movement, it is Zukofsky's closest approximation to the *Cantos* of Ezra Pound, written at a time of Pound's greatest influence on him. The figure of Bach reappears, but the chief focus of "A"-8 is on the thinking of Karl Marx and its applicability to the troubled decade of the 1930's. This political focus is especially apparent at the beginning of the movement, in which Zukofsky recasts his earlier "Nature as creator . . . Nature as created" of "A"-6 into:

And of labor:
Light lights in air,
                              on streets, on earth, in earth—
Obvious as that horses eats oats—
                  Labor as creator,
                              Labor as creature,
To right praise.

"A"-8 also contains a revolutionary song, the first stanza of which is:

        Railways and highways have tied
        Blood of farmland and town
              And the chains
              Speed wheat to machine
        This is May
        The poor's armies veining the earth!

The distinct features of "A"-8 are the unique musicality of its beginning and magnificent close, and Zukofsky's handling of twentieth-century science. In that, he went beyond Pound, whose mechanical notions of causation are derived directly from late nineteenth-century classical physics and never proceed beyond them. Zukofsky, in his reading and writing in physics, had absorbed completely the quantum and relativistic theories of the twentieth century.

Zukofsky's life had settled into a fairly comfortable routine by the late 1930's. His work on the WPA project in 1937 took only a couple of hours a day; he checked in at the office occasionally, but did most of his work, unsupervised, at the New York Public Library, essentially as he pleased. He availed himself of the lively New York cultural scene, going to the May Day parade in 1937; attending a lecture by Leo Frobenius; going to see *Tsar to Lenin*, a collection of newsreel films from before World War I through the Bolshevik Revolution, edited by Max Eastman; and viewing D. W. Griffith's *Birth of a Nation*. New York attracted poets. Basil Bunting, whom he had finally met in Rapallo earlier in the decade, visited him in May 1938.

Zukofsky found both the time and the technical skill to write the canzone about economics that he had projected several years earlier. He began work on what would become the first half of "A"-9 in 1938; the foreword to his privately printed *First Half of "A"-9* is dated November 24, 1939. It is a reworking of Guido Cavalcanti's canzone "Donna mi prega," the most difficult poem in Italian. Pound had tried to translate it three separate times, over a period of twenty years, without conspicuous success. In the first half of "A"-9 Zukofsky accomplishes a nearly impossible feat, using the precise rhyme scheme of the original canzone to write an original poem on Marxist economics. Cavalcanti's canzone form is incredibly circumscribed; more than a third of the syllables in each stanza rhyme, and the rhymes occur in the same place in each of the subsequent stanzas.

Zukofsky brilliantly had decided to recast the extremely technical, scholastic, philosophical vocabulary of the original in an equally difficult Marxist philosophical vocabulary, bringing the canzone up to date. And, as his notes reveal, he did not feel challenged sufficiently, so he decided on a further technical constraint: the distribution of the two consonants *r* and *n* would be governed by a mathematical formula for a conic surface:

$$\frac{\dfrac{d^2y}{dt^2}}{\dfrac{d^2x}{dt^2}} = \tan \theta \text{ where } \theta = \text{arc } \tan \frac{y}{x}$$

Zukofsky was working simultaneously on a Brooklynese translation of the same canzone, the first three lines of which read:

A foin lass bodders me I gotta tell her
Of a fact surely, so unrurly, often'
'R't comes 'tcan't soften it's proud neck's called
    love mm. .

Zukofsky believed that he had captured some unnoticed element of humor in Cavalcanti's original language by rendering the poem in this way. Although there is no such humor in "Donna me prega," the rendering is interesting, and the prowess needed to carry it off in English demonstrates Zukofsky as rare among poets in sheer technical capacity. Besides, Zukofsky could be very funny.

The completion of that piece and his marriage to Celia Thaew marked a distinct break in his life, a turn away from the political to the familial. Likewise, his poetry became increasingly concerned with family matters. Zukofsky was manifestly happy with his newfound domesticity, and it afforded him the energy necessary to finish "A" despite the scant attention given to his work (considering its importance) throughout most of his life.

The Zukofskys had been married in a civil ceremony on August 20, 1939, in Wilmington,

Delaware. They did not have a honeymoon but returned to Manhattan, to Louis's new apartment on 111th Street where they stayed for a few months until they found a more desirable place opposite a Bronx park. Celia was musically inclined, a capable composer and accomplished pianist.

Zukofsky's work on his life's project continued. He wrote to Carl Rakosi on August 6, 1940, that "A"-10 was to be published in *La France en Liberté*. Intended as the review of free France, that publication's editorial board consisted of René Taupin and Ivan Goll for the French section and Louis Zukofsky for the English section. Albert Einstein accepted Taupin's invitation to join the advisory board. Although it seemed that the review had sufficient funds for a year's publication, the project quickly folded. "A"-10 is one of the least successful movements in "*A*." Its clichéd propagandistic ploys and Marxist resentment may have appealed to the imagined audience of *La France en Liberté*, but they seem glaringly out of place in the rest of the work.

Celia helped Zukofsky by typing the movement and running off fifty-five copies (a few spoiled) for the limited edition of that remarkable work, the first half of "A"-9. It was finished early in December 1940. The postcard from the Gotham Book Mart advertising Zukofsky's amazing technical achievement read as follows:

Zukofsky has spent five years on the first half of the ninth movement of his long poem "A." He uses the canzone form which, according to Dante, embraced the whole of poetry. The form appears only once before [*sic*] in literature, in Guido Cavalcanti's Donna mi Prega. Intent on "the whole art of poetry," "A"-9 places the canzone in the thought of our time.

The poet's notes, showing the development of his poem, are included in this volume and will *not* be reprinted in any complete edition of "A." *Strictly limited to 55 autographed copies* numbers 16 to 55 for sale Quarto, oaktag covers, 41pp. mimeographed.

Very few of the mimeographed edition sold. Louis wrote to Rakosi on October 15, 1941 with the observation that it was easiest to publish with a commercial publishing house to avoid disappointment.

Zukofsky's Marxist rendering of the canzone had been appropriate, for he had not lost his political sympathies. But he was cautious with whom he shared his views. Late in the war he told a banker who employed him that, as a Confucian, he did not see the need for a profit motive.

In fall 1941, Zukofsky tried once again for a Guggenheim, but was once again turned down, despite the recommendation of George Dillon, the new editor of *Poetry*, who had recently accepted some of his work. More encouraging was the publication (by James A. Decker) of his book *55 Poems*. In his review of them in the September 1942 *Poetry*, "An Extraordinary Sensitivity: Zukofsky's 55 Poems," William Carlos Williams wrote of the necessary obscurity of those doing superlative work in the arts: "There is a kind of monkhood in excellence." He continued:

The poems are uneven. They try a difficult approach to the reader's attention, a very difficult approach, so that there are many factors involved in their failure—even tho' their successes are of superlative quality when achieved.

Privately, on October 20, 1941, he gave Zukofsky good advice:

This is a dangerous sort of writing for if it doesn't click, if it doesn't do the magic and arouse the reader or doesn't find one who is serious enough, trained enough and ready enough to place himself exactly in tune with it—or if, in writing it, the writer isn't instructed by deep enough feeling (as it sometimes happens here) it becomes a mere jargon and a reaching. . . . When sense, even ploddingly, cannot solve a sentence because of *lack* of its *parts*—the fault cannot be said to lie with the reader. But to fly, we require a certain lightness and wings. HERE, at their best, we have them.

In both his strictures and his praise, Williams had reached the heart of the problems and the successes of Zukofsky's poetry.

Zukofsky finished work for the WPA in April 1942, but instead of finding another job, he spent the summer and early fall of 1942 with Celia in Diamond Point, Lake George, New York. When they returned to New York City, they found an apartment at 202 Columbia Heights in Brooklyn. Zukofsky renewed his old substitute license and tried teaching English for $8.50 a day in the high schools, but found the discipline problems discomfiting. He found work instead as a laboratory assistant in physics at Brooklyn Technical High School. The job paid a dollar less a day, but it was nearby, he liked both students and staff, and he did not have to teach, only set up lab demonstrations. Nevertheless, he decided he was not cut out for high school employment. He then found work as a technical writer and editor: at Hazeltine Electronics between June 1943 and October 1944, at Jordanoff Aviation between October 1944 and March 1946, and at Techlit Consultants between March 1946 and January 1947.

Family life suited Zukofsky well. Celia was an ideal mate, and they were very close. The poet Robert Creeley later remarked that if one of them left the room, the other seemed to disappear. He and Celia bought a house in Brooklyn. Their son, Paul, was born on October 22, 1943. When he was little more than five years old, he was learning to play a quarter-sized violin at the Mannes School, where he was enrolled, and Celia bought him a full-sized violin of his own. The Zukofskys had a piano, and Celia would play and compose music for poems by Louis and oc-

casionally for poems by Williams (the two families were good friends and visited each other often). After another month or so of substitute teaching again at Brooklyn Technical High School, Zukofsky found a job that became permanent, within walking distance of his home. With so many returning soldiers going to college on the G.I. bill, instructors were in demand and in February 1947, Zukofsky found a post at the Polytechnic Institute of Brooklyn; he taught English there for roughly the next twenty years, rising from instructor to associate professor. In the same year, he began a long critical and philosophical work, *Bottom: On Shakespeare*; the project took him more than a decade to complete and was not published until 1963. During this same period the Zukofskys briefly owned a small country home in Old Lyme, Connecticut, where they hoped to escape a polio epidemic. The epidemic was soon over, and plagued by the cottage's bad plumbing and the high tides flooding its backyard, they quickly put it up for sale again.

Zukofsky's *Test of Poetry* was published in October 1948. He wrote to Pound, then under indictment for treason and confined to St. Elizabeths in Washington, D. C., for permission to include selections from the *Cantos* and from "Homage to Sextus Propertius," from "Dieu qu'il la fait," and from his translation of the Cavalcanti canzone. When neither Pound nor Dorothy responded to his letters, Zukofsky left the material out. The estate of Emily Dickinson wanted twenty-five dollars for the poems of hers that he planned to include, so he left them out as well. Aside from those omissions, the volume was as he wanted. The print run was small, and sales were disappointing. But he did use the book to support a promotion to assistant professor effective September 1, 1949, at a salary of $4,200 per year.

The decade of the 1940's was one of scant poetic activity for Zukofsky, understandable because of his new responsibilities, but by the end of the decade, with his son older and his job situation finally settled, he returned to poetry. He finished "A"-9 on August 22, 1950, only two days after his eleventh wedding anniversary, the date when he had hoped to finish. The first half of the diptych, written at the close of the 1930's had Marxist economics as its subject; the second half of the diptych, written at the close of the 1940's, celebrated the mysteries of love. Thus "A"-9 represents Zukofsky's personal journey from the Marxism of his Columbia days and the 1930's through his eleven years of marriage and love for Celia.

In 1950 Zukofsky wrote "A"-11, a ballata based on Cavalcanti's: "Perch'io non spero di tornar giammai." Again, it is a bravura technical performance in a very constrained rhymed form, made even more difficult by Zukofsky in that he ends each stanza with the word "honor." The words "love," "honor," "song," and "light" are repeated constantly throughout the ballata, with hypnotic effect. Knowing that Pound would appreciate what he was doing, he sent a copy to St. Elizabeths. He also submitted "A"-11 to the new editor of *Poetry*, Karl Shapiro, who rejected it. In "A"-11 he introduces his family; the constrained poetic form and the repetition of key words tend to remove the poem from the realm of public reference toward a private, familial realm, though its musicality can be readily appreciated.

Zukofsky's father took suddenly ill, was operated on, and died of a heart attack early in April 1950. When Zukofsky and Celia visited him in the hospital, Pinchos had been worried that some money he had set aside for the synagogue would not get there. After he died they looked in his room and found what he had left—three dollars and less than a dollar in pennies. Zukofsky wrote to Niedecker on 12 April of the affection for his father that was expressed by many at the funeral.

"A"-12 is an affectionate and affecting portrayal of Zukofsky's father and his family. It is longer than the sum of all eleven of the previous movements and is the most emotional of any:

> The miracle of his first job
> On the lower East Side:
> Six years night watchman
> In a men's shop
> Where by day he pressed pants
> Every crease a blade
> The irons weighed
> At least twenty pounds
> But moved both of them
> Six days a week
> From six in the morning
> To nine, sometimes eleven at night,
> Or midnight;
> Except Fridays
> When he left, enough time before sunset
> Margolis begrudged.
> His own business
> My father told Margolis
> Is to keep Sabbath.

A father himself, Louis could empathize with his father's heavy responsibilities, and he could also begin to understand his father's profound religious feeling. "A"-12 was begun in 1950 and completed in 1951. Having reached the midpoint of his projected work, Zukofsky set it aside until 1960.

Paul, demonstrating remarkable gifts as a musician, started formal lessons. Around 1951, Celia arranged, after persistent effort with the Board of Education, to take over his education at home so he could practice in the morning fresh and rested. In the summer of 1952 he attended Meadowmount, in Elizabethtown, New York, where the family rented an apartment. Father and son read Shakespeare together, the elder Zukofsky reading aloud a Cambridge edition; Paul followed in an Oxford one, checking every variant. On election day in November the Zukofskys voted for Stevenson; their son Paul was furious because he liked Ike. After voting, they went to see Chaplin's *Limelight*. Zukofsky's admiration for Chaplin, evident in his 1936 essay "Modern Times," had not diminished.

On September 25, 1955, Zukofsky was promoted to associate professor at Poly, though he felt obligated to return the first year of his two-hundred-dollars-per-year raise to the building fund celebrating Poly's centennial. He was continuing work on his most ambitious prose piece, *Bottom: On Shakespeare*, an early version of which had appeared in 1953 in *New Directions* 14.

Although his poetry was read and admired by the Black Mountain poets, he felt underappreciated. Charles Olson's influential essay "Projective Verse" had appeared in 1951 and was making quite a stir. In a letter to the poet Edward Dahlberg on July 11, 1954, Zukofsky claimed that Olson's essay was taken, in large part, from his "Objectivists" issue of *Poetry*, twenty years before, and that Olson had misinterpreted it.

Zukofsky's letters of the time reveal that Celia was having health problems in August of 1955 (she had an ulcer and was down to eighty-eight pounds), and the Zukofskys were having problems with the bank about renewing the ten-year mortgage on their home in Brooklyn. Such financial pressures led them to try to sell the house. Zukofsky wrote to Edward Dahlberg on February 7, 1956 that the prospect of showing the house to potential buyers and moving to an apartment was unappealing. The Zukofsky's had a number of visitors, both family and friends coming to stay, and the work of keeping up the home fell entirely on Celia, who began to believe that the greatest line in modern poetry was "Do not make my house your inn." When it became too much for her, they sold the house and moved into an apartment at 135 Willow Street, where Zukofsky was only a ten-minute walk from Poly.

Zukofsky had finished the first section of *Bottom* and was ready to start on the second section,

"An Alphabet of Subjects." The third section was to be Celia's musical setting of Shakespeare's *Pericles*. Zukofsky offered the new editor of *Poetry*, Henry Rago, the second half of "A"-9, but since a part of it had appeared in the *Montevallo Review*, *Poetry* would not take it: they used only unpublished material. Rago suggested, instead, that Zukofsky excerpt a five-to ten-page selection from "A"-12. Zukofsky made a careful selection of exactly three hundred lines, but Rago turned it down.

Paul Zukofsky's career was taking off, and his parents were busy with plans for this first Carnegie Hall recital. The program described the thirteen-year-old violinist as "a scholarship student at the Julliard School of Music working with Ivan Galamian." *The New York Times* reviewed the concert:

A deadpan bundle of talent made his debut last night in Carnegie Hall. . . .

There was, indeed, something almost frightening about the serious way the boy went through the music. . . . The playing was remarkably accurate and remarkably lifeless. . . .

Despite this clichéd response to a prodigy, both the *Times* review and the much shorter *Herald Tribune* review were quite favorable.

The Zukofskys managed a trip to Europe in the summer of 1957, arriving in Plymouth, England, on June 25 and leaving from Le Havre, France, on September 10. They traveled from Plymouth to Worcester to see Gael Turnbull, to Newcastle to see Basil Bunting, and then to London where they saw Herbert Read and met T. S. Eliot. In France, arriving around July 16 in Calais, they went through Normandy down to Poitiers, Limoges, and Provence, then through northern Italy, and back north through Switzerland to spend their last week in Paris. In Florence they met Cid Corman, whose friendship would develop into one of the most remarkable and fortunate of this period of Zukofsky's life, one that would be almost as productive for his poetry as his friendship with Pound had been.

In February 1958, continuing to work on *Bottom*, he reported to Corman that for relief he had turned to translating Catullus, with Celia acting as Latinist, providing Zukofsky with a line-by-line crib for each of the 116 poems. Paul was preparing for another Carnegie Hall recital, scheduled for February 1959. In May 1958 Louis received some further recognition for his work in the form of an offer from San Francisco State College to teach a summer course in poetry for fifteen hundred dollars. The family left for San Francisco on June 10, arriving by train on June 20 by way of Chicago, Denver, Salt Lake City, and a two-and-a-half-day side trip to Yellowstone. The lively San Francisco poetry community welcomed him, and the Zukofskys spent time with Robert Duncan, the Patchens, and the Rexroths.

Shortly after their return, Zukofsky mentioned to Celia that his recent group of twelve poems would make a nice book. She took the initiative and signed a contract to print a limited, facsimile edition of them. Although initially he disapproved of the expenditure, he liked the new volume. The Zukofskys sent copies to Cid Corman and to Robert Duncan, who wrote the beautiful tribute "After Reading *Barely and Widely*" (included in his *The Opening of the Field*):

> Will you give yourself airs
> from that lute of Zukofsky?
> In comely pairs
>
> the words courteously
> dancing, to lose the sense, thus,
> and return, thus, in time to see
>
> "God is
> "but one's deepest conviction—
> "your art, its use" so the text says.

These lines show once again that Zukofsky's best readers and most sensitive critics have been poets.

Zukofsky's difficulty in attracting a wider audience stemmed in part from the fact that he published his work in limited editions, often privately, that went rapidly out of print. Celia sent out two hundred postcards announcing the publication of *Barely and Widely*, but there was scant interest. In a letter to Corman of 19 November 1958, Zukofsky spoke of the pain of neglect after giving a reading that ended with selections from his book; everyone had listened attentively, but no one had bought a copy.

Bitterness and disappointment continued to grow in Zukofsky's later years. He was a gentle and kind man who lived a life of complete integrity and devotion to his work. He had long since given up on any large audience for his poetry, but he knew his work was appreciated by a coterie of poets. With the financial pressures of launching their son Paul's concert career, and with Celia spending so much time and taking the initiative of bringing out her husband's work, the Zukofskys had some reason to hope for small support. To see even those hopes shattered must have been painful indeed.

The Zukofskys moved again in March 1959, but only one flight up at 135 Willow. The new apartment had a more spacious layout, more like their former house. Paul's February recital at Carnegie Hall had received favorable reviews from the critics, though not enough to please his father.

Although Pound was no longer corresponding with Louis, he did carry on an intermittent correspondence with Paul, who had played the Jannequin Canto for him on the lawn of St. Elizabeths. Pound followed Paul's career after that, publicizing him and giving him advice. Pound told Paul that he had stopped writing to his father because Zukofsky would not rightly examine his ideas. Pound did contact Zukofsky by postcard in September, suggesting that the Pound-Zukofsky correspondence contained a great deal of important criticism and would make a good book, asking if he wanted to do it. Zukofsky, discouraged about the chances of ever getting a publisher, declined.

Celia had started a publicity campaign designed to attract a major publisher's notice to Zukofsky's work. A press release she prepared, entitled "*A MAJOR POET IN MINOR PUBLICATIONS?*" contained critical praise of Zukofsky's work by William Carlos Williams, Kenneth Rexroth, Marianne Moore, Mark Van Doren, Robert Duncan, Cid Corman, Robert Creeley, Babette Deutsch, Sir Herbert Read, and Ezra Pound. Rexroth was quoted twice; his second statement was: "To speak as a literateur—what are the 'influences,' the antecedents? Pound, Williams, Stein, Zukofsky." The release closes: "enquiries to Celia Zukofsky" with their Willow Street address.

Louis Zukofsky's correspondence with Cid Corman was to have more result than Celia's press release. Corman asked how much the Zukofskys could afford to contribute toward publishing an edition of the complete "*A*"-1–12. Although obviously excited by the prospect, Zukofsky, with his characteristic kindness and gentility, repeatedly told Cid not to deprive himself of time to do his own work by publishing "*A*" and not to neglect his own interests by doing so.

After almost thirty years' absence, George Oppen—from Zukofsky's "Objectivists" days—turned up in Brooklyn in late June 1959 and asked the Zukofskys to drive back with him to his home in Mexico City. They left on June 29 and flew back on Eastern Airlines on July 16. The car trip took seven days. They saw the pre-Aztec pyramids of Teotihuacán and traveled as far south as Cuernavaca. Zukofsky's favorite part of the trip was the airplane flight back, a new experience for him. He reported to Cid Corman on July 20, 1959, that he was worried about the creeping Americanization of Mexican culture.

Zukofsky was trying to finish *Bottom* in the fall of 1959, but the academic year began before he could complete the "Definition" section. His duties at school were beginning to wear on him, and he longed for retirement so he could get on with his own work full time. He reported to Corman on November 18, 1959 that writing brought in next to no income, only twenty-five dollars for all of that year. The Zukofskys' plan was to move eventually into a smaller apartment and live from Social Security and Louis's tiny pension from Poly.

A few days before Christmas 1959 copies of "*A*"-1–12 arrived from Cid Corman in Japan. Zukofsky was tremendously excited, and rightly so. Since it had appeared only in bits and pieces in various small magazines, there had been no way to get an impression of the work as a whole until Corman published it in one volume. Zukofsky's enthusiasm was charmingly childlike. He looked at the volume again and again. It is not far-fetched to conclude that the energy Zukofsky received from seeing the first half of "*A*" in print allowed him to finish the second half, and for that thanks is due to Cid Corman.

Bottom: On Shakespeare was finally completed on May 11, 1960. In it Zukofsky announces his intention to treat all the items in Shakespeare's "canon as one work, sometimes poor, sometimes good, sometimes great." His overall attempt is to consider Shakespeare's definition of love, a parallel to which he believed to have found in Baruch Spinoza. He summarizes Shakespeare on love using a mathematical ratio:—love is to reason as eyes are to mind—and he ranges through the entire Shakespearean corpus to find various instances of that relation. He concludes that Shakespeare's concept was that "when reason judges with eyes, love and mind are one."

The philosophical range of *Bottom: On Shakespeare* is extraordinary, and includes both Charles Sanders Peirce, the seminal American philosopher of language, and Ludwig Wittgenstein (the early Wittgenstein of the 1921 *Tractatus*). There is something in the nature of a commonplace book to *Bottom*, a collection of quotations from his readings with commentary. Its extended exploration of epistemology is not very compelling; Zukofsky's metaphysics are rather old-fashioned. Yet Zukofsky does have some importance to contemporary linguistic philosophy because of his extended experimentation with nonreferential language, one of the widest-ranging demonstrations of the problem of reference that exists. His poetry is philosophically interesting; *Bottom: On Shakespeare* is not.

Zukofsky was in his mid fifties, and his pace was gradually slowing down. His lifelong tendency toward hypochondria seems even more pronounced in his correspondence of this period, and he complained about the difficulties of getting published. In light of the reception that his efforts of the last thirty years had received, such complaints seem justified.

Zukofsky had fully embarked on his translation of Catullus. His approach was unique; he was very conscious of the breath required for each Latin word, and he was attempting to re-breath the lines. Meanwhile, he was also at work on "A"-13, which he finished in 1960. Titled "partita" and written in five sections, it consists largely of advice and concern for his son and is as a whole successful. It appeared in the journal *Origin*, which Corman published from Kyoto, Japan.

Zukofsky felt uncomfortable at the visits of younger poets, though he was generous with his time and advice. He believed that his work told them what they needed from him, and he wished to add nothing to it. The epigraphs from his taciturn *Autobiography* repeat his belief: "I too have been charged with obscurity, tho it's a case of listeners wanting to know too much about me, more than the words say.—*Little*," and "As a poet I have always felt that the work says all there needs to be said of one's life." Of course,

his work was difficult to find. He wrote to Corman on December 3, 1960, that he was less and less inclined to pursue publishers and prizes. Nevertheless, he surely had been thinking about awards: Marianne Moore had made great efforts to get "A"-1–12 the National Book Award for poetry, but it did not qualify because it had been printed abroad, a bitter turn of events given that no American publisher had paid any attention to Zukofsky.

In the 1960's some recognition finally started to arrive. The Library of Congress acquired a recording of Zukofsky reading from his poetry for its Archive of Recorded Poetry, and the Humanities Research Center at the University of Texas at Austin bought his manuscripts and books from 1923 to 1960, creating the Louis Zukofsky Manuscript Collection. The Longview Foundation awarded a prize of three hundred dollars to *Bottom*, announced in the December issue of *Poetry*.

The money was probably needed, since Paul Zukofsky was scheduled for his third Carnegie Hall recital in February 1961. The Zukofskys publicized the event and offered free tickets to their close friends, who sometimes paid anyway. Young poets being an impoverished lot, the bolder ones occasionally asked for free tickets. Celia, the practical Zukofsky and the one who had to handle the budget, exploded in one instance about Allen Ginsberg's request for two free tickets. Zukofsky's reaction to his wife's outburst was to make a note for possible use in a future "A."

On June 26, 1961, Celia finished her section of *Bottom*, the score for *Pericles*. Her music is suited to the era in which the play was written and the piece could be performed in about two hours. She deliberately makes the music simple; the piece was probably meant for a small, intimate audience. Not an oratorio, but meant to be staged, *Pericles* shows clearly that Celia Zukofsky had ability as a composer. Louis Zukofsky, though, was not yet finished: he had twenty more pages to go on his index to the book, an index that he called a guide to reading.

Paul left for a summer music camp, his first extended absence, and Zukofsky missed him a great deal. His work on Catullus progressed. He started on poem thirty at the end of June 1961 and was on poem thirty-one by mid-July. However, unaccustomed to Paul's absence, it was difficult for him to concentrate on his translations. Public appreciation, even when it came by way of a successful reading he did in early August, seemed to give him no joy. Renting a cabin on Lake Champlain, near Paul and his friends, gave him a great deal more happiness.

On November 30, 1961, he announced to Corman that because of a rent increase, he and Celia were moving again, to a sunnier apartment only a block way with a southeast view of the harbor rather than a northeast view of the city. The new address, really an old one for the Zukofskys, who had lived on the street before, was 160 Columbia Heights. His book *After I's*, published in 1964 and containing poetry from 1961 to 1964, contains the appropriate poem "THE OLD POET MOVES TO A NEW APARTMENT 14 TIMES."

Despite the attention that had turned toward him in 1961, Zukofsky had almost stopped caring about recognition. All of his books were out of print, and he and Celia no longer made much effort to publicize his work. However, there was increased attention to the "Objectivists" during this time; Reznikoff and Oppen in particular published books that almost overshadowed Zukofsky's key role, causing further resentment on his part. Reznikoff sent an inscribed copy of his book, and Oppen's sister June called to ask the Zukofskys to a cocktail party honoring the authors. Zukofsky refused, but a formal invitation arrived anyway, accompanied by a flyer that, as he complained to Corman on September 27, 1962, described the Objectivists without mentioning his role in the movement.

William Carlos Williams died in his sleep during the early morning of March 4, 1963. Pound wired to Floss Williams: "He fought a good fight for you, & he was the best poet-friend I ever had." Zukofsky was saddened by the death of one of his poetic fathers. When Henry Rago, the editor of *Poetry*, wrote to Zukofsky requesting an excerpt of some length from a work in progress, the poet jumped ahead of sequence to complete "A"-17, numbered to honor Williams' September 17 birthday. A May 21, 1963, letter to Rago indicates that the jump from "A"-13 to "A"-17 was not unusual, that some of the other movements of *"A"* were written outside of chronological sequence. "A"-17, titled "A CORONAL / for Floss" was accepted by *Poetry*.

"A"-16, a movement consisting of four words, was also completed in 1963, as was "A"-20 (which appeared in *Agenda*), a list of musical pieces two pages long with a concluding short lyric. Perhaps the poet tired. "A"-16 does present an interesting question: How can a four-word phrase

An

inequality

wind flower

be said to constitute one twenty-fourth of an eight-hundred page poem? It appeared in *Origin*.

At the last minute, Paul Zukofsky was invited to represent the United States in the Paganini festival in Genoa, and he left on September 30, 1963. His performance there was a tremendous success; he won fourth place, behind two musicians from Russia and one from Japan. The award resulted in an invitation to the Thibaud competition in Paris. In 1965, Paul moved to his own apartment in the same building as his parents. A review that year by Michael Steinberg from the *Boston Globe* of his performance (along with pianist Gilbert Kalish) of Charles Ives's second, third, and fourth sonatas for violin and piano shows that Paul's career had started:

The intelligent, thinking performer in America today is in the youngest generation represented at his most impressive by Paul Zukofsky. In the most familiar and traditional sense of what virtuosity means, he has no superiority among living string players. In intelligence, intellectual penetration, and musicianship, Zukofsky, who is barely into his twenties, goes far in his accomplishments beyond those of most of the big name players.

When the pair recorded all four of the sonatas, the reviews were equally positive. Zukofsky was very proud of his son, and with Paul's growing independence, he felt that he could retire to a full-time pursuit of his real work.

During the last fifteen years of his life, Zukofsky increasingly received a portion of the recognition to which he was entitled. W. W. Norton published the first volume of *ALL, The Collected Shorter Poems, 1923–1958*, in 1965. Henry Rago, at *Poetry*, recognized the value of Zukofsky's achievement, and in 1964 published portions of his Catullus translation, his review of the work of William Blake in the form of a short play, and "A"-14. The latter, a consideration of the poet's life and Bach's, is written in a rather odd form: (1) the first stanza has six one-word lines, (2) the next three stanzas have ten one-word lines, followed by (3) three-line stanzas consisting of first two-word lines (the first eighteen pages), then three-word lines (the next twenty-six pages), until the end when (4) three two-word lines are used for the antepenultimate stanza, closing with (5) a six-line stanza with one word in each line and (6) a final ten-line

stanza, also with one word in each line. "A"-15, treating, in part, the assassination of John F. Kennedy, along with selections from Edward Gibbon's *The Decline and Fall of the Roman Empire*, was also completed in 1964, and it appeared in *Poetry*.

Good news also came in August 1965: Henry Rago was going to devote the entire October issue of *Poetry* to Louis Zukofsky. Consisting of "A"-14 in its entirety, the issue also contained appreciative reviews of the first volume of *ALL* by Robert Creeley: "I can think of no man more useful to learn from than Zukofsky" and Thomas Clark: "Zukofsky's understanding / feeling of existence *as shape* (melody) at least gives us words as emotionally active as substance, existence, itself." A review of *After I's* and *Bottom: On Shakespeare* by Gerard Malanga does justice to Celia Zukofsky's music for *Pericles*: "Vocally, the fabric and texture of *Pericles*, consistently lucid and tasteful, is flawlessly spun out to display the composer's superb stylistic assimilation and limitless melodic gift." The issue also announces the first production of Zukofsky's *Arise, Arise*, on August 19, 1965, by A New / Kinda Theatre Company at the Cinematheque East Theatre in New York. The year 1965 was a gratifying one for the Zukofskys, but recognition so long delayed caused bitterness.

Zukofsky had retired from Poly in August 1965. He and Celia then visited old friends in Saratoga Springs, New York, and together they finished the Catullus, finally, after ten years. Typeset with the Latin and English on facing pages, the Zukofskys' *Catullus* saw publication in 1969. After retiring the Zukofskys moved from Brooklyn to Manhattan. Later they moved again, to Port Jefferson, New York. Zukofsky wrote to Carl Rakosi in December 1965 that he would write only if specifically commissioned to do so. His exasperation had become final. Nevertheless, he achieved more recognition in this period than ever before. In 1966, Norton published a second volume *ALL, The Collected Short Poems 1956–1964,* and *Prepositions: The Collected Critical Essays of Louis Zukofsky* was published in 1967.

"A"-18 and -19 were written in the period 1964–1966. "A"-18 contains numerous references to the war in Vietnam and to Zukofsky's own life; it won a National Endowment for the Arts award for its author and for *Poetry.* "A"-19 begins with Stephane Mallarmé (Zukofsky has often been referred to as the American Mallarmé) and then proceeds to an account of the Paganini competition in Genoa in a series of thirteen-line stanzas with two words to the line (three to the last line in each stanza). Neither are particularly striking, though in the story of the miraculous fish of the Quang Nam pond, Zukofsky may have found a perfect representation of the Vietnam War. Both appeared in *Poetry.*

"A"-21, from 1967, is a free-form version of the comedy *Rudens* by Plautus. The first three acts appeared in *Poetry.* As with his translation of Catullus, a chief force of Zukofsky's "translation" of the Roman comedian is to drive the reader to the original (or to other translations). In this movement, he first experiments with his five-word line, which he later uses so successfully in "A"-22 and -23.

Zukofsky's important fiction works, *Ferdinand* and *It Was,* were published together in 1968. "A"-24, which concludes his long work, was also completed in 1968. Titled "L.Z. Masque," it is as much Celia Zukofsky's work as her husband's and forms a fitting ending to "A." The movement is a five-part score, with one voice consisting of music from Handel, and the other four voices consisting of arrangements of Zukofsky's work: "Thought" is from *Prepositions,* "Drama" is from *Arise, Arise,* "Story" is from *It Was,* and "Poem" is from "A." "A"-24 was meant to be performed, so is difficult to evaluate. It is divided into two acts, with five scenes in the first act and four in the second. In

act 1, the scenes are labeled as follows: (1) Cousin: Lesson, (2) Nurse: Prelude & Allegro, (3) Father: Suite, (4) Girl: Fantasia, (5) Attendants: Chaconne, and in act 2: (1) Mother: Sonata, (2) Doctor: Capriccio, (3) Aunt: Passacaille, and (4) Son: Fugues. The titles denote characters and musical forms.

Zukofsky was feted at the International Poetry Festival at Austin, Texas, November 20–22, 1969, along with nine other poets including Jorge Luis Borges, Octavio Paz, Czeslaw Milosz, Robert Creeley, and Robert Duncan. He considered his most important work at the time the completion of "A." He was at work on "A"-22 during the period 1970–1973, and "A"-23 from 1973 to 1974. They represent his most difficult sustained work and show Zukofsky at his most experimental. Employing throughout his five-word line, "A"-22 and "A"-23—the first movement a hymn to Nature and the second to just polity— are mostly made up of five line stanzas, whose language avoids all usual collocation. Since we have as yet no poetics adequate to describe fully what Zukofsky is doing in these two movements (published as a volume in 1975), we are thrown back on his own definition, which he gave in "A"-12:

> I'll tell you.
> About my *poetics*—
>
> $$\int \begin{array}{l} \text{music} \\ \text{speech} \end{array}$$
>
> An integral
> Lower limit speech
> Upper limit music
>
> No?

"A"-22 and -23 can be read with pleasure for their sound; in them we are approaching the upper limit of his poetics. Of necessity, then, does "A"-24 consist of words set to music, the appropriate completion of the infinite summation that is Zukofsky's poetics.

When Pound died on November 1, 1972, Zukofsky lost his first poetic father. He grieved in his own way, seeking to commune with his lost friend by taking down Pound's poetry and reading it once again.

In his last years, after the move to Port Jefferson, where Louis and Celia kept a garden, Zukofsky was working on his experimental work, *80 Flowers*. It was to have been published on his 80th birthday. He also contemplated a further work, *90 Trees*, for his 90th birthday. Louis Zukofsky died unexpectedly on May 12, 1978, while his complete *"A"* was being prepared for publication. He was a gentle man much hurt by the world, but one who had found great solace in his family and friends. He dedicated his life to his art with an integrity and singleness of purpose that have seldom been equaled, but he achieved no commensurate recognition in his lifetime.

Zukofsky loved to tell a joke about a young Talmudic scholar in Russia, about to be drafted. He went to the rabbi for wisdom. "There are two possibilities," said the rabbi. "You go to war; you don't go to war. If you go to war, well, not great. Still, two possibilities. You train with Jews; you train with strangers. If with strangers, not great. Still two possibilities. You're sent to the front; you remain behind the lines. If the front, still two possibilities: you're killed or you live. But if you're killed, there are still two possibilities. You may be buried with the faithful, or you may not be. And if you are not buried with the faithful, are you properly buried?"

Will Zukofsky himself be properly buried? The question remains one of the canon, which poets are read and which die. If, as one might argue, poets ultimately decide what the canon will be, then Louis Zukofsky's work will truly live, for poets most appreciate the risks taken in dedication to art. Robert Duncan recognized the risks that Zukofsky took in "After Reading *Barely and Widely*":

He who writes a touching line dares overmuch.

He does not observe
the intimate boundaries of natural speech
—then we in hearing must have reserve.

Poetry, that must *touch* the string
for music's service
is of violence and obedience a delicate
    balancing.

Selected Bibliography

WORKS OF LOUIS ZUKOFSKY

An "Objectivists" Anthology. Le Beausset, Var, France, and New York: TO, 1932; Folcroft Library Editions, 1975.

Ferdinand, Including It Was. London: Jonathan Cape, 1968.

Catullus (Gai Valeri Catulli Veronensis Liber). Translated by Celia and Louis Zukofsky. London and New York: Cape Goliard Press and Grossman Publishers, 1969.

Autobiography. New York: Grossman Publishers, 1970.

Little: For Careenagers. New York: Grossman, 1970.

Arise, Arise. New York: Grossman Publishers, 1973.

80 Flowers. New York: C.Z. Publications, 1978.

"A". Berkeley, California: University of California Press, 1978.

Prepositions: The Collected Critical Essays. Berkeley, Calif.: University of California Press, 1981.

Bottom: On Shakespeare, Vol. I. Berkeley, California: University of California Press, 1987.

Pound / Zukofsky: Selected Letters of Ezra Pound and Louis Zukofsky. Edited by Barry Ahearn. New York: New Directions, 1987.

COLLECTED WORKS

ALL: The Collected Short Poems. New York: W. W. Norton & Co., 1971.

Collected Fiction. With an afterword by Paul Zukofsky. Elmwood Park, Ill.: Dalkey Archive, 1990.

Complete Short Poetry. With a Foreword by Robert Creeley. Baltimore, Md.: The Johns Hopkins University Press, 1991.

MANUSCRIPTS AND PAPERS

The Humanities Research Center at the University of Texas at Austin contains the Zukofsky Archive.

The Beinecke Library at Yale University contains a large Zukofsky holding.

The Lilly Library at Indiana University contains the *Poetry* archive after 1961 and other Zukofsky material.

The Regenstein Library at the University of Chicago contains the *Poetry* archive from 1912 to 1961.

A significant amount of other material is housed at Bellarmine College, Louisville; Columbia University; Kent State University; State University of New York at Buffalo; University of California, Los Angeles; University of California, San Diego; University of Delaware; University of Maryland; Washington University, St. Louis.

BOOK-LENGTH BIOGRAPHICAL AND CRITICAL STUDIES

Ahearn, Barry. *Zukofsky's "A": An Introduction.* Berkeley, Calif.: University of California Press, 1983.

Lang, Warren Paul. *Zukofsky's Conception of Poetry and a Reading of his Poem of Life "A."* Ann Arbor, Michigan: Xerox University Microfilms, 1974 (University of Indiana Ph.D. diss., 1974).

Leggott, Michele J. *Reading Zukofsky's "80 Flowers."* Baltimore, Md.: Johns Hopkins University Press, 1989.

Mandell, Stephen Roy. *The Finer Mathematician: An Introduction to the Work of Louis Zukofsky.* Ann Arbor, Michigan: Xerox University Microfilms, 1975 (Temple University Ph.D. diss., 1975).

Terrell, Carroll F. *Louis Zukofsky: Man and Poet.* Orono, Maine: National Poetry Foundation, n.d.

Tomas, John. *Zukofsky in the Twenties.* University of Chicago Ph.D. diss., 1991.

—TIM REDMAN

Index

Index

Arabic numbers printed in bold-face type refer to extended treatment of a subject.

635

"Angel of the Bridge, The" (Cheever), **Supp. I, Part 1,** 186–187

"Angel of the Odd, The" (Poe), **III,** 425

"Angel on the Porch, An" (Wolfe), **IV,** 451

"Angel Surrounded by Paysans" (Stevens), **IV,** 93

Angel That Troubled the Waters, The (Wilder), **IV,** 356, 357–358

"Angel, The" (Buck), **Supp. II, Part 1,** 127

Angell, Carol, **Supp. I, Part 2,** 655

Angell, Katharine Sergeant, *see* White, Mrs. E. B. (Katharine Sergeant Angell)

Angell, Roger, **Supp. I, Part 2,** 655

Angels and Earthly Creatures (Wylie), **Supp. I, Part 2,** 709, 713, 724–730

"Angels of the Love Affair" (Sexton), **Supp. II, Part 2,** 692

Angle of Ascent (Hayden), **Supp. II, Part 1,** 363, 367, 370

Angle, Paul M., **III,** 597

Anglo-Saxon Century, The (Dos Passos), **I,** 474–475, 483

Angoff, Charles, **I,** 262; **III,** 107, 121, 408; **IV,** 23

"Angola Question Mark" (Hughes), **Supp. I, Part 1,** 344

Angry Wife, The (Sedges), **Supp. II, Part 1,** 125

"Angst and Animism in the Poetry of Sylvia Plath" (Perloff), **Supp. I, Part 2,** 548

Angus, D. and S., **III,** 240

"Animal, Vegetable, and Mineral" (Bogan), **Supp. III, Part 1,** 66

Animal and Vegetable Physiology Considered with Reference to Natural Theology (Roget), **Supp. I, Part 1,** 312

"Animals, The" (Merwin), **Supp. III, Part 1,** 348

Ankor Wat (Ginsberg), **Supp. II, Part 1,** 323

"Ann Garner" (Agee), **I,** 27

Ann Vickers (Lewis), **II,** 453

Anna Christie (O'Neill), **III,** 386, 389, 390

Anna Karenina (Tolstoi), **I,** 10; **II,** 290

"*Anna Karenina*" (Trilling), **Supp. III, Part 2,** 508

"Anna Who Was Mad" (Sexton), **Supp. II, Part 2,** 692

Anne, Queen, **II,** 524; **IV,** 145

Anne Bradstreet (Piercy), **Supp. I, Part 1,** 123

Anne Bradstreet: "The Tenth Muse" (White), **Supp. I, Part 1,** 123

Anne Bradstreet: The Worldly Puritan (Stanford), **Supp. I, Part 1,** 123

"Anne Bradstreet's 'Contemplations': Patterns of Form and Meaning" (Rosenfeld), **Supp. I, Part 1,** 123

"Anne Bradstreet's Poetic Voices" (Requa), **Supp. I, Part 1,** 107, 123

"Anniad, The" (Brooks), **Supp. III, Part 1,** 77, 78

Annie Allen (Brooks), **Supp. III, Part 1,** 76–79

Annie Kilburn, a Novel (Howells), **II,** 275, 286, 287

"Another August" (Merrill), **Supp. III, Part 1,** 326

Another Country (Baldwin), **Supp. I, Part 1,** 51, 52, 56–58, 63, 67, 337; **Supp. II, Part 1,** 40

"*Another Country*, Another Time" (Strandley), **Supp. I, Part 1,** 71

"*Another Country:* Baldwin's New York Novel" (Thelwell), **Supp. I, Part 1,** 71

"Another Night in the Ruins" (Kinnell), **Supp. III, Part 1,** 239, 251

Another Part of the Forest (Hellman), **Supp. I, Part 1,** 282–283, 297

Another Time (Auden), **Supp. II, Part 1,** 15

"Another upon the Same" (Taylor), **IV,** 161

"Another Voice" (Wilbur), **Supp. III, Part 2,** 557

"Another Wife" (Anderson), **I,** 114

Anouilh, Jean, **Supp. I, Part 1,** 286–288, 297

Ansky, S., **IV,** 6

"Answer, The" (Jeffers), **Supp. II, Part 2,** 423

Answered Prayers: The Unfinished Novel (Capote), **Supp. III, Part 1,** 113, 125, 131–132

Antaeus (Wolfe), **IV,** 461

"Ante-Bellum Sermon, An" (Dunbar), **Supp. II, Part 1,** 203–204

Antheil, George, **III,** 471, 472; **IV,** 404

Anthology of Twentieth-Century Brazilian Poetry (eds. Bishop and Brasil), **Supp. I, Part 1,** 94

Anthon, Kate, **I,** 452

Anthony, Katharine, **Supp. I, Part 1,** 46

Anthony, Saint, **III,** 395

"Anthropologist as Hero, The" (Sontag), **Supp. III, Part 2,** 451

Anthropos: The Future of Art (Cummings), **I,** 430

Antichrist (Nietzsche), **III,** 176

"Anti-Feminist Woman, The" (Rich), **Supp. I, Part 2,** 550

Antigone (Sophocles), **Supp. I, Part 1,** 284

Antiphon, The (Barnes), **Supp. III, Part 1,** 43–44

"Antiquities" (Mather), **Supp. II, Part 2,** 452

"Antiquity of Freedom, The" (Bryant), **Supp. I, Part 1,** 168

"Antislavery Tocsin, An" (Douglass), **Supp. III, Part 1,** 171

Antoine, Andre, **III,** 387

Antony and Cleopatra (Shakespeare), **I,** 285

"Antony on Behalf of the Play" (Burke), **I,** 284

"Anywhere Out of This World" (Baudelaire), **II,** 552

Apollinaire, Guillaume, **I,** 432; **II,** 529; **III,** 196; **IV,** 80

Apologies to the Iroquois (Wilson), **IV,** 429

"Apology, An" (Malamud), **Supp. I, Part 2,** 435, 437

"Apology for Bad Dreams" (Jeffers), **Supp. II, Part 2,** 427, 438

"Apology for Crudity, An" (Anderson), **I,** 109

Apology for Poetry (Sidney), **Supp. II, Part 1,** 105

"Apostle of the Tules, An" (Harte), **Supp. II, Part 1,** 356

"Apostrophe to a Pram Rider" (White), **Supp. I, Part 2,** 678

"Apostrophe to Man (on reflecting that the world is ready to go to war again)" (Millay), **III,** 127

"Apostrophe to Vincentine, The" (Stevens), **IV,** 90

"Apotheosis of Martin Luther King, The" (Hardwick), **Supp. III, Part 1,** 203–204

"Appeal to Progressives, An" (Wilson), **IV,** 429

Appeal to Reason (Paine), **I,** 490

Appeal to the World, An (Du Bois), **Supp. II, Part 1,** 184

Appearance and Reality (Bradley), **I,** 572

"August 1968" (Auden), **Supp. II, Part 1,** 25

Augustine, Saint, **I,** 279, 290; **II,** 537; **III,** 259, 270, 292, 300; **IV,** 69, 126

"Aunt Cynthy Dallett" (Jewett), **II,** 393

"Aunt Imogen" (Robinson), **III,** 521

"Aunt Jemima of the Ocean Waves" (Hayden), **Supp. II, Part 1,** 368, 379

Aunt Jo's Scrapbooks (Alcott), **Supp. I, Part 1,** 43

"Aunt Mary" (Stowe), **Supp. I, Part 2,** 587

"Aunt Sarah" (Lowell), **II,** 554

"Auroras of Autumn, The" (Stevens), **Supp. III, Part 1,** 12

Auser, Cortland P., **Supp. I, Part 1,** 198

"Auspex" (Lowell), **Supp. I, Part 2,** 424

"Austen and Alcott on Matriarchy" (Auerbach), **Supp. I, Part 1,** 46

Austen, Jane, **I,** 130, 339, 375, 378; **II,** 272, 278, 287, 568–569, 577; **IV,** 8; **Supp. I, Part 1,** 267, **Part 2,** 656, 715

Austin, George L., **II,** 509

Austin, Neal F., **IV,** 473

Austin, Samuel, **I,** 564

"Authentic Unconscious, The" (Trilling), **Supp. III, Part 2,** 512

"Author at Sixty, The" (Wilson), **IV,** 426

"Author to Her Book, The" (Bradstreet), **Supp. I, Part 1,** 119

"Auto Wreck" (Shapiro), **Supp. II, Part 2,** 706

"Autobiographic Chapter, An" (Bourne), **I,** 236

"Autobiographical Note" (Miller), **III,** 174–175

"Autobiographical Notes" (Baldwin), **Supp. I, Part 1,** 54

"Autobiographical Notes" (Holmes), **Supp. I, Part 1,** 301

Autobiography (Cournos), **Supp. I, Part 1,** 275

Autobiography (Franklin), **II,** 102, 103, 108, 121–122, 302

Autobiography (James), **I,** 462

"Autobiography" (MacLeish), **III,** 20

Autobiography (Van Buren), **III,** 473

Autobiography (Williams), **Supp. I, Part 1,** 254, 275

Autobiography (Zukofsky), **Supp. III, Part 2,** 627

Autobiography of Alice B. Toklas, The (Stein), **IV,** 26, 30, 35, 43

Autobiography of an Ex-Colored Man, The (Johnson), **Supp. II, Part 1,** 33, 194

Autobiography of Malcolm X (Little), **Supp. I, Part 1,** 66

Autobiography of Mark Twain, The (Twain), **IV,** 209

Autobiography of Mark Van Doren, The (Van Doren), **Supp. I, Part 2,** 626

Autobiography of W. E. B. Du Bois, The (Du Bois), **Supp. II, Part 1,** 159, 186

Autocrat of the Breakfast-Table, The (Holmes), **Supp. I, Part 1,** 306–307

"Automotive Passacaglia" (Miller), **III,** 186

"Autopsy Room, The" (Carver), **Supp. III, Part 1,** 137

"Autre Temps" (Wharton), **IV,** 320, 324

"Autumn Afternoon" (Farrell), **II,** 45

"Autumn Begins in Martins Ferry, Ohio" (Wright), **Supp. III, Part 2,** 599

"Autumn Courtship, An" (Caldwell), **I,** 309

Autumn Garden, The (Hellman), **Supp. I, Part 1,** 285–286, 290

"Autumn Garden, The: Mechanics and Dialectics" (Felheim), **Supp. I, Part 1,** 297

"Autumn Holiday, An" (Jewett), **II,** 391

"Autumn Musings" (Harte), **Supp. II, Part 1,** 336

"Autumn Within" (Longfellow), **II,** 499

"Autumn Woods" (Bryant), **Supp. I, Part 1,** 164

"Autumnal" (Eberhart), **I,** 540–541

"Aux Imagistes" (Williams), **Supp. I, Part 1,** 266

Avedon, Richard, **Supp. I, Part 1,** 58

Avenue Bearing the Initial of Christ into the New World: Poems 1946–1964 (Kinnell), **Supp. III, Part 1,** 235, 239–241

Avery, John, **Supp. I, Part 1,** 153

Avon's Harvest (Robinson), **III,** 510

Awake and Sing! (Odets), **Supp. II, Part 2,** 530, 531, 536–538, 550

Awakening, The (Chopin), **Supp. I, Part 1,** 200, 201, 202, 211, 220–225

Awful Rowing Toward God, The (Sexton), **Supp. II, Part 2,** 694–696

Awkward Age, The (James), **II,** 332

Axel's Castle: A Study in the Imaginative Literature of 1870 to 1930 (Wilson), **I,** 185; **II,** 577; **IV,** 428, 431, 438, 439, 443

Axthelm, Peter M., **I,** 165

B. F.'s Daughter (Marquand), **III,** 59, 65, 68, 69

Babbitt (Lewis), **II,** 442, 443–445, 446, 447, 449; **III,** 63–64, 394; **IV,** 326

Babbitt, Irving, **I,** 247; **II,** 456; **III,** 315, 461, 613; **IV,** 439; **Supp. I, Part 2,** 423

Babcock, Elisha, **Supp. II, Part 1,** 69

Babel, Isaac, **IV,** 1

Babeuf, François, **Supp. I, Part 2,** 518

Baby Doll (Williams), **IV,** 383, 386, 387, 389, 395

"Baby Face" (Sandburg), **III,** 584

"Babylon Revisited" (Fitzgerald), **II,** 95

"Baccalaureate" (MacLeish), **III,** 4

Bach, Johann Sebastian, **Supp. I, Part 1,** 363; **Supp. III, Part 2,** 611, 612, 619

Bache, Richard, **Supp. I, Part 2,** 504

Bachelard, Gaston, **III,** 431

Bachofen, J. J., **Supp. I, Part 2,** 560, 567

Back Bog Beast Bait (Shepard), **Supp. III, Part 2,** 437, 438

Back to Methuselah (Shaw), **IV,** 64

"Background with Revolutionaries" (MacLeish), **III,** 14–15

"Backgrounds of Lowell's Satire in 'The Bigelow Papers' " (Voss), **Supp. I, Part 2,** 426

"Backlash Blues, The" (Hughes), **Supp. I, Part 1,** 343

Backman, Melvin, **II,** 76

"Backwacking" (Ellison), **Supp. II, Part 1,** 248

"Backward Glance o'er Travel'd Roads, A" (Whitman), **IV,** 348

Bacon, Francis, **II,** 1, 8, 11, 15–16, 111; **III,** 284; **Supp. I, Part 1,** 310, 388

Bacon, Leonard, **II,** 530

Bacon, Roger, **IV,** 69

"Bacterial War, The" (Nemerov), **III,** 272

Becker, Paula, *see* Modersohn, Mrs. Otto (Paula Becker)

Beckett, Samuel, **I,** 71, 91, 142, 298, 461; **III,** 387; **IV,** 95

Beckford, William, **I,** 204

Beckonings (Brooks), **Supp. III, Part 1,** 85

"Becky" (Toomer), **Supp. III, Part 2,** 481, 483

Beddoes, Thomas Lovell, **III,** 469

"Bee Hunt, The" (Irving), **II,** 313

"Bee, The" (Lanier), **Supp. I, Part 1,** 364

Beebe, Maurice, **II,** 76; **IV,** 472

Beecher, Catharine, **Supp. I, Part 2,** 581, 582–583, 584, 586, 588, 589, 591, 599

Beecher, Charles, **Supp. I, Part 2,** 588, 589

Beecher, Edward, **Supp. I, Part 2,** 581, 582, 583, 584, 588, 591

Beecher, Harriet, *see* Stowe, Harriet Beecher

Beecher, Henry Ward, **II,** 275; **Supp. I, Part 2,** 581

Beecher, Lyman, **Supp. I, Part 2,** 580–581, 582, 583, 587, 588, 599

Beecher, Mrs. Lyman (Roxanna Foote), **Supp. I, Part 2,** 580–581, 582, 588, 599

Beer, Thomas, **I,** 405, 426

Beerbohm, Max, **III,** 472; **IV,** 436; **Supp. I, Part 2,** 714

Beethoven, Ludwig van, **II,** 536; **III,** 118; **IV,** 274, 358; **Supp. I, Part 1,** 363

Befo' de War: Echoes in Negro Dialect (Gordon), **Supp. II, Part 1,** 201

Before Adam (London), **II,** 466

Before Disaster (Winters), **Supp. II, Part 2,** 786, 800

"Before Disaster" (Winters), **Supp. II, Part 2,** 801, 815

"Before I Knocked" (Thomas), **III,** 534

"Before March" (MacLeish), **III,** 15

"Before the Altar" (Lowell), **II,** 516

"Before the Birth of one of her children" (Bradstreet), **Supp. I, Part 1,** 118

"Begat" (Sexton), **Supp. II, Part 2,** 693

Beggar on Horseback (Kaufman and Connelly), **III,** 394

"Beggar Said So, The" (Singer), **IV,** 12

Beggar's Opera, The (Gay), **Supp. I, Part 2,** 523

"Beginning and the End, The" (Jeffers), **Supp. II, Part 2,** 420–421, 424

"Beginning of Decadence, The" (Jeffers), **Supp. II, Part 2,** 420

Beginning of Wisdom, The (Benét) **I,** 358

"Behavior" (Emerson), **II,** 2, 4

Behind a Mask (Alcott), **Supp. I, Part 1,** 36–37, 43–44

"Behind a Wall" (Lowell), **II,** 516

"Behind Spoon River" (Van Doren), **Supp. I, Part 2,** 478

"Behold the Key" (Malamud), **Supp. I, Part 2,** 437

Beiliss, Mendel, **Supp. I, Part 2,** 427, 446, 447, 448

Belcher, William F., **III,** 574

"Beleaguered City, The" (Longfellow), **II,** 498

Belfrey Owl (magazine), **Supp. I, Part 1,** 320

Belfry of Bruges and Other Poems, The (Longfellow), **II,** 489

Belkind, Alan, **I,** 496

Bell, Arthur, **IV,** 401

Bell, Clive, **IV,** 87

Bell, Daniel, **Supp. I, Part 2,** 648

Bell Jar, The (Plath), **Supp. I, Part 2,** 526, 527, 529, 531–536, 539, 540, 541, 542, 544

Bell, Michael D., **Supp. I, Part 1,** 148

Bell, Millicent, **IV,** 329

Bell, Quentin, **Supp. I, Part 2,** 636

"Bell Tower, The" (Melville), **III,** 91

Bell, Vereen, **IV,** 234

Bell, Whitfield J., Jr., **II,** 123

Bellamy, Edward, **II,** 276; **Supp. I, Part 2,** 641

Bellamy, Gladys C., **IV,** 213

"Belle Dollinger" (Masters), **Supp. I, Part 2,** 463

"Belle Zoraïde, La" (Chopin), **Supp. I, Part 1,** 215–216

Belleforest, François de, **IV,** 370

Belloc, Hilary, **III,** 176; **IV,** 432

Bellow, Saul, **I,** 113, 138–139, **144–166,** 375, 517; **II,** 579; **III,** 40; **IV,** 3, 19, 22, 217, 340; **Supp. I, Part 2,** 428, 451; **Supp. II, Part 1,** 109

"Bells, The" (Poe), **III,** 593; **Supp. I, Part 2,** 388

"Bells, The" (Sexton), **Supp. II, Part 2,** 673

"Bells for John Whiteside's Daughter" (Ransom), **III,** 490

"Bells of Lynn, The" (Longfellow), **II,** 498

"Bells of San Blas, The" (Longfellow), **II,** 490–491, 493, 498

Beloved (Morrison), **Supp. III, Part 1,** 364, 372–379

Beloved Lady: A History of Jane Addams' Ideas on Reform and Peace (Farrell), **Supp. I, Part 1,** 24, 27

Ben Franklin's Wit and Wisdom (Franklin), **II,** 111

Benchley, Nathaniel, **Supp. I, Part 2,** 626

Benchley, Robert, **I,** 48, 482; **II,** 435; **III,** 53

Bend Sinister (Nabokov), **III,** 253–254

Benedetti, Anna, **I,** 70

Benefactor, The (Sontag), **Supp. III, Part 2,** 451, 455, 468, 469

"Benefit Performance" (Malamud), **Supp. I, Part 2,** 431

Benét, Rosemary, **Supp. I, Part 2,** 626

Benét, Stephen Vincent, **I,** 358; **II,** 177; **III,** 22, 24; **IV,** 129; **Supp. I, Part 2,** 626

Benét, William Rose, **II,** 530; **Supp. I, Part 2,** 626, 709, 730

Benito Cereno (Lowell), **II,** 546

"Benito Cereno" (Melville), **III,** 91

Benjamin Franklin (Van Doren), **Supp. I, Part 2,** 486

"Benjamin Pantier" (Masters), **Supp. I, Part 2,** 461

Bennett, Anne Virginia, **II,** 184

Bennett, Arnold, **I,** 103; **II,** 337

Bennett, George N., **II,** 294

Bennett, John C., **III,** 313

Bennett, Mildred R., **I,** 333

Bennett, Whitman, **Supp. I, Part 2,** 705

Benson, A. C., **II,** 340

Benson, Ivan, **IV,** 213

Benson, Jackson J., **II,** 270

Bentham, Jeremy, **I,** 279; **Supp. I, Part 2,** 635

Bentley, Eric, **Supp. I, Part 1,** 297

Bentley, Eric R., **III,** 407; **IV,** 258, 396

Bentley, Richard, **III,** 79, 86

Benton, Richard P., **III,** 432

Beowulf, **Supp. II, Part 1,** 6

Bercovitch, Sacvan, **Supp. I, Part 1,** 99, **Part 2,** 659

Berdyaev, Nikolai, **I,** 494; **III,** 292

Braving the Elements (Merrill), **Supp. III, Part 1**, 320, 323, 325–327, 329

Bravo, The (Cooper), **I**, 345–346, 348

Brawley, Benjamin, **Supp. I, Part 1**, 327, 332

Brawne, Fanny, **I**, 284; **II**, 531

Brazil (Bishop), **Supp. I, Part 1**, 92

"Bread Alone" (Wylie), **Supp. I, Part 2**, 727

Bread of Idleness, The (Masters), **Supp. I, Part 2**, 460

"Break, The" (Sexton), **Supp. II, Part 2**, 689

Breakfast at Tiffany's (Capote), **Supp. III, Part 1**, 113, 117, 119–121, 124, 126

Breakfast of Champions (Vonnegut), **Supp. II, Part 2**, 755, 759, 769, 770, 777–778

"Breaking Up of the Winships, The" (Thurber), **Supp. I, Part 2**, 616

Breast, The (Roth), **Supp. III, Part 2**, 416, 418

"Breast, The" (Sexton), **Supp. II, Part 2**, 687

Breathing the Water (Levertov), **Supp. III, Part 1**, 274, 283, 284

Brecht, Bertolt, **I**, 60, 96, 301; **III**, 161, 162; **IV**, 394; **Supp. I, Part 1**, 292; **Supp. II, Part 1**, 10, 26, 56

Breen, Joseph I., **IV**, 390

Breit, Harvey, **I**, 47, 433, 449; **III**, 47, 72, 242, 384, 575; **Supp. I, Part 1**, 69, 198

Bremer, Fredrika, **Supp. I, Part 1**, 407

Brenner, Gerry, **IV**, 234

Brentano, Franz, **II**, 350

Breslin, James E., **IV**, 424

Bretall, Robert W., **III**, 313

Breton, André, **III**, 425

Brett, George, **II**, 466

Brevoort, Henry, **II**, 298

"Brewing of Soma, The" (Whittier), **Supp. I, Part 2**, 704

Brewsie and Willie (Stein), **IV**, 27

Brewster, Martha, **Supp. I, Part 1**, 114

"Briar Patch, The" (Warren), **IV**, 237

"Briar Rose (Sleeping Beauty)" (Sexton), **Supp. II, Part 2**, 690

Brice, Fanny, **II**, 427

"Brick Layer's Lunch Hour, The" (Ginsberg), **Supp. II, Part 1**, 318

Brickell, Herschel, **III**, 72

"Bridal Ballad, The" (Poe), **III**, 428

"Bride Comes to Yellow Sky, The" (Crane), **I**, 34, 415, 416, 423

"Bride in the 30's, A" (Auden), **Supp. II, Part 1**, 9

Bride of Lammermoor (Scott), **II**, 291

Bride of the Innisfallen, The (Welty), **IV**, 261, 275–279

"Bride of the Innisfallen, The" (Welty), **IV**, 278–279

Brides of the South Wind: Poems 1917–1922 (Jeffers), **Supp. II, Part 2**, 419

Bridge, Horatio, **II**, 226, 245

"BRIDGE, THE" (Baraka), **Supp. II, Part 1**, 32, 36

Bridge, The (Crane), **I**, 62, 109, 266, 385, 386, 387, 395–399, 400, 402; **IV**, 123, 341, 418, 419, 420

"Bridge Burners, The" (Van Vechten), **Supp. II, Part 2**, 733

Bridge of San Luis Rey, The (Wilder), **I**, 360; **IV**, 356, 357, 360–363, 365, 366

Bridges, Harry, **I**, 493

Bridges, Robert, **II**, 537; **III**, 527; **Supp. I, Part 2**, 721; **Supp. II, Part 1**, 21

Bridgman, P. W., **I**, 278

Bridgman, Richard, **Supp. I, Part 2**, 477

"Bridle, The" (Carver), **Supp. III, Part 1**, 138

"Brief Début of Tildy, The" (O. Henry), **Supp. II, Part 1**, 408

"Brief Encounters on the Inland Waterway" (Vonnegut), **Supp. II, Part 2**, 760

Briffault, Robert, **Supp. I, Part 2**, 560, 567

"Brigade de Cuisine" (McPhee), **Supp. III, Part 1**, 307–308

Brigadier and the Golf Widow, The (Cheever), **Supp. I, Part 1**, 184–185, 192

Briggs, Austin, **II**, 148

Briggs, Charles F., **Supp. I, Part 2**, 411

"Bright and Morning Star" (Wright), **IV**, 488

Bright Book of Life (Kazin), **Supp. I, Part 1**, 198

Bright Procession (Sedges), **Supp. II, Part 1**, 125

Brignano, Russell, **IV**, 496

"Brilliant Leaves" (Gordon), **II**, 199

"Bring the Day!" (Roethke), **III**, 536

Brinnin, John Malcolm, **I**, 189; **IV**, 26, 27, 28, 42, 46, 47

Brissot, Jacques Pierre, **Supp. I, Part 2**, 511

"Britain's Negro Problem in Sierra Leone" (Du Bois), **Supp. II, Part 1**, 176

"British Poets, The" (Holmes), **Supp. I, Part 1**, 306

"British Prison Ship, The" (Freneau), **Supp. II, Part 1**, 261

Brittain, Joan, **III**, 360

Britten, Benjamin, **II**, 586; **Supp. II, Part 1**, 17

Broadwater, Bowden, **II**, 562

Broadway Journal (publication), **III**, 413

Broadway Magazine, **I**, 501

"Broadway Sights" (Whitman), **IV**, 350

Brodtkorb, Paul, Jr., **III**, 97

"Broken Balance, The" (Jeffers), **Supp. II, Part 2**, 426

"Broken Home, The" (Merrill), **Supp. III, Part 1**, 319, 325

"Broken Promise" (MacLeish), **III**, 15

Broken Span, The (Williams), **IV**, 419

"Broken Tower, The" (Crane), **I**, 385, 386, 400, 401–402

Bromfield, Louis, **IV**, 380

"Broncho That Would Not Be Broken, The" (Lindsay), **Supp. I, Part 2**, 383

Brontë, Branwell, **I**, 462

Brontë, Charlotte, **I**, 458; **II**, 175

Brontë, Emily, **I**, 458

"Bronze" (Merrill), **Supp. III, Part 1**, 336

"Bronze Buckaroo, The" (Baraka), **Supp. II, Part 1**, 49

"Bronze Horses, The" (Lowell), **II**, 524

"Bronze Tablets" (Lowell), **II**, 523

Bronzeville Boys and Girls (Brooks), **Supp. III, Part 1**, 79

"Bronzeville Mother Loiters in Mississippi, A. Meanwhile, a Mississippi Mother Burns Bacon" (Brooks), **Supp. III, Part 1**, 80

"Brooch, The" (Singer), **IV**, 20

Brook Evans (Glaspell), **Supp. III, Part 1**, 182–185

Brooke, Rupert, **II**, 82; **III**, 3

Brooklyn *Eagle* (newspaper), **IV**, 334

Brooklyn *Times*, **IV**, 341

Brooks, Cleanth, **I**, 280, 282; **II**, 76, 390; **III**, 217, 517; **IV**, 236, 258, 279, 284; **Supp. I, Part 2**, 423; **Supp. III, Part 2**, 542

Brooks, Gwendolyn, **Supp. III, Part 1,** 69–90

Brooks, Mrs. Van Wyck (Eleanor Kenyon Stimson), **I,** 240, 245, 250, 252

Brooks, Mrs. Van Wyck (Gladys Billings), **I,** 258, 262

Brooks, Phillips, **II,** 542

Brooks, Van Wyck, **I,** 24, 106, 117, 119, 213, 215, 222, 228, 230, 231, 233, 236, 237, **239–263,** 266, 480; **II,** 30, 195, 271, 285, 294, 309, 318, 337, 341, 482, 533; **III,** 394, 606; **IV,** 171, 189, 213, 312, 330, 427, 433; **Supp. I, Part 2,** 423, 424, 426, 650; **Supp. II, Part 1,** 137

Broom (periodical), **Supp. II, Part 1,** 138

Brosnan, Jim, **II,** 424–425

Brother Carl (Sontag), **Supp. III, Part 2,** 452

"Brother Death" (Anderson), **I,** 114

Brother to Dragons: A Tale in Verse and Voices (Warren), **IV,** 243–244, 245, 246, 251, 252, 254, 257

"Brothers" (Anderson), **I,** 114

Brothers Ashkenazi, The (Singer), **IV,** 2

Brothers Karamazov, The (Dostoevski), **II,** 60; **III,** 146, 150, 283

Broughton, Rhoda, **II,** 174; **IV,** 309, 310

Broun, Heywood, **I,** 478; **II,** 417; **IV,** 432

Broussais, François, **Supp. I, Part 1,** 302

Broussard, Louis, **III,** 432

Browder, Earl, **I,** 515

Brower, Brock, **II,** 584

Brower, Reuben A., **II,** 172

Brown, Alice, **II,** 523

Brown, Ashley, **II,** 221; **IV,** 95; **Supp. I, Part 1,** 79, 80, 82, 84, 92, 96

Brown, C. H., **III,** 47

Brown, Charles Brockden, **I,** 54, 211, 335; **II,** 74, 267, 298; **III,** 415; **Supp. I, Part 1, 124–149; Supp. II, Part 1,** 65, 292

Brown, Charles H., **Supp. I, Part 1,** 173

Brown, Clarence, **Supp. I, Part 2,** 477

Brown, E. K., **I,** 333; **IV,** 376, 448

Brown, Elijah, **Supp. I, Part 1,** 125

Brown, George Douglas, **III,** 473

Brown, Herbert Ross, **Supp. I, Part 2,** 601

Brown, John, **II,** 13; **IV,** 125, 126, 172, 237, 249, 254; **Supp. I, Part 1,** 345

Brown, John Mason, **III,** 407; **IV,** 376

Brown, Mary Armitt, **Supp. I, Part 1,** 125

Brown, Merle E., **I,** 287

Brown, Mrs. Charles Brockden (Elizabeth Linn), **Supp. I, Part 1,** 145, 146

Brown, Percy, **II,** 20, 23

Brown, Slater, **IV,** 123

Brown, Solyman, **Supp. I, Part 1,** 156

Brown, Susan Jenkins, **I,** 403

Brown, W. C., **IV,** 166

Brown Decades, The (Mumford), **Supp. II, Part 2,** 475, 478, 491–492

"Brown Dwarf of Rügen, The" (Whittier), **Supp. I, Part 2,** 696

Browne, Charles Farrar, **II,** 289; **IV,** 193, 196

Browne, E. K., **IV,** 330

Browne, E. Martin, **I,** 590

Browne, Nina E., **II,** 245

Browne, R. B., **III,** 241–242

Browne, Sir Thomas, **II,** 15–16, 304; **III,** 77, 78, 198, 487; **IV,** 147

Browne, William, **Supp. I, Part 1,** 98

Brownell, W. C., **II,** 14; **Supp. I, Part 2,** 426

Brownies' Book, The (Hughes), **Supp. I, Part 1,** 321

Browning, Elizabeth, **I,** 458, 459

Browning, Robert, **I,** 50, 66, 103, 458, 460, 468; **II,** 338, 478, 522; **III,** 5, 8, 467, 469, 484, 511, 521, 524, 606, 609; **IV,** 135, 245, 366, 416; **Supp. I, Part 1,** 2, 6, 79, 311, **Part 2,** 416, 468, 622; **Supp. III, Part 1,** 5, 6

Brownstone Eclogues and Other Poems (Aiken), **I,** 65, 67

Broyard, Anatole, **Supp. I, Part 1,** 198

Bruccoli, Matthew J., **II,** 100

Brueghel, Pieter, **I,** 174, 189; **Supp. I, Part 2,** 475

Brunner, Emil, **III,** 291, 303, 313

Bruno's Bohemia (publication), **I,** 384

Bruno's Weekly (publication), **I,** 384

Brustein, Robert, **I,** 95; **III,** 407

Brutus, **IV,** 373, 374; **Supp. I, Part 2,** 471

"Brutus and Antony" (Masters), **Supp. I, Part 2,** 472

"Bryan, Bryan, Bryan, Bryan" (Lindsay), **Supp. I, Part 2,** 394, 395, 398

Bryan, Katharine, *see* O'Hara, Mrs. John (Katharine Bryan)

Bryan, William Jennings, **I,** 483; **IV,** 124; **Supp. I, Part 2,** 385, 395–396, 455, 456

Bryant, Austin, **Supp. I, Part 1,** 152, 153

Bryant, Frances, **Supp. I, Part 1,** 153

Bryant, Jerry H., **Supp. I, Part 1,** 69

Bryant, Mrs. William Cullen (Frances Fairchild), **Supp. I, Part 1,** 153, 169

Bryant, Peter, **Supp. I, Part 1,** 150, 151, 152, 153

Bryant, William Cullen, **I,** 335, 458; **II,** 311; **III,** 81; **IV,** 309; **Supp. I, Part 1,** 150–173, 312, 362, **Part 2,** 413, 416, 420

Bryant, William Cullen, II, **Supp. I, Part 1,** 154

Bryer, Jackson R., **I,** 119, 142; **II,** 100; **III,** 406; **IV,** 95, 472

Bryher, Jackson R. (pseudonym), *see* Ellerman, Winifred

Brylowski, Walter, **II,** 76

Buber, Martin, **II,** 228; **III,** 45, 308, 528; **IV,** 11; **Supp. I, Part 1,** 83, 88

Buccaneers, The (Wharton), **IV,** 327

Buchan, A. M., **II,** 413

Buchen, Irving, **IV,** 23

Buck, Dudley, **Supp. I, Part 1,** 362

Buck, Gene, **II,** 427

Buck, Pearl S., **Supp. II, Part 1, 113–134**

Buck, Philo Melvin, Jr., **III,** 407

"Buck in the Snow, The" (Millay), **III,** 135

Bucke, R. M., **IV,** 353

Buckingham, Willis J., **I,** 564

Buckley, Tom, **IV,** 401

Buckminster, Joseph, **Supp. II, Part 1,** 66–67, 69

Bucolics (Auden), **Supp. II, Part 1,** 21, 24

Budd, Louis J., **IV,** 210, 213

Budd, Nelson H., **Supp. I, Part 2,** 626

Buddha, **I,** 136; **II,** 1; **III,** 173, 179, 239, 567; **Supp. I, Part 1,** 363, **Part 2,** 397

Buechner, Frederick, **III,** 310

"Buffalo Bill," *see* Cody, William

Buffalo Express (publication), **II,** 465

"Buffalo, The" (Moore), **III,** 215

Buffington, Robert, **III,** 502

Buffon, Comte de, **II,** 101

"Buick" (Shapiro), **Supp. II, Part 2,** 705

Builders, The (Glasgow), **II**, 183–184, 193

Builders of the Bay Colony (Morison), **Supp. I, Part 1,** 123, **Part 2,** 484–485

"Builders of the Bridge, The" (Mumford), **Supp. II, Part 2,** 475

"Building of the Ship, The" (Longfellow), **II**, 498

Building of Uncle Tom's Cabin, The (Kirkham), **Supp. I, Part 2,** 601

Bukowski, Charles, **Supp. III, Part 1,** 147

"Bulgarian Poetess, The" (Updike), **IV**, 215, 227

Bulkin, Elly, **Supp. I, Part 2,** 578

Bull, Ole, **II**, 504

Bullet Park (Cheever), **Supp. I, Part 1,** 185, 187–193, 194, 195

Bullins, Ed, **Supp. II, Part 1,** 34, 42

Bultmann, Rudolf, **III**, 309

Bulwark, The (Dreiser), **I**, 497, 506, 516–517

Bulwer-Lytton, Edward George, **IV**, 350

Bunche, Ralph, **Supp. I, Part 1,** 343

"Bunner Sisters, The" (Wharton), **IV**, 317

Bunting, Basil, **Supp. III, Part 2,** 616, 620, 624

Buñuel, Luis, **III**, 184

Bunyan, John, **I**, 445, **II**, 15, 104, 228; **IV**, 80, 84, 156, 437; **Supp. I, Part 1,** 32

Buranelli, Vincent, **III**, 432

Burbank, Luther, **I**, 483

Burbank, Rex, **I**, 119, 120; **IV**, 363, 376

Burchard, Rachael C., **IV**, 234

Burchfield, Alice, **Supp. I, Part 2,** 652, 660

Bürger, Gottfried August, **II**, 306

Burgess, Anthony, **III**, 47; **IV**, 234

Burgess, Charles E., **Supp. I, Part 2,** 477

Burgh, James, **Supp. I, Part 2,** 522

"Burglar of Babylon, The" (Bishop), **Supp. I, Part 1,** 93

Burgum, E. B., **IV**, 469, 470

Burhans, Clinton S., Jr., **Supp. I, Part 1,** 198

Buried Child (Shepard), **Supp. III, Part 2,** 433, 447, 448

"Buried Lake, The" (Tate), **IV**, 136

Burke, Edmund, **I**, 9; **III**, 310; **Supp. I, Part 2,** 496, 511, 512, 513, 523; **Supp. II, Part 1,** 80

Burke, Kenneth, **I**, **264–287**, 291, 311; **III**, 217, 289, 497, 499, 546, 550; **IV**, 48, 123, 408, 424; **Supp. I, Part 2,** 630; **Supp. II, Part 1,** 136

Burke, Paine, and the Rights of Man: A Difference of Political Opinions (Fennessy), **Supp. I, Part 2,** 525

Burks, Mary Fair, **Supp. I, Part 1,** 69

"Burly Fading One, The" (Hayden), **Supp. II, Part 1,** 366

Burnett, Frances Hodgson, **Supp. I, Part 1,** 44

Burnett, Hallie S., **III**, 573

Burnett, Whit, **III**, 551, 573

Burnham, James, **IV**, 142; **Supp. I, Part 2,** 648

Burnham, John Chynoweth, **I**, 59

Burnham, Philip E., **IV**, 188

"Burning, The" (Welty), **IV**, 277–278

Burning Bright (Steinbeck), **IV**, 51, 61–62

Burning Daylight (London), **II**, 474, 481

"Burning of Paper Instead of Children, The" (Rich), **Supp. I, Part 2,** 558

Burns, David, **III**, 165–166

Burns, Robert, **II**, 150, 306; **III**, 592; **IV**, 453; **Supp. I, Part 1,** 158, **Part 2,** 410, 455, 683, 685, 691, 692

Burnshaw, Stanley, **Supp. III, Part 2,** 615

Burnt Norton (Eliot), **I**, 575, 580–581, 582, 584, 585; **III**, 10

Burr, Aaron, **I**, 7, 549, 550; **II**, 300; **IV**, 264; **Supp. I, Part 2,** 461, 483

Burr Oaks (Eberhart), **I**, 533, 535

Burroughs, John, **I**, 220, 236, 506; **IV**, 346

Burroughs, William, **III**, 45, 174, 258; **Supp. II, Part 1,** 320, 328

Burroughs, William S., **Supp. III, Part 1,** **91–110**, 217, 226

Burrow, Trigant, **Supp. II, Part 1,** 6

Burrows, David, **II**, 293

Burt, Struthers, **Supp. I, Part 1,** 198

Burton, Robert, **II**, 535; **III**, 77, 78; **Supp. I, Part 1,** 349

Burton, William Evans, **III**, 412

Burton's Gentleman's Magazine, **III**, 412

Bury the Dead (Shaw), **IV**, 381

"Burying Ground by the Ties" (MacLeish), **III**, 14

Busch, Arthur J., **III**, 242

Bush, Douglas, **Supp. I, Part 1,** 268, 275

Bush, Warren V., **III**, 25

"Busher Comes Back, The" (Lardner), **II**, 422

"Busher's Letters Home, A" (Lardner), **II**, 418–419, 421

Bushman, Richard L., **I**, 564

"Business Deal" (West), **IV**, 287

"But Only Mine" (Wright), **Supp. III, Part 2,** 595

"But What Is the Reader to Make of This?" (Ashbery), **Supp. III, Part 1,** 25

Butler, Benjamin, **I**, 457

Butler, Dorothy, *see* Farrell, Mrs. James T. (Dorothy Butler)

Butler, E. M., **Supp. I, Part 1,** 275

Butler, Elizabeth, **Supp. I, Part 1,** 260

Butler, Joseph, **II**, 8, 9

Butler, Maud, *see* Falkner, Mrs. Murray C. (Maud Butler)

Butler, Nicholas Murray, **I**, 223; **Supp. I, Part 1,** 23; **Supp. III, Part 2,** 499

Butler, Samuel, **II**, 82, 86; **IV**, 121, 440

Butscher, Edward, **Supp. I, Part 2,** 526, 548

Butterfield, R. W., **I**, 386, 404

Butterfield, Roger, **III**, 72

Butterfield 8 (O'Hara), **III**, 361

Buttrick, George, **III**, 301

"Buzz" (Alcott), **Supp. I, Part 1,** 43

By Avon River (Doolittle), **Supp. I, Part 1,** 272

"By Disposition of Angels" (Moore), **III**, 214

By Land and by Sea (Morison), **Supp. I, Part 1,** 492

By Love Possessed (Cozzens), **I**, 358, 365, 372–374, 375, 376, 377, 378, 379

By the North Gate (Oates), **Supp. II, Part 2,** 504

By Way of Orbit (O'Neill), **III**, 405

By-Line: Ernest Hemingway (Hemingway), **II**, 257–258

Bynner, Witter, **II**, 513, 527

Byrd, Cecil K., **Supp. I, Part 1,** 401

Byrne, Donn, **IV**, 67

Byron, George Gordon, Lord, **I**, 343, 568, 577; **II**, 135, 193, 296, 301, 303, 310, 315, 331, 566; **III**, 82, 137, 170, 409, 410, 412, 469; **IV**, 245, 435; **Supp. I, Part 1,** 150, 312, 349, **Part 2,** 580, 591, 683, 685, 719

Capitalist Meditates by a Civil War Monument" (Lowell), **II**, 538

"Christmas Eve under Hooker's Statue" (Lowell), **II**, 539–540

"Christmas Gift" (Warren), **IV**, 252–253

"Christmas Greeting, A" (Wright), **Supp. III, Part 2**, 601

"Christmas Hymn, A" (Wilbur), **Supp. III, Part 2**, 557

Christmas Memory, A (Capote), **Supp. III, Part 1**, 118, 119, 129

"Christmas 1944" (Levertov), **Supp. III, Part 1**, 274

"Christmas, or the Good Fairy" (Stowe), **Supp. I, Part 2**, 586

Christmas Story (Mencken), **III**, 111

Christographia (Taylor), **IV**, 164–165

Christopher Columbus, Mariner (Morison), **Supp. I, Part 2**, 488

Christus: A Mystery (Longfellow), **II**, 490, 493, 495, 505–507

"Chronicle of Race Relations, A" (Du Bois), **Supp. II, Part 1**, 182

Chronicle of the Conquest of Granada (Irving), **II**, 310

Chronologies of the Life and Writings of William Cullen Bryant . . . (Sturges), **Supp. I, Part 1**, 173

"Chrysanthemums, The" (Steinbeck), **IV**, 53

"Chrysaor" (Longfellow), **II**, 498

Church, Margaret, **IV**, 466

"Church Porch, The" (Herbert), **IV**, 153

Church Psalmody, Selected from Dr. Watts and Other Authors (ed. Mason and Greene), **I**, 458

Churchill, Winston, **I**, 9, 490; **Supp. I, Part 2**, 491

Ciannic, Saint, **II**, 215

Ciano, Edda, **IV**, 249

Ciardi, John, **I**, 169, 179, 189, 535, 542; **III**, 268, 289; **IV**, 424

"Cicadas" (Wilbur), **Supp. III, Part 2**, 549

Cicero, **I**, 279; **II**, 8, 14–15; **III**, 23; **Supp. I, Part 2**, 405

"Cigales" (Wilbur), **Supp. III, Part 2**, 549

"Cimetière Marin, Le" (Valéry), **IV**, 91–92

"Cinderella" (Jarrell), **II**, 386

"Cinderella" (Perrault), **IV**, 266, 267

"Cinderella" (Sexton), **Supp. II, Part 2**, 691

Cinthio, **IV**, 370

CIOPW (Cummings), **I**, 429

"Circle in the Fire, A" (O'Connor), **III**, 344–345, 349–350, 351, 353, 354

"Circles" (Emerson), **I**, 455, 460

"Circles" (Lowell), **II**, 554

"Circus, The" (Porter), **III**, 443, 445

"Circus Animals' Desertion" (Yeats), **I**, 389

"Circus in the Attic" (Warren), **IV**, 253

Circus in the Attic, The (Warren), **IV**, 243, 251–253

"Circus in Three Rings" (Plath), **Supp. I, Part 2**, 536

"Cirque d'Hiver" (Bishop), **Supp. I, Part 1**, 85

Cities of the Red Night (Burroughs), **Supp. III, Part 1**, 106

"Citizen Cain" (Baraka), **Supp. II, Part 1**, 49

"Citizen of the World" (Goldsmith), **II**, 299

City in History, The (Mumford), **Supp. II, Part 2**, 495

"City in the Sea, The" (Poe), **III**, 411

City of Discontent (Harris), **Supp. I, Part 2**, 402

City of God, The (St. Augustine), **IV**, 126

"City on a Hill" (Lowell), **II**, 552

City Without Walls (Auden), **Supp. II, Part 1**, 24

Civil Disobedience (Thoreau), **IV**, 185; **Supp. I, Part 2**, 507

"Civil Rights" (Lanier), **Supp. I, Part 1**, 357

Civilization in the United States (Stearns), **I**, 245

Claiborne, William, **I**, 132

Clancy's Wake, At (Crane), **I**, 422

Clara Howard; or, The Enthusiasm of Love (Brown), **Supp. I, Part 1**, 145

Clara's Ole Man (Bullins), **Supp. II, Part 1**, 42

Clare, John, **II**, 387; **III**, 528

Clarel: A Poem and Pilgrimage in the Holy Land (Melville), **III**, 92–93

Clarissa (Richardson), **II**, 111; **Supp. I, Part 2**, 714

Clark, Barrett H., **III**, 406–407

Clark, Charles, **I**, 470

Clark, David Lee, **Supp. I, Part 1**, 148

Clark, Eleanor, *see* Warren, Mrs. Robert Penn (Eleanor Clark)

Clark, Francis Edward, **II**, 9

Clark, Harry Hayden, **Supp. I, Part 1**, 319, **Part 2**, 423, 426, 525

Clark, John Bates, **Supp. I, Part 2**, 633

Clark, Thomas, **Supp. III, Part 2**, 629

Clark, William, **III**, 14; **IV**, 179, 283

Clark, Willis Gaylord, **Supp. I, Part 2**, 684

Clarke, James Freeman, **Supp. II, Part 1**, 280

Clarke, John H., **IV**, 118, 119

Clarke, John J., **III**, 356

Clarke, Samuel, **II**, 108

Clash by Night (Odets), **Supp. II, Part 2**, 531, 538, 544–546, 550, 551

"CLASS STRUGGLE" (Baraka), **Supp. II, Part 1**, 55

Classical Tradition, The (Highet), **Supp. I, Part 1**, 268

Classical World of H. D., The (Swann), **Supp. I, Part 1**, 275

Classics and Commercials: A Literary Chronicle of the Forties (Wilson), **IV**, 433

Claudel, Paul, **I**, 60

Claudelle Inglish (Caldwell), **I**, 304

Clavel, Marcel, **I**, 343, 357

"Claw of the Sea-Puss, The: James Thurber's Sense of Experience" (Black), **Supp. I, Part 2**, 626

"CLAY" (Baraka), **Supp. II, Part 1**, 54

Clay, Cassius, *see* Muhammad Ali

Clay, Henry, **I**, 8; **Supp. I, Part 2**, 684, 686

Clayton, John J., **I**, 165

"Clear Days" (White), **Supp. I, Part 2**, 664, 665

"Clear, with Light Variable Winds" (Lowell), **II**, 522

"Clearing the Title" (Merrill), **Supp. III, Part 1**, 336

"Clearness" (Wilbur), **Supp. III, Part 2**, 544, 550

Clemenceau, Georges, **I**, 490

Clemens, Clara, **IV**, 213

Clemens, Jane, **I**, 247

Clemens, John Marshall, **IV**, 193

Clemens, Mrs. John Marshall (Jane Lampton), **IV**, 193

Clemens, Mrs. Samuel Langhorne (Olivia Langdon), **I**, 197, 208; **Supp. I, Part 2**, 457

Clemens, Olivia, **I**, 247

Douglass (cont.) 157, 195, 196, 292, 378; **Supp. III, Part 1, 153–174**

Dove, Belle, **I**, 451

Dow, Lorenzo, **IV**, 265

Dowd, Douglas, **Supp. I, Part 2,** 645, 650

Dowling, Eddie, **IV**, 394

"Down at the Cross" (Baldwin), **Supp. I, Part 1,** 60, 61

"Down at the Dinghy" (Salinger), **III**, 559, 563

"Down by the Station, Early in the Morning" (Ashbery), **Supp. III, Part 1,** 25

"Down East Humor (1830–1867)" (Blair), **Supp. I, Part 2,** 426

"Down in Alabam" (Bierce), **I**, 193

"Down Where I Am" (Hughes), **Supp. I, Part 1,** 344

Downer, Alan S., **I**, 95; **III**, 407

Downey, Jean, **II**, 509

Downing, Major Jack (pseudonym), *see* Smith, Seba

"Downward Path to Wisdom, The" (Porter), **III**, 442, 443, 446

Dowson, Ernest C., **I**, 384

Doyle, C. W., **I**, 199

Drach, Ivan, **Supp. III, Part 1,** 268

"Draft Lyrics for *Candide*" (Agee), **I**, 28

Draft of XVI Cantos, A (Pound), **III**, 472

Draft of XXX Cantos, A (Pound), **III**, 196

Dragon Country (Williams), **IV**, 383

Dragon Seed (Buck), **Supp. II, Part 1,** 124

Drake, Benjamin, **Supp. I, Part 2,** 584

Drake, Daniel, **Supp. I, Part 2,** 584

Drake, Sir Francis, **Supp. I, Part 2,** 497

Drake, St. Clair, **IV**, 475, 496

Dramatic Duologues (Masters), **Supp. I, Part 2,** 461

"Draught" (Cowley), **Supp. II, Part 1,** 141, 142

Drayton, Michael, **IV**, 135

"Dream, A" (Ginsberg), **Supp. II, Part 1,** 312

"Dream, A" (Tate), **IV**, 129

"Dream, The" (Hayden), **Supp. II, Part 1,** 368, 377

"Dream Boogie" (Hughes), **Supp. I, Part 1,** 339–340

"Dream Interpreted, The" (Paine), **Supp. I, Part 2,** 505

Dream Keeper, The (Hughes), **Supp. I, Part 1,** 328, 332, 333, 334

Dream Life of Balso Snell, The (West), **IV**, 286, 287, 288–290, 291, 297

Dream of a Common Language, Poems 1974–77, The (Rich), **Supp. I, Part 2,** 551, 554, 569–576

Dream of Arcadia: American Writers and Artists in Italy (Brooks), **I**, 254

"Dream of Italy, A" (Masters), **Supp. I, Part 2,** 458

Dream of the Golden Mountains, The (Cowley), **Supp. II, Part 1,** 139, 141, 142, 144

"Dream Pang, A" (Frost), **II**, 153

"Dream Variations" (Hughes), **Supp. I, Part 1,** 323

"Dreaming the Breasts" (Sexton), **Supp. II, Part 2,** 692

"Dreams About Clothes" (Merrill), **Supp. III, Part 1,** 328–329

"Dreams of Adulthood" (Ashbery), **Supp. III, Part 1,** 26

Dred: A Tale of the Great Dismal Swamp (Stowe), **Supp. I, Part 2,** 592

Dreiser, Al, **I**, 498

Dreiser, Claire, **I**, 499

Dreiser, Ed, **I**, 499

Dreiser, Emma, **I**, 498, 502, 504

Dreiser, John Paul, **I**, 498–499, 503

Dreiser, Mame, **I**, 498, 504

Dreiser, Mrs. Theodore (Sara White), **I**, 500, 501

Dreiser, Paul, **I**, 498, 500, 503, 517

Dreiser, Rome, **I**, 498

Dreiser, Sara, **I**, 510, 511–512, 515

Dreiser, Sara Maria Schänäb, **I**, 498, 499, 503, 504

Dreiser, Sylvia, **I**, 498

Dreiser, Theodore, **I**, 59, 97, 109, 116, 119, 355, 374, 375, 475, 482, **497–520;** **II**, 26, 27, 29, 34, 38, 44, 74, 89, 93, 180, 276, 283, 428, 444, 451, 456–457, 467–468; **III**, 40, 103, 106, 251, 314, 319, 327, 335, 453, 576, 582; **IV**, 29, 35, 40, 135, 208, 237, 475, 482, 484; **Supp. I, Part 1,** 320, **Part 2,** 461, 468; **Supp. III, Part 2,** 412

Dreiser, Theresa, **I**, 498

Dresser, Paul, *see* Dreiser, Paul

Drew, Elizabeth, **I**, 590

Dreyfus, Alfred, **Supp. I, Part 2,** 446

Drift and Mastery (Lippmann), **I**, 222–223

"Drinker, The" (Lowell), **II**, 535, 550

"Driver" (Merrill), **Supp. III, Part 1,** 331

"Drowsy Day, A" (Dunbar), **Supp. II, Part 1,** 198

"Drug Store" (Shapiro), **Supp. II, Part 2,** 705

Drugiye Berega (Nabokov), **III**, 247–250, 252

Drum (magazine), **Supp. I, Part 1,** 344

"Drumlin Woodchuck, A" (Frost), **II**, 159–160

Drummond, William, **Supp. I, Part 1,** 369

Drum-Taps (Whitman), **IV**, 346, 347, 444

Drunk in the Furnace, The (Merwin), **Supp. III, Part 1,** 345–346

"Drunk in the Furnace, The" (Merwin), **Supp. III, Part 1,** 346

Drunkard's Holiday, The (Fitzgerald), **II**, 93

"Drunken Fisherman, The" (Lowell), **II**, 534, 550

"Drunken Sisters, The" (Wilder), **IV**, 374

Dry Salvages, The (Eliot), **I**, 581

"Dry September" (Faulkner), **II**, 72, 73

Dryden, Edgar A., **III**, 97

Dryden, John, **II**, 111, 542, 556; **III**, 15; **IV**, 145; **Supp. I, Part 1,** 150, **Part 2,** 422

Du Bartas, Guillaume, **Supp. I, Part 1,** 98, 104, 111, 118, 119

Du Bois, Nina Gomer (Mrs. W. E. B. Du Bois), **Supp. II, Part 1,** 158

Du Bois, Shirley Graham (Mrs. W. E. B. Du Bois), **Supp. II, Part 1,** 186

Du Bois, W. E. B., **I**, 260; **Supp. I, Part 1,** 5, 345; **Supp. II, Part 1,** 33, 56, 61, **157–189,** 195

Du Maurier family, **II**, 404

Dualism, **I**, 460, 527; **II**, 21

Duberman, Martin, **Supp. I, Part 2,** 408, 409, 425

"Dubin's Lives" (Malamud), **Supp. I, Part 2,** 451

Dubliners (Joyce), **I**, 130, 480; **III**, 471

Duchamp, Marcel, **IV**, 408

Duchess of Malfi, The (Webster), **IV**, 131

Dudley, Anne, *see* Bradstreet, Anne

Dudley, Joseph, **III**, 52

Dudley, Thomas, **III**, 52; **Supp. I, Part 1,** 98, 99, 110, 116

"Ecologues of These States 1969–1971" (Ginsberg), **Supp. II, Part 1,** 325

"Economic Theory of Women's Dress, The" (Veblen), **Supp. I, Part 2,** 636

"Economics of Negro Emancipation in the United States, The" (Du Bois), **Supp. II, Part 1,** 174

"Economy of Love, The: The Novels of Bernard Malamud" (Baumbach), **Supp. I, Part 2,** 452

Eddy, Mary Baker, I, 583; III, 506

Edel, Leon, I, 20, 333; II, 293, 338–339, 340, 341; IV, 330

Edelstein, J. M., IV, 376

Edelstein, Sanford, IV, 425

Edgar Huntly; or, Memoirs of a Sleep-Walker (Brown), **Supp. I, Part 1,** 140–144, 145

"Edgar Lee Masters" (Powys), **Supp. I, Part 2,** 478

Edgar Lee Masters: A Centenary Memoir-Anthology (Masters), **Supp. I, Part 2,** 478

"Edgar Lee Masters and the Chinese" (Hartley), **Supp. I, Part 2,** 478

"Edgar Lee Masters—Biographer and Historian" (Hartley), **Supp. I, Part 2,** 478

"Edgar Lee Masters Centenary Exhibition: Catalogue and Checklist of Books" (Robinson), **Supp. I, Part 2,** 478

"Edgar Lee Masters Collection, The: Sixty Years of Literary History" (Robinson), **Supp. I, Part 2,** 478

"Edgar Lee Masters—Political Essayist" (Hartley), **Supp. I, Part 2,** 478

Edgar Lee Masters: The Spoon River Poet and His Critics (Flanagan), **Supp. I, Part 2,** 478

Edge, Mary E., II, 316

"Edge" (Plath), **Supp. I, Part 2,** 527, 547

Edgell, D. P., IV, 376

Edgeworth, Maria, II, 8

"Edict by the King of Prussia, An" (Franklin), II, 120

Edison, Thomas A., I, 483; **Supp. I, Part 2,** 392

"Editor and the Schoolma'am, The" (Frederic), II, 130

"Editor Whedon" (Masters), **Supp. I, Part 2,** 463

"Editor's Easy Chair" (Howells), II, 276

"Editor's Study, The" (Howells), II, 275, 276, 285

Edman, Irwin, III, 605, 621

Edsel (Shapiro), **Supp. II, Part 2,** 703, 704, 717–719

"Educated American Woman, An" (Cheever), **Supp. I, Part 1,** 194

Education and Living (Bourne), I, 252

Education of Black People, The (Du Bois), **Supp. II, Part 1,** 186

Education of Henry Adams, The (Adams), I, 1, 5, 6, 11, 14, 15–18, 19, 20–21, 111; II, 276; III, 504

"Education of Jane Addams, The" (Phillips), **Supp. I, Part 1,** 27

Education sentimentale (Flaubert), III, 315

Edward IV, King, II, 379; IV, 200

Edwards, Davis, **Supp. I, Part 2,** 402

Edwards, Esther, I, 545

Edwards, John, I, 478

Edwards, Jonathan, I, **544–566**; II, 432; **Supp. I, Part 1,** 301, 302, **Part 2,** 552, 594, 700

Edwards, Sarah, I, 545

Edwards, Timothy, I, 545

"Edwin Arlington Robinson" (Cowley), **Supp. II, Part 1,** 144

Edwin Arlington Robinson (Winters), **Supp. II, Part 2,** 812

"Efforts of Affection" (Moore), III, 214

"Egg, The" (Anderson), I, 113, 114

Egoist, The (Meredith), II, 186

Egoist, The (publication), I, 384, 568; III, 194, 197, 471; **Supp. I, Part 1,** 257, 262

"Egotism, or the Bosom Sergent" (Hawthorne), II, 227, 239

"Egyptian Pulled Glass Bottle in the Shape of a Fish, An" (Moore), III, 195, 213

Ehrenpreis, Irvin, II, 557

Eichelberger, Clayton, II, 413

"Eidolon" (Warren), IV, 239

Eight Cousins (Alcott), **Supp. I, Part 1,** 29, 38, 42, 43

Eight Harvard Poets: E. Estlin Cummings, S. Foster Damon, J. R. Dos Passos, Robert Hillyer, R. S. Mitchell, William A. Norris, Dudley Poore, Cuthbert Wright, I, 429, 475

Eight Men (Wright), IV, 478, 488, 494

"18 West 11th Street" (Merrill), **Supp. III, Part 1,** 323, 328

"Eighth Air Force" (Jarrell), II, 373–374, 377

"Eighth Ditch, The" (Baraka), **Supp. II, Part 1,** 40

80 Flowers (Zukofsky), **Supp. III, Part 2,** 631

Eileen (Masters), **Supp. I, Part 2,** 460

Eimi (Cummings), I, 429, 433, 434, 439–440

Einstein, Albert, I, 493; III, 8, 10, 21, 161; IV, 69, 375, 410, 411, 421; **Supp. I, Part 2,** 609, 643; **Supp. III, Part 2,** 621

"Einstein" (MacLeish), III, 5, 8, 10–11, 18–19

Eiseley, Loren, III, 227–228

Eisenberg, J. A., IV, 23

Eisenhower, Dwight D., I, 136, 376; II, 548; III, 215; IV, 75; **Supp. I, Part 1,** 291; **Supp. III, Part 2,** 624

Eisenstein, Sergei, I, 481

Eisinger, Chester E., I, 165, 302; II, 221, 604, 607; III, 47, 72, 243

Eissenstat, Martha Turnquist, III, 168

El Greco, I, 387; III, 212

"El-Hajj Malik El-Shabazz" (Hayden), **Supp. II, Part 1,** 379

"El Salvador: Requiem and Invocation" (Levertov), **Supp. III, Part 1,** 284

Elbert, Sarah, **Supp. I, Part 1,** 34, 41, 46

Elder, Donald, II, 417, 426, 435, 437, 438

Elder Statesman, The (Eliot), I, 572, 573, 583

Eldridge, Florence, III, 154, 403; IV, 357

Eleanor of Aquitaine, III, 470

Eleanor of Guienne, I, 14

Elective Affinities (Goethe, trans. Bogan and Mayer), **Supp. III, Part 1,** 63

Electra (Euripides), III, 398

Electra (Sophocles), III, 398; IV, 370

"Electra on Azalea Path" (Plath), **Supp. I, Part 2,** 538

Electric Kool-Aid Acid Test, The (Wolfe), **Supp. III, Part 2,** 575–577, 582–584

"Electrical Storm" (Bishop), **Supp. I, Part 1,** 93

"Electrical Storm" (Hayden), **Supp. II, Part 1,** 370

"Fit Against the Country, A" (Wright), **Supp. III, Part 2,** 591–592, 601

Fitch, Elizabeth, *see* Taylor, Mrs. Edward (Elizabeth Fitch)

Fitch, James, **IV,** 147

Fitts, Dudley, **I,** 169, 173, 189; **III,** 289; **Supp. I, Part 1,** 342, 345

FitzGerald, Edward, **Supp. I, Part 2,** 416; **Supp. III, Part 2,** 610

Fitzgerald, F. Scott, **I,** 107, 117, 118, 123, 188, 221, 263, 288, 289, 358, 367, 374–375, 382, 423, 476, 482, 487, 495, 509, 511; **II,** **77–100,** 257, 263, 272, 283, 415, 416, 417–418, 420, 425, 427, 430, 431, 432, 433, 434, 436, 437, 438, 450, 458–459, 482, 560; **III,** 2, 26, 35, 45, 36, 37, 40, 44, 69, 106, 244, 284, 334, 350–351, 453, 454, 471, 551, 552, 572; **IV,** 27, 49, 97, 101, 126, 140, 191, 222, 223, 287, 297, 427, 471; **Supp. I, Part 1,** **196,** 197, **Part 2,** 622; **Supp. III, Part 2,** 409, 411, 585

Fitzgerald, Mrs. F. Scott (Zelda Sayre), **I,** 482; **II,** 77, 79, 82–85, 88, 90–91, 93, 95

Fitzgerald, Robert, **I,** 27–28, 47; **II,** 390; **III,** 338, 348, 359, 360; **IV,** 142

Fitzgerald, Sally, **III,** 338

"Fitzgerald: The Romance of Money" (Cowley), **Supp. II, Part 1,** 143

"Five Awakenings of Edna Pontellier, The" (Wheeler), **Supp. I, Part 1,** 226

Five Black Writers: Essays on Wright, Ellison, Baldwin, Hughes and Le Roi Jones (Gibson), **Supp. I, Part 1,** 348

Five Came Back (West), **IV,** 287

Five Temperaments (Kalstone), **Supp. I, Part 1,** 97

Five Young American Poets, **I,** 170; **II,** 367

Fixer, The (Malamud), **Supp. I, Part 2,** 428, 435, 445, 446–448, 450, 451

Fixler, Michael, **IV,** 23

Flacius, Matthias, **IV,** 163

Flag of Our Union, The (publication), **II,** 397

Flagons and Apples (Jeffers), **Supp. II, Part 2,** 413, 414, 417–418

Flaherty, Joe, **III,** 48

Flammarion, Camille, **Supp. I, Part 1,** 260

Flanagan, John T., **III,** 598; **Supp. I, Part 2,** 402, 464, 465, 468, 478

Flanagan, William, **I,** 95

"Flannery O'Connor: Poet to the Outcast" (Sister Rose Alice), **III,** 348

Flappers and Philosophers (Fitzgerald), **II,** 88

Flasch, Mrs. Harold A., **I,** 95

Flaubert, Gustave, **I,** 66, 123, 130, 272, 312, 314, 315, 477, 504, 506, 513, 514; **II,** 182, 185, 194, 198–199, 205, 209, 221, 230, 289, 311, 316, 319, 325, 337, 392, 401, 577, 594; **III,** 196, 207, 251, 315, 461, 467, 511, 564; **IV,** 4, 29, 31, 37, 40, 134, 285, 428; **Supp. III, Part 2,** 411, 412

Flavor of Man, The (Toomer), **Supp. III, Part 2,** 487

Flavoring of New England, The (Brooks), **I,** 253, 256

Flaxman, Josiah, **Supp. I, Part 2,** 716

"Flèche d'Or" (Merrill), **Supp. III, Part 1,** 328

Flecker, James Elroy, **Supp. I, Part 1,** 257

"Flee on Your Donkey" (Sexton), **Supp. II, Part 2,** 683, 685

Fleming, Thomas, **II,** 125

Flender, Harold, **IV,** 23

Fletcher, H. D., **II,** 517, 529

Fletcher, John, **Supp. I, Part 2,** 422

Fletcher, John Gould, **I,** 243; **II,** 517, 529; **III,** 458; **Supp. I, Part 1,** 263, 275, 373

Fletcher, Marie, **II,** 221; **Supp. I, Part 1,** 226

Fletcher, Phineas, **Supp. I, Part 1,** 369

Fletcher, Valerie, *see* Eliot, Mrs. T. S. (Valerie Fletcher)

Fletcher, Virginia, *see* Caldwell, Mrs. Erskine (Virginia Fletcher)

Fleurs du Mal, Les (trans. Millay and Dillon), **III,** 141–142

"Flight" (Updike), **IV,** 218, 222, 224

"Flight, The" (Roethke), **III,** 537–538

Flight of the Rocket, The (Fitzgerald), **II,** 89

Flint, F. Cudworth, **IV,** 142, 258

Flint, F. S., **II,** 517; **III,** 459, 464, 465; **Supp. I, Part 1,** 261, 262

Flint, R. W., **II,** 390; **III,** 289

Floating Bear (periodical), **Supp. II, Part 1,** 30

Floating Opera, The (Barth), **I,** 121, 122–126, 127, 129, 130, 131

"Floating Poem, Unnumbered, The" (Rich), **Supp. I, Part 2,** 572–573

Flood (Warren), **IV,** 252, 256–257

"Flood of Years, The" (Bryant), **Supp. I, Part 1,** 159, 170, 171, **Part 2,** 416

"Floral Decorations for Bananas" (Stevens), **IV,** 8

"Florida Sunday, A" (Lanier), **Supp. I, Part 1,** 364, 366

"Flossie Cabanis" (Masters), **Supp. I, Part 2,** 461–462

Flournoy, Théodore, **II,** 365

"Flowchart" (Ashbery), **Supp. III, Part 1,** 26

Flower Fables (Alcott), **Supp. I, Part 1,** 33

"Flower Herding on Mount Monadnock" (Kinnell), **Supp. III, Part 1,** 242

Flower Herding on Mount Monadnock (Kinnell), **Supp. III, Part 1,** 235, 239, 241–244

"Flowering Death" (Ashbery), **Supp. III, Part 1,** 22

"Flowering Dream, The" (McCullers), **II,** 591

"Flowering Judas" (Porter), **III,** 434, 435–436, 438, 441, 445, 446, 450–451

Flowering Judas and Other Stories (Porter), **III,** 433, 434

Flowering of New England, The (Brooks), **IV,** 171–172; **Supp. I, Part 2,** 426

Flowering of the Rod (Doolittle), **Supp. I, Part 1,** 272

Flowering Peach, The (Odets), **Supp. II, Part 2,** 533, 547, 549–550

Flower-de-Luce (Longfellow), **II,** 490

"Flower-Fed Buffaloes, The" (Lindsay), **Supp. I, Part 2,** 398

"Flower-gathering" (Frost), **II,** 153

"Flowers for Marjorie" (Welty), **IV,** 262

"Fly, The" (Kinnell), **Supp. III, Part 1,** 249

"Fly, The" (Shapiro), **Supp. II, Part 2,** 705

Flye, Father James Harold, **I,** 25, 26, 35–36, 37, 42, 46; **IV,** 215

"Flying High" (Levertov), **Supp. III, Part 1,** 284

"Flying Home" (Ellison), **Supp. II, Part 1,** 235, 238–239

"Flying Home" (Kinnell), **Supp. III, Part 1,** 250

Focillon, Henri, **IV,** 90

Focus (Miller), **III,** 150–151, 156

Foerster, Norman, **I**, 222, 263; **II**, 23; **III**, 432; **Supp. I, Part 2,** 423, 424, 426

"Fog" (Sandburg), **III**, 586

Fogle, Richard H., **II**, 245

Folded Leaf, The (Maxwell), **Supp. III, Part 1,** 62

Foley, Martha, **I**, 188; **II**, 587; **III**, 573

Folk of Southern Fiction, The (Skaggs), **Supp. I, Part 1,** 226

Folks from Dixie (Dunbar), **Supp. II, Part 1,** 211–212

Folkways (Sumner), **III**, 102

Follett, Wilson, **I**, 405, 425

Following the Equator (Twain), **II**, 434; **IV**, 208

Folsom, Charles, **Supp. I, Part 1,** 156

Folsom, James K., **III**, 336

Fonda, Henry, **Supp. I, Part 1,** 67

Fonda, Jane, **III**, 284

Foner, Eric, **Supp. I, Part 2,** 523

Foner, Philip S. **II**, 484

Fontanne, Lynn, **III**, 397

Fool for Love (Shepard), **Supp. III, Part 2,** 433, 447, 448

"Foot Fault" (pseudonym), *see* Thurber, James

Foote, Horton, **Supp. I, Part 1,** 281

Foote, Roxanna, *see* Beecher, Mrs. Lyman (Roxanna Foote)

Foote, Samuel, **Supp. I, Part 2,** 584

"Footing up a Total" (Lowell), **II**, 528

"Footnote to Howl" (Ginsberg), **Supp. II, Part 1,** 316–317

Footprints (Levertov), **Supp. III, Part 1,** 272, 281

"Footsteps of Angels" (Longfellow), **II**, 496

"For a Dead Lady" (Robinson), **III**, 508, 513, 517

"For a Lamb" (Eberhart), **I**, 523, 530, 531

"For a Marriage" (Bogan), **Supp. III, Part 1,** 52

"For an Emigrant" (Jarrell), **II**, 371

"For Anna Akmatova" (Lowell), **II**, 544

"For Annie" (Poe), **III**, 427

"For Dudley" (Wilbur), **Supp. III, Part 2,** 558

"For Elizabeth Bishop" (Lowell), **Supp. I, Part 1,** 97

"For Esmé—with Love and Squalor" (Salinger), **III**, 560

"For George Santayana" (Lowell), **II**, 547

"FOR HETTIE" (Baraka), **Supp. II, Part 1,** 32

"FOR HETTIE IN HER FIFTH MONTH" (Baraka), **Supp. II, Part 1,** 32, 38

"For John, Who Begs Me not to Enquire Further" (Sexton), **Supp. II, Part 2,** 676

"For Johnny Pole on the Forgotten Beach" (Sexton), **Supp. II, Part 2,** 675

"For Malamud It's Story" (Shenker), **Supp. I, Part 2,** 453

"For Mr. Death Who Stands with His Door Open" (Sexton), **Supp. II, Part 2,** 695

"For My Lover, Returning to His Wife" (Sexton), **Supp. II, Part 2,** 688

"For Once, Then, Something" (Frost), **II**, 156–157

"For Radicals" (Bourne), **I**, 221

For Spacious Skies (Buck), **Supp. II, Part 1,** 131

"For the Ahkoond" (Bierce), **I**, 209

"For the Dedication of the New City Library, Boston" (Holmes), **Supp. I, Part 1,** 308

"For the Marriage of Faustus and Helen" (Crane), **I**, 395–396, 399, 402

"For the Meeting of the National Sanitary Association, 1860" (Holmes), **Supp. I, Part 1,** 307

"For the New Railway Station in Rome" (Wilbur), **Supp. III, Part 2,** 554

"FOR THE REVOLUTIONARY OUTBURST BY BLACK PEOPLE" (Baraka), **Supp. II, Part 1,** 55

For the Time Being (Auden), **Supp. II, Part 1,** 2, 17, 18

"For the Union Dead" (Lowell), **II**, 551

For the Union Dead (Lowell), **II**, 543, 550–551, 554, 555

"For the Word Is Flesh" (Kunitz), **Supp. III, Part 1,** 262–264

"For Theodore Roethke: 1908–1963" (Lowell), **II**, 554

For Whom the Bell Tolls (Hemingway), **II**, 249, 254–255, 261; **III**, 18, 363

Forbes, Waldo Emerson, **II**, 22; **IV**, 189

Ford, Ford Madox, **I**, 288, 405, 409, 417, 421, 423; **II**, 58, 144, 198, 221, 222, 257, 263, 265, 517, 536; **III**, 458, 464–465, 470–471, 472, 476; **IV**, 27, 126, 261; **Supp. II, Part 1,** 107; **Supp. III, Part 2,** 617

Ford, Henry, **I**, 295, 480–481; **III**, 292, 293; **Supp. I, Part 1,** 21, **Part 2,** 644; **Supp. III, Part 2,** 612, 613

Ford, John, **Supp. I, Part 2,** 422; **Supp. III, Part 2,** 619

Ford, Newell F., **IV**, 259

Ford, Paul Leicester, **II**, 124

Ford, Webster (pseudonym), *see* Masters, Edgar Lee

Ford, Worthington C., **I**, 24

"Ford Madox Ford" (Lowell), **II**, 547

Fordyce, David, **II**, 113

Foregone Conclusion, A (Howells), **II**, 278–279, 282

"Foreign Affairs" (Kunitz), **Supp. III, Part 1,** 265

"Foreigner, The" (Jewett), **II**, 409–410

Forensic and the Navigators (Shepard), **Supp. III, Part 2,** 439

"Forest Hymn, A" (Bryant), **Supp. I, Part 1,** 156, 162, 163, 164, 165, 170

"Forest of the South, The" (Gordon), **II**, 199, 201

Forest of the South, The (Gordon), **II**, 197

Forester's Letters (Paine), **Supp. I, Part 2,** 508

"Forgotten Novel, A: Kate Chopin's *The Awakening*" (Eble), **Supp. I, Part 1,** 226

Forgotten Village, The (Steinbeck), **IV**, 51

Forgue, Guy J., **III**, 118, 119, 121

"Forlorn Hope of Sidney Lanier, The" (Leary), **Supp. I, Part 1,** 373

"Form Is Emptiness" (Baraka), **Supp. II, Part 1,** 51

"Formal Elegy" (Berryman), **I**, 170

"Formalist Criticism: Its Principles and Limits" (Burke), **I**, 282

Forms of Discovery (Winters), **Supp. II, Part 2,** 812, 813

Forrestal, James, **I**, 491; **Supp. I, Part 2,** 489

Forrey, Carolyn, **Supp. I, Part 1,** 226

"Forsaken Merman" (Arnold), **Supp. I, Part 2,** 529

Forster, E. M., **I**, 292; **IV**, 201; **Supp. III, Part 2,** 503

Forster, John, **II**, 315

Garibaldi, Giuseppe, **I**, 4; **II**, 284

Garis, Robert, **I**, 143

Garland, Hamlin, **I**, 407; **II**, 276, 289; **III**, 576; **Supp. I, Part 1,** 217

Garner, Stanton, **II**, 148

Garnett, Edward, **I**, 405, 409, 417, 426; **III**, 27

Garrett, George, **Supp. I, Part 1,** 196, 198

Garrett, George P., **III**, 243

Garrigue, Jean, **IV**, 424

Garrison, Fielding, **III**, 105

Garrison, William, Lloyd, **Supp. I, Part 2,** 524, 588, 683, 685, 686, 687

"Garrison of Cape Ann, The" (Whittier), **Supp. I, Part 2,** 691, 694

"Garter Motif" (White), **Supp. I, Part 2,** 673

Garvey, Marcus, **Supp. II, Part 1,** 175, 180

Gary Schools, The (publication), **I**, 232

Gas (Kaiser), **I**, 479

Gas-House McGinty (Farrell), **II**, 41–42

Gaskell, Elizabeth, **II**, 192; **Supp. I, Part 2,** 580

Gass, W. H., **IV**, 48

Gassner, John, **III**, 169, 407; **IV**, 376, 381, 401; **Supp. I, Part 1,** 284, 292

Gates, Elmer, **I**, 515–516

Gates, Lewis E., **III**, 315, 330

Gates of Wrath, The; Rhymed Poems (Ginsberg), **Supp. II, Part 1,** 311, 319

Gathering of Fugitives, A (Trilling), **Supp. III, Part 2,** 506, 512

Gaudier-Brzeska, Henri, **III**, 459, 464, 465, 477

Gauguin, Paul, **I**, 34; **IV**, 290

Gaunt, Marcia E., **Supp. I, Part 1,** 198

Gauss, Christian, **II**, 82; **IV**, 427, 439–440, 444

Gaustad, Edwin Scott, **I**, 565

Gautier, Théophile, **II**, 543; **III**, 466, 467; **Supp. I, Part 1,** 277

Gay, John, **II**, 111; **Supp. I, Part 2,** 523

Gay, Peter, **I**, 560, 565

Gay, Sydney Howard, **Supp. I, Part 1,** 158

Gay, Walter, **IV**, 317

"Gay Chaps at the Bar" (Brooks), **Supp. III, Part 1,** 74, 75

Gayatri Prayer, The, **III**, 572

Gayle, Addison, Jr., **Supp. I, Part 1,** 70

Gaylord, Winfield R., **III**, 579–580

"Gazebo" (Carver), **Supp. III, Part 1,** 138, 144, 145

Gazzo, Michael V., **III**, 155

Geddes, Virgil, **III**, 407; **Supp. I, Part 2,** 627

Gefvert, Constance J., **IV**, 166

"Gegenwart" (Goethe), **Supp. II, Part 1,** 26

Gehman, Richard B., **IV**, 307

Geismar, Maxwell, **I**, 119, 333, 426, 520; **II**, 178, 195, 431, 438, 484; **III**, 71, 72, 336; **IV**, 71, 118, 213, 472, 473; **Supp. I, Part 1,** 198

Gelb, Arthur, **III**, 407; **IV**, 380, 401

Gelb, Philip, **III**, 169

Gelfant, Blanche H., **I**, 496; **II**, 27, 41, 53

Gellhorn, Martha, *see* Hemingway, Mrs. Ernest (Martha Gellhorn)

Gelpi, Albert, **I**, 473; **Supp. I, Part 2,** 552, 554, 560

Gelpi, Barbara, **Supp. I, Part 2,** 560

"General Aims and Theories" (Crane), **I**, 389

General Died at Dawn, The (Odets), **Supp. II, Part 2,** 546

"General Gage's Confession" (Freneau), **Supp. II, Part 1,** 257

"General Gage's Soliloquy" (Freneau), **Supp. II, Part 1,** 257

"General William Booth Enters into Heaven" (Lindsay), **Supp. I, Part 2,** 374, 382, 384, 385–388, 389, 392, 399

General William Booth Enters into Heaven and Other Poems (Lindsay), **Supp. I, Part 2,** 379, 381, 382, 387–388, 391

Genesis (biblical book), **I**, 279; **II**, 540

Genesis: Book One (Schwartz), **Supp. II, Part 2,** 640, 651–655

Genet, Jean, **I**, 71, 82, 83, 84

"Genial Host, The" (McCarthy), **II**, 564

"Genie in the Bottle, The" (Wilbur), **Supp. III, Part 2,** 542

"Genius," The (Dreiser), **I**, 497, 501, 509–511, 519

"Genius, The" (MacLeish), **III**, 19

"Genteel Tradition in American Philosophy, The" (Santayana), **I**, 222

Gentle Crafter, The (O. Henry), **Supp. II, Part 1,** 410

"Gentle Lena, The" (Stein), **IV**, 37, 40

Gentleman Caller, The (Williams), **IV**, 383

"Gentleman from Cracow, The" (Singer), **IV**, 9

"Gentleman of Bayou Têche, A" (Chopin), **Supp. I, Part 1,** 211–212

"Gentleman of Shalott, The" (Bishop), **Supp. I, Part 1,** 85, 86

Gentleman's Agreement (Hobson), **III**, 151

Gentleman's Magazine, **II**, 114

"Genuine Man, The" (Emerson), **II**, 10

"Geode" (Frost), **II**, 161

Geographical History of America, The (Stein), **IV**, 31, 45

Geography and Plays (Stein), **IV**, 29–30, 32, 43, 44

Geography of a Horse Dreamer (Shepard), **Supp. III, Part 2,** 432

Geography III (Bishop), **Supp. I, Part 1,** 72, 73, 76, 82, 93, 94, 95

George Bernard Shaw: His Plays (Mencken), **III**, 102

George II, King, **I**, 352, 547

George III, King, **II**, 120; **Supp. I, Part 1,** 102, **Part 2,** 404, 504, 506, 507

George V, King, **II**, 337

George, Henry, **II**, 276; **Supp. I, Part 2,** 518

"George Thurston" (Bierce), **I**, 202

George's Mother (Crane), **I**, 408

Georgia Boy (Caldwell), **I**, 288, 305–306, 308, 309, 310

"Georgia: Invisible Empire State" (Du Bois), **Supp. II, Part 1,** 179

"Georgia Night" (Toomer), **Supp. III, Part 2,** 481

Georgia Scenes (Longstreet), **II**, 70, 313; **Supp. I, Part 1,** 352

Gérando, Joseph Marie de, **II**, 10

"German Girls! The German Girls!, The" (MacLeish), **III**, 16

"German Refugee, The" (Malamud), **Supp. I, Part 2,** 436, 437

"Germany's Reichswehr" (Agee), **I**, 35

Germer, Rudolf, **I**, 590

Germinal (Zola), **III**, 318, 322

"Gerontian" (Eliot), **I**, 569, 574, 577, 578, 585, 588; **III**, 9, 435, 436

Gerry, Elbridge, **Supp. I, Part 2,** 486

Gershwin, Ira, **Supp. I, Part 1,** 281

Gerstenberger, Donna, **III**, 289

Gerstner, John H., **I**, 565

Gertrude Stein (Sprigge), **IV**, 31

Guard of Honor (Cozzens), **I**, 370–372, 375, 376–377, 378, 379

Guardian Angel, The (Holmes), **Supp. I, Part 1,** 315–316

Guérin, Maurice de, **I**, 241

"Guerrilla Handbook, A" (Baraka), **Supp. II, Part 1,** 36

Guess Who's Coming to Dinner (film), **Supp. I, Part 1,** 67

"Guests of Mrs. Timms, The" (Jewett), **II**, 408

Guide in the Wilderness, A (Cooper), **I**, 337

Guide to Kulchur (Pound), **III**, 475

Guide to the Ruins (Nemerov), **III**, 269, 270–271, 272

Guillén, Nicolas, **Supp. I, Part 1,** 345

Guillevic, Eugene, **Supp. III, Part 1,** 283

"Guilty Man, The" (Kunitz), **Supp. III, Part 1,** 263

Guimond, James, **IV**, 424

Gulistan (Saadi), **II**, 19

Gullason, Thomas A., **I**, 425, 426

Gullible's Travels (Lardner), **II**, 426, 427

Gulliver's Travels (Swift), **I**, 209, 348, 366; **II**, 301; **Supp. I, Part 2,** 656

"Gulls" (Hayden), **Supp. II, Part 1,** 367

"Gulls, The" (Nemerov), **III**, 272

Günderode: A Translation from the German (Fuller), **Supp. II, Part 1,** 293

Gungrick, Arnold, **II**, 99

"Guns as Keys; and the Great Gate Swings" (Lowell), **II**, 524

Gunter, Richard, **I**, 450

Gurko, Leo, **III**, 62, 72, 384

Gurwitsch, Aron, **II**, 366

Gussow, Mel, **I**, 95; **IV**, 401

Gutenberg, Johann, **Supp. I, Part 2,** 392

Guthrie, Ramon, **II**, 460

Guthrie, Tyrone, **IV**, 376

Gutman, Herbert, **Supp. I, Part 1,** 47

Guttmann, Allen, **I**, 166

Guy Domville (James), **II**, 331

Gwynn, Frederick I., **II**, 75; **III**, 574

Gypsy Ballads (trans. Hughes), **Supp. I, Part 1,** 345

H.D., *see* Doolittle, Hilda

"H.D.: A Note on Her Critical Reputation" (Bryher), **Supp. I, Part 1,** 275

"H.D.: A Preliminary Checklist" (Bryher and Roblyer), **Supp. I, Part 1,** 275

"H.D.'s 'Hermetic Definition' " (Quinn), **Supp. I, Part 1,** 275

H. L. Mencken, a Portrait from Memory (Angoff), **III**, 107

"H. L. Mencken Meets a Poet in the West Side Y.M.C.A." (White), **Supp. I, Part 2,** 677

H. L. Mencken: The American Scene (Cairns), **III**, 119

H. M. Pulham, Esquire (Marquand), **II**, 482–483; **III**, 58, 59, 65, 68–69

Haardt, Sara, *see* Mencken, Mrs. H. L. (Sara Haardt)

Haas, Robert B., **IV**, 47

Habakkuk (Hebrew prophet and biblical book), **III**, 200, 347

"Habit" (James), **II**, 351

Hackett, Francis, **I**, 120; **Supp. I, Part 2,** 626

Haeckel, Ernst Heinrich, **II**, 480

Hagedorn, Hermann, **III**, 525

Hagemann, E. R., **I**, 425

Hagen, Beulah, **Supp. I, Part 2,** 679

Hager, Philip E., **III**, 574

Haggard, Rider, **III**, 189

Hagopian, John V., **Supp. I, Part 1,** 70

Hagoromo (play), **III**, 466

Haigh-Wood, Vivienne Haigh, *see* Eliot, Mrs. T. S. (Vivienne Haigh Haigh-Wood)

Haines, George, IV, **I**, 444, 450; **IV**, 48

Haines, Paul, **II**, 148

"Hair, The" (Carver), **Supp. III, Part 1,** 137

"Haircut" (Lardner), **II**, 430, 436

Hairy Ape, The (O'Neill), **III**, 391, 392, 393

"Haïta the Shepherd" (Bierce), **I**, 203

Haldeman, Anna, **Supp. I, Part 1,** 2

Hale, Edward Everett, **Supp. I, Part 2,** 425, 584

Hale, John Parker, **Supp. I, Part 2,** 685

Hale, Nathan G., Jr., **II**, 365

Hale family, **III**, 52

Haley, Alex, **Supp. I, Part 1,** 47, 66

"Half a Century Gone" (Lowell), **II**, 554

Half-Century of Conflict, A (Parkman), **Supp. II, Part 2,** 600, 607, 610

"Half Deity" (Moore), **III**, 210, 214, 215

"Halfway" (Rich), **Supp. I, Part 2,** 553

Haliburton, Thomas Chandler, **II**, 301; **IV**, 193; **Supp. I, Part 2,** 411

Halifax, Lord, **II**, 111

Hall, Donald, **I**, 542, 567; **III**, 194, 217; **Supp. I, Part 2,** 681, 706

Hall, James, **I**, 542; **II**, 313; **Supp. I, Part 2,** 584, 585

Hall, Max, **II**, 125

Halleck, Fitz-Greene, **Supp. I, Part 1,** 156, 158

Haller, Robert S., **IV**, 95

Hallock, Rev. Moses, **Supp. I, Part 1,** 153

Hallwas, John E., **Supp. I, Part 2,** 402, 454, 478

Hamburger, Philip, **III**, 72

Hamerik, Asger, **Supp. I, Part 1,** 356

Hamilton, Alexander, **I**, 485; **Supp. I, Part 2,** 456, 483, 509

Hamilton, Alice, **IV**, 235; **Supp. I, Part 1,** 5

Hamilton, Hamish, **Supp. I, Part 2,** 617

Hamilton, Kenneth, **I**, 95; **III**, 574; **IV**, 235

Hamilton, Lady Emma, **II**, 524

Hamilton, Walton, **Supp. I, Part 2,** 632

"Hamlen Brook" (Wilbur), **Supp. III, Part 2,** 564

"Hamlet" (Laforgue), **I**, 573; **III**, 11

Hamlet (Miller and Fraenkel), **III**, 178, 183

Hamlet (Shakespeare), **I**, 53, 183, 205, 377, 586–587; **II**, 158, 531; **III**, 7, 11, 12, 183; **IV**, 116, 131, 227; **Supp. I, Part 1,** 369, **Part 2,** 422, 457, 471

Hamlet, The (Faulkner), **II**, 69–71, 73, 74; **IV**, 131

"Hamlet and His Problems" (Eliot), **I**, 586–587

Hamlet of A. MacLeish, The (MacLeish), **III**, 11–12, 14, 15, 18

Hammar, George, **III**, 312

Hammett, Dashiell, **IV**, 286; **Supp. I, Part 1,** 286, 289, 291, 292, 293, 294, 295; **Supp. III, Part 1,** 91

Hampshire *Gazette*, **Supp. I, Part 1,** 152

Hampson, Alfred Leete, **I**, 472

"Hamrick's Polar Bear" (Caldwell), **I**, 309–310

Hams, William T., **Supp. I, Part 1,** 46

Hamsun, Knut, **IV**, 22

Hanau, Stella, **III**, 406

Hancock, John, **Supp. I, Part 2,** 524

Handcarved Coffins: A Nonfiction Account of an American Crime (Capote), **Supp. III, Part 1,** 131

Hascom, Leslie, **III**, 169
Hasley, Louis, **Supp. I, Part 2,** 627, 681
Hassan, Ihab, **I**, 166; **II**, 608; **III**, 48, 192, 243; **IV**, 99–100, 115, 119; **Supp. I, Part 1,** 198
Hasty-Pudding, The (Barlow), **Supp. II, Part 1,** 74, 77–80
Hatfield, James T., **II**, 509
Hatfield, Ruth, **II**, 53
Hatful of Rain, A (Gazzo), **III**, 155
Hathorne, Captain Nathaniel, **II**, 223
Hathorne, Elizabeth Manning, **II**, 223, 224
Hathorne family, **II**, 223, 225
"Haunted Landscape" (Ashbery), **Supp. III, Part 1,** 22
"Haunted Mind, The" (Hawthorne), **II**, 230–231
"Haunted Oak, The" (Dunbar), **Supp. II, Part 1,** 207, 208
"Haunted Palace, The" (Poe), **III**, 421
"Haunted Valley, The" (Bierce), **I**, 200
Hauptmann, Gerhart, **III**, 472
Haven's End (Marquand), **III**, 55, 56, 63, 68
Havighurst, Walter, **Supp. I, Part 2,** 478
"Having Lost My Sons, I Confront the Wreckage of the Moon: Christmas, 1960" (Wright), **Supp. III, Part 2,** 600
"Having Snow" (Schwartz), **Supp. II, Part 2,** 652
Hawk in the Rain, The (Hughes), **Supp. I, Part 2,** 537, 540
Hawk Moon (Shepard), **Supp. III, Part 2,** 445
Hawke, David Freeman, **Supp. I, Part 2,** 511, 516
Hawkes, John, **I**, 113; **III**, 360; **Supp. III, Part 1,** 2
Hawkins, William, **II**, 587
Hawk's Well, The (Yeats), **III**, 459–460
Hawley, Joseph, **I**, 546
Hawley, Michael, **Supp. I, Part 2,** 627
Hawthorne (James), **II**, 372–378
"Hawthorne" (Lowell), **II**, 550
"Hawthorne in Solitude" (Cowley), **Supp. II, Part 1,** 143
Hawthorne, Julian, **II**, 225, 245; **Supp. I, Part 1,** 38
Hawthorne, Manning, **II**, 509
Hawthorne, Mrs. Nathaniel (Sophia Peabody), **II**, 224, 244, 245; **III**, 75, 86

Hawthorne, Nathaniel, **I**, 106, 204, 211, 340, 355, 363, 384, 413, 458, 561–562; **II**, 7, 8, 40, 60, 63, 74, 89, 127–128, 138, 142, 198, **223–246**, 255, 259, 264, 267, 272, 274, 277, 281, 282, 295, 307, 309, 311, 313, 322, 324, 326, 340, 402, 408, 446, 501, 545; **III**, 51, 81–82, 83, 84, 85, 87, 88, 91, 92, 113, 316, 359, 412, 415, 421, 438, 453, 454, 507, 565, 572; **IV**, 2, 4, 167, 172, 179, 194, 333, 345, 453; **Supp. I, Part 1,** 38, 147, 188, 197, 317, 372, **Part 2,** 420, 421, 545, 579, 580, 582, 587, 595, 596; **Supp. III, Part 2,** 501
Hawthorne, Rose, **II**, 225
Hawthorne, Una, **II**, 225
Hay, John, **I**, 1, 10, 12, 14–15; **Supp. I, Part 1,** 352
Hay, Mrs. John, **I**, 14
Hayakawa, S. I., **I**, 448; **Supp. I, Part 1,** 315
Hayashi, Tetsumaro, **III**, 168
Hayden, Robert, **Supp. II, Part 1,** 361–383
Haydn, Hiram, **IV**, 100, 358
Haydock, J., **II**, 484
Hayes, Rutherford B., **Supp. I, Part 2,** 419
Hayford, Harrison, **III**, 95, 96
Hayman, Ronald, **III**, 169
Hayne, Paul Hamilton, **Supp. I, Part 1,** 352, 354, 355, 360, 372
Haywood, Bill, **I**, 483
Hazard, Grace, **II**, 530
Hazard of New Fortunes, A (Howells), **II**, 275, 276, 286–287, 290
Hazel, Robert, **I**, 311
Hazen, General W. B., **I**, 192, 193
Hazlitt, William, **I**, 58, 378; **II**, 315
Hazo, Samuel, **I**, 386, 404
"He" (Porter), **III**, 434, 435
"He Came Also Still" (Zukofsky), **Supp. III, Part 2,** 612
He Who Gets Slapped (Andreyev), **II**, 425
"Head-Hunter, The" (O. Henry), **Supp. II, Part 1,** 403
Headings, Philip R., **I**, 590
"Headless Hawk, The" (Capote), **Supp. III, Part 1,** 124
Headlines (Williams), **IV**, 381
Headlong Hall (Peacock), **Supp. I, Part 1,** 307
Headmaster, The (McPhee), **Supp. III, Part 1,** 291, 294, 298

Headsman, The (Cooper), **I**, 345–346
Heal, Edith, **IV**, 423
Healy, Tim, **II**, 129, 137
"Hear the Nightingale Sing" (Gordon), **II**, 200
Hearn, Lafcadio, **I**, 211; **II**, 311
Hearst, William Randolph, **I**, 198, 207, 208; **IV**, 298
Hearst's International (publication), **II**, 87
"Heart and the Lyre, The" (Bogan), **Supp. III, Part 1,** 65
Heart for the Gods of Mexico, A (Aiken), **I**, 54
Heart Is a Lonely Hunter, The (McCullers), **II**, 586, 588–593, 604, 605
"Heart of Darkness" (Conrad), **I**, 575, 578; **II**, 595
Heart of Happy Hollow, The (Dunbar), **Supp. II, Part 1,** 214
Heart of the West (O. Henry), **Supp. II, Part 1,** 410
Heart to Artemis, The (Bryher), **Supp. I, Part 1,** 259, 275
Heartland, The: Ohio, Indiana, Illinois (Havighurst), **Supp. I, Part 2,** 478
Heartman, Charles F., **III**, 431
"Hearts and Heads" (Ransom), **Supp. I, Part 1,** 373
"Hearts' and Flowers'" (MacLeish), **III**, 8
Heart's Needle (Snodgrass), **I**, 400
Heart-Shape in the Dust (Hayden), **Supp. II, Part 1,** 365, 366
Heathcote, Anne, *see* De Lancey, Mrs. James
"Heathen Chinee, The" (Harte), **Supp. II, Part 1,** 350–351, 352
Heathen Days, 1890–1936 (Mencken), **III**, 100, 111
Heavenly Conversation, The (Mather), **Supp. II, Part 2,** 460
"Heavy Bear Who Goes with Me, The" (Schwartz), **Supp. II, Part 2,** 646
Hecht, Anthony, **IV**, 138, 143; **Supp. III, Part 2,** 541, 561
Hecht, Ben, **I**, 103; **II**, 42; **Supp. I, Part 2,** 646
Hecht, S. Theodore, **Supp. III, Part 2,** 614
Heckewelder, John, **II**, 503
"Hedge Island" (Lowell), **II**, 524
Hedges, William, **Supp. I, Part 1,** 148
Hedges, William I., **II**, 311–312, 318

Keats (cont.) **III,** 4, 10, 45, 122, 133–134, 179, 214, 237, 272, 275, 469, 485, 523; **IV,** 360, 405, 416; **Supp. I, Part 1,** 82, 183, 266, 267, 312, 349, 362, 363, 365, **Part 2,** 410, 422, 424, 539, 552, 675, 719, 720; **Supp. III, Part 1,** 73

"Keela, the Outcast Indian Maiden" (Welty), **IV,** 263

"Keep A-Inchin' Along" (Van Vechten), **Supp. II, Part 2,** 744

"Keeping Informed in D.C." (Nemerov), **III,** 287

"'Keeping Their World Large'" (Moore), **III,** 201–202

Kees, Weldon, **Supp. I, Part 1,** 199

Kegley, Charles W., **III,** 313

Keith, Minor C., **I,** 483

Keller, A. G., **III,** 108

Keller, Dean H., **Supp. I, Part 1,** 147

Keller, Helen, **I,** 254, 258

Keller, Karl, **Supp. I, Part 2,** 705

Kelley, Florence, **Supp. I, Part 1,** 5, 7

Kellogg, Paul U., **Supp. I, Part 1,** 5, 7, 12

Kellogg, Reverend Edwin H., **III,** 200

Kelly, **II,** 464

Kemble, Gouverneur, **II,** 298

Kemble, Peter, **II,** 298

Kemler, Edgar, **III,** 121

Kempton-Wace Letters, The (London and Strunsky), **II,** 465

Kendle, Burton, **Supp. I, Part 1,** 199

Kennard, Jean E., **I,** 143

Kennedy, Albert J., **Supp. I, Part 1,** 19, 27

Kennedy, Arthur, **III,** 153

Kennedy, John F., **I,** 136, 170; **II,** 49, 152–153; **III,** 38, 41, 42, 234, 411, 415, 581; **III,** 229; **Supp. I, Part 1,** 291, **Part 2,** 496

Kennedy, John Pendleton, **II,** 313

Kennedy, Mrs. John F., **I,** 136

Kennedy, Raymond A., **IV,** 425

Kennedy, Richard S., **IV,** 472, 473

Kennedy, Robert F., **I,** 294; **Supp. I, Part 1,** 52

Kennedy, William Sloane, **Supp. I, Part 2,** 705

Kenner, Hugh, **I,** 590; **III,** 217, 475, 478; **IV,** 412, 424, 425; **Supp. I, Part 1,** 255, 275

Kent, Charles W., **Supp. I, Part 1,** 373

Kent, Rockwell, **III,** 96

Kenton, Edna, **I,** 263; **II,** 340

Kenyon Review (publication), **I,** 170, 174; **II,** 536–537; **III,** 497, 498; **IV,** 141

Keokuk *Evening Post* (newspaper), **IV,** 194

Kepler, Johannes, **III,** 484; **IV,** 18

Keppel, Frederick P., **I,** 214

"Kéramos" (Longfellow), **II,** 494

Kéramos and Other Poems (Long-fellow), **II,** 490

Kermode, Frank, **IV,** 95, 133, 143, 449

Kern, Jerome, **II,** 427

Kerner, David, **I,** 143

Kerouac, Jack, **III,** 174; **Supp. II, Part 1,** 31, 307, 309, 318, 328; **Supp. III, Part 1,** 91–94, 96, 100, **217–234**

Kerr, Orpheus C. (pseudonym), *see* Newell, Henry

Kerr, Walter, **III,** 407

Kesey, Ken, **III,** 558; **Supp. III, Part 1,** 217

Kessler, Jascha, **I,** 189

"Key, The" (Welty), **IV,** 262

Key to Uncle Tom's Cabin, A (Stowe), **Supp. I, Part 2,** 580

"Key West" (Crane), **I,** 400

Key West: An Island Sheaf (Crane), **I,** 385, 399–402

Khrushchev, Nikita, **I,** 136

Kid, The (Aiken), **I,** 61

Kid, The (Chaplin), **I,** 386

Kidder, Tracy, **Supp. III, Part 1,** 302

Kiely, Benedict, **I,** 143

Kieran, John, **II,** 417

Kierkegaard, Sören Aabye, **II,** 229; **III,** 292, 305, 309, 572; **IV,** 438, 491

Kieseritsky, L., **III,** 252

"Killed at Resaca" (Bierce), **I,** 202

"Killers, The" (Hemingway), **II,** 249

Killing of Sister George, The (Marcus), **Supp. I, Part 1,** 277

Kilmer, Joyce, **Supp. I, Part 2,** 387

Kim, Kichung, **Supp. I, Part 1,** 70

Kimball, Arthur, **Supp. I, Part 1,** 148

"Kin" (Welty), **IV,** 277

Kind of Order, A Kind of Folly, A: Essays and Conversations (Kunitz), **Supp. III, Part 1,** 262, 268

"Kind Sir: These Woods" (Sexton), **Supp. II, Part 2,** 673

Kindred Spirits: Knickerbocker Writers and American Artists, 1807–1855 (Callow), **Supp. I, Part 1,** 173

Kindt, Kathleen A., **Supp. I, Part 1,** 70

Kinfolk (Buck), **Supp. II, Part 1,** 126

King, Alexander, **IV,** 287

King, Clarence, **I,** 1

King, Ernest, **Supp. I, Part 2,** 491

King, Fisher, **II,** 425

King, Lawrence T., **II,** 222

King, Martin Luther, **Supp. I, Part 1,** 52, 60, 65

King, Starr, **Supp. II, Part 1,** 341, 342

King Coffin (Aiken), **I,** 53–54, 57

King Jasper (Robinson), **III,** 523

King Lear (Shakespeare), **I,** 538; **II,** 540, 551

King Leopold's Soliloquy (Twain), **IV,** 208

"King of Folly Island" (Jewett), **II,** 394

"King of the Bingo Game" (Ellison), **Supp. II, Part 1,** 235, 238, 240–241

"King of the Clock Tower" (Yeats), **III,** 473

"King of the Desert, The" (O'Hara), **III,** 369

"King of the River" (Kunitz), **Supp. III, Part 1,** 263, 267–268

"King of the Sea" (Marquand), **III,** 60

"King over the Water" (Blackmur), **Supp. II, Part 1,** 107

"King Pandar" (Blackmur), **Supp. II, Part 1,** 92, 102

King, Queen, Knave (Nabokov), **III,** 251

"King Volmer and Elsie" (Whittier), **Supp. I, Part 2,** 696

Kingdom of Earth (Williams), **IV,** 382, 386, 387, 388, 391, 393, 398

"Kingdom of Earth, The" (Williams), **IV,** 384

"Kingfishers, The" (Olson), **Supp. II, Part 2,** 557, 558–563, 582

King's Henchman, The (Millay), **III,** 138–139

"King's Missive, The" (Whittier), **Supp. I, Part 2,** 694

Kingsblood Royal (Lewis), **II,** 456

Kingsbury, John, **Supp. I, Part 1,** 8

Kingsley, Sidney, **Supp. I, Part 1,** 277, 281

Kinmont, Alexander, **Supp. I, Part 2,** 588–589

Kinnamon, Kenneth, **Supp. I, Part 1,** 69

Kinnell, Galway, **Supp. III, Part 1,** **235–256, Part 2,** 541

Kinsey, Alfred, **IV,** 230

"Kipling" (Trilling), **Supp. III, Part 2,** 495

Le courant abolitioniste dans la littérature américaine de 1808 à 1861 (Rivière), **Supp. I, Part 2,** 426

Le cultivateur américain: Étude sur l'oeuvre de Saint John de Crèvecoeur (Rice), **Supp. I, Part 1,** 252

Le Style Apollinaire (Zukofsky), **Supp. III, Part 2,** 616

"Le marais du cygne" (Whittier), **Supp. I, Part 2,** 687

Lea, Luke, **IV,** 248

"LEADBELLY GIVES AN AUTO-GRAPH" (Baraka), **Supp. II, Part 1,** 49

Leaflets (Rich), **Supp. I, Part 2,** 551, 556–557

"League of American Writers, The: Communist Organizational Activity Among American Writers 1929–1942" (Wolfe), **Supp. III, Part 2,** 568

League of Brightened Philistines and Other Papers, The (Farrell), **II,** 49

Leaks, Sylvester, **Supp. I, Part 1,** 70

Leaning Tower and Other Stories, The (Porter), **III,** 433, 442, 443–447

"Leaning Tower, The" (Porter), **III,** 442, 443, 446–447

Lear, Edward, **III,** 428, 536

Learned Ladies, The (Molière, trans. Wilbur), **Supp. III, Part 2,** 560

"Learning a Dead Language" (Merwin), **Supp. III, Part 1,** 345

"Learning to Read" (Harper), **Supp. II, Part 1,** 201–202

Leary, Lewis, **I,** 263; **III,** 478; **IV,** 212, 213; **Supp. I, Part 1,** 226, 319, 373, **Part 2,** 706

Leather-Stocking Tales, The (Cooper), **I,** 335

Leatherwood God, The (Howells), **II,** 276, 277, 288

Leaves from the Notebook of a Tamed Cynic (Niebuhr), **III,** 293

Leaves of Grass (Whitman), **II,** 8; **IV,** 331, 332, 333, 334, 335, 336, 340, 341–342, 348, 350, 405, 464; **Supp. I, Part 1,** 365, **Part 2,** 416, 579; **Supp. III, Part 1,** 156

"Leaves of Grass" (Whitman), **IV,** 463

Leaves of the Tree, The (Masters), **Supp. I, Part 2,** 460

"Leaving" (Wilbur), **Supp. III, Part 2,** 563

Leavis, F. R., **I,** 263, 522; **III,** 462–463, 475, 478; **Supp. I, Part 2,** 536

"Leavis-Snow Controversy, The" (Trilling), **Supp. III, Part 2,** 512

Leavitt, Jonathan, **I,** 564

Lechlitner, Ruth, **IV,** 424

"Lecture, The" (Singer), **IV,** 21

"LECTURE PAST DEAD CATS" (Baraka), **Supp. II, Part 1,** 52

Lectures in America (Stein), **IV,** 27, 32, 33, 35, 36, 41, 42

"Lectures on Poetry" (Bryant), **Supp. I, Part 1,** 159, 161

Lectures on Rhetoric (Blair), **II,** 8

"Leda and the Swan" (Yeats), **III,** 347

Lee, Brian, **Supp. I, Part 1,** 70

Lee, C. P., **Supp. I, Part 2,** 402

Lee, Charlotte I, **III,** 550

Lee, Don L., *see* Madhubuti, Haki R.

Lee, Gypsy Rose, **II,** 586; **III,** 161

Lee, James W., **III,** 574

Lee, Robert E., **II,** 150, 206; **IV,** 126; **Supp. I, Part 2,** 471, 486

Lee, Samuel, **IV,** 158

Lee (Masters), **Supp. I, Part 2,** 471

Leeds, Barry, H., **III,** 48

Leeds, Daniel, **II,** 110

Leeds, Titan, **II,** 110, 111

"Lees of Happiness, The" (Fitzgerald), **II,** 88

LeFevre, Louis, **II,** 318

Left Front Anvil (publication), **IV,** 476

Legacy of Fear, A (Farrell), **II,** 39

Legacy of the Civil War, The: Meditations on the Centennial (Warren), **IV,** 236

"Legal Tender Act, The" (Adams), **I,** 5

"Legend of Duluoz, The" (Kerouac), **Supp. III, Part 1,** 218, 226, 227, 229

"Legend of Lillian Hellman, The" (Kazin), **Supp. I, Part 1,** 297

"Legend of Monte del Diablo, The" (Harte), **Supp. II, Part 1,** 339

"Legend of Sammtstadt, A" (Harte), **Supp. II, Part 1,** 355

"Legend of Sleepy Hollow, The" (Irving), **II,** 306–308

"Legendary Mr. Thurber, The" (Walker), **Supp. I, Part 2,** 627

Legends (Lowell), **II,** 525–526

Legends of New England (Whittier), **Supp. I, Part 2,** 684, 692

Legends of the West (Hall), **II,** 313

Legge, James, **III,** 472

Leggett, William, **Supp. I, Part 1,** 157

Lehan, Richard, **I,** 520; **II,** 100

Lehmann, Paul, **III,** 311, 313

Leibniz, Gottfried Wilhelm von, **II,** 103; **III,** 428

Leibowitz, Herbert A., **I,** 386, 404; **IV,** 23

Leisy, E. E., **II,** 318

Leivick, H., **IV,** 6

Lekachman, Robert, **Supp. I, Part 2,** 648

Leland, Charles, **Supp. II, Part 1,** 193

Leland, Charles Godfrey, **I,** 257

Lemay, J. A. Leo, **II,** 125

Lenin, V. I., **I,** 366, 439, 440; **III,** 14–15, 262, 475; **IV,** 429, 436, 443–444; **Supp. I, Part 2,** 647

"Lenore" (Poe), **III,** 411

Leonidas, King, **II,** 121

"Leopard Man's Story, The" (London), **II,** 475

Leopardi, Giacomo, **II,** 543

Lerner, Arthur, **I,** 70

Lerner, Max, **I,** 237; **III,** 60; **Supp. I, Part 2,** 629, 630, 631, 647, 650, 654

Les Misérables (Hugo), **II,** 179; **Supp. I, Part 1,** 280

Leskov, Nikolai, **IV,** 299

Lessing, Gotthold, **Supp. I, Part 2,** 422

"Lesson, The" (Dunbar), **Supp. II, Part 1,** 199

Lesson of the Masters: An Anthology of the Novel from Cervantes to Hemingway (ed. Cowley–Hugo), **Supp. II, Part 1,** 140

"Lesson on Concealment, A" (Brown), **Supp. I, Part 1,** 133

"'Lesson on Concealment, A': Brockden Brown's Method in Fiction" (Berthoff), **Supp. I, Part 1,** 148

"Let America Be America Again" (Hughes), **Supp. I, Part 1,** 331

"Let No Charitable Hope" (Wylie), **Supp. I, Part 2,** 713–714, 729

Let Us Now Praise Famous Men (Agee and Evans), **I,** 25, 27, 35, 36–39, 42, 45, 293

Let Your Mind Alone! (Thurber), **Supp. I, Part 2,** 608

Létargeez, J., **IV,** 259

Letter (publication), **I,** 206

"Letter…" (Whittier), **Supp. I, Part 2,** 687

Lowell (cont.) 530, 532, 534, 551; **III,** 409, 431; **IV,** 129, 171, 175, 180, 182–183, 186; **Supp. I, Part 1,** 168, 299, 300, 303, 306, 311 312, 317, 318, 362, **Part 2, 404–426; Supp. II, Part 1,** 197, 291, 352

Lowell, Mrs. James Russell (Maria White), **Supp. I, Part 2,** 405, 406, 414, 424

Lowell, Mrs. Robert (Elizabeth Hardwick), **II,** 365, 543, 554, 566, 584; **IV,** 425

Lowell, Mrs. Robert (Jean Stafford), **II,** 537

Lowell, Percival, **II,** 513, 525, 534

Lowell, Robert, **I,** 172, 381, 382, 400, 442, 521, 544–545, 550; **II,** 371, 376, 377, 384, 386–387, 390, 532, **534–557; III,** 39, 44, 142, 508, 527, 528–529, 606; **IV,** 120, 138, 143, 259, 402, 424, 430; **Supp. I, Part 1,** 89, 97, **Part 2,** 538, 543, 554; **Supp. III, Part 1,** 6, 64, 84, 138, 147, 193, 194, 197–202, 205–208, **Part 2,** 541, 543, 555, 561, 599

Lowell, Rose, **Supp. I, Part 2,** 409

Lowell family, **II,** 403

"Lowell" (Brownell), **Supp. I, Part 2,** 426

Lowell and France (Stewart), **Supp. I, Part 2,** 426

"Lowell and Longinus" (Pritchard), **Supp. I, Part 2,** 426

"Lowell as Critic" (Robertson), **Supp. I, Part 2,** 426

"Lowell on Thoreau" (Warren), **Supp. I, Part 2,** 426

Lower Depths, The (Gorki), **III,** 402

"Lower the Standard" (Shapiro), **Supp. II, Part 2,** 715

Lowes, John Livingston, **II,** 512, 516, 532, 533; **IV,** 453, 455

"Low-Lands" (Pynchon), **Supp. II, Part 2,** 620, 624

Lowle, Percival, **Supp. I, Part 2,** 404

Lowth, Richard, **II,** 8

Loy, Mina, **III,** 194

Loyola, Ignatius, **IV,** 151

"Luani of the Jungle" (Hughes), **Supp. I, Part 1,** 328

Lubbock, Percy, **I,** 504; **II,** 337, 340, 341; **IV,** 308, 314, 319, 322, 330

Lubin, Isidor, **Supp. I, Part 2,** 632

Lucas, Victoria (pseudonym), *see* Plath, Sylvia

Lucid, Robert F., **III,** 48

"Lucid Eye in Silver Town, The" (Updike), **IV,** 218

"Lucinda Matlock" (Masters), **Supp. I, Part 2,** 461, 465

Luck of Barry Lyndon, The (Thackeray), **II,** 290

"Luck of Roaring Camp, The" (Harte), **Supp. II, Part 1,** 335, 344, 345–347

Lucretius, **I,** 59; **II,** 162, 163; **III,** 600, 610–611, 612; **Supp. I, Part 1,** 363

Lucy, Saint, **II,** 211

Lucy Gayheart (Cather), **I,** 331

Ludwig, Jack, **I,** 166; **III,** 48

Ludwig, Richard M., **II,** 125, 533

Luke (biblical book), **III,** 606

"Luke Havergal" (Robinson), **III,** 524

Luks, George, **IV,** 411

"Lullaby" (Auden), **Supp. II, Part 1,** 9

"Lullaby" (Bishop), **Supp. I, Part 1,** 85

"Lulls" (Walker), **Supp. III, Part 2,** 525

Lulu's Library (Alcott), **Supp. I, Part 1,** 43

Lume Spento, A (Pound), **III,** 470

"Lumumba's Grave" (Hughes), **Supp. I, Part 1,** 344

Lupercal (Hughes), **Supp. I, Part 2,** 540

Luria, Isaac, **IV,** 7

Lustgarten, Edith, **III,** 107

Luther, Martin, **II,** 11–12, 506; **III,** 306, 607; **IV,** 490

Lyceumite (magazine), **III,** 579

"Lycidas" (Milton), **II,** 540; **IV,** 347; **Supp. I, Part 1,** 370

Lydenberg, John, **I,** 380

Lyford, Harry, **Supp. I, Part 2,** 679

"Lying" (Wilbur), **Supp. III, Part 2,** 547, 562

"Lying in a Hammock at William Duffy's Farm in Pine Island, Minnesota" (Wright), **Supp. III, Part 2,** 589, 599, 600

Lyly, John, **III,** 536; **Supp. I, Part 1,** 369

Lynch, William James, **II,** 53

"Lynching, The" (McKay), **Supp. I, Part 1,** 63

"Lynching of Jube Benson, The" (Dunbar), **Supp. II, Part 1,** 214

"Lynching Song" (Hughes), **Supp. I, Part 1,** 331

Lynd, Staughton, **Supp. I, Part 1,** 27, **Part 2,** 525

Lynen, John, **II,** 125

Lynn, Kenneth S., **II,** 294; **III,** 336; **IV,** 213

Lyon, Kate, **I,** 409; **II,** 138, 143, 144

"Lyonnesse" (Plath), **Supp. I, Part 2,** 541

Lyons, Charles R., **I,** 95

Lyrical Ballads (Wordsworth), **III,** 583; **IV,** 120

Lyrics of Love and Laughter (Dunbar), **Supp. II, Part 1,** 207

Lyrics of Lowly Life (Dunbar), **Supp. II, Part 1,** 197, 199, 200, 207

Lyrics of the Hearthside (Dunbar), **Supp. II, Part 1,** 206

Lytle, Andrew, **I,** 426; **II,** 222; **IV,** 125, 143; **Supp. II, Part 1,** 139

Lytton of Knebworth, *see* Bulwer-Lytton, Edward George

Mabbott, Thomas O., **III,** 431

McAlmon, Mrs. Robert (Winifred Ellerman), **III,** 194

McAlmon, Mrs. Robert, *see* Ellerman, Winifred

McAlmon, Robert, **IV,** 404; **Supp. I, Part 1,** 259; **Supp. III, Part 2,** 614

McCall, Dan, **IV,** 497

McCall's (magazine), **III,** 58

Macaulay, Catherine, **Supp. I, Part 2,** 522

Macaulay, Thomas, **II,** 15–16; **III,** 113, 591–592

McCarthy, Harold T., **Supp. I, Part 1,** 70

McCarthy, Joseph, **Supp. I, Part 1,** 294, 295, **Part 2,** 444, 611, 612, 620

McCarthy, Mary, **II,** 558–584; **III,** 169, 407; **Supp. I, Part 1,** 84

McCarthy, Senator Joseph, **I,** 31, 492; **II,** 562, 568

Macbeth (Shakespeare), **I,** 271; **IV,** 227; **Supp. I, Part 1,** 67, **Part 2,** 457

McClatchy, J. D., **Supp. I, Part 1,** 97

McClellan, John L., **I,** 493

McClure, Michael, **Supp. II, Part 1,** 32

McClure, S. S., **I,** 313; **II,** 465; **III,** 327

McClure's Magazine, **I,** 313, 322

McCluskey, John, **Supp. I, Part 1,** 70

McConnell, Fanny, *see* Ellison, Fanny McConnell

McCormack, T., **III,** 242

McCullers, Carson, **I,** 113, 190, 211; **II,** 585–608; **IV,** 282, 384, 385, 386, 400; **Supp. II, Part 1,** 17

"Market" (Hayden), **Supp. II, Part 1,** 368, 369

Marketplace, The (Frederic), II, 145–146

Markham, Edwin, I, 199, 207

Markings (Hammarskjold), **Supp. II, Part 1,** 26

Marks, Alison, **Supp. I, Part 2,** 660

Marks, Barry A., I, 435, 438, 442, 446, 450

Markus, Thomas B., I, 96

Marlowe, Christopher, I, 68, 368, 384; II, 590; III, 259, 491; **Supp. I, Part 2,** 422

Marmee: the Mother of Little Women (Salyer), **Supp. I, Part 1,** 46

Marne, The (Wharton), IV, 319, 320

Marquand, J. P., I, 362, 375; II, 459, 482–483; III, **50–73,** 383; **Supp. I, Part 1,** 196

Marquand, Mrs. John P. (Adelaide Hooker), III, 57, 61

Marquand, Mrs. John P. (Christina Sedgwick), III, 54, 57

Marquand, Philip, III, 52

Marquis, Don, **Supp. I, Part 2,** 668

Marriage (Moore), III, 194

"Marriage" (Moore), III, 198–199, 213

"Marriage in the 'Sixties, A" (Rich), **Supp. I, Part 2,** 554

"Marriage of Heaven and Hell, The" (Blake), III, 544–545

Marryat, Captain Frederick, III, 423

"Mars and Hymen" (Freneau), **Supp. II, Part 1,** 258

Marsden, Dora, III, 471

Marsden, Malcolm M., III, 574

Marsena (Frederic), II, 135, 136–137

Marsh, Edward, **Supp. I, Part 1,** 257, 263

Marsh, Mae, **Supp. I, Part 2,** 391

Marsh Island, A (Jewett), II, 405

Marshall, George, III, 3

Marshall, John, **Supp. I, Part 2,** 455

Marshall, Margaret, III, 455

"Marshall Carpenter" (Masters), **Supp. I, Part 2,** 463

"Marshes of Glynn, The" (Lanier), **Supp. I, Part 1,** 364, 365–368, 370, 373

"'Marshes of Glynn, The': A Study in Symbolic Obscurity" (Ross), **Supp. I, Part 1,** 373

Marta y Maria (Valdes), II, 290

Marthe, Saint, II, 213

Martial, II, 1, 169

Martien, Norman, III, 48

Martin du Gard, Roger, **Supp. I, Part 1,** 51

Martin, Benjamin, **Supp. I, Part 2,** 503

Martin, Carter W., III, 360

Martin, Ernest, II, 509

Martin, Jay, I, 55, 58, 60, 61, 67, 70, 426, 590; III, 307

Martin, John Stephen, **Supp. I, Part 1,** 319

Martin, R. A., III, 169

Martin, Terrence, II, 318; **Supp. I, Part 1,** 148

Martin Eden (London), II, 466, 477–481

Martineau, Harriet, **Supp. II, Part 1,** 282, 288, 294

Martson, Frederic C., II, 293

"Martyr, The" (Porter), III, 454

Martz, Louis L., IV, 151, 156, 165, 166; **Supp. I, Part 1,** 107

Martz, William J., I, 189; II, 557; III, 550

Marvell, Andrew, IV, 135, 151, 156, 161, 253; **Supp. I, Part 1,** 80

Marvell family, IV, 318

Marx, Karl, I, 60, 267, 279, 283, 588; II, 376, 462, 463, 483, 577; IV, 429, 436, 443–444, 469; **Supp. I, Part 2,** 518, 628, 632, 633, 634, 635, 639, 643 645, 646; **Supp. III, Part 2,** 619

Marx, Leo, **Supp. I, Part 1,** 233, 252

Marxism, I, 371, 488, 518; II, 26, 34, 39, 567; III, 3, 17, 27, 30, 262, 297–298, 304, 580, 602; IV, 5, 7, 288, 302, 349, 363, 428, 429, 441; **Supp. I, Part 2,** 493, 518, 600, 628, 633, 635, 643, 645

Marxist Quarterly (publication), **Supp. I, Part 2,** 645

Mary (Jesus' mother), IV, 152; **Supp. I, Part 2,** 581

Mary, Queen, IV, 145, 163

Mary Magdalene, I, 303

"Mary O'Reilly" (Anderson), II, 44

"Mary's Song" (Plath), **Supp. I, Part 2,** 541

Masefield, John, II, 552; III, 523

Mask for Janus, A (Merwin), **Supp. III, Part 1,** 339, 341, 342

Maslow, Abraham, **Supp. I, Part 2,** 540

Mason, Lowell, I, 458

Mason, Otis Tufton, **Supp. I, Part 1,** 18

Mason, Ronald, III, 97

Masque of Mercy, A (Frost), II, 155, 165, 167–168

"Masque of Mummers, The" (MacLeish), III, 18

Masque of Pandora, The (Longfellow), II, 490, 494, 506

Masque of Poets, A (ed. Lathrop), **Supp. I, Part 1,** 365, 368

Masque of Reason, A (Frost), II, 155, 162, 165–167

"Masque of the Red Death, The" (Poe), III, 412, 419, 424

"Mass for the Day of St. Thomas Didymus" (Levertov), **Supp. III, Part 1,** 283

Massa, Ann, **Supp. I, Part 2,** 402

Massachusetts, Its Historians and Its History (Adams), **Supp. I, Part 2,** 484

Massachusetts Quarterly Review (publication), **Supp. I, Part 2,** 420

"Massachusetts to Virginia" (Whittier), **Supp. I, Part 2,** 688–689

"Massacre at Scio, The" (Bryant), **Supp. I, Part 1,** 168

Masses (publication), I, 105

Masses and Man (Toller), I, 479

Massinger, Philip, **Supp. I, Part 2,** 422

"Master Misery" (Capote), **Supp. III, Part 1,** 117

"Master Player, The" (Dunbar), **Supp. II, Part 1,** 200

Masters, Edgar Lee, I, 106, 384, 475, 480, 518; II, 276, 529; III, 505, 576, 579; IV, 352; **Supp. I, Part 2,** 378, 386, 387, 402, **454–478;** **Supp. III, Part 1,** 63, 71, 73, 75

Masters, Ellen Coyne, **Supp. I, Part 2,** 478

Masters, Hardin W., **Supp. I, Part 2,** 468, 478

"Masters and Whitman: A Second Look" (Burgess), **Supp. I, Part 2,** 477

Masters of Sociological Thought (Coser), **Supp. I, Part 2,** 650

Matchmaker, The (Wilder), IV, 357, 369, 370, 374

Mate of the Daylight, The, and Friends Ashore (Jewett), II, 404

Materialism, I, 383; II, 202, 282; III, 394, 396–397, 610, 611

Mather, Cotton, II, 10, 104, 302, 506, 536; III, 442, 455; IV, 144, 152–153, 157; **Supp. I, Part 1,** 102, 117, 174,

"Meeting-House Hill" (Lowell), II, 522, 527

Meiners, R. K., IV, 136, 137, 138, 140, 143

Meister, Charles W., II, 112, 125

"Melancholia" (Dunbar), Supp. II, Part 1, 194

"Melanctha" (Stein), IV, 30, 34, 35, 37, 38–40, 45

"Melancthon" (Moore), III, 212, 215

Melander, Ingrid, Supp. I, Part 2, 548

Melcher, Frederic G., Supp. I, Part 2, 402

Meliboeus-Hipponax (Lowell), see Bigelow Papers, The

Mellaart, James, Supp. I, Part 2, 567

Mellon, Andrew, III, 14

Melodrama Play (Shepard), Supp. III, Part 2, 440–441, 443, 445

Melodramatists, The (Nemerov), III, 268, 281–283, 284

Melting-Pot, The (Zangwill), I, 229

Meltzer, Milton, IV, 189; Supp. I, Part 1, 348

Meiville, Allan, III, 74, 77

Melville, Gansevoort, III, 76

Melville, Herman, I, 104, 106, 211, 288, 340, 343, 348, 354, 355, 561–562; II, 27, 74, 224–225, 228, 230, 232, 236, 255, 259, 271, 272, 277, 281, 295, 307, 311, 319, 320, 321, 418, 477, 497, 539–540, 545; III, 29, 45, 70, 74–98, 359, 438, 453, 454, 507, 562–563, 572, 576; IV, 57, 105, 194, 199, 202, 250, 309, 333, 345, 350, 380, 444, 453; Supp. I, Part 1, 147, 238, 242, 249, 309, 317, 372, Part 2, 383, 495, 579, 580, 582, 602

Melville, Maria Gansevoort, III, 74, 77, 85

Melville, Mrs. Herman (Elizabeth Shaw), III, 77, 91, 92

Melville, Thomas, III, 77, 79, 92; Supp. I, Part 1, 309

Melville, Whyte, IV, 309

Melville family, III, 75

Melville Goodwin, USA (Marquand), III, 60, 65–66

Member of the Wedding, The (McCullers), II, 587, 592, 592, 600–604, 605, 606

"Memoir" (Untermeyer), II, 516–517

Memoir of Mary Ann, A, III, 357

Memoirs of Arii Taimai (Adams), I, 2–3

"Memoirs of Carwin, the Biloquist" (Brown), Supp. I, Part 1, 132

Memoirs of Hecate County (Wilson), IV, 429

Memoirs of Margaret Fuller Ossoli (Fuller), Supp. II, Part 1, 280, 283, 285

"Memoirs of Stephen Calvert" (Brown), Supp. I, Part 1, 133, 144

Memorabilia (Xenophon), II, 105

Memorabilia of John Greenleaf Whittier (ed. Pickard), Supp. I, Part 2, 706

Memorable Providences (Mather), Supp. II, Part 2, 458

"Memorial for the City" (Auden), Supp. II, Part 1, 20

"Memorial Rain" (MacLeish), III, 15

"Memorial to Ed Bland" (Brooks), Supp. III, Part 1, 77

"Memories" (Whittier), Supp. I, Part 2, 699

Memories of a Catholic Girlhood (McCarthy), II, 560–561, 566

"Memories of Uncle Neddy" (Bishop), Supp. I, Part 1, 73, 93

"Memories of West Street and Lepke" (Lowell), II, 550

"Memory, A" (Welty), IV, 261–262

Memory of Two Mondays, A (Miller), III, 153, 156, 158–159, 160, 166

Memphis Commercial Appeal (newspaper), IV, 378

Men and Brethen (Cozzens), I, 363–365, 368, 375, 378, 379

"Men in the Storm, The" (Crane), I, 411

"Men Loved Wholly Beyond Wisdom" (Bogan), Supp. III, Part 1, 50

"Men Made Out of Words" (Stevens), IV, 88

Men Must Act (Mumford), Supp. II, Part 2, 479

"Men of Color, to Arms!" (Douglass), Supp. III, Part 1, 171

Men of Good Hope: A Story of American Progressives (Aaron), Supp. I, Part 2, 650

Men Who Made the Nation, The (Dos Passos), I, 485

Men Without Women (Hemingway), II, 249

Men, Women and Ghosts (Lowell), II, 523–524

"Men, Women, and Thurber," Supp. I, Part 2, 627

Mencius (Meng-tzu), IV, 183

Mencken, August, III, 100, 108

Mencken, August, Jr., III, 99, 109, 118–119

Mencken, Burkhardt, III, 100, 108

Mencken, Charles, III, 99

Mencken, Gertrude, III, 99

Mencken, H. L., I, 199, 210, 212, 213, 235, 245, 261, 405, 514, 515, 517; II, 25, 27, 42, 89, 90, 91, 271, 289, 430, 443, 449, 485; III, 99–121, 394, 482; IV, 76, 432, 440, 475, 482; Supp. I, Part 2, 484, 629–630, 631, 647, 651, 653, 659, 673; Supp. II, Part 1, 136

Mencken, Mrs. August (Anna Abhau), III, 100, 109

Mencken, Mrs. H. L. (Sara Haardt), III, 109, 111

Mendele, IV, 3, 10

Mendelief, Dmitri Ivanovich, IV, 421

"Mending Wall" (Frost), II, 153–154

Menikoff, Barry, Supp. I, Part 1, 319

Mennes, John, II, 111

"Menstruation at Forty" (Sexton), Supp. II, Part 2, 686

"Merced" (Rich), Supp. I, Part 2, 563

Merchant of Venice, The (Shakespeare), IV, 227

Mercy Street (Sexton), Supp. II, Part 2, 683, 689

"Mère Pochette" (Jewett), II, 400

Meredith, George, II, 175, 186

Meredith, Mary, see Webb, Mary

Meredith, William, I, 189; II, 390, 545

"Merely to Know" (Rich), Supp. I, Part 2, 554

Merideth, Robert, Supp. I, Part 2, 601

Meridian (Walker), Supp. III, Part 2, 520, 524, 527, 528, 531–537

Mérimée, Prosper, II, 322

Meriweather family, II, 197

Meriwether, James B., I, 380; II, 76

"Meriwether Connection, The" (Cowley), Supp. II, Part 1, 142

"Merlin" (Emerson), II, 19, 20

Merlin (Robinson), III, 522

"Merlin Enthralled" (Wilbur), Supp. III, Part 2, 544, 554

Merrill, Bob, III, 406

Merrill, James, Supp. III, Part 1, 317–338, Part 2, 541, 561

Merry Widow, The (Lehar), III, 183

"Merry-Go-Round" (Hughes), Supp. I, Part 1, 333

Merry-Go-Round, The (Van Vechten), Supp. II, Part 2, 734, 735

Merry's Museum (magazine), II, 397

Mertins, Louis, II, 172

Merton, Father, **III**, 357

Merwin, W. S., **Supp. III, Part 1, 339–360, Part 2,** 541

Meserve, Frederick H., **III**, 598

Meserve, Walter J., **II**, 292, 293

Meserve, Walter, **Supp. I, Part 1,** 70

Message in the Bottle, The (Percy), **Supp. III, Part 1,** 387–388, 393, 397

"Message in the Bottle, The" (Percy), **Supp. III, Part 1,** 388

"Message of Flowers and Fire and Flowers, The" (Brooks), **Supp. III, Part 1,** 69

Messenger (publication), **Supp. I, Part 1,** 328

Metamorphic Tradition in Modern Poetry (Quinn), **IV**, 421

Metamorphoses (Ovid), **II**, 542–543; **III**, 467, 468

Metamorphoses (trans. Pound), **III**, 468–469

"Metamorphosis" (Kafka), **IV**, 438

"Metaphor as Mistake" (Percy), **Supp. III, Part 1,** 387–388

"Metaphors of a Magnifico" (Stevens), **IV**, 92

"Metaphysical Poets, The" (Eliot), **I**, 527, 586

Metaphysicism, **I**, 384, 396, 447; **II**, 40, 211, 542; **III**, 4, 13, 18, 32, 37, 38, 115, 173, 204, 245, 252–253, 255, 263, 348, 392, 393, 394, 405, 481, 493, 541, 611; **IV**, 28, 100, 115, 137, 144, 151, 152, 154, 165, 283, 333, 349, 433, 482, 485, 487, 488, 493, 495, 496; **Supp. I, Part 1,** 261, 366, **Part 2,** 421, 634, 635, 661, 679, 704

"Metaphysics" (Ginsberg), **Supp. II, Part 1,** 313

Metcalf, Allan A., **I**, 450

Metcalf, Eleanor M., **III**, 96, 97

Metrical History of Christianity, The (Taylor), **IV**, 163

Metropolitan Magazine, **II**, 90

"Metzengerstein" (Poe), **III**, 411, 417

Metzger, Arnold, **II**, 365

"Mexico" (Lowell), **II**, 553, 554

Mexico City Blues (Kerouac), **Supp. III, Part 1,** 225, 229

"Mexico Is a Foreign Country: Five Studies in Naturalism" (Warren), **IV**, 241, 252

Meyer, Donald B., **III**, 298, 313

Meyers, Sister Bertrande, **III**, 360

Meynell, Alice, **Supp. I, Part 1,** 220

"Mezzo Cammin" (Longfellow), **II**, 490

"Michael" (Wordsworth), **III**, 523

Michael Angelo (Longfellow), **II**, 490, 494, 495, 506

Michael Scarlett (Cozzens), **I**, 358–359, 378

Michelangelo, **I**, 18; **II**, 11–12; **III**, 124; **Supp. I, Part 1,** 363

Michelson, Albert, **IV**, 27

Michigan Daily (newspaper), **III**, 146

Mickiewicz, Adam, **Supp. II, Part 1,** 299

Mid-American Chants (Anderson), **I**, 109, 114

Mid-Century American Poets, **III**, 532

"Mid-Day" (Doolittle), **Supp. I, Part 1,** 266–267

"Midas" (Winters), **Supp. II, Part 2,** 801

Midcentury (Dos Passos), **I**, 474, 475, 478, 490, 492–494; **Supp. I, Part 2,** 646

"Middle Age" (Lowell), **II**, 550

Middle of the Journey, The (Trilling), **Supp. III, Part 2,** 495, 504–506

"Middle of the Way" (Kinnell), **Supp. III, Part 1,** 242

"Middle Passage" (Hayden), **Supp. II, Part 1,** 363, 375–376

"Middle Toe of the Right Foot, The" (Bierce), **I**, 203

Middle Years, The (James), **II**, 337–338

Middlemarch (Eliot), **I**, 457, 459; **II**, 290, 291; **Supp. I, Part 1,** 174

Middlesex Standard (publication), **Supp. I, Part 2,** 687

"Midnight Consultations, The" (Freneau), **Supp. II, Part 1,** 257

Midnight Cry, A (Mather), **Supp. II, Part 2,** 460

"Midnight Gladness" (Levertov), **Supp. III, Part 1,** 284–285

"Midnight Show" (Shapiro), **Supp. II, Part 2,** 705

Midpoint and Other Poems (Updike), **IV**, 214

Midsummer Night's Dream, A (Shakespeare), **Supp. I, Part 1,** 369–370

"Migration, The" (Tate), **IV**, 130

Miles, Julie, **I**, 199

Miles, Kitty, **I**, 199

Miles, Richard D., **II**, 125

Miles Wallingford (Cooper), *see Afloat and Ashore* (Cooper)

Milestone, Lewis, **Supp. I, Part 1,** 281

Milford, Nancy, **II**, 83, 100

"Militant Nudes" (Hardwick), **Supp. III, Part 1,** 210–211

"Milk Bottles" (Anderson), **I**, 114

Milk Train Doesn't Stop Here Anymore, The (Williams), **IV**, 382, 383, 384, 386, 390, 391, 392, 393, 394, 395, 398

Mill, James, **II**, 357

Mill, John Stuart, **III**, 294–295

Millay, Cora, **III**, 123, 133–134, 135–136

Millay, Edna St. Vincent, **I**, 482; **II**, 530; **III**, **122–144**; **IV**, 433, 436; **Supp. I, Part 2,** 707, 714, 726

Miller, Arthur, **I**, 81, 94; **III**, **145–169**

Miller, C. William, **II**, 125

Miller, Edwin H., **IV**, 354

Miller, Henry, **I**, 97, 119, 157; **III**, 40, **170–192**; **IV**, 138; **Supp. I, Part 2,** 546

Miller, Herman, **Supp. I, Part 2,** 614, 617

Miller, J. Hillis, **IV**, 424

Miller, James E., Jr., **I**, 404; **II**, 100; **III**, 241; **IV**, 352, 354

Miller, Joaquin, **I**, 193, 195, 459; **Supp. II, Part 1,** 351

Miller, John Duncan, **Supp. I, Part 2,** 604

Miller, Jordan Y., **I**, 96; **III**, 406, 407

Miller, Mrs. Arthur (Ingeborg Morath), **III**, 162–163

Miller, Mrs. Arthur (Marilyn Monroe), **III**, 161, 162–163

Miller, Mrs. Arthur (Mary Grace Slattery), **III**, 146, 161

Miller, Orilla, **Supp. I, Part 1,** 48

Miller, Perry, **I**, 546, 547, 549, 550, 560, 564, 566; **II**, 23, 460; **III**, 407; **IV**, 166, 186, 188; **Supp. I, Part 1,** 31, 46, 104, **Part 2,** 484

Miller, R. B., **Supp. I, Part 1,** 348

Miller, Robert Ellis, **II**, 588

Miller, Rosamond, **IV**, 47

Miller, Russell H., **I**, 143

Miller of Old Church, The (Glasgow), **II**, 175, 181

"Miller's Tale" (Chaucer), **III**, 283

Millet, Kate, **III**, 48, 192

Millgate, Michael, **II**, 76; **III**, 48, 72–73, 336; **IV**, 123, 130, 132, 143

"Principles" (Du Bois), **Supp. II, Part 1,** 172

Principles of Literary Criticism (Richards), **I,** 274; **Supp. I, Part 1,** 264, 275

Principles of Psychology, The (James), **II,** 321, 350–352, 353, 354, 357, 362, 363–364; **IV,** 28, 29, 32, 37

Principles of Zoölogy (Agassiz), **Supp. I, Part 1,** 312

Prior, Matthew, **II,** 111; **III,** 521

Prior, Sir James, **II,** 315

"Prison, The" (Malamud), **Supp. I, Part 2,** 431, 437

Prisoner of Sex, The (Mailer), **III,** 46

Prisoner of Zenda, The (film), **Supp. I, Part 2,** 615

Pritchard, John P., **Supp. I, Part 1,** 173, **Part 2,** 426

Pritchett, V. S., **II,** 587, 608; **Supp. II, Part 1,** 143

"Privatation and Publication" (Cowley), **Supp. II, Part 1,** 149

"Private History of a Campaign That Failed" (Twain), **IV,** 195

"Private Theatricals" (Howells), **II,** 280

"Problem from Milton, A" (Wilbur), **Supp. III, Part 2,** 550

"Problem of Being, The" (James), **II,** 360

"Problem of Housing the Negro, The" (Du Bois), **Supp. II, Part 1,** 168

Probst, Leonard, **IV,** 401

Processional (Lawson), **I,** 479

"Prodigal, The" (Bishop), **Supp. I, Part 1,** 90, 92

Prodigal Parents, The (Lewis), **II,** 454–455

"Proem" (Crane), **I,** 397

"Proem, The: By the Carpenter" (O. Henry), **Supp. II, Part 1,** 409

"Profession of a New Yorker" (Krutch), **Supp. I, Part 2,** 681

Profession of Authorship in America, 1800–1870, The (Charvat), **Supp. I, Part 1,** 148

"Professor" (Hughes), **Supp. I, Part 1,** 330

"Professor, The" (Bourne), **I,** 223

Professor at the Breakfast Table, The (Holmes), **Supp. I, Part 1,** 313, 316

"Professor Clark's Economics" (Veblen), **Supp. I, Part 2,** 634

Professor of Desire, The (Roth), **Supp. III, Part 2,** 403, 418–420

"Professor Veblen" (Mencken), **Supp. I, Part 2,** 630

Professor's House, The (Cather), **I,** 325–236

Proffer, Karl, **III,** 266

Profile of Vachel Lindsay (ed. Flanagan), **Supp. I, Part 2,** 402

"Prognosis" (Warren), **IV,** 245

Progressive (publication), **Supp. I, Part 1,** 60

"Project for a Trip to China" (Sontag), **Supp. III, Part 2,** 454, 469

"Projection" (Nemerov), **III,** 275

"Projective Verse" (Olson), **Supp. II, Part 1,** 30, **Part 2,** 555, 556, 557; **Supp. III, Part 2,** 624

Proletarian Literature in the United States (Hicks), **Supp. I, Part 2,** 609–610

"Prolegomena, Section 1" (Pound), **Supp. III, Part 2,** 615–616

"Prolegomena, Section 2" (Pound), **Supp. III, Part 2,** 616

"Prologue" (MacLeish), **III,** 8, 14

"Prologue to Our Time" (Mumford), **Supp. II, Part 2,** 473

"Prometheus" (Longfellow), **II,** 494

Prometheus Bound (Lowell), **II,** 543, 544, 545, 555

Promise, The (Buck), **Supp. II, Part 1,** 124

Promise of American Life, The (Croly), **I,** 229

Promised Land, The (Porter), **III,** 447

Promised Lands (Sontag), **Supp. III, Part 2,** 452

Promises: Poems 1954–1956 (Warren), **IV,** 244–245, 249, 252

Proof, The (Winters), **Supp. II, Part 2,** 786, 791, 792–794

"Propaganda of History, The" (Du Bois), **Supp. II, Part 1,** 182

Propertius, Sextus, **III,** 467

"Prophecy of Samuel Sewall, The" (Whittier), **Supp. I, Part 2,** 699

"Prophetic Pictures, The" (Hawthorne), **II,** 227

"Proportion" (Lowell), **II,** 525

"Proposal" (Carver), **Supp. III, Part 1,** 149

Proposals Relating to the Education of Youth in Pensilvania (Franklin), **II,** 113

"Proposed New Version of the Bible" (Franklin), **II,** 110

Prose and Poetry of Elinor Wylie, The (Benét), **Supp. I, Part 2,** 730

"Prose for Departure" (Merrill), **Supp. III, Part 1,** 336

"Prose Style in the Essays of E. B. White" (Fuller), **Supp. I, Part 2,** 681

"Proserpina and the Devil" (Wilder), **IV,** 358

"Prosody" (Shapiro), **Supp. II, Part 2,** 710

Prospect, The (journal), **Supp. I, Part 2,** 520

Prospect before Us, The (Dos Passos), **I,** 491

Prospect of Peace, The (Barlow), **Supp. II, Part 1,** 67, 68, 75

"Prospective Immigrants Please Note" (Rich), **Supp. I, Part 2,** 555

Prospects on the Rubicon (Paine), **Supp. I, Part 2,** 510–511

Prospectus of a National Institution, to Be Established in the United States (Barlow), **Supp. II, Part 1,** 80, 82

Prospice (Browning), **IV,** 366

"Protestant Easter" (Sexton), **Supp. II, Part 2,** 684

"Prothalamion" (Schwartz), **Supp. II, Part 2,** 649, 652

Proud, Robert, **Supp. I, Part 1,** 125

"Proud Farmer, The" (Lindsay), **Supp. I, Part 2,** 381

"Proud Flesh" (Warren), **IV,** 243

"Proud Lady" (Wylie), **Supp. I, Part 2,** 711–712

Proust, Marcel, **I,** 89, 319, 327, 377, 461; **II,** 377, 514, 606; **III,** 174, 181, 184, 244–245, 259, 471; **IV,** 32, 201, 237, 301, 312, 328, 359, 428, 431, 434, 439, 443, 466, 467; **Supp. III, Part 1,** 10, 12, 14, 15

Prufrock and Other Observations (Eliot), **I,** 569–570, 571, 573, 574, 576–577, 583, 584, 585

"Psalm" (Ginsberg), **Supp. II, Part 1,** 312

"Psalm of Life, A" (Longfellow), **II,** 489, 496

"Psalm of Life, A: What the Heart of the Young Man Said to the Psalmist" (Longfellow), **Supp. I, Part 2,** 409

"Psalm of the West" (Lanier), **Supp. I, Part 1,** 362, 364

"Psalm: Our Fathers" (Merwin), **Supp. III, Part 1,** 350

"Quinnapoxet" (Kunitz), **Supp. III, Part 1**, 263

Quintero, José, **III**, 403

Quintet: Essays on Five American Women Poets (Saul), **Supp. I, Part 2**, 730

"Quintet Honors Thurber Fables" (Hawley), **Supp. I, Part 2**, 627

Quintilian, **IV**, 123

Quod Erat Demonstrandum (Stein), **IV**, 34

"Rabbi, The" (Hayden), **Supp. II, Part 1**, 363, 369

"Rabbit, The" (Barnes), **Supp. III, Part 1**, 34

Rabbit Redux (Updike), **IV**, 214

Rabbit, Run (Updike), **IV**, 214, 223, 230–234

"Rabbits Who Caused All the Trouble, The" (Thurber), **Supp. I, Part 2**, 610

Rabelais, François, **I**, 130; **II**, 111, 112, 302, 535; **III**, 77, 78, 174, 182; **IV**, 68; **Supp. I, Part 2**, 461

"Race" (Emerson), **II**, 6

"'RACE LINE' IS A PRODUCT OF CAPITALISM, THE" (Baraka), **Supp. II, Part 1**, 61

"Race of Life, The" (Thurber), **Supp. I, Part 2**, 614

"Race Problems and Modern Society" (Toomer), **Supp. III, Part 2**, 486

"Races, The" (Lowell), **II**, 554

Racine, Jean Baptiste, **II**, 543, 573; **III**, 145, 151, 152, 160; **IV**, 317, 368, 370; **Supp. I, Part 2**, 716

"Radical" (Moore), **III**, 211

"Radical Chic" (Wolfe), **Supp. III, Part 2**, 577–578, 584, 585

Radical Chic & Mau-mauing the Flak Catchers (Wolfe), **Supp. III, Part 2**, 577–578

Radical Empiricism of William James, The (Wild), **II**, 362, 363–364

Radical Innocence: Studies in the Contemporary American Novel (Hassan), **Supp. I, Part 1**, 198

Radical Tradition, The: From Tom Paine to Lloyd George (Derry), **Supp. I, Part 2**, 525

Radicalism in America, The (Lasch), **I**, 259

"Radio" (O'Hara), **III**, 369

Radkin, Paul, **Supp. I, Part 2**, 539

"Raft, The" (Lindsay), **Supp. I, Part 1**, 393

Rage to Live, A (O'Hara), **III**, 361

Raglan, Lord, **I**, 135

Rago, Henry, **IV**, 48; **Supp. III, Part 2**, 624, 628, 629

Rahv, Philip, **Supp. II, Part 1**, 136

Rain in the Trees, The (Merwin), **Supp. III, Part 1**, 340, 342, 345, 349, 354–356

Rainbow, The (Lawrence), **III**, 27

"Rainbows" (Marquand), **III**, 56

"Rain-Dream, A" (Bryant), **Supp. I, Part 1**, 164

Raine, Kathleen, **I**, 522, 527

Rainer, Luise (Mrs. Clifford Odets), **Supp. II, Part 2**, 544

"Rainy Day" (Longfellow), **II**, 498

"Rainy Day, The" (Buck), **Supp. II, Part 1**, 127

"Rainy Season: Sub-Tropics" (Bishop), **Supp. I, Part 1**, 93

"Raise High the Roof Beam, Carpenters" (Salinger), **III**, 567–569, 571

Raise High the Roof Beam, Carpenters; and Seymour: An Introduction (Salinger), **III**, 552, 567–571, 572

Raise Race Rays Raze: Essays Since 1965 (Baraka), **Supp. II, Part 1**, 47, 52, 55

Rajan, R., **I**, 390

Rake's Progress, The (opera), **Supp. II, Part 1**, 24

Rakosi, Carl, **Supp. III, Part 2**, 614, 615, 616, 617, 618, 621, 629

Ralegh, Sir Walter, **Supp. I, Part 1**, 98

Raleigh, John Henry, **II**, 149; **III**, 408; **IV**, 366

Ramakrishna, Sri, **III**, 567

"Ramble of Aphasia, A" (O. Henry), **Supp. II, Part 1**, 410

Ramsay, Richard David, **IV**, 448

Ramsey, Paul, **I**, 564; **III**, 313

Ramus, Petrus, **Supp. I, Part 1**, 104

Rand, Ayn, **Supp. I, Part 1**, 294

Randall, Jarrell, 1914–1965 (eds. Lowell, Taylor, and Warren), **II**, 368, 385

Randall, John H., **I**, 333; **III**, 605

Randolph, John, **I**, 5–6

Randolph family, **II**, 173

Rank, Otto, **I**, 135

Ranke, Leopold von, **Supp. I, Part 2**, 492

Rankin, Daniel S., **Supp. I, Part 1**, 200, 203, 225, 226

Rans, Geoffrey, **III**, 432

Ransom, John Crowe, **I**, 265, 287, 301, 473; **II**, 34, 367, 385, 389, 390, 536–537, 542; **III**, 144, 217, 454, **480–502**, 549; **IV**, 121, 122, 123, 124, 125, 127, 134, 140, 141, 143, 236, 237, 284, 433; **Supp. I, Part 1**, 80, 361, 373, **Part 2**, 423; **Supp. II, Part 1**, 90, 91, 136, 137, 139, 318, **Part 2**, 639; **Supp. III, Part 1**, 318, **Part 2**, 542, 591

Rap on Race, A (Baldwin and Mead), **Supp. I, Part 1**, 66

"Rape, The" (Baraka), **Supp. II, Part 1**, 40

"Rape of Philomel, The" (Shapiro), **Supp. II, Part 2**, 720

Raphael, **I**, 15; **III**, 505, 521, 524; **Supp. I, Part 1**, 363

"Rappaccini's Daughter" (Hawthorne), **II**, 229

Rapping, Elayne A., **Supp. I, Part 1**, 252

"Rapunzel" (Sexton), **Supp. II, Part 2**, 691

"Raree Show" (MacLeish), **III**, 9

Rascoe, Burton, **III**, 106, 115, 121

"Ration" (Baraka), **Supp. II, Part 1**, 50

Rational Fictions: A Study of Charles Brockden Brown (Kimball), **Supp. I, Part 1**, 148

"Rationale of Verse, The" (Poe), **III**, 427–428

Rattigan, Terence, **III**, 152

Raugh, Joseph, **Supp. I, Part 1**, 286

Rauschenbusch, Walter, **III**, 293; **Supp. I, Part 1**, 7

"Raven, The" (Poe), **III**, 413, 421–422, 426

Raven, The, and Other Poems (Poe), **III**, 413

"Raven Days, The" (Lanier), **Supp. I, Part 1**, 351

Ravitz, Abe C., **II**, 149

Ray, David, **Supp. I, Part 1**, 199

Ray, Gordon M., **II**, 340

Ray, John, **II**, 111, 112

Ray, Man, **IV**, 404

Raymond, Thomas L., **I**, 426

Raynolds, Robert, **IV**, 473

Reactionary Essays on Poetry and Ideas (Tate), **Supp. II, Part 1,** 106, 146

Read, Deborah, **II**, 122

Read, Forrest, **III**, 478; **Supp. I, Part 1,** 275

Read, Herbert, **I**, 523; **II**, 372–373, 377–378; **IV**, 143; **Supp. III, Part 1,** 273, **Part 2,** 624, 626

Reade, Charles, **Supp. I, Part 2,** 580

Reader, Dennis J., **Supp. I, Part 2,** 402, 454, 478

Reader's Digest (magazine), **III**, 164; **Supp. I, Part 2,** 534

"Reading Myself" (Lowell), **II**, 555

"Reading of *Wieland*, A" (Ziff), **Supp. I, Part 1,** 148

Reading the Spirit (Eberhart), **I**, 525, 527, 530

"Readings of History" (Rich), **Supp. I, Part 2,** 554

"Ready Or Not" (Baraka), **Supp. II, Part 1,** 50

Real Dope, The (Lardner), **II**, 422–423

"Real Horatio Alger Story, The" (Cowley), **Supp. II, Part 1,** 143

Real Life of Sebastian Knight, The (Nabokov), **III**, 246

"Real Source of Vachel Lindsay's Poetic Technique, The" (Edwards), **Supp. I, Part 2,** 402

"Realities" (MacLeish), **III**, 4

"Reality in America" (Trilling), **Supp. III, Part 2,** 495, 502

"Reality! Reality! What Is It?" (Eberhart), **I**, 536

Reality Sandwiches, 1953–60 (Ginsberg), **Supp. II, Part 1,** 315, 320

"Reapers," **Supp. III, Part 2,** 481

"Reasons for Music" (MacLeish), **III**, 19

Reaver, Joseph Russell, **III**, 406

"Recapitulation, The" (Eberhart), **I**, 522

"Recapitulations" (Shapiro), **Supp. II, Part 2,** 701, 702, 708, 710–711

"Recencies in Poetry" (Zukofsky), **Supp. III, Part 2,** 615

Recent Killing, A (Baraka), **Supp. II, Part 1,** 55

"Recent Negro Fiction" (Ellison), **Supp. II, Part 1,** 233, 235

"Recital, The" (Ashbery), **Supp. III, Part 1,** 14

"Recitative" (Crane), **I**, 390

"Reconciliation" (Whitman), **IV**, 347

"Reconstructed but Unregenerate" (Ransom), **III**, 496

"Reconstruction and Its Benefits" (Du Bois), **Supp. II, Part 1,** 171

Record of Mr. Alcott's School (Peabody), **Supp. I, Part 1,** 46

"RED AUTUMN" (Baraka), **Supp. II, Part 1,** 55

Red Badge of Courage, The (Crane), **I**, 201, 207, 212, 405, 406, 407, 408, 412–416, 419, 421, 422, 423, 477, 506; **II**, 264; **III**, 317; **IV**, 350

"Red Carpet for Shelley, A" (Wylie), **Supp. I, Part 2,** 724

Red Cross (Shepard), **Supp. III, Part 2,** 440, 446

"Red Leaves" (Faulkner), **II**, 72

Red Pony, The (Steinbeck), **IV**, 50, 51, 58, 70

Red Roses for Bronze (Doolittle), **Supp. I, Part 1,** 253, 268, 271

Red Rover, The (Cooper), **I**, 342–343, 355

"Red Wheelbarrow, The" (Williams), **IV**, 411–412

Redbook (magazine), **III**, 522–523

"Redbreast in Tampa" (Lanier), **Supp. I, Part 1,** 364

Redburn: His First Voyage (Melville), **III**, 79–80, 84

Redding, Saunders, **IV**, 497; **Supp. I, Part 1,** 332, 333

"Redeployment" (Nemerov), **III**, 267, 272

Redfield, Robert, **IV**, 475

Redskins, The (Cooper), **I**, 351, 353

"Redwings" (Wright), **Supp. III, Part 2,** 603

Reed, Ishmael, **Supp. II, Part 1,** 34

Reed, John, **I**, 48, 476, 483

Reed, Rex, **IV**, 401

"Reed of Pan, A" (McCullers), **II**, 585

Reedy, William Marion, **Supp. I, Part 2,** 456, 461, 465

Reef, The (Wharton), **IV**, 317–318, 322

Rees, Robert A., **II**, 125; **Supp. I, Part 2,** 425

Reeves, George M., Jr., **IV**, 473

Reeves, John K., **II**, 292

Reeves, Paschal, **IV**, 472, 473

Reeve's Tale (Chaucer), **I**, 131

Reflections at Fifty and Other Essays (Farrell), **II**, 49

Reflections in a Golden Eye (McCullers), **II**, 586, 588, 593–596, 604; **IV**, 384, 396

Reflections on Poetry and Poetics (Nemerov), **III**, 269

"Reflections on the Constitution of Nature" (Freneau), **Supp. II, Part 1,** 274

"Reflections on the Death of the Reader" (Morris), **III**, 237

Reflections on the End of an Era (Niebuhr), **III**, 297–298

"Reflections on the Life and Death of Lord Clive" (Paine), **Supp. I, Part 2,** 505

Reflections on the Revolution in France (Burke), **Supp. I, Part 2,** 511, 512

Reflections: Thinking Part I (Arendt), **Supp. I, Part 2,** 570

"Reflex Action and Theism" (James), **II**, 345, 363

"Refugees, The" (Jarrell), **II**, 371

Regan, Robert, **III**, 432

Régnier, Henri de, **II**, 528–529

Reichart, Walter A., **II**, 317

Reichel, Hans, **III**, 183

Reid, B. L., **II**, 41, 47

Reid, Randall, **IV**, 307

Reid, Thomas, **II**, 9; **Supp. I, Part 1,** 151

Reign of Wonder, The (Tanner), **I**, 260

Reisman, Jerry, **Supp. III, Part 2,** 618

Reiter, Irene Morris, **II**, 53

Reivers, The (Faulkner), **I**, 305; **II**, 57, 73

Relearning the Alphabet (Levertov), **Supp. III, Part 1,** 280, 281

"Release, The" (MacLeish), **III**, 16

"Relevance of an Impossible Ethical Ideal, The" (Niebuhr), **III**, 298

"Religion" (Dunbar), **Supp. II, Part 1,** 199

"Religion" (Emerson), **II**, 6

Religion of Nature Delineated, The (Wollaston), **II**, 108

"Religious Symbolism and Psychic Reality in Baldwin's *Go Tell It on the Mountain*" (Allen), **Supp. I, Part 1,** 69

"Reluctance" (Frost), **II**, 153

Welles, Gideon, **Supp. I, Part 2,** 484

Welles, Orson, **IV,** 476; **Supp. I, Part 1,** 67

"Wellfleet Whale, The" (Kunitz), **Supp. III, Part 1,** 263, 269

Wellfleet Whale and Companion Poems, The (Kunitz), **Supp. III, Part 1,** 263

Wellman, Flora, **II,** 463–464, 465

Wells, H. G., **I,** 103, 226, 241, 243, 253, 405, 409, 415; **II,** 82, 144, 276, 337, 338, 340, 458; **III,** 456; **IV,** 340, 455

Wells, Henry W., **I,** 473; **IV,** 96

Welsh, Mary, *see* Hemingway, Mrs. Ernest (Mary Welsh)

Welty, Eudora, **II,** 194, 217, 606; **IV,** **260–284**

Wendell, Barrett, **III,** 507; **Supp. I, Part 2,** 414

Wendell, Sarah, *see* Holmes, Mrs. Abiel (Sarah Wendell)

Wept of Wish-ton-Wish, The (Cooper), **I,** 339, 342, 350

"We're Friends Again" (O'Hara), **III,** 372–373

"Were the Whole Realm of Nature Mine" (Watts), **I,** 458

Wershba, Joseph, **Supp. I, Part 2,** 453

Wescott, Glenway, **I,** 263, 288; **II,** 85; **III,** 448, 454, 455

West, Benjamin, **Supp. I, Part 2,** 511

West, James, **II,** 562

West, Mrs. Nathanael (Eileen McKenney), **IV,** 288

West, Nathanael, **I,** 97, 107, 190, 211, 298; **II,** 436; **III,** 357, 425; **IV,** **285–307**

West, Ray B., Jr., **III,** 455

West, Rebecca, **II,** 412, 445; **III,** 598

"West Wall" (Merwin), **Supp. III, Part 1,** 355

"West Wind, The" (Bryant), **Supp. I, Part 1,** 155

Westall, Julia Elizabeth, *see* Wolfe, Mrs. William Oliver (Julia Elizabeth Westall)

Westbrook, Max, **I,** 427

Westcott, Edward N., **II,** 102

"Western Association of Writers" (Chopin), **Supp. I, Part 1,** 217

"Western Ballad, A" (Ginsberg), **Supp. II, Part 1,** 311

Western Humanities Review (publication), **Supp. I, Part 1,** 201

Western Lands, The (Burroughs), **Supp. III, Part 1,** 106

Western Monthly Magazine, The, **Supp. I, Part 2,** 584

West-Going Heart, The: A Life of Vachel Lindsay (Ruggles), **Supp. I, Part 2,** 402

Westhoff, Clara, *see* Rilke, Mrs. Rainer Maria (Clara Westhoff)

Westminster Gazette (publication), **I,** 408

Weston, Jessie L., **II,** 540; **III,** 12; **Supp. I, Part 2,** 438

West-running Brook (Frost), **II,** 155

"West-running Brook" (Frost), **II,** 150, 162–164

"Westward Beach, A" (Jeffers), **Supp. II, Part 2,** 418

"Wet Casements" (Ashbery), **Supp. III, Part 1,** 18–20

Whalen, Marcella, **Supp. I, Part 1,** 49

Wharton, Edith, **I,** 12, 375; **II,** 96, 180, 183, 186, 189–190, 193, 283, 338, 444, 451; **III,** 69, 175, 576; **IV,** 8, 53, 58, **302–330**

Wharton, Edward Robbins, **IV,** 310, 313–314, 319

What a Kingdom It Was (Kinnell), **Supp. III, Part 1,** 235, 238, 239

What a Way to Go (Morris), **III,** 230–232

What Are Masterpieces (Stein), **IV,** 30–31

What Are Years (Moore), **III,** 208–209, 210, 215

"What Are Years?" (Moore), **III,** 211, 213

"What Can I Tell My Bones?" (Roethke), **III,** 546, 549

"What Color Is God?" (Wills), **Supp. I, Part 1,** 71

"What Do You Do in San Francisco?" (Carver), **Supp. III, Part 1,** 143

"What God Is Like to Him I Serve" (Bradstreet), **Supp. I, Part 1,** 106–107

"What I Believe" (Mumford), **Supp. II, Part 2,** 479

"What Is an Emotion" (James), **II,** 350

What Is Art? (Tolstoi), **I,** 58

"What Is Civilization? Africa's Answer" (Du Bois), **Supp. II, Part 1,** 176

"What Is College For?" (Bourne), **I,** 216

"What Is Exploitation?" (Bourne), **I,** 216

"What Is It?" (Carver), **Supp. III, Part 1,** 139

What Is Man? (Twain), **II,** 434; **IV,** 209

"What Is Poetry" (Ashbery), **Supp. III, Part 1,** 19

What Maisie Knew (James), **II,** 332

"What Must" (MacLeish), **III,** 18

"What the Arts Need Now" (Baraka), **Supp. II, Part 1,** 47

"What Thurber Saw" (Brady), **Supp. I, Part 2,** 626

What Time Collects (Farrell), **II,** 46, 47–48

What Was the Relationship of the Lone Ranger to the Means of Production? (Baraka), **Supp. II, Part 1,** 58

What We Talk About When We Talk About Love (Carver), **Supp. III, Part 1,** 142–146

"What You Want" (O. Henry), **Supp. II, Part 1,** 402

"What's Happening in America" (Sontag), **Supp. III, Part 2,** 460–461

"What's in Alaska?" (Carver), **Supp. III, Part 1,** 141, 143

What's O'Clock (Lowell), **II,** 511, 527, 528

Wheaton, Mabel Wolfe, **IV,** 473

Wheel of Life, The (Glasgow), **II,** 176, 178, 179, 183

Wheeler, John, **II,** 433

Wheeler, Otis B., **Supp. I, Part 1,** 226

Wheelock, John Hall, **IV,** 143, 461, 472

When Boyhood Dreams Come True (Farrell), **II,** 45

"When De Co'n Pone's Hot" (Dunbar), **Supp. II, Part 1,** 202–203

"When Death Came April Twelve 1945" (Sandburg), **III,** 591, 593

"When I Buy Pictures" (Moore), **III,** 205

"When I Came from Colchis" (Merwin), **Supp. III, Part 1,** 343

"When I Left Business for Literature" (Anderson), **I,** 101

When Knighthood Was in Flower (Major), **III,** 320

"[When] Let by rain" (Taylor), **IV,** 160–161

"When Lilacs Last in the Dooryard Bloom'd" (Whitman), **IV,** 347–348, 351